D1200858

THE MODERN LIBRARY
of the World's Best Books

A JOHNSON READER

A JOHNSON READER

EDITED BY

E. L. McAdam, Jr.
& George Milne

THE MODERN LIBRARY
New York

FIRST MODERN LIBRARY EDITION, *February, 1966*

Reprinted by arrangement with Pantheon Books

THE MODERN LIBRARY
is published by
RANDOM HOUSE, INC.

BENNETT CERF DONALD S. KLOPFER

MANUFACTURED IN THE UNITED STATES OF AMERICA

TO EDITH AND ALLEN

Contents

Introduction

THE OLD STEREOTYPE of Dr. Johnson as a sort of Tory crustacean has begun to crack. It ought to. Any man who could describe Sir Robert Walpole, the great Whig leader, as "a statesman, as able perhaps as any that ever existed" (1753), and in the next sentence refer to the invasion of Bonnie Prince Charlie as "a rebellion, which was not less contemptible in its beginning than threatening in its progress and consequences" should be read out of the party. Neither of these printed comments was known to Boswell or Macaulay, both of whom might have been embarrassed to fit them into a preconceived image of Johnson.

It is the purpose of this volume to give a wide-ranging selection from Johnson's works, deliberately emphasizing that he thought for himself and departed from tradition whenever he thought tradition wrong. We have also tried to present his first, unrevised thoughts, and have therefore reprinted from the first editions of his works, although in later editions he made many changes, mostly stylistic. (As a sample of his revision, we have given all of his changes for the second edition of *Rasselas.*)

Johnson had composed poetry as a schoolboy, and continued to do so at Oxford, but his first extended work was a translation and condensation of Lobo's *Voyage to Abyssinia* (1735), a distant precursor of *Rasselas.* In the spring of 1738 he published *London,* his first imitation of Juvenal, and began to work on Cave's *Gentleman's Magazine,* writing verse, short biographies, and accounts of Parliamentary debates. All of these were anonymous, and, except for *London,* all hack-work, though sometimes hack-work of a superior kind.

In 1744 he published his first major prose work, his *Life of Savage.* The recent biography of Savage by Clarence Tracy is called *The Artificial Bastard,* the story, that is, of a man probably legitimately born who, nevertheless, believed himself a bastard and exerted every effort to prove himself one. It was almost a classical changeling drama. A Lady Macclesfield had an illegitimate child, and put the boy to nurse with a woman who had also just had a baby boy. One child died. The survivor grew up believing that he was Lady Macclesfield's son, and spent his life trying vainly to prove it. He was a minor poet, and managed to elicit some support from Pope, and, even more important, a pension from Queen Caroline. But he would now be forgotten except that he and Johnson became friends in 1738, and in the winter of their discontents paced the streets of London, speaking out for liberty, and, hungry, sometimes slept on the bulks by the river. Johnson believed his story, and wrote a vivid biography, his only life of a close friend. It is here printed in full.

Five years later Johnson published his second imitation of Juvenal, *The Vanity of Human Wishes* (1749). As Pope had done earlier with some of the satires of Horace, Johnson took the basic structure of the Latin poem and generally used modern examples instead of classical ones. (He did, however, retain Xerxes.) The angry violence of Juvenal gives way to a somber tone, and Johnson discards Juvenal's Stoical conclusion for a Christian one. The poem is much more original than *London,* and it is not at all hampered by reference to passing political events. In it Johnson's always competent heroic couplets rise to a noble and moving statement.

In 1746 Johnson had begun to compile a *Dictionary* to challenge those of the French and Italian academies. He had no college degree, but he was backed by the major publishers of England, and by the powerful patronage of Lord Chesterfield. Nine years later, a widower, childless, abandoned by Chesterfield except for belated recommendations, unknown except to a few, he produced his two massive volumes. Their vast comprehensiveness, their wit, their stunning collection of examples from classical

English literature, do not need comment here. But his Preface is a distillation of experience which is worth a new reading. In it Johnson shows his first hope of an authoritative dictionary, then his realization that such a dictionary was not possible, since the language was in a state of flux, bad as that might appear, and finally his statement of what he had accomplished. The great aim, the strong personal tone, the tension of purpose and accomplishment, the stirring, rolling prose, make the Preface unmatched in eighteenth-century literature.

In the decade of the *Dictionary* Johnson also published his two major series of periodical essays, *The Rambler* (1750–52), which appeared separately twice a week, and *The Idler* (1758–60), which appeared once a week in *The Universal Chronicle.* These are generally on moral, occasionally on literary, themes. One of the *Idlers,* No. 22, attacking war, is his most violent satire, so violent that he omitted it from the collected edition of 1761. We reprint it as entirely characteristic of Johnson's attitude toward war. Part of Johnson's admiration for Walpole, mentioned earlier, must stem from Walpole's steady avoidance of war in the face of provocation from abroad and jingoism at home. Another paper on war we have reprinted from Johnson's *Literary Magazine* (1756), and a third from *The British Magazine* (1760). Last among the essays we have included a legal brief which Johnson wrote for Boswell advocating the freeing of a Negro slave.

The Prince of Abissinia (1759), soon renamed *Rasselas,* elaborates the themes of some of the essays. According to Sir Joshua Reynolds, it was written in one week to defray the funeral expenses of Johnson's mother, who had died in Lichfield at the age of eighty-nine. But Johnson's translation of Father Lobo's *Voyage to Abyssinia* had been made twenty-four years earlier—that strange, remote land held a strong appeal to a man who was never to travel further from Great Britain than Paris—and his ideas for this book had been developing through *The Vanity of Human Wishes, The Rambler,* and *The Idler.* At some time he read Norden's *Travels into Egypt and Nubia,* and was impelled to note in his diary that Norden saw crocodiles "thirty feet long." But the attraction of *Rasselas* is not only that it is the first long Oriental moral tale in English, but that Johnson uses Abyssinia and Egypt to achieve an appropriate distance, geographical and cultural, for a commentary on human life pertinent to eighteenth-century England. The pertinence, or the liveliness, of the comment may be judged by the fact that the book has appeared in some two hundred editions and translations. The reader will not need to be warned that Johnson has a sly sense of humor; when Imlac becomes pedantic, he is cut short by a bored Rasselas. And not every sentence in the book should be quoted, out of context, as Johnson's last word on literary criticism or the human condition. Sometimes the characters speak for themselves.

Johnson had proposed a new edition of Shakespeare in 1745, but had been put off by publishers claiming a perpetual copyright. In 1756 the dispute was resolved, and Johnson confidently expected to publish in 1757. The eight volumes appeared, after prodigious labor, in 1765. The text of Shakespeare had degenerated steadily since the first folio of 1623, and Johnson attempted to establish a sound text from that volume, with side glances at quartos borrowed from Garrick. The Preface, the text, and the notes were aimed primarily at the reader, since the audience in the theater would hear Shakespeare only as rewritten by Nahum Tate (*King Lear* with a happy ending) or revised by Garrick. To a modern reader, Johnson's common-sense approach forms his greatest appeal. He is not a bardolater, yet he fully recognizes Shakespeare's greatness. He examines, weighs, and finally places the laurel, usually where it belongs. His is the first modern edition of Shakespeare, and has been cited in all subsequent editions. His Preface can stand by itself.

In the twelve years following his *Shakespeare,* Johnson wrote four political pamphlets, *A Journey to the Western Islands,* following his trip to the Hebrides with Boswell, and many shorter works. In 1777 a group of publishers proposed that he write prefaces for a large collection of English poets, and in 1779 the first four volumes appeared: *Prefaces, Biographical and Critical, to the Works of the English Poets* (later called *Lives of the Poets*). Johnson's *Milton* was in the second volume. If Milton had been a conservative, a Royalist, and an undeviating member of the Church of England, Johnson would have treated him with more kindness in his biography. But Milton's advocacy of divorce, his republicanism, and his radicalism in religion insured that Johnson would treat his ideas with rigor, if not abuse. In a little more than a century after his death, his reputation as a poet was steadily growing, but he had not yet been canonized, by Wordsworth, as a leader of free men. Johnson had, however, long admired his poetry. In 1750 he had written a Prologue to *Comus,* for the benefit of Milton's sole surviving granddaughter, and even earlier he had tried, unwisely, to imitate Milton's blank verse in *Irene.*

When he came as a critic to examine Milton's poems, he was not subject to the intimidation of a mass of earlier work. When in college he had translated into Latin Dryden's six-line verse panegyric on Milton, and he had read Addison's appreciative papers in the *Spectator.* But, on the whole, he could read the poems freshly, and he did. Having suffered through innumerable eighteenth-century pastoral poems, however (partly as editor of the *Gentleman's Magazine*), he saw "Lycidas" only as another pastoral, and one disfigured by a combination of Christian elements and pagan myth. He did not see Milton springing through the veils of allusion in his search for identity and fame. He thought *Paradise Lost* a very great poem.

Johnson's biography was attacked immediately after its publication. It is still attacked—and read. It shows much about Milton, and perhaps more about Johnson.

Johnson's *Life of Gray* was published in May 1781, in volume X of his *Prefaces,* just short of ten years after Gray's death. The relatively unsympathetic treatment of some of Gray's poems produced immediate outcries, two books in the same year, another in 1782, and a fourth in 1783. These Johnson characteristically ignored. He did change one word in his criticism (*or* to *and*) when he revised his *Lives* for the third edition (1783). He made more changes, largely factual, in his biographical account.

A curious blind spot in Johnson's criticism is his tepid reaction to Gray's "Ode on a Favourite Cat." This poem is perhaps the most brilliant self-parody in English literature: Gray takes his own studied poetic diction, and his moralizing, and destroys them. Johnson missed the point. In commenting on "The Bard" and "The Fatal Sisters," Johnson merely reiterates his known position: he wholly approved of resurrecting the old ballads, as Percy had done, but he thought that using such materials for modern poetry was ridiculous. He may have been wrong.

The last three sections of this *Reader* are made up of pieces which Johnson never published, and, indeed, he would not have called them "works." But his light verse, often impromptu, has an ease and sometimes a bite not at all in the stereotype of the Great Cham. His letters range from controlled indignation (to Chesterfield), through suavity (to Bute) and quiet advice (to Susy Thrale) to reckless fury (to Mrs. Thrale on her marriage to Piozzi), and final resignation. Finally we hear Johnson talking. His voice is known in great part from Boswell's biography. Boswell as friend and recorder commemorated Johnson's conversation as no English writer had ever done for anyone. From Boswell, many of Johnson's remarks have become famous, and others deserve to be. We have selected some from the list given by G. B. Hill as "Dicta Philosophiae" at the end of his edition of Boswell's *Life* in 1887, and others from a similar list at the end of his *Johnsonian Miscellanies*, 1892. We have rearranged these and elaborated them from his sources in some instances. That many were spoken in the heat of debate is clear enough; others may have undergone changes in transmission. But the voice still sounds authentic. A few quotations from Johnson's letters are in the same tone.

We do not offer an estimate of Johnson's position as a writer or a thinker. We suggest, instead, that the reader find in this volume a man thinking, and writing with wit, precision, and humanity.

E. L. M. Jr.
G. M.

ACKNOWLEDGMENTS

We are grateful for generous help we have received from Dr. Ashley T. Day of the New York University Library, Mr. Herman W. Liebert, Curator of Rare Books at Yale University, and Mr. André Schiffrin, our editor at Pantheon Books.

A Note on the Text

WE HAVE printed works published during Johnson's lifetime from the first edition, thinking that a reader would be interested in Johnson's first, unrevised thoughts, and his way of putting them down. For he was, as he said, a man who waited till the printer's boy was waiting for copy, and then wrote in precipitous haste. But he was also an inveterate reviser: few works reprinted during his lifetime, under his supervision, are without changes. Indeed, some six thousand verbal differences have been noted in the 208 numbers of *The Rambler*. Not all of these are improvements, though they tend to greater conciseness, and what Fowler called "elegant variation." For the curious, we have printed the changes Johnson made for the second edition of *Rasselas,* and have noted a few of the significant variants in other works. Except for Dublin piracies, few of these original texts were reprinted during Johnson's life. The Prefaces to the *Dictionary* and to *Shakespeare* have few changes, which may suggest his satisfaction with these two works. He never reprinted *Idler* 22, perhaps because its satire is so bitter, or his *Observations on the Present State of Affairs,* perhaps because he thought it too topical. They are given from the original texts.

We have followed the original spelling and punctuation, except for silently adding quotation marks in *Rasselas* and *Idler* 22 where they are required for conversation. We have throughout reduced capitalization and italics to modern usage.

A Johnson Reader

Life of Savage

"He was a vicious man, but very kind to me. If you call a dog HERVEY, I shall love him." Johnson said this of Henry Hervey, who had befriended him in London, when he was penniless and almost friendless, in 1737. This appears to be the key to Johnson's Life of Savage, *for Savage, who was well-known for his poems, as well as his claim to be the illegitimate son of Lady Macclesfield, befriended Johnson in the next year. Johnson believed Savage's story of his birth (Boswell did not), and apparently it was friendship that led him to treat Savage's poems with more kindness than they deserve. But, as with Hervey, Johnson was not deceived as to Savage's character. The biography concludes: "negligence and irregularity, long continued, will make knowledge useless, wit ridiculous, and genius contemptible." Johnson was writing just six months after Savage died.*

The Life of Savage *was published, anonymously, in February 1744 in a small octavo volume. It was Johnson's first full-length biography, and his only biography of a close friend. Later he did not use such long footnotes as appear here: they may mark a man who has not yet acquired full mastery of his medium. The* Life *was revised for a second edition in 1745 and was subsequently reprinted in* Prefaces to the Works of the English Poets, *1781, where the long extracts from Savage's poems are omitted, since the collected poems appear in a separate volume. Savage's verse is now largely forgotten, though his anger against his supposed mother gave vigor to* The Bastard, *of which one line is still quoted: "No tenth transmitter of a foolish face."*

We have put Johnson's notes at the end of the selection, in order to focus attention on his narrative. Reprinted from the first edition.

An Account of the Life of Mr. Richard Savage,

Son of the Earl Rivers

It has been observed in all ages, that the advantages of nature or of fortune have contributed very little to the promotion of happiness; and that those whom the splendor of their rank, or the extent of their capacity, have placed upon the summits of human life, have not often given any just occasion to envy in those who look up to them from a lower station. Whether it be that apparent superiority incites great designs, and great designs are naturally liable to fatal miscarriages, or that the general lot of mankind is misery, and the misfortunes of those whose eminence drew upon them an universal attention, have been more carefully recorded, because they were more generally observed, and have in reality been only more conspicuous than those of others, not more frequent, or more severe.

That affluence and power, advantages extrinsic and adventitious, and therefore easily separable from those by whom they are possessed, should very often flatter the mind with expectations of felicity which they cannot give, raises no astonishment; but it seems rational to hope, that intellectual greatness should produce better effects, that minds qualified for great attainments should first endeavour their own benefit, and that they who are most able to teach others the way to happiness, should with most certainty follow it themselves.

But this expectation, however plausible, has been very frequently disappointed. The heroes of literary as well as civil history have been very often no less remarkable for what they have suffered, than for what they have atchieved; and volumes have been

---

Because of their length and complexity, the footnotes for the *Life of Savage* will be found grouped together at the end of the selection (pp. 87-105).

written only to enumerate the miseries of the learned, and relate their unhappy lives, and untimely deaths.

To these mournful narratives, I am about to add the life of Richard Savage, a man whose writings entitle him to an eminent rank in the classes of learning, and whose misfortunes claim a degree of compassion, not always due to the unhappy, as they were often the consequences of the crimes of others, rather than his own.

In the year 1697, Anne Countess of Macclesfield having lived for some time upon very uneasy terms with her husband, thought a public confession of adultery the most obvious and expeditious method of obtaining her liberty, and therefore declared, that the child, with which she was then great, was begotten by the Earl Rivers. This, as may be easily imagined, made her husband no less desirous of a separation than herself, and he prosecuted his design in the most effectual manner; for he applied not to the Ecclesiastical Courts for a divorce, but to the Parliament for an Act, by which his marriage might be dissolved, the nuptial contract totally annulled, and the children of his wife illegitimated. This Act, after the usual deliberation, he obtained, tho' without the approbation of some, who considered marriage as an affair only cognizable by ecclesiastical judges;[1] and on March 3d was separated from his wife, whose fortune, which was very great, was repaid her; and who having as well as her husband the liberty of making another choice, was in a short time married to Colonel Bret.

While the Earl of Macclesfield was prosecuting this affair, his wife was, on the tenth of January 1697–8, delivered of a son, and the Earl Rivers, by appearing to consider him as his own, left none any reason to doubt of the sincerity of her declaration; for he was his godfather, and gave him his own name, which was by his direction inserted in the register of St. Andrew's Parish in Holbourn, but unfortunately left him to the care of his mother, whom, as she was now set free from her husband, he probably imagined likely to treat with great tenderness the child that had contributed to so pleasing an event. It is not indeed easy to discover what motives could be found to over-balance that natural affection of a parent, or what interest could be promoted by neglect or cruelty. The dread of shame or of poverty, by which some wretches have been incited to abandon or to murder their children, cannot be supposed to have affected a woman who had proclaimed her crimes and solicited reproach, and on whom the clemency of the legislature had undeservedly bestowed a fortune, which would have been very little diminished by the expences which the care of her child could have brought upon her. It was therefore not likely that she would be wicked without temptation, that she would look upon her son from his birth with a kind of resentment and abhorrence; and instead of supporting, assisting, and defending him, delight to see him struggling with misery, or that she would take every opportunity of aggravating his misfortunes, and obstructing his resources, and with an implacable and restless cruelty continue her persecution from the first hour of his life to the last.

But whatever were her motives, no sooner was her son born, than she discovered a resolution of disowning him; and in a very short time removed him from her sight, by committing him to the care of a poor woman, whom she directed to educate him as her own, and injoined never to inform him of his true parents.

Such was the beginning of the life of Richard Savage: Born with a legal claim to honour and to affluence, he was in two months illegitimated by the Parliament, and disowned by his mother, doomed to poverty and obscurity, and launched upon the ocean of life, only that he might be swallowed by its quicksands, or dashed upon its rocks.

His mother could not indeed infect others with the same cruelty. As it was impossible to avoid the inquiries which the curiosity or tenderness of her relations made after her child, she was obliged to give some account of the measures that she had taken, and her mother, the Lady Mason, whether in approbation of her design, or to prevent more criminal contrivances, engaged to transact with the nurse, to pay her for her care, and to superintend the education of the child.

In this charitable office she was assisted by his godmother Mrs. Loyd, who while she lived always looked upon him with that tenderness, which the barbarity of his mother made peculiarly necessary; but her death, which happened in his tenth year, was another of the misfortunes of his childhood; for though she kindly endeavoured to alleviate his loss by a legacy of three hundred pounds, yet as he had none to prosecute his claim, to shelter him from oppression, or call in law to the assistance of justice, her will was eluded by the executors, and no part of the money was ever paid.

He was however not yet wholly abandoned. The Lady Mason still continued her care, and directed him to be placed at a small grammar school near St. Alban's, where he was called by the name of his nurse, without the least intimation that he had a claim to any other.

Here he was initiated in literature, and passed through several of the classes, with what rapidity or what applause cannot now be known. As he always spoke with respect of his master, it is probable that the mean rank, in which he then appeared, did not hinder his genius from being distinguished, or his industry from being rewarded, and if in so low a state he obtained distinction and rewards, it is not likely that they were gained but by genius and industry.

It is very reasonable to conjecture, that his application was equal to his abilities, because his improvement was more than proportioned to the opportunities which he enjoyed; nor can it be doubted, that if his earliest productions had been preserved, like those of happier students, we might in some have found vigorous sallies of that sprightly humour, which distinguishes the *Author to be let,* and in others, strong touches of that ardent imagination which painted the solemn scenes of *The Wanderer*.

While he was thus cultivating his genius, his father the Earl Rivers was seized with a distemper, which in a short time put an end to his life. He had frequently inquired after his son, and had always been amused with fallacious and evasive answers; but being now in his own opinion on his death-bed, he thought it his duty to provide for him among his other natural children, and therefore demanded a positive account of him, with an importunity not to be diverted or denied. His mother, who could no longer refuse an answer, determined at least to give such as should cut him off for ever from that happiness which competence affords, and therefore declared that he was dead; which is perhaps the first instance of a lie invented by a mother to deprive her son of a provision which was designed him by another, and which she could not expect herself, though he should lose it.

This was therefore an act of wickedness which could not be

defeated, because it could not be suspected; the Earl did not imagine, that there could exist in a human form a mother that would ruin her son without enriching herself, and therefore bestowed upon some other person six thousand pounds, which he had in his will bequeathed to Savage.

The same cruelty which incited his mother to intercept this provision which had been intended him, prompted her in a short time to another project, a project worthy of such a disposition. She endeavoured to rid herself from the danger of being at any time made known to him, by sending him secretly to the American plantations.[2]

By whose kindness this scheme was counteracted, or by what interposition she was induced to lay aside her design, I know not; it is not improbable that the Lady Mason might persuade or compel her to desist, or perhaps she could not easily find accomplices wicked enough to concur in so cruel an action; for it may be conceived, that those who had by a long gradation of guilt hardened their hearts against the sense of common wickedness, would yet be shocked at the design of a mother to expose her son to slavery and want, to expose him without interest, and without provocation; and Savage might on this occasion find protectors and advocates among those who had long traded in crimes, and whom compassion had never touched before.

Being hindered, by whatever means, from banishing him into another country, she formed soon after a scheme for burying him in poverty and obscurity in his own; and that his station of life, if not the place of his residence, might keep him for ever at a distance from her, she ordered him to be placed with a shoemaker in Holbourn, that after the usual time of trial, he might become his apprentice.[3]

It is generally reported, that this project was for some time successful, and that Savage was employed at the awl longer than he was willing to confess; nor was it perhaps any great advantage to him, that an unexpected discovery determined him to quit his occupation.

About this time his nurse, who had always treated him as her own son, died; and it was natural for him to take care of those effects which by her death were, as he imagined, become his own; he therefore went to her house, opened her boxes, and examined her papers, among which he found some letters written to her by the Lady Mason, which informed him of his birth, and the reasons for which it was concealed.

He was now no longer satisfied with the employment which had been allotted him, but thought he had a right to share the affluence of his mother, and therefore without scruple applied to her as her son, and made use of every art to awaken her tenderness, and attract her regard. But neither his letters, nor the interposition of those friends which his merit or his distress procured him, made any impression upon her mind: She still resolved to neglect, though she could no longer disown him.

It was to no purpose that he frequently solicited her to admit him to see her; she avoided him with the most vigilant precaution, and ordered him to be excluded from her house, by whomsoever he might be introduced, and what reason soever he might give for entering it.

Savage was at the same time so touched with the discovery of his real mother, that it was his frequent practice to walk in the dark evenings[4] for several hours before her door, in hopes of seeing her as she might come by accident to the window, or cross her apartment with a candle in her hand.

But all his assiduity and tenderness were without effect, for he could neither soften her heart, nor open her hand, and was reduced to the utmost miseries of want, while he was endeavouring to awaken the affection of a mother: He was therefore obliged to seek some other means of support, and having no profession, became, by necessity, an author.

At this time the attention of all the literary world was engrossed by the Bangorian Controversy, which filled the press with pamphlets, and the coffee-houses with disputants. Of this subject, as most popular, he made choice for his first attempt, and without any other knowledge of the question, than he had casually collected from conversation, published a poem against the bishop.

What was the success or merit of this performance I know not, it was probably lost among the innumerable pamphlets to which that dispute gave occasion. Mr. Savage was himself in a little time ashamed of it, and endeavoured to suppress it, by destroying all the copies that he could collect.

He then attempted a more gainful kind of writing,[5] and in his eighteenth year offered to the stage a comedy borrowed from a Spanish plot, which was refused by the players, and was therefore given by him to Mr. Bullock, who having more interest, made some slight alterations, and brought it upon the stage, under the title of[6] *Woman's a Riddle,* but allowed the unhappy author no part of the profit.

Not discouraged however at his repulse, he wrote two years afterwards *Love in a Veil,* another comedy, borrowed likewise from the Spanish, but with little better success than before; for though it was received and acted, yet it appeared so late in the year, that the author obtained no other advantage from it, than the acquaintance of Sir Richard Steele, and Mr. Wilks; by whom he was pitied, caressed, and relieved.

Sir Richard Steele having declared in his favour with all the ardour of benevolence which constituted his character, promoted his interest with the utmost zeal, related his misfortunes, applauded his merit, took all opportunities of recommending him, and asserted[7] that *the inhumanity of his mother had given him a right to find every good man his father.*

Nor was Mr. Savage admitted to his acquaintance only, but to his confidence, of which he sometimes related an instance too extraordinary to be omitted, as it affords a very just idea of his patron's character.

He was once desired by Sir Richard, with an air of the utmost importance, to come very early to his house the next morning. Mr. Savage came as he had promised, found the chariot at the door, and Sir Richard waiting for him, and ready to go out. What was intended, and whither they were to go, Savage could not conjecture, and was not willing to enquire; but immediately seated himself with Sir Richard; the coachman was ordered to drive, and they hurried with the utmost expedition to Hyde-park Corner, where they stopped at a petty tavern, and retired to a private room. Sir Richard then informed him, that he intended to publish a pamphlet, and that he had desired him to come thither that he might write for him. They soon sat down to the work, Sir Richard dictated, and Savage wrote, till the dinner that had been ordered was put upon the table. Savage was surprised at the meanness of the entertainment, and after some hesitation, ventured to ask for wine, which Sir Richard, not without reluctance, ordered to be brought. They then finished their dinner, and proceeded in their pamphlet, which they concluded in the afternoon.

Mr. Savage then imagined his task over, and expected that Sir Richard would call for the reckoning, and return home; but his expectations deceived him, for Sir Richard told him, that he was without money, and that the pamphlet must be sold before the dinner could be paid for; and Savage was therefore obliged to go and offer their new production to sale for two guineas, which with some difficulty he obtained. Sir Richard then returned home, having retired that day only to avoid his creditors, and composed the pamphlet only to discharge his reckoning.

Mr. Savage related another fact equally uncommon, which, though it has no relation to his life, ought to be preserved. Sir Richard Steele having one day invited to his house a great number of persons of the first quality, they were surprised at the number of liveries which surrounded the table; and after dinner, when wine and mirth had set them free from the observation of rigid ceremony, one of them enquired of Sir Richard, how such an expensive train of domestics could be consistent with his fortune. Sir Richard very frankly confessed, that they were fellows of whom he would very willingly be rid. And being then asked, why he did not discharge them, declared that they were bailiffs who had introduced themselves with an execution, and whom, since he could not send them away, he had thought it convenient to embellish with liveries, that they might do him credit while they staid.

His friends were diverted with the expedient, and by paying the debt discharged their attendance, having obliged Sir Richard to promise that they should never again find him graced with a retinue of the same kind.

Under such a tutor, Mr. Savage was not likely to learn prudence or frugality, and perhaps many of the misfortunes which the want of those virtues brought upon him in the following parts of his life, might be justly imputed to so unimproving an example.

Nor did the kindness of Sir Richard end in common favours. He proposed to have established him in some settled scheme of life, and to have contracted a kind of alliance with him, by marrying him to a natural daughter, on whom he intended to bestow a thousand pounds. But though he was always lavish of future bounties, he conducted his affairs in such a manner, that he was very seldom able to keep his promises, or execute his own intentions; and as he was never able to raise the sum which he had offered, the marriage was delayed. In the mean time he was officiously informed that Mr. Savage had ridiculed him; by which he was so much exasperated, that he withdrew the allowance which he had paid him, and never afterwards admitted him to his house.

It is not indeed unlikely that Savage might by his imprudence expose himself to the malice of a tale-bearer; for his patron had many follies, which as his discernment easily discovered, his imagination might sometimes incite him to mention too ludicrously. A little knowledge of the world is sufficient to discover that such weakness is very common, and that there are few who do not sometimes in the wantonness of thoughtless mirth, or the heat of transient resentment, speak of their friends and benefactors with levity and contempt, though in their cooler moments, they want neither sense of their kindness, nor reverence for their virtue. The fault therefore of Mr. Savage was rather negligence than ingratitude; but Sir Richard must likewise be acquitted of severity, for who is there that can patiently bear contempt from one whom he has relieved and supported, whose establishment he has laboured, and whose interest he has promoted?

He was now again abandoned to fortune, without any other friend than Mr. Wilks; a man, who, whatever were his abilities or skill as an actor, deserves at least to be remembered for his virtues,[8] which are not often to be found in the world, and perhaps less often in his profession than in others. To be humane, generous and candid, is a very high degree of merit in any state; but those qualities deserve still greater praise, when they are found in that condition, which makes almost every other man, for whatever reason, contemptuous, insolent, petulant, selfish, and brutal.

As Mr. Wilks was one of those to whom calamity seldom complained without relief, he naturally took an unfortunate wit into his protection, and not only assisted him in any casual distresses, but continued an equal and steady kindness to the time of his death.

By his interposition Mr. Savage once obtained from his mother[9] fifty pounds, and a promise of one hundred and fifty more; but it was the fate of this unhappy man, that few promises of any advantage to him were performed. His mother was infected among others with the general madness of the South-Sea traffick, and having been disappointed in her expectations, refused to pay what perhaps nothing but the prospect of sudden affluence prompted her to promise.

Being thus obliged to depend upon the friendship of Mr. Wilks, he was consequently an assiduous frequenter of the theatres, and in a short time the amusements of the stage took such possession of his mind, that he never was absent from a play in several years.

This constant attendance naturally procured him the acquaintance of the players, and among others, of Mrs. Oldfield, who was so much pleased with his conversation, and touched with his misfortunes, that she allowed him a settled pension of fifty pounds a year, which was during her life regularly paid.

That this act of generosity may receive its due praise, and that the good actions of Mrs. Oldfield may not be sullied by her general character, it is proper to mention what Mr. Savage often declared in the strongest terms, that he never saw her alone, or in any other place than behind the scenes.

At her death, he endeavoured to shew his gratitude in the most decent manner, by wearing mourning as for a mother, but did not celebrate her in elegies, because he knew that too great profusion of praise would only have revived those faults which his natural equity did not allow him to think less, because they were committed by one who favoured him; but of which, though his virtue would not endeavour to palliate them, his gratitude would not suffer him to prolong the memory, or diffuse the censure.

In his *Wanderer*, he has indeed taken an opportunity of mentioning her, but celebrates her not for her virtue, but her beauty, an excellence which none ever denied her: This is the only encomium with which he has rewarded her liberality, and perhaps he has even in this been too lavish of his praise. He seems to have thought that never to mention his benefactress, would have an appearance of ingratitude, though to have dedicated any particular performance to her memory, would have only betrayed an officious partiality, that without exalting her character, would have depressed his own.

He had sometimes, by the kindness of Mr. Wilks, the advantage of a benefit, on which occasions he often received uncommon marks of regard and compassion; and was once told by the Duke of Dorset, that it was just to consider him as an injured nobleman, and that in his opinion the nobility ought to think themselves obliged without solicitation to take every opportunity of supporting him by their countenance and patronage. But he had generally the mortification to hear that the whole interest of his mother was employed to frustrate his applications, and that she never left any expedient untried, by which he might be cut off from the possibility of supporting life. The same disposition she endeavoured to diffuse among all those over whom nature or fortune gave her any influence, and indeed succeeded too well in her design; but could not always propagate her effrontery with her cruelty, for some of those whom she incited against him, were ashamed of their own conduct, and boasted of that relief which they never gave him.

In this censure I do not indiscriminately involve all his relations; for he has mentioned with gratitude the humanity of one lady, whose name I am now unable to recollect, and to whom therefore I cannot pay the praises which she deserves for having acted well in opposition to influence, precept and example.

The punishment which our laws inflict upon those parents who murder their infants, is well known, nor has its justice ever been contested; but if they deserve death who destroy a child in its birth, what pains can be severe enough for her who forbears to destroy him only to inflict sharper miseries upon him; who prolongs his life only to make it miserable; and who exposes him without care and without pity, to the malice of oppression, the caprices of chance, and the temptations of poverty; who rejoices to see him overwhelmed with calamities; and when his own industry, or the charity of others, has enabled him to rise for a short time above his miseries, plunges him again into his former distress?

The kindness of his friends not affording him any constant supply, and the prospect of improving his fortune, by enlarging his acquaintance, necessarily leading him to places of expence, he found it necessary[1] to endeavour once more at dramatic poetry, for which he was now better qualified by a more extensive knowl-

attempt a species of writing of which all the
long before exhausted, and which was made at
y the multitudes that had failed in it, and those
ded.

advancing in reputation, and though frequently
y distressful perplexities, appeared however to be
mankind, when both his fame and his life were
y an event, of which it is not yet determined,
ht to be mentioned as a crime or a calamity.

of November 1727, Mr. Savage came from Rich-
e then lodged that he might persue his studies with
ion, with an intent to discharge another lodging
d in Westminster, and accidentally meeting two
s acquaintances, whose names were Merchant and
went in with them to a neighbouring coffee-house,
ing till it was late, it being in no time of Mr. Savage's
of his character to be the first of the company that
eparate. He would willingly have gone to bed in the
but there was not room for the whole company, and
ey agreed to ramble about the streets, and divert
with such amusements as should offer themselves till

walk they happened unluckily to discover light in
Coffee-house, near Charing-Cross, and therefore went
ant with some rudeness, demanded a room, and was
there was a good fire in the next parlour, which the
were about to leave, being then paying their reckoning.
not satisfied with this answer, rushed into the room, and
wed by his companions. He then petulantly placed him-
een the company and the fire, and soon after kicked down
. This produced a quarrel, swords were drawn on both
d one Mr. James Sinclair was killed. Savage having
d likewise a maid that held him, forced his way with
t out of the house; but being intimidated and confused,
resolution either to fly or stay, they were taken in a back
y one of the company and some soldiers, whom he had
o his assistance.

g secured and guarded that night, they were in the morning
before three justices, who committed them to the Gate-

edge, and longer observation. But having been unsuccessful in comedy, though rather for want of opportunities than genius, he resolved now to try whether he should not be more fortunate in exhibiting a tragedy.

The story which he chose for the subject, was that of Sir Thomas Overbury, a story well adapted to the stage, though perhaps not far enough removed from the present age, to admit properly the fictions necessary to complete the plan; for the mind which naturally loves truth is always most offended with the violation of those truths of which we are most certain, and we of course conceive those facts most certain which approach nearest to our own time.

Out of this story he formed a tragedy, which, if the circumstances in which he wrote it be considered, will afford at once an uncommon proof of strength of genius, an evenness of mind, of a serenity not to be ruffled, and an imagination not to be suppressed.

During a considerable part of the time, in which he was employed upon this performance, he was without lodging, and often without meat; nor had he any other conveniences for study than the fields or the street allowed him, there he used to walk and form his speeches, and afterwards step into a shop, beg for a few moments the use of the pen and ink, and write down what he had composed upon paper which he had picked up by accident.

If the performance of a writer thus distressed is not perfect, its faults ought surely to be imputed to a cause very different from want of genius, and must rather excite pity than provoke censure.

But when under these discouragements the tragedy was finished, there yet remained the labour of introducing it on the stage, an undertaking which to an ingenuous mind was in a very high degree vexatious and disgusting; for having little interest or reputation, he was obliged to submit himself wholly to the players, and admit, with whatever reluctance, the emendations of Mr. Cibber, which he always considered as the disgrace of his performance.

He had indeed in Mr. Hill another critic of a very different class, from whose friendship he received great assistance on many occasions, and whom he never mentioned but with the utmost tenderness and regard.[2] He had been for some time distinguished by him with very particular kindness, and on this occasion it was natural to apply to him as an author of an established character. He therefore sent this tragedy to him with a short copy of verses,[3] in which he desired his correction. Mr. Hill, whose humanity and politeness are generally known, readily complied with his request; but as he is remarkable for singularity of sentiment, and bold experiments in language, Mr. Savage did not think his play much improved by his innovation, and had even at that time the courage to reject several passages which he could not approve, and what is still more laudable, Mr. Hill had the generosity not to resent the neglect of his alterations, but wrote the Prologue and Epilogue, in which he touches on the circumstances of the author with great tenderness.[4]

After all these obstructions and compliances, he was only able to bring his play upon the stage in the summer, when the chief actors had retired, and the rest were in possession of the house for their own advantage. Among these Mr. Savage was admitted to play the part of Sir Thomas Overbury, by which he gained no great reputation, the theatre being a province for which nature seemed not to have designed him; for neither his voice, look, nor gesture, were such as are expected on the stage, and he was himself so much ashamed of having been reduced to appear as a player, that he always blotted out his name from the list, when a copy of his tragedy was to be shown to his friends.

In the publication of his performance he was more successful, for the rays of genius that glimmered in it, that glimmered through all the mists which poverty and Cibber had been able to spread over it, procured him the notice and esteem of many persons eminent for their rank, their virtue, and their wit.

Of this play, acted, printed, and dedicated, the accumulated profits arose to an hundred pounds, which he thought at that time a very large sum, having been never master of so much before.

In the Dedication,[5] for which he received ten guineas, there is nothing remarkable. The Preface contains a very liberal encomium on the blooming excellencies of Mr. Theophilus Cibber, which Mr. Savage could not in the latter part of his life see his friends about to read without snatching the play out of their hands.

The generosity of Mr. Hill did not end on this occasion; for afterwards when Mr. Savage's necessities returned, he encouraged a subscription to a Miscellany of Poems in a very extraordinary

manner, by publi
affecting lines,[7] w
Savage upon the tr
of which he was h
declared. These line
had a very powerfu
making her cruelty
aversion.

Mr. Hill not only pr
but furnished likewise
is composed, and parti
lished as a specimen.

The subscriptions of t
to patronise merit in dist
directed to be left at Butt
thither a few days afterw
from his proposal, found t
had been sent him in cons
Mr. Hill's pathetic represen

To this Miscellany he wr
account of his mother's cru
humour, and with a gaiety o
his subscription probably pro

The Dedication is addres
Montague, whom he flatters w
truth, with very little[1] art. The s
to all his Dedications: his comp
lent, heaped together without th
of introduction: he seems to hav
perusal only of his patrons, and t
other task than to pamper them w
that flattery would make its way t
ance of elegance or invention.

Soon afterwards the death of t
subject for a poetical contest, in whi
is allowed to have carried the prize
tors; but I know not whether he gai
other advantage than the increase o
must certainly have been with farthe

house, from whence, upon the death of Mr. Sinclair, which happened the same day, they were removed in the night to Newgate, where they were however treated with some distinction, exempted from the ignominy of chains, and confined, not among the common criminals, but in the Press-Yard.

When the day of trial came, the court was crouded in a very unusual manner, and the publick appeared to interest itself as in a cause of general concern. The witnesses against Mr. Savage and his friends were, the woman who kept the house, which was a house of ill fame, and her maid, the men who were in the room with Mr. Sinclair, and a woman of the town, who had been drinking with them, and with whom one of them had been seen in bed. They swore in general, that Merchant gave the provocation, which Savage and Gregory drew their swords to justify; that Savage drew first, and that he stabbed Sinclair when he was not in a posture of defence, or while Gregory commanded his sword; that after he had given the thrust he turned pale, and would have retired, but that the maid clung round him, and one of the company endeavoured to detain him, from whom he broke, by cutting the maid on the head, but was afterwards taken in a court.

There was some difference in their depositions; one did not see Savage give the wound, another saw it given when Sinclair held his point towards the ground; and the woman of the town asserted, that she did not see Sinclair's sword at all: This difference however was very far from amounting to inconsistency, but it was sufficient to shew, that the hurry of the dispute was such, that it was not easy to discover the truth with relation to particular circumstances, and that therefore some deductions were to be made from the credibility of the testimonies.

Sinclair had declared several times before his death, that he received his wound from Savage, nor did Savage at his trial deny the fact, but endeavoured partly to extenuate it by urging the suddenness of the whole action, and the impossibility of any ill design, or premeditated malice, and partly to justify it by the necessity of self-defence, and the hazard of his own life, if he had lost that opportunity of giving the thrust: He observed, that neither reason nor law obliged a man to wait for the blow which was threatened, and which, if he should suffer it, he might never be able to return; that it was always allowable to prevent an assault, and to preserve life by taking away that of the adversary, by whom it was endangered.

With regard to the violence with which he endeavoured his escape, he declared, that it was not his design to fly from justice, or decline a trial, but to avoid the expences and severities of a prison, and that he intended to have appeared at the bar without compulsion.

This defence, which took up more than an hour, was heard by the multitude that thronged the court with the most attentive and respectful silence: Those who thought he ought not to be acquitted owned that applause could not be refused him; and those who before pitied his misfortunes, now reverenced his abilities.

The witnesses which appeared against him were proved to be persons of characters which did not entitle them to much credit; a common strumpet, a woman by whom strumpets were entertained, and a man by whom they were supported; and the character of Savage was by several persons of distinction asserted, to be that of a modest inoffensive man, not inclined to broils, or to insolence, and who had, to that time, been only known for his misfortunes and his wit.

Had his audience been his judges, he had undoubtedly been acquitted; but Mr. Page, who was then upon the bench, treated him with his usual insolence and severity, and when he had summed up the evidence, endeavoured to exasperate the jury, as Mr. Savage used to relate it, with this eloquent harangue.

"Gentlemen of the jury, you are to consider, that Mr. Savage is a very great man, a much greater man than you or I, gentlemen of the jury; that he wears very fine clothes, much finer clothes than you or I, gentlemen of the jury; that he has abundance of money in his pocket, much more money than you or I, gentlemen of the jury; but, gentlemen of the jury, is it not a very hard case, gentlemen of the jury, that Mr. Savage should therefore kill you or me, gentlemen of the jury?"

Mr. Savage hearing his defence thus misrepresented, and the men who were to decide his fate incited against him by invidious comparisons, resolutely asserted, that his cause was not candidly explained, and began to recapitulate what he had before said with regard to his condition and the necessity of endeavouring to escape the expences of imprisonment; but the judge having ordered him to be silent, and repeated his orders without effect, commanded that he should be taken from the bar by force.

The jury then heard the opinion of the judge, that good characters were of no weight against positive evidence, though they might turn the scale, where it was doubtful; and that though when two men attack each other, the death of either is only manslaughter; but where one is the aggressor, as in the case before them, and in pursuance of his first attack, kills the other, the law supposes the action, however sudden, to be malicious. They then deliberated upon their verdict, and determined that Mr. Savage and Mr. Gregory were guilty of murder, and Mr. Merchant, who had no sword, only of manslaughter.

Thus ended this memorable trial, which lasted eight hours. Mr. Savage and Mr. Gregory were conducted back to prison, where they were more closely confined, and loaded with irons of fifty pounds weight: Four days afterwards they were sent back to the court to receive sentence; on which occasion Mr. Savage made, as far as it could be retained in memory, the following speech.

"It is now, my Lord, too late to offer any thing by way of defence, or vindication; nor can we expect ought from your Lordships, in this court, but the sentence which the law requires you, as judges, to pronounce against men of our calamitous condition. —But we are also persuaded, that as mere men, and out of this seat of rigorous justice, you are susceptive of the tender passions, and too humane, not to commiserate the unhappy situation of those, whom the law sometimes perhaps—exacts—from you to pronounce upon. No doubt you distinguish between offences, which arise out of premeditation, and a disposition habituated to vice or immorality, and transgressions, which are the unhappy and unforeseen effects of a casual absence of reason, and sudden impulse of passion: We therefore hope you will contribute all you can to an extension of that mercy, which the gentlemen of the jury have been pleased to shew Mr. Merchant, who (allowing facts as sworn against us by the evidence) has led us into this our calamity. I hope, this will not be construed as if we meant to reflect upon that gentleman, or remove any thing from us upon him, or that we repine the more at our fate, because he has no participation of it: No, my Lord! For my part, I declare nothing could more soften my grief, than to be without any companion in so great a misfortune."[2]

Mr. Savage had now no hopes of life, but from the mercy of the Crown, which was very earnestly solicited by his friends, and which, with whatever difficulty the story may obtain belief, was obstructed only by his mother.

To prejudice the Queen against him, she made use of an incident, which was omitted in the order of time, that it might be mentioned together with the purpose which it was made to serve. Mr. Savage, when he had discovered his birth, had an incessant desire to speak to his mother, who always avoided him in publick, and refused him admission into her house. One evening walking, as it was his custom, in the street that she inhabited, he saw the door of her house by accident open; he entered it, and finding no persons in the passage, to hinder him, went up stairs to salute her. She discovered him before he could enter her chamber, alarmed the family with the most distressful outcries, and when she had by her screams gathered them about her, ordered them to drive out of the house that villain, who had forced himself in upon her, and endeavoured to murder her. Savage, who had attempted with the most submissive tenderness to soften her rage, hearing her utter so detestable an accusation, thought it prudent to retire, and, I believe, never attempted afterwards to speak to her.

But shocked as he was with her falshood and her cruelty, he imagined that she intended no other use of her lie, than to set herself free from his embraces and solicitations, and was very far from suspecting that she would treasure it in her memory, as an instrument of future wickedness, or that she would endeavour for this fictitious assault to deprive him of his life.

But when the Queen was solicited for his pardon, and informed of the severe treatments which he had suffered from his judge, she answered, that however unjustifiable might be the manner of his trial, or whatever extenuation the action for which he was condemned might admit, she could not think that man a proper object of the King's mercy, who had been capable of entering his mother's house in the night, with an intent to murder her.

By whom this atrocious calumny had been transmitted to the Queen, whether she that invented, had the front to relate it; whether she found any one weak enough to credit it, or corrupt enough to concur with her in her hateful design, I know not; but methods had been taken to persuade the Queen so strongly of the truth of it, that she for a long time refused to hear any of those who petitioned for his life.

Thus had Savage perished by the evidence of a bawd, a strumpet, and his mother, had not justice and compassion procured him an advocate of rank too great to be rejected unheard, and of virtue too eminent to be heard without being believed. His merit and his calamities happened to reach the ear of the Countess of Hertford, who engaged in his support with all the tenderness that is excited by pity, and all the zeal which is kindled by generosity, and demanding an audience of the Queen, laid before her the whole series of his mother's cruelty, exposed the improbability of an accusation by which he was charged with an intent to commit a murder, that could produce no advantage, and soon convinced her how little his former conduct could deserve to be mentioned as a reason for extraordinary severity.

The interposition of this lady was so successful, that he was soon after admitted to bail, and on the 9th of March 1728, pleaded the King's pardon.

It is natural to enquire upon what motives his mother could persecute him in a manner so outragious and implacable; for what reason she could employ all the acts of malice and all the snares of calumny, to take away the life of her own son, of a son who never injured her, who was never supported by her expence, nor obstructed any prospect of pleasure or advantage; why she should endeavour to destroy him by a lie; a lie which could not gain credit, but must vanish of itself at the first moment of examination, and of which only this can be said to make it probable, that it may be observed from her conduct, that the most execrable crimes are sometimes committed without apparent temptation.

This mother is still alive, and may perhaps even yet, though her malice was so often defeated, enjoy the pleasure of reflecting, that the life which she often endeavoured to destroy, was at least shortened by her maternal offices; that though she could not transport her son to the plantations, bury him in the shop of a mechanick, or hasten the hand of the publick executioner, she has yet had the satisfaction of imbittering all his hours, and forcing him into exigencies, that hurried on his death.

It is by no means necessary to aggravate the enormity of this woman's conduct, by placing it in opposition to that of the Countess of Hertford; no one can fail to observe how much more amiable it is to relieve, than to oppress, and to rescue innocence from destruction, than to destroy without an injury.

Mr. Savage, during his imprisonment, his trial, and the time in which he lay under sentence of death, behaved with great firmness and equality of mind, and confirmed by his fortitude the esteem of those, who before admired him for his abilities. The peculiar circumstances of his life were made more generally known by a short Account,[3] which was then published, and of which several thousands were in a few weeks dispersed over the nation; and the compassion of mankind operated so powerfully in his favour, that he was enabled, by frequent presents, not only to support himself, but to assist Mr. Gregory in prison; and when he was pardoned and released he found the number of his friends not lessened.

The nature of the act for which he had been tried was in itself doubtful; of the evidences which appeared against him, the character of the man was not unexceptionable, that of the women notoriously infamous; she whose testimony chiefly influenced the jury to condemn him, afterwards retracted her assertions. He always himself denied that he was drunk, as had been generally reported. Mr. Gregory, who is now Collector of Antegua, is said to declare him far less criminal than he was imagined, even by some who favoured him: And Page himself afterwards confessed, that he had treated him with uncommon rigour. When all these particulars are rated together, perhaps the memory of Savage may not be much sullied by his trial.

Some time after he had obtained his liberty, he met in the street the woman that had sworn with so much malignity against him. She informed him, that she was in distress, and, with a degree of confidence not easily attainable, desired him to relieve her. He, instead of insulting her misery, and taking pleasure in the calamities of one who had brought his life into danger, reproved her gently for her perjury, and changing the only guinea that he had, divided it equally between her and himself.

This is an action which in some ages would have made a saint, and perhaps in others a hero, and which, without any hyperbolical encomiums, must be allowed to be an instance of uncommon generosity, an act of complicated virtue; by which he at once relieved the poor, corrected the vicious, and forgave an enemy; by which he at once remitted the strongest provocations, and exercised the most ardent charity.

Compassion was indeed the distinguishing quality of Savage; he never appeared inclined to take advantage of weakness, to attack the defenceless, or to press upon the falling; whoever was distressed was certain at least of his good-wishes; and when he could give no assistance, to extricate them from misfortunes, he endeavoured to sooth them by sympathy and tenderness.

But when his heart was not softened by the sight of misery, he was sometimes obstinate in his resentment, and did not quickly lose the remembrance of an injury. He always continued to speak with anger of the insolence and partiality of Page, and a short time before his death revenged it by a satire.[4]

It is natural to enquire in what terms Mr. Savage spoke of this fatal action, when the danger was over, and he was under no necessity of using any art to set his conduct in the fairest light. He was not willing to dwell upon it, and if he transiently mentioned it, appeared neither to consider himself as a murderer, nor as a man wholly free from the guilt of blood.[5] How much and how long he regretted it, appeared in a[6] poem which he published many years afterwards. On occasion of a copy of verses in which the failings of good men were recounted, and in which the author had endeavoured to illustrate his position, that *the best may sometimes deviate from virtue,* by an instance of murder committed by Savage in the heat of wine, Savage remarked, that it was no very just representation of a good man, to suppose him liable to drunkenness, and disposed in his riots to cut throats.

He was now indeed at liberty, but was, as before, without any other support than accidental favours and uncertain patronage afforded him; sources by which he was sometimes very liberally supplied, and which at other times were suddenly stopped; so that he spent his life between want and plenty, or what was yet worse, between beggary and extravagance; for as whatever he received was the gift of chance, which might as well favour him at one time as another, he was tempted to squander what he had, because he always hoped to be immediately supplied.

Another cause of his profusion was the absurd kindness of his friends, who at once rewarded and enjoyed his abilities, by treating him at taverns, and habituated him to pleasures which he could not afford to enjoy, and which he was not able to deny himself, though he purchased the luxury of a single night by the anguish of cold and hunger for a week.

The experience of these inconveniences determined him to endeavour after some settled income, which, having long found submission and intreaties fruitless, he attempted to extort from his mother by rougher methods. He had now, as he acknowledged, lost that tenderness for her, which the whole series of her cruelty had not been able wholly to repress, till he found, by the efforts which she made for his destruction, that she was not content with refusing to assist him, and being neutral in his struggles with poverty, but was as ready to snatch every opportunity of adding to his misfortunes, and that she was to be considered as an enemy implacably malicious, whom nothing but his blood could satisfy. He therefore threatened to harass her with lampoons, and to publish a copious narrative of her conduct, unless she consented to purchase an exemption from infamy, by allowing him a pension.

This expedient proved successful. Whether shame still survived, though virtue was extinct, or whether her relations had more delicacy than herself, and imagined that some of the darts which satire might point at her would glance upon them: Lord Tyrconnel, whatever were his motives, upon his promise to lay aside his design of exposing the cruelty of his mother, received him into his family, treated him as his equal, and engaged to allow him a pension of two hundred pounds a year.

This was the golden part of Mr. Savage's life; and for some time he had no reason to complain of fortune; his appearance was splendid, his expences large, and his acquaintance extensive. He was courted by all who endeavoured to be thought men of genius, and caressed by all who valued themselves upon a refined taste. To admire Mr. Savage was a proof of discernment, and to be acquainted with him was a title to poetical reputation. His presence was sufficient to make any place of publick entertainment popular; and his approbation and example constituted the fashion. So powerful is genius, when it is invested with the glitter of affluence; men willingly pay to fortune that regard which they owe to merit, and are pleased when they have an opportunity at once of gratifying their vanity, and practising their duty.

This interval of prosperity furnished him with opportunities of enlarging his knowledge of human nature, by contemplating life from its highest gradations to its lowest, and had he afterwards applied to dramatic poetry, he would perhaps not have had many superiors; for as he never suffered any scene to pass before his eyes without notice, he had treasured in his mind all the different combinations of passions, and the innumerable mixtures of vice and virtue, which distinguish one character from another; and as his conception was strong, his expressions were clear, he easily received impressions from objects, and very forcibly transmitted them to others.

Of his exact observations on human life he has left a proof, which would do honour to the greatest names, in a small pamphlet, called, *The Author to be let,* where he introduces Iscariot Hackney, a prostitute scribler, giving an account of his birth, his education, his disposition and morals, habits of life and maxims of conduct. In the Introduction are related many secret histories of the petty writers of that time, but sometimes mixed with ungenerous reflections on their birth, their circumstances, or those of their relations; nor can it be denied, that some passages are such as Iscariot Hackney might himself have produced.

He was accused likewise of living in an appearance of friendship with some whom he satirised, and of making use of the confidence which he gained by a seeming kindness to discover failings and expose them; it must be confessed, that Mr. Savage's esteem was no very certain possession, and that he would lampoon at one time those whom he had praised at another.

It may be alledged, that the same man may change his principles, and that he who was once deservedly commended, may be afterwards satirised with equal justice, or that the poet was dazzled with the appearance of virtue, and found the man whom he had celebrated, when he had an opportunity of examining him more nearly, unworthy of the panegyric which he had too hastily bestowed; and that as a false satire ought to be recanted, for the sake of him whose reputation may be injured, false praise ought likewise to be obviated, lest the distinction between vice and virtue should be lost, lest a bad man should be trusted upon the credit of his encomiast, or lest others should endeavour to obtain the like praises by the same means.

But though these excuses may be often plausible, and sometimes just, they are very seldom satisfactory to mankind; and the writer, who is not constant to his subject, quickly sinks into contempt, his satire loses its force, and his panegyric its value, and he is only considered at one time as a flatterer, and as a calumniator at another.

To avoid these imputations, it is only necessary to follow the rules of virtue, and to preserve an unvaried regard to truth. For though it is undoubtedly possible, that a man, however cautious, may be sometimes deceived by an artful appearance of virtue, or by false evidences of guilt, such errors will not be frequent; and it will be allowed, that the name of an author would never have been made contemptible, had no man ever said what he did not think, or misled others, but when he was himself deceived.

The[7] *Author to be let* was first published in a single pamphlet, and afterwards inserted in a collection of pieces relating to the *Dunciad,* which were addressed by Mr. Savage to the Earl of Middlesex, in a[8] Dedication, which he was prevailed upon to sign, though he did not write it, and in which there are some positions, that the true author would perhaps not have published under his own name; and on which Mr. Savage afterwards reflected with no great satisfaction.

The enumeration of the bad effects of the *uncontrolled freedom of the press,* and the assertion that the *liberties taken by the writers of journals with their superiors were exorbitant and unjustifiable,* very ill became men, who have themselves not always shewn the exactest regard to the laws of subordination in their writings, and who have often satirised those that at least thought themselves their superiors, as they were eminent for their hereditary rank, and employed in the highest offices of the kingdom. But this is only an instance of that partiality which almost every man indulges with regard to himself; the liberty of the press is a blessing when we are inclined to write against others, and a calamity when we find ourselves overborn by the multitude of our assailants; as the power of the Crown is always thought too great by those who suffer by its influence, and too little by those in whose favour it is exerted; and a standing army is generally accounted necessary by those who command, and dangerous and oppressive by those who support it.

Mr. Savage was likewise very far from believing, that the letters annexed to each species of bad poets in the *Bathos*, were, as he was directed to assert, *set down at random;* for when he was charged by one of his friends with putting his name to such an improbability, he had no other answer to make, than that *he did not think of it*, and his friend had too much tenderness to reply, that next to the crime of writing contrary to what he thought, was that of writing without thinking.

After having remarked what is false in this Dedication, it is proper that I observe the impartiality which I recommend, by declaring what Savage asserted, that the account of the circumstances which attended the publication of the *Dunciad*, however strange and improbable, was exactly true.

The publication of this piece at this time raised Mr. Savage a great number of enemies among those that were attacked by Mr. Pope, with whom he was considered as a kind of confederate, and whom he was suspected of supplying with private intelligence and secret incidents: So that the ignominy of an informer was added to the terror of a satirist.

That he was not altogether free from literary hypocrisy, and that he sometimes spoke one thing, and wrote another, cannot be denied, because he himself confessed, that when he lived in great familiarity with Dennis, he wrote an epigram[9] against him.

Mr. Savage however set all the malice of all the pigmy writers at defiance, and thought the friendship of Mr. Pope cheaply purchased by being exposed to their censure and their hatred; nor had he any reason to repent of the preference, for he found Mr. Pope a steady and unalienable friend almost to the end of his life.

About this time, notwithstanding his avowed neutrality with regard to party, he published a panegyric on Sir Robert Walpole, for which he was rewarded by him with twenty guineas, a sum not very large, if either the excellence of the performance, or the affluence of the patron be considered; but greater than he afterwards obtained from a person of yet higher rank, and more desirous in appearance of being distinguished as a patron of literature.

As he was very far from approving the conduct of Sir Robert Walpole, and in conversation mentioned him sometimes with acrimony, and generally with contempt, as he was one of those who were always zealous in their assertions of the justice of the late opposition, jealous of the rights of the people, and alarmed by the long continued triumph of the Court; it was natural to ask him what could induce him to employ his poetry in praise of that man who was, in his opinion, an enemy to liberty, and an oppressor of his country? He alleged, that he was then dependent upon the Lord Tyrconnel, who was an implicite follower of the ministry, and that being enjoined by him, not without menaces, to write in praise of his leader, he had not resolution sufficient to sacrifice the pleasure of affluence to that of integrity.

On this and on many other occasions he was ready to lament the misery of living at the tables of other men, which was his fate from the beginning to the end of his life; for I know not whether he ever had, for three months together, a settled habitation, in which he could claim a right of residence.

To this unhappy state it is just to impute much of the inconstancy of his conduct; for though a readiness to comply with the inclination of others was no part of his natural character, yet he was sometimes obliged to relax his obstinacy, and submit his own judgment and even his virtue to the government of those by whom he was supported: So that if his miseries were sometimes the consequences of his faults, he ought not yet to be wholly excluded from compassion, because his faults were very often the effects of his misfortunes.

In this gay period[1] of his life, while he was surrounded by affluence and pleasure, he published the *Wanderer,* a moral poem of which the design is comprised in these lines:

> I fly all public care, all venal strife,
> To try the *still* compar'd with *active life,*
> To prove by these, the sons of men may owe
> The fruits of bliss to bursting clouds of woe;
> That even calamity by thought refin'd
> Inspirits and adorns the thinking mind.

and more distinctly in the following passage;

> By woe the soul to daring action swells,
> By woe in plaintless patience it excels;
> From patience prudent, clear experience springs,

And traces knowledge through the course of things.
Thence hope is form'd, thence fortitude, success,
Renown—whate'er men covet and caress.

This performance was always considered by himself as his master-piece, and Mr. Pope, when he asked his opinion of it, told him, that he read it once over, and was not displeased with it, that it gave him more pleasure at the second perusal, and delighted him still more at the third.

It has been generally objected to the *Wanderer*, that the disposition of the parts is irregular, that the design is obscure, and the plan perplexed, that the images, however beautiful, succeed each other without order; and that the whole performance is not so much a regular fabric as a heap of shining materials thrown together by accident, which strikes rather with the solemn magnificence of a stupendous ruin, than the elegant grandeur of a finished pile.

This criticism is universal, and therefore it is reasonable to believe it at least in a great degree just; but Mr. Savage was always of a contrary opinion, and thought his drift could only be missed by negligence or stupidity, and that the whole plan was regular, and the parts distinct.

It was never denied to abound with strong representations of nature, and just observations upon life, and it may easily be observed, that most of his pictures have an evident tendency to illustrate his first great position, *that good is the consequence of evil.* The sun that burns up the mountains, fructifies the vales, the deluge that rushes down the broken rocks with dreadful impetuosity, is separated into purling brooks; and the rage of the hurricane purifies the air.

Even in this poem he has not been able to forbear one touch upon the cruelty of his mother,[2] which though remarkably delicate and tender, is a proof how deep an impression it had made upon his mind.

This must be at least acknowledged, which ought to be thought equivalent to many other excellencies, that this poem can promote no other purposes than those of virtue, and that it is written with a very strong sense of the efficacy of religion.

But my province is rather to give the history of Mr. Savage's performances, than to display their beauties, or to obviate the criticisms, which they have occasioned, and therefore I shall not dwell upon the particular passages which deserve applause: I shall neither show the excellence of his descriptions,[3] nor expatiate on the terrific portrait of Suicide,[4] nor point out the artful touches,[5] by which he has distinguished the intellectual features of the rebels, who suffer death in his last canto. It is, however, proper to observe, that Mr. Savage always declared the characters wholly fictitious, and without the least allusion to any real persons or actions.

From a poem so diligently laboured, and so successfully finished, it might be reasonably expected that he should have gained considerable advantage; nor can it, without some degree of indignation and concern, be told that he sold the copy for ten guineas, of which he afterwards returned two, that the two last sheets of the work might be reprinted, of which he had in his absence intrusted the correction to a friend, who was too indolent to perform it with accuracy.

A superstitious regard to the correction of his sheets was one of Mr. Savage's peculiarities; he often altered, revised, recurred to his first reading or punctuation, and again adopted the alteration; he was dubious and irresolute without end, as on a question of the last importance, and at last was seldom satisfied; the intrusion or omission of a comma was sufficient to discompose him, and he would lament an error of a single letter as a heavy calamity. In one of his letters relating to an impression of some verses he remarks, that he had with regard to the correction of the proof *a spell upon him,* and indeed the anxiety, with which he dwelt upon the minutest and most trifling niceties, deserved no other name than that of fascination.

That he sold so valuable a performance for so small a price was not to be imputed either to necessity by which the learned and ingenious are often obliged to submit to very hard conditions, or to avarice by which the book-sellers are frequently incited to oppress that genius by which they are supported, but to that intemperate desire of pleasure, and habitual slavery to his passions, which involved him in many perplexities; he happened at that time to be engaged in the pursuit of some trifling gratification, and being without money for the present occasion, sold his poem to the first bidder, and perhaps for the first price that was proposed, and would probably have been content with less, if less had been offered him.

This poem was addressed to the Lord Tyrconnel not only in the first lines,[6] but in a formal dedication filled with the highest strains of panegyric, and the warmest professions of gratitude, but by no means remarkable for delicacy of connection or elegance of stile.

These praises in a short time he found himself inclined to retract, being discarded by the man on whom he had bestowed them, and whom he then immediately discovered not to have deserved them. Of this quarrel, which every day made more bitter, Lord Tyrconnel and Mr. Savage assigned very different reasons, which might perhaps all in reality concur, though they were not all convenient to be alleged by either party. Lord Tyrconnel affirmed, that it was the constant practice of Mr. Savage, to enter a tavern with any company that proposed it, drink the most expensive wines, with great profusion, and when the reckoning was demanded, to be without money: If, as it often happened, his company were willing to defray his part, the affair ended, without any ill consequences; but if they were refractory, and expected that the wine should be paid for by him that drank it, his method of composition was, to take them with him to his own apartment, assume the government of the house, and order the butler in an imperious manner to set the best wine in the cellar before his company, who often drank till they forgot the respect due to the house in which they were entertained, indulged themselves in the utmost extravagance of merriment, practised the most licentious frolics, and committed all the outrages of drunkenness.

Nor was this the only charge which Lord Tyrconnel brought against him: Having given him a collection of valuable books, stamped with his own arms, he had the mortification to see them in a short time exposed to sale upon the stalls, it being usual with Mr. Savage, when he wanted a small sum, to take his books to the pawnbroker.

Whoever was acquainted with Mr. Savage, easily credited both these accusations; for having been obliged from his first entrance into the world to subsist upon expedients, affluence was not able to exalt him above them; and so much was he delighted with wine and conversation, and so long had he been accustomed to live by chance, that he would at any time go to the tavern, without scruple, and trust for his reckoning to the liberality of his company, and frequently of company to whom he was very little known. This conduct indeed very seldom drew upon him those inconveniences that might be feared by any other person, for his conversation was so entertaining, and his address so pleasing, that few thought the pleasure which they received from him dearly purchased by paying for his wine. It was his peculiar happiness, that he scarcely ever found a stranger, whom he did not leave a friend; but it must likewise be added, that he had not often a friend long, without obliging him to become a stranger.

Mr. Savage, on the other hand, declared that Lord Tyrconnel[7] quarrelled with him, because he would not substract from his own luxury and extravagance what he had promised to allow him, and that his resentment was only a plea for the violation of his promise: He asserted that he had done nothing that ought to exclude him from that subsistence which he thought not so much a favour, as a debt, since it was offered him upon conditions, which he had never broken; and that his only fault was, that he could not be supported with nothing.

He acknowledged, that Lord Tyrconnel often exhorted him to regulate his method of life, and not to spend all his nights in taverns, and that he appeared very desirous, that he would pass those hours with him which he so freely bestowed upon others. This demand Mr. Savage considered as a censure of his conduct, which he could never patiently bear; and which in the latter and cooler part of his life was so offensive to him, that he declared it as his resolution, *to spurn that friend who should presume to dictate to him;* and it is not likely, that in his earlier years he received admonitions with more calmness.

He was likewise inclined to resent such expectations, as tending to infringe his liberty, of which he was very jealous when it was necessary to the gratification of his passions, and declared, that the request was still more unreasonable, as the company to which he was to have been confined was insupportably disagreeable. This assertion affords another instance of that inconsistency of his writings with his conversation, which was so often to be observed. He forgot how lavishly he had, in his[8] Dedication to the

Wanderer, extolled the delicacy and penetration, the humanity and generosity, the candour and politeness of the man, whom, when he no longer loved him, he declared to be a wretch without understanding, without good-nature, and without justice; of whose name he thought himself obliged to leave no trace in any future edition of his writings; and accordingly blotted it out of that copy of the *Wanderer* which was in his hands.

During his continuance with the Lord Tyrconnel he wrote *The*[9] *Triumph of Health and Mirth*, on the recovery of Lady Tyrconnel from a languishing illness. This performance is remarkable, not only for the gayety of the ideas, and the melody of the numbers, but for the agreeable fiction upon which it is formed. Mirth overwhelmed with sorrow, for the sickness of her favourite, takes a flight in quest of her sister Health, whom she finds reclined upon the brow of a lofty mountain, amidst the fragrance of perpetual spring, with the breezes of the morning sporting about her. Being solicited by her sister Mirth, she readily promises her assistance, flies away in a cloud, and impregnates the waters of Bath with new virtues, by which the sickness of Belinda is relieved.

As the reputation of his abilities, the particular circumstances of his birth and life, the splendour of his appearance, and the distinction which was for some time paid him by Lord Tyrconnel, intitled him to familiarity with persons of higher rank, than those to whose conversation he had been before admitted, he did not fail to gratify that curiosity, which induced him to take a nearer view of those whom their birth, their employments, or their fortunes, necessarily place at a distance from the greatest part of mankind, and to examine, whether their merit was magnified or diminished by the medium through which it was contemplated; whether the splendour with which they dazzled their admirers, was inherent in themselves, or only reflected on them by the objects that surrounded them; and whether great men were selected for high stations, or high stations made great men.

For this purpose, he took all opportunities of conversing familiarly with those who were most conspicuous at that time, for their power, or their influence; he watched their looser moments, and examined their domestic behaviour, with that acuteness which nature had given him, and which the uncommon variety of his life had contributed to increase, and that inquisitiveness which must always be produced in a vigorous mind by an absolute freedom from all pressing or domestic engagements. His discernment was quick, and therefore he soon found in every person, and in every affair, something that deserved attention; he was supported by others, without any care for himself, and was therefore at leisure to pursue his observations.

More circumstances to constitute a critic on human life could not easily concur, nor indeed could any man who assumed from accidental advantages more praise than he could justly claim from his real merit, admit an acquaintance more dangerous than that of Savage; of whom likewise it must be confessed, that abilities really exalted above the common level, or virtue refined from passion, or proof against corruption could not easily find an abler judge, or a warmer advocate.

What was the result of Mr. Savage's enquiry, though he was not much accustomed to conceal his discoveries, it may not be entirely safe to relate, because the persons whose characters he criticised are powerful; and power and resentment are seldom strangers; nor would it perhaps be wholly just, because what he asserted in conversation might, though true in general, be heightened by some momentary ardour of imagination, and as it can be delivered only from memory, may be imperfectly represented; so that the picture at first aggravated, and then unskilfully copied, may be justly suspected to retain no great resemblance of the original.

It may however be observed, that he did not appear to have formed very elevated ideas of those to whom the administration of affairs, or the conduct of parties, has been intrusted; who have been considered as the advocates of the Crown, or the guardians of the people, and who have obtained the most implicit confidence, and the loudest applauses. Of one particular person, who has been at one time so popular as to be generally esteemed, and at another so formidable as to be universally detested, he observed, that his acquisitions had been small, or that his capacity was narrow, and that the whole range of his mind was from obscenity to politics, and from politics to obscenity.

But the opportunity of indulging his speculations on great characters was now at an end. He was banished from the table of Lord Tyrconnel, and turned again adrift upon the world, without prospect of finding quickly any other harbour. As prudence was not one of the virtues by which he was distinguished, he had made no provision against a misfortune like this. And though it is not to be imagined, but that the separation must for some time have been preceded by coldness, peevishness, or neglect, though it was undoubtedly the consequence of accumulated provocations on both sides, yet every one that knew Savage will readily believe, that to him it was sudden as a stroke of thunder; that though he might have transiently suspected it, he had never suffered any thought so unpleasing to sink into his mind, but that he had driven it away by amusements, or dreams of future felicity and affluence, and had never taken any measures by which he might prevent a precipitation from plenty to indigence.

This quarrel and separation, and the difficulties to which Mr. Savage was exposed by them, were soon known both to his friends and enemies; nor was it long before he perceived, from the behaviour of both, how much is added to the lustre of genius, by the ornaments of wealth.

His condition did not appear to excite much compassion; for he had not always been careful to use the advantages which he enjoyed with that moderation, which ought to have been with more than usual caution preserved by him, who knew, if he had reflected, that he was only a dependant on the bounty of another, whom he could expect to support him no longer than he endeavoured to preserve his favour, by complying with his inclinations, and whom he nevertheless set at defiance, and was continually irritating by negligence or encroachments.

Examples need not be sought at any great distance to prove that superiority of fortune has a natural tendency to kindle pride, and that pride seldom fails to exert itself in contempt and insult; and if this is often the effect of hereditary wealth, and of honours enjoyed only by the merit of others, it is some extenuation of any indecent triumphs to which this unhappy man may have been betrayed, that his prosperity was heightened by the force of novelty, and made more intoxicating by a sense of the misery in which he had so long languished, and perhaps of the insults which he had formerly born, and which he might now think himself entitled to revenge. It is too common for those who have unjustly suffered pain, to inflict it likewise in their turn, with the same injustice, and to imagine that they have a right to treat others as they have themselves been treated.

That Mr. Savage was too much elevated by any good fortune is generally known; and some passages of his introduction to the *Author to be let* sufficiently shew, that he did not wholly refrain from such satire as he afterwards thought very unjust, when he was exposed to it himself; for when he was afterwards ridiculed in the character of a distressed poet, he very easily discovered, that distress was not a proper subject for merriment, or topic of invective. He was then able to discern that if misery be the effect of virtue, it ought to be reverenced; if of ill-fortune, to be pitied; and if of vice, not to be insulted, because it is perhaps itself a punishment adequate to the crime by which it was produced. And the humanity of that man can deserve no panegyric, who is capable of reproaching a criminal in the hands of the executioner.

But these reflections, though they readily occurred to him in the first and last parts of his life, were, I am afraid, for a long time forgotten; at least they were, like many other maxims, treasured up in his mind, rather for shew than use, and operated very little upon his conduct, however elegantly he might sometimes explain, or however forcibly he might inculcate them.

His degradation therefore from the condition which he had enjoyed with such wanton thoughtlessness, was considered by many as an occasion of triumph. Those who had before paid their court to him, without success, soon returned the contempt which they had suffered, and they who had received favours from him, for of such favours as he could bestow he was very liberal, did not always remember them. So much more certain are the effects of resentment than of gratitude: It is not only to many more pleasing to recollect those faults which place others below them, than those virtues by which they are themselves comparatively depressed; but it is likewise more easy to neglect, than to recompense; and though there are few who will practise a laborious virtue, there will never be wanting multitudes that will indulge an easy vice.

Savage however was very little disturbed at the marks of contempt which his ill-fortune brought upon him, from those whom he never esteemed, and with whom he never considered himself as levelled by any calamities; and though it was not without some uneasiness, that he saw some, whose friendship he valued, change their behaviour; he yet observed their coldness without much emotion, considered them as the slaves of fortune and the worshippers of prosperity; and was more inclined to despise them, than to lament himself.

It does not appear, that after this return of his wants, he found mankind equally favourable to him, as at his first appearance in the world. His story, though in reality not less melancholy, was less affecting, because it was no longer new; it therefore procured him no new friends, and those that had formerly relieved him thought they might now consign him to others. He was now likewise considered by many rather as criminal, than as unhappy; for the friends of Lord Tyrconnel and of his mother were sufficiently industrious to publish his weaknesses, which were indeed very numerous, and nothing was forgotten, that might make him either hateful or ridiculous.

It cannot but be imagined, that such representations of his faults must make great numbers less sensible of his distress; many who had only an opportunity to hear one part, made no scruple to propagate the account which they received; many assisted their circulation from malice or revenge, and perhaps many pretended to credit them, that they might with a better grace withdraw their regard, or withhold their assistance.

Savage however was not one of those, who suffered himself to be injured without resistance, nor was less diligent in exposing the faults of Lord Tyrconnel, over whom he obtained at least this advantage, that he drove him first to the practice of outrage and violence; for he was so much provoked by the wit and virulence of Savage, that he came with a number of attendants, that did no honour to his courage, to beat him at a coffee-house. But it happened that he had left the place a few minutes, and his lordship had without danger the pleasure of boasting, how he would have treated him. Mr. Savage went next day to repay his visit at his own house, but was prevailed on by his domestics, to retire without insisting upon seeing him.

Lord Tyrconnel was accused by Mr. Savage of some actions, which scarcely any provocations will be thought sufficient to justify; such as seizing what he had in his lodgings, and other instances of wanton cruelty, by which he encreased the distress of Savage, without any advantage to himself.

These mutual accusations were retorted on both sides for many years, with the utmost degree of virulence and rage, and time seemed rather to augment than diminish their resentment; that the anger of Mr. Savage should be kept alive is not strange, because he felt every day the consequences of the quarrel, but it might reasonably have been hoped, that Lord Tyrconnel might have relented, and at length have forgot those provocations, which, however they might have once inflamed him, had not in reality much hurt him.

The spirit of Mr. Savage indeed never suffered him to solicite a reconciliation; he returned reproach for reproach, and insult for insult; his superiority of wit supplied the disadvantages of his fortune, and inabled him to form a party, and prejudice great numbers in his favour.

But though this might be some gratification of his vanity, it afforded very little relief to his necessities, and he was very frequently reduced to uncommon hardships, of which, however, he never made any mean or importunate complaints, being formed rather to bear misery with fortitude, than enjoy prosperity with moderation.

He now thought himself again at liberty to expose the cruelty of his mother, and therefore, I believe, about this time, published *The Bastard,* a poem remarkable for the vivacious sallies of thought in the beginning,[1] where he makes a pompous enumeration of the imaginary advantages of base birth, and the pathetic sentiments at the end, where he recounts the real calamities which he suffered by the crime of his parents.

The vigour and spirit of the verses, the peculiar circumstances of the author, the novelty of the subject, and the notoriety of the story, to which the allusions are made, procured this performance a very favourable reception; great numbers were immediately dispersed, and editions were multiplied with unusual rapidity.

One circumstance attended the publication, which Savage used to relate with great satisfaction. His mother, to whom the poem was *with due reverence* inscribed, happened then to be at Bath, where she could not conveniently retire from censure, or conceal herself from observation; and no sooner did the reputation of the poem begin to spread, than she heard it repeated in all places of concourse, nor could she enter the assembly rooms, or cross the walks, without being saluted with some lines from *The Bastard.*

This was perhaps the first time that ever she discovered a sense of shame, and on this occasion the power of wit was very conspicuous; the wretch who had, without scruple, proclaimed herself an adulteress, and who had first endeavoured to starve her son, then to transport him, and afterwards to hang him, was not able to bear the representation of her own conduct, but fled from reproach, though she felt no pain from guilt, and left Bath with the utmost haste, to shelter herself among the crouds of London.

Thus Savage had the satisfaction of finding, that though he could not reform his mother, he could punish her, and that he did not always suffer alone.

The pleasure which he received from this increase of his poetical reputation, was sufficient for some time to overbalance the miseries of want, which this performance did not much alleviate, for it was sold for a very trivial sum to a bookseller, who, though the success was so uncommon, that five impressions were sold, of which many were undoubtedly very numerous, had not generosity sufficient to admit the unhappy writer to any part of the profit.

The sale of this poem was always mentioned by Mr. Savage with the utmost elevation of heart, and referred to by him as an incontestable proof of a general acknowledgement of his abilities. It was indeed the only production of which he could justly boast a general reception.

But though he did not lose the opportunity which success gave him of setting a high rate on his abilities, but paid due deference to the suffrages of mankind when they were given in his favour, he did not suffer his esteem of himself to depend upon others, nor found any thing sacred in the voice of the people when they were inclined to censure him; he then readily shewed the folly of expecting that the publick should judge right, observed how slowly poetical merit had often forced its way into the world, he contented himself with the applause of men of judgment; and was somewhat disposed to exclude all those from the character of men of judgment, who did not applaud him.

But he was at other times more favourable to mankind, than

to think them blind to the beauties of his works, and imputed the slowness of their sale to other causes; either they were published at a time when the town was empty, or when the attention of the publick was engrossed by some struggle in the Parliament, or some other object of general concern; or they were by the neglect of the publisher not diligently dispersed, or by his avarice not advertised with sufficient frequency. Address, or industry, or liberality, was always wanting; and the blame was laid rather on any other person than the author.

By arts like these, arts which every man practises in some degree, and to which too much of the little tranquillity of life is to be ascribed, Savage was always able to live at peace with himself. Had he indeed only made use of these expedients to alleviate the loss or want of fortune or reputation, or any other advantages, which it is not in man's power to bestow upon himself, they might have been justly mentioned as instances of a philosophical mind, and very properly proposed to the imitation of multitudes, who, for want of diverting their imaginations with the same dexterity, languish under afflictions which might be easily removed.

It were doubtless to be wished, that truth and reason were universally prevalent; that every thing were esteemed according to its real value; and that men would secure themselves from being disappointed in their endeavours after happiness, by placing it only in virtue, which is always to be obtained; but if adventitious and foreign pleasures must be persued, it would be perhaps of some benefit, since that persuit must frequently be fruitless, if the practice of Savage could be taught, that folly might be an antidote to folly, and one fallacy be obviated by another.

But the danger of this pleasing intoxication must not be concealed; nor indeed can any one, after having observed the life of Savage, need to be cautioned against it. By imputing none of his miseries to himself, he continued to act upon the same principles, and to follow the same path; was never made wiser by his sufferings, nor preserved by one misfortune from falling into another. He proceeded throughout his life to tread the same steps on the same circle; always applauding his past conduct, or at least forgetting it, to amuse himself with phantoms of happiness, which were dancing before him; and willingly turned his eyes from the light of reason, when it would have discovered the illusion, and shewn him, what he never wished to see, his real state.

He is even accused, after having lulled his imagination with those ideal opiates, of having tried the same experiment upon his conscience; and having accustomed himself to impute all deviations from the right to foreign causes, it is certain that he was upon every occasion too easily reconciled to himself, and that he appeared very little to regret those practices which had impaired his reputation. The reigning error of his life was, that he mistook the love for the practice of virtue, and was indeed not so much a good man, as the friend of goodness.

This at least must be allowed him, that he always preserved a strong sense of the dignity, the beauty and the necessity of virtue, and that he never contributed deliberately to spread corruption amongst mankind; his actions, which were generally precipitate, were often blameable, but his writings being the productions of study, uniformly tended to the exaltation of the mind, and the propagation of morality and piety.

These writings may improve mankind, when his failings shall be forgotten, and therefore he must be considered upon the whole as a benefactor to the world; nor can his personal example do any hurt, since whoever hears of his faults, will hear of the miseries which they brought upon him, and which would deserve less pity, had not his condition been such as made his faults pardonable. He may be considered as a child *exposed* to all the temptations of indigence, at an age when resolution was not yet strengthened by conviction, nor virtue confirmed by habit; a circumstance which in his *Bastard* he laments in a very affecting manner.

> ——No mother's care
> Shielded my infant ignorance with prayer:
> No father's guardian hand my youth maintain'd,
> Call'd forth my virtues, and from vice restrain'd.

The *Bastard*, however it might provoke or mortify his mother, could not be expected to melt her to compassion, so that he was still under the same want of the necessaries of life, and he therefore exerted all the interest, which his wit, or his birth, or his misfortunes could procure, to obtain upon the death of Eusden the place of Poet Laureat, and prosecuted his application with so much diligence, that the King publickly declared it his intention to bestow it upon him; but such was the fate of Savage, that even the King, when he intended his advantage, was disappointed in his schemes; for the Lord Chamberlain, who has the disposal of the laurel as one of the appendages of his office, either did not know the King's design, or did not approve it, or thought the nomination of the Laureat an encroachment upon his rights, and therefore bestowed the laurel upon Colly Cibber.

Mr. Savage thus disappointed took a resolution of applying to the Queen, that having once given him life, she would enable him to support it, and therefore published a short poem on her birth-day, to which he gave the odd title of *Volunteer Laureat.* The event of this essay he has himself related in the following letter, which he prefixed to the poem, when he afterwards reprinted it in the *Gentleman's Magazine,* from whence I have copied it intire, as this was one of the few attempts in which Mr. Savage succeeded.

"Mr. Urban,

"In your magazine for February you published the last *Volunteer Laureat,* written on a very melancholy occasion, the death of the royal patroness of arts and literature in general, and of the author of that poem in particular; I now send you the first that Mr. Savage wrote under that title. —— This gentleman, notwithstanding a very considerable interest, being, on the death of Mr. Eusden, disappointed of the Laureat's place, wrote the following verses; which were no sooner published, but the late Queen sent to a book-seller for them: The author had not at that time a friend either to get him introduced, or his poem presented at Court; yet such was the unspeakable goodness of that princess, that, notwithstanding this act of ceremony was wanting, in a few days after publication, Mr. Savage received a bank-bill of fifty pounds, and a gracious message from her Majesty, by the Lord North and Guilford, to this effect: 'That her Majesty was highly pleased with the verses; that she took particularly kind his lines there relating to the King; that he had permission to write annually on the same subject; and that he should yearly receive the like present, till something better (which was her Majesty's intention) could be done for him.' After this he was permitted to present one of his annual poems to her Majesty, had the honour of kissing her hand, and met with the most gracious reception.

"Your's, &c."

The Volunteer Laureat

A Poem: On the Queen's Birth-Day. Humbly addressed to her Majesty

Twice twenty tedious moons have roll'd away,
Since Hope, kind flatt'rer! tun'd my pensive lay,
Whisp'ring, that you, who rais'd me from despair,
Meant, by your smiles, to make life worth my care;
With pitying hand an orphan's tears to screen,
And o'er the motherless extend the Queen.
'Twill be—the prophet guides the poet's strain!
Grief never touch'd a heart like your's in vain:
Heav'n gave you power, because you love to bless,
And pity, when you feel it, is redress.
  Two fathers join'd to rob my claim of one!
My mother too thought fit to have no son!
The Senate next, whose aid the helpless own,
Forgot my infant wrongs, and mine alone!
Yet parents pitiless, nor peers unkind,
Nor titles lost, nor woes mysterious join'd,
Strip me of hope—by heav'n thus lowly laid,
To find a Pharaoh's daughter in the shade.
  You cannot hear unmov'd, when wrongs implore,
Your heart is woman, though your mind be more;
Kind, like the Pow'r who gave you to our pray'rs,
You would not lengthen life to sharpen cares:
They who a barren leave to live bestow,
Snatch but from death to sacrifice to woe.
Hated by her, from whom my life I drew,
Whence should I hope, if not from heav'n and you?
Nor dare I groan beneath affliction's rod,
My Queen, my mother; and my father, God.
  The pitying muses saw me wit pursue,
A *Bastard Son,* alas! on that side too,
Did not your eyes exalt the poet's fire,
And what the muse denies, the queen inspire;
While rising thus your heavenly soul to view,
I learn, how angels think, by copying you.
  Great Princess! 'tis decreed—once ev'ry year

I march uncall'd your Laureat Volunteer;
Thus shall your poet his low genius raise,
And charm the world with truths too vast for praise.
Nor need I dwell on glories all your own,
Since surer means to tempt your smiles are known;
Your poet shall allot your lord his part,
And paint him in his noblest throne, your heart.
Is there a greatness that adorns him best,
A rising wish that ripens in his breast?
Has he fore-meant some distant age to bless,
Disarm oppression, or expel distress?
Plans he some scheme to reconcile mankind,
People the seas, and busy ev'ry wind?
Would he, by pity, the deceiv'd reclaim,
And smile contending factions into shame?
Would his example lend his laws a weight,
And breathe his own soft morals o'er his state?
The muse shall find it all, shall make it seen,
And teach the world his praise, to charm his Queen.
Such be the annual truths my verse imparts,
Nor frown, fair *fav'rite* of a people's hearts!
Happy if plac'd, perchance, beneath your eye,
My muse unpension'd might her pinions try,
Fearless to fail, while you indulge her flame,
And bid me proudly boast your Laureat's name;
Renobled thus by wreaths my Queen bestows,
I lose all memory of wrongs and woes.

Such was the performance, and such its reception; a reception which, though by no means unkind, was yet not in the highest degree generous: To chain down the genius of a writer to an annual panegyric, shewed in the Queen too much desire of hearing her own praises, and a greater regard to herself than to him on whom her bounty was conferred. It was a kind of avaricious generosity, by which flattery was rather purchased than genius rewarded.

Mrs. Oldfield had formerly given him the same allowance with much more heroic intention; she had no other view than to enable him to prosecute his studies, and to set himself above the want of assistance, and was contented with doing good without stipulating for encomiums.

Mr. Savage however was not at liberty to make exceptions, but was ravished with the favours which he had received, and probably yet more with those which he was promised; he considered himself now as a favourite of the Queen, and did not doubt but a few annual poems would establish him in some profitable employment.

He therefore assumed the title of *Volunteer Laureat,* not without some reprehensions from Cibber, who informed him, that the title of *Laureat* was a mark of honour conferred by the King, from whom all honour is derived, and which therefore no man has a right to bestow upon himself; and added, that he might with equal propriety stile himself a volunteer lord, or volunteer baronet. It cannot be denied that the remark was just, but Savage did not think any title, which was conferred upon Mr. Cibber, so honourable as that the usurpation of it could be imputed to him as an instance of very exorbitant vanity, and therefore continued to write under the same title, and received every year the same reward.

He did not appear to consider these encomiums as tests of his abilities, or as any thing more than annual hints to the Queen of her promise, or acts of ceremony, by the performance of which he was intitled to his pension, and therefore did not labour them with great diligence, or print more than fifty each year, except that for some of the last years he regularly inserted them in the *Gentleman's Magazine,* by which they were dispersed over the kingdom.

Of some of them he had himself so low an opinion, that he intended to omit them in the collection of poems, for which he printed Proposals, and solicited subscriptions; nor can it seem strange, that being confined to the same subject, he should be at some times indolent, and at others unsuccessful, that he should sometimes delay a disagreeable task, till it was too late to perform it well; or that he should sometimes repeat the same sentiment on the same occasion, or at others be misled by an attempt after novelty to forced conceptions, and far-fetched images.

He wrote indeed with a double intention, which supplied him with some variety, for his business was to praise the Queen for the favours which he had received, and to complain to her of the delay of those which she had promised: In some of his pieces, therefore, gratitude is predominant, and in some discontent; in some he represents himself as happy in her patronage, and in others as disconsolate to find himself neglected.

Her promise, like other promises made to this unfortunate man, was never performed, though he took sufficient care that it should not be forgotten. The publication of his *Volunteer Laureat* procured him no other reward than a regular remittance of fifty pounds.

He was not so depressed by his disappointments as to neglect any opportunity that was offered of advancing his interest. When the Princess Anne was married, he wrote a poem upon her departure, only, as he declared, *because it was expected from him,* and he was not willing to bar his own prospects by any appearance of neglect.

He never mentioned any advantage gain'd by this poem, or any regard that was paid to it, and therefore it is likely that it was considered at Court as an act of duty to which he was obliged by his dependence, and which it was therefore not necessary to reward by any new favour: Or perhaps the Queen really intended his advancement, and therefore thought it superfluous to lavish presents upon a man whom she intended to establish for life.

About this time not only his hopes were in danger of being frustrated, but his pension likewise of being obstructed by an accidental calumny. The writer of the *Daily Courant,* a paper then published under the direction of the ministry, charged him with a crime, which though not very great in itself, would have been remarkably invidious in him, and might very justly have incensed the Queen against him. He was accused by name of influencing elections against the Court, by appearing at the head of a Tory mob; nor did the accuser fail to aggravate his crime, by representing it as the effect of the most atrocious ingratitude, and a kind of rebellion against the Queen, who had first preserved him from an infamous death, and afterwards distinguished him by her favour, and supported him by her charity. The charge, as it was open and confident, was likewise by good fortune very particular. The place of the transaction was mentioned, and the whole series of the rioter's conduct related. This exactness made Mr. Savage's vindication easy, for he never had in his life seen the place which was declared to be the scene of his wickedness, nor ever had been present in any town when its representatives were chosen. This answer he therefore made haste to publish, with all the circumstances necessary to make it credible, and very reasonably demanded, that the accusation should be retracted in the same paper, that he might no longer suffer the imputation of sedition and ingratitude. This demand was likewise pressed by him in a private letter to the author of the paper, who either trusting to the protection of those whose defence he had undertaken, or having entertained some personal malice against Mr. Savage, or fearing lest, by retracting so confident an assertion, he should impair the credit of his paper, refused to give him that satisfaction.

Mr. Savage therefore thought it necessary, to his own vindication, to prosecute him in the King's Bench; but as he did not find any ill effects from the accusation, having sufficiently cleared his innocence, he thought any farther procedure would have the appearance of revenge, and therefore willingly dropped it.

He saw soon afterwards a process commenced in the same court against himself, on an information in which he was accused of writing and publishing an obscene pamphlet.

It was always Mr. Savage's desire to be distinguished, and when any controversy became popular, he never wanted some reason for engaging in it with great ardour, and appearing at the head of the party which he had chosen. As he was never celebrated for his prudence, he had no sooner taken his side, and informed himself of the chief topics of the dispute, than he took all opportunities of asserting and propagating his principles, without much regard to his own interest, or any other visible design than that of drawing upon himself the attention of mankind.

The dispute between the Bishop of London and the Chancellor is well known to have been for some time the chief topic of political conversation, and therefore Mr. Savage, in pursuance of his character, endeavoured to become conspicuous among the controvertists with which every coffee-house was filled on that occasion. He was an indefatigable opposer of all the claims of ecclesiastical power, though he did not know on what they were founded, and was therefore no friend to the Bishop of London. But he had another reason for appearing as a warm advocate for Dr. Rundle, for he was the friend of Mr. Foster and Mr. Thompson, who were the friends of Mr. Savage.

Thus remote was his interest in the question, which however, as he imagined, concerned him so nearly, that it was not sufficient to harangue and dispute, but necessary likewise to write upon it.

He therefore engaged with great ardour in a new poem, called by him, *The Progress of a Divine,* in which he conducts a profligate priest by all the gradations of wickedness from a poor curacy in the country, to the highest preferments of the church, and describes with that humour which was natural to him, and that knowledge which was extended to all the diversities of human life, his behaviour in every station, and insinuates, that this priest thus accomplished found at last a patron in the Bishop of London.

When he was asked by one of his friends, on what pretence he could charge the Bishop with such an action, he had no more to say, than that he had only inverted the accusation, and that he thought reasonable to believe, that he, who obstructed the rise of a good man without reason, would for bad reasons promote the exaltation of a villain.

The clergy were universally provoked by this satire, and Savage, who, as was his constant practice, had set his name to his performance, was censured in the *Weekly Miscellany*[2] with severity, which he did not seem inclined to forget.

But a return of invective was not thought a sufficient punishment. The court of King's Bench was therefore moved against him, and he was obliged to return an answer to a charge of obscenity. It was urged in his defence, that obscenity was criminal when it was intended to promote the practice of vice, but that Mr. Savage had only introduced obscene ideas with the view of exposing them to detestation, and of amending the age by shewing the deformity of wickedness. This plea was admitted, and Sir Philip Yorke, who then presided in that court, dismissed the information with encomiums upon the purity and excellence of Mr. Savage's writings.

The prosecution however answered in some measure the purpose of those by whom it was set on foot, for Mr. Savage was so far intimidated by it, that when the edition of his poem was sold, he did not venture to reprint it, so that it was in a short time forgotten, or forgotten by all but those whom it offended.

It is said, that some endeavours were used to incense the Queen against him, but he found advocates to obviate at least part of their effect; for though he was never advanced, he still continued to receive his pension.

This poem drew more infamy upon him than any incident of his life, and as his conduct cannot be vindicated, it is proper to secure his memory from reproach, by informing those whom he made his enemies, that he never intended to repeat the provocation; and that, though whenever he thought he had any reason to complain of the clergy, he used to threaten them with a new edition of *The Progress of a Divine,* it was his calm and settled resolution to suppress it for ever.

He once intended to have made a better reparation for the folly or injustice with which he might be charged, by writing another poem, called, *The Progress of a Free-Thinker,* whom he intended to lead through all the stages of vice and folly, to convert him from virtue to wickedness, and from religion to infidelity by all the modish sophistry used for that purpose; and at last to dismiss him by his own hand into the other world.

That he did not execute this design is a real loss to mankind, for he was too well acquainted with all the scenes of debauchery to have failed in his representations of them, and too zealous for virtue not to have represented them in such a manner as should expose them either to ridicule or detestation.

But this plan was like others, formed and laid aside, till the vigour of his imagination was spent, and the effervescence of invention had subsided, but soon gave way to some other design which pleased by its novelty for a while, and then was neglected like the former.

He was still in his usual exigencies, having no certain support but the pension allowed him by the Queen, which though it might have kept an exact oeconomist from want, was very far from being sufficient for Mr. Savage, who had never been accustomed to dismiss any of his appetites without the gratification which they solicited, and whom nothing but want of money withheld from partaking of every pleasure that fell within his view.

His conduct with regard to his pension was very particular. No sooner had he changed the bill, than he vanished from the sight of all his acquaintances, and lay for some time out of the reach of all the enquiries that friendship or curiosity could make after him; at length he appeared again pennyless as before, but never informed even those whom he seemed to regard most, where he had been, nor was his retreat ever discovered.

This was his constant practice during the whole time that he received the pension from the Queen: He regularly disappeared and returned. He indeed affirmed, that he retired to study, and that the money supported him in solitude for many months; but his friends declared, that the short time in which it was spent sufficiently confuted his own account of his conduct.

His politeness and his wit still raised him friends, who were desirous of setting him at length free from that indigence by which he had been hitherto oppressed, and therefore solicited Sir Robert Walpole in his favour with so much earnestness, that they obtained a promise of the next place that should become vacant, not exceeding two hundred pounds a year. This promise was made with an uncommon declaration, *that it was not the promise of a minister to a petitioner, but of a friend to his friend.*

Mr. Savage now concluded himself set at ease for ever, and as he observes in a poem[3] written on that incident of his life, *trusted* and *was trusted,* but soon found that his confidence was ill-grounded, and this *friendly* promise was not inviolable. He spent a long time in solicitations, and at last despaired and desisted.

He did not indeed deny that he had given the minister some reason to believe that he should not strengthen his own interest by advancing him, for he had taken care to distinguish himself in coffee-houses as an advocate for the ministry of the last years of Queen Anne, and was always ready to justify the conduct, and exalt the character of Lord Bolingbroke, whom he mentions with great regard in an epistle upon authors, which he wrote about that time, but was too wise to publish, and of which only some fragments[4] have appeared, inserted by him in the *Magazine* after his retirement.

To despair was not, however, the character of Savage, when one patronage failed, he had recourse to another. The Prince was now extremely popular, and had very liberally rewarded the merit of some writers whom Mr. Savage did not think superior to himself, and therefore he resolved to address a poem to him.

For this purpose he made choice of a subject, which could regard only persons of the highest rank and greatest affluence, and which was therefore proper for a poem intended to procure the patronage of a prince; and having retired for some time to Richmond, that he might prosecute his design in full tranquillity, without the temptations of pleasure, or the solicitations of creditors, by which his meditations were in equal danger of being disconcerted, he produced *a Poem on public spirit, with regard to public works.*

The plan of this poem is very extensive, and comprises a multitude of topics, each of which might furnish matter sufficient for a long performance, and of which some have already employed more eminent writers; but as he was perhaps not fully acquainted with the whole extent of his own design, and was writing to obtain a supply of wants too pressing to admit of long or accurate enquiries, he passes negligently over many public works, which, even in his own opinion, deserved to be more elaborately treated.

But though he may sometimes disappoint his reader by transient touches upon these subjects, which have often been considered, and therefore naturally raise expectations, he must be allowed amply to compensate his omissions by expatiating in the conclusion of his work upon a kind of beneficence not yet celebrated by any eminent poet, though it now appears more susceptible of embellishments, more adapted to exalt the ideas, and affect the passions, than many of those which have hitherto been thought most worthy of the ornaments of verse. The settlement of colonies in uninhabited countries, the establishment of those in security whose misfortunes have made their own country no longer pleasing or safe, the acquisition of property without injury to any, the appropriation of the waste and luxuriant bounties of nature, and the enjoyment of those gifts which heaven has scattered upon regions uncultivated and unoccupied, cannot be considered without giving rise to a great number of pleasing ideas, and bewildering the imagination in delightful prospects; and, therefore, whatever speculations they may produce in those who have confined themselves to political studies, naturally fixed the attention, and excited the applause of a poet. The politician, when he considers men driven into other countries for shelter, and obliged to retire to forests and deserts, and pass their lives and fix their posterity in the remotest corners of the world, to avoid those hardships which they suffer or fear in their native place, may very properly enquire why the legislature does not provide a remedy for these miseries, rather than encourage an escape from them. He may conclude, that the flight of every honest man is a loss to the community, that those who are unhappy without guilt ought to be relieved, and the life which is overburthened by accidental calamities, set at ease by the care of the publick, and that those, who have by misconduct forfeited their claim to favour, ought rather to be made useful to the society which they have injured, than be driven from it. But the poet is employed in a more pleasing undertaking than that of proposing laws, which, however just or expedient, will never be made, or endeavouring to reduce to rational schemes of government societies which were formed by chance, and are conducted by the private passions of those who preside in them. He guides the unhappy fugitive from want and persecution, to plenty, quiet, and security, and seats him in scenes of peaceful solitude, and undisturbed repose.

Savage has not forgotten amidst the pleasing sentiments which this prospect of retirement suggested to him to censure those crimes which have been generally committed by the discoverers of new regions, and to expose the enormous wickedness of making war upon barbarous nations because they cannot resist, and of invading countries because they are fruitful; of extending navigation only to propagate vice, and of visiting distant lands only to lay them waste. He has asserted the natural equality of mankind, and endeavoured to suppress that pride which inclines men to imagine that right is the consequence of power.[5]

His description of the various miseries which force men to seek for refuge in distant countries affords another instance of his proficiency in the important and extensive study of human life, and the tenderness with which he recounts them, another proof of his humanity and benevolence.

It is observable, that the close of this poem discovers a change which experience had made in Mr. Savage's opinions. In a poem written by him in his youth, and published in his Miscellanies, he declares his contempt of the contracted views and narrow prospects of the middle state of life, and declares his resolution either to tower like the cedar, or be trampled like the shrub; but in this poem, though addressed to a prince, he mentions this state of life as comprising those who ought most to attract reward, those who merit most the confidence of power, and the familiarity of greatness, and accidentally mentioning this passage to one of his friends, declared that in his opinion all the virtue of mankind was comprehended in that state.

In describing villas and gardens he did not omit to condemn that absurd custom which prevails among the English of permitting servants to receive money from strangers for the entertainment that they receive, and therefore inserted in his poem these lines:

> But what the flow'ring pride of gardens rare,
> However royal, or however fair:
> If gates which to access should still give way,
> Ope but, like Peter's Paradise, for pay.
> If perquisited varlets frequent stand,
> And each new walk must a new tax demand?
> What foreign eye but with contempt surveys?
> What muse shall from oblivion snatch their praise?

But before the publication of his performance he recollected, that the Queen allowed her garden and cave at Richmond to be shewn for money, and that she so openly countenanced the practice, that she had bestowed the privilege of shewing them as a place of profit on a man whose merit she valued herself upon rewarding, though she gave him only the liberty of disgracing his country.

He therefore thought, with more prudence than was often exerted by him, that the publication of these lines might be officiously represented as an insult upon the Queen to whom he owed his life and his subsistence, and that the propriety of his observation would be no security against the censures which the unseasonableness of it might draw upon him; he therefore suppressed the passage in the first edition, but after the Queen's death thought the same caution no longer necessary, and restored it to the proper place.

The poem was therefore published without any political faults, and inscribed to the Prince, but Mr. Savage having no friend upon whom he could prevail to present it to him, had no other method of attracting his observation than the publication of frequent advertisements, and therefore received no reward from his patron, however generous on other occasions.

This disappointment he never mentioned without indignation,

being by some means or other confident that the Prince was not ignorant of his address to him, and insinuated, that if any advances in popularity could have been made by distinguishing him, he had not written without notice, or without reward.

He was once inclined to have presented his poem in person, and sent to the printer for a copy with that design; but either his opinion changed, or his resolution deserted him, and he continued to resent neglect without attempting to force himself into regard.

Nor was the public much more favourable than his patron, for only seventy-two were sold, though the performance was much commended by some whose judgment in that kind of writing is generally allowed. But Savage easily reconciled himself to mankind without imputing any defect to his work, by observing that his poem was unluckily published two days after the prorogation of the Parliament, and by consequence at a time when all those who could be expected to regard it were in the hurry of preparing for their departure, or engaged in taking leave of others upon their dismission from public affairs.

It must be however allowed, in justification of the public, that this performance is not the most excellent of Mr. Savage's works, and that though it cannot be denied to contain many striking sentiments, majestic lines, and just observations, it is in general not sufficiently polished in the language, or enlivened in the imagery, or digested in the plan.

Thus his poem contributed nothing to the alleviation of his poverty, which was such as very few could have supported with equal patience, but to which it must likewise be confessed, that few would have been exposed who received punctually fifty pounds a year; a salary which though by no means equal to the demands of vanity and luxury, is yet found sufficient to support families above want, and was undoubtedly more than the necessities of life require.

But no sooner had he received his pension, than he withdrew to his darling privacy, from which he return'd in a short time to his former distress, and for some part of the year, generally lived by chance, eating only when he was invited to the tables of his acquaintances, from which the meanness of his dress often excluded him, when the politeness and variety of his conversation would have been thought a sufficient recompence for his entertainment.

He lodged as much by accident as he dined and passed the night, sometimes in mean houses, which are set open at night to any casual wanderers, sometimes in cellars among the riot and filth of the meanest and most profligate of the rabble; and sometimes, when he had not money to support even the expences of these receptacles, walked about the streets till he was weary, and lay down in the summer upon a bulk, or in the winter with his associates in poverty, among the ashes of a glass-house.

In this manner were passed those days and those nights, which nature had enabled him to have employed in elevated speculations, useful studies, or pleasing conversation. On a bulk, in a cellar, or in a glass-house among thieves and beggers, was to be found the author of the *Wanderer,* the man of exalted sentiments, extensive views and curious observations, the man whose remarks on life might have assisted the statesman, whose ideas of virtue might have enlightened the moralist, whose eloquence might have influenced senates, and whose delicacy might have polished courts.

It cannot be imagined [but] that such necessities might sometimes force him upon disreputable practices, and it is probable that these lines in the *Wanderer* were occasioned by his reflections on his own conduct.

> Though mis'ry leads to fortitude and truth,
> Unequal to the load this languid youth,
> (O! let none censure if untried by grief,
> Or amidst woes untempted by relief,)
> He stoop'd, reluctant, to mean acts of shame,
> Which then, ev'n then, he scorn'd, and blush'd to name.

Whoever was acquainted with him, was certain to be solicited for small sums, which the frequency of the request made in time considerable, and he was therefore quickly shunned by those who were become familiar enough to be trusted with his necessities; but his rambling manner of life, and constant appearance at houses of public resort, always procured him a new succession of friends, whose kindness had not been exhausted by repeated requests, so that he was seldom absolutely without resources, but had in his utmost exigences this comfort, that he always imagined himself sure of speedy relief.

It was observed that he always asked favours of this kind without the least submission or apparent consciousness of dependence, and that he did not seem to look upon a compliance with his request as an obligation that deserved any extraordinary acknowledgments, but a refusal was resented by him as an affront, or complained of as an injury; nor did he readily reconcile himself to those who either denied to lend, or gave him afterwards any intimation, that they expected to be repaid.

He was sometimes so far compassionated by those who knew both his merit and his distresses, that they received him into their families, but they soon discovered him to be a very incommodious inmate; for being always accustomed to an irregular manner of life, he could not confine himself to any stated hours, or pay any regard to the rules of a family, but would prolong his conversation till midnight, without considering that business might require his friend's application in the morning; and when he had persuaded himself to retire to bed, was not, without equal difficulty, called up to dinner; it was therefore impossible to pay him any distinction without the entire subversion of all oeconomy, a kind of establishment which, wherever he went, he always appeared ambitious to overthrow.

It must therefore be acknowledged, in justification of mankind, that it was not always by the negligence or coldness of his friends that Savage was distressed, but because it was in reality very difficult to preserve him long in a state of ease. To supply him with money was a hopeless attempt, for no sooner did he see himself master of a sum sufficient to set him free from care for a day, than he became profuse and luxurious. When once he had entered a tavern, or engaged in a scheme of pleasure, he never retired till want of money obliged him to some new expedient. If he was entertained in a family, nothing was any longer to be regarded there but amusements and jollity; wherever Savage entered he immediately expected that order and business should fly before him, that all should thenceforward be left to hazard, and that no dull principle of domestic management should be opposed to his inclination, or intrude upon his gaiety.

His distresses, however afflictive, never dejected him; in his lowest state he wanted not spirit to assert the natural dignity of wit, and was always ready to repress that insolence which superiority of fortune incited, and to trample that reputation which rose upon any other basis than that of merit: He never admitted any gross familiarities, or submitted to be treated otherwise than as an equal. Once when he was without lodging, meat, or cloaths, one of his friends, a man not indeed remarkable for moderation in his prosperity, left a message, that he desired to see him about nine in the morning. Savage knew that his intention was to assist him, but was very much disgusted, that he should presume to prescribe the hour of his attendance, and, I believe, refused to visit him, and rejected his kindness.

The same invincible temper, whether firmness or obstinacy, appeared in his conduct to the Lord Tyrconnel, from whom he very frequently demanded that the allowance which was once paid him should be restored, but with whom he never appeared to entertain for a moment the thought of soliciting a reconciliation, and whom he treated at once with all the haughtiness of superiority, and all the bitterness of resentment. He wrote to him not in a stile of supplication or respect, but of reproach, menace, and contempt, and appeared determined, if he ever regained his allowance, to hold it only by the right of conquest.

As many more can discover, that a man is richer than he is wiser than themselves, superiority of understanding is not so readily acknowledged as that of fortune; nor is that haughtiness, which the consciousness of great abilities incites, borne with the same submission as the tyranny of affluence; and therefore Savage, by asserting his claim to deference and regard, and by treating those with contempt whom better fortune animated to rebel against him, did not fail to raise a great number of enemies in the different classes of mankind. Those who thought themselves raised above him by the advantages of riches, hated him because they found no protection from the petulance of his wit. Those who were esteemed for their writings feared him as a critic, and maligned him as a rival, and almost all the smaller wits were his professed enemies.

Among these Mr. Millar so far indulged his resentment as to introduce him in a farce, and direct him to be personated on the stage in a dress like that which he then wore; a mean insult which only insinuated, that Savage had but one coat, and which was therefore despised by him rather than resented; for though he wrote a lampoon against Millar, he never printed it: and as no other person ought to prosecute that revenge from which the person who was injured desisted, I shall not preserve what Mr. Savage suppressed; of which the publication would indeed have been a punishment too severe for so impotent an assault.

The great hardships of poverty were to Savage not the want of lodging or of food, but the neglect and contempt which it drew upon him. He complained that as his affairs grew desperate he found his reputation for capacity visibly decline, that his opinion in questions of criticism was no longer regarded, when his coat was out of fashion; and that those who in the interval of his prosperity were always encouraging him to great undertakings by encomiums on his genius and assurances of success, now received any mention of his designs with coldness, thought that the subjects on which he proposed to write were very difficult; and were ready to inform him, that the event of a poem was uncertain, that an author ought to employ much time in the consideration of his plan, and not presume to sit down to write in confidence of a few cursory ideas, and a superficial knowledge; difficulties were started on all sides, and he was no longer qualified for any performance but the *Volunteer Laureat.*

Yet even this kind of contempt never depressed him; for he always preserved a steady confidence in his own capacity, and believed nothing above his reach which he should at any time earnestly endeavour to attain. He formed schemes of the same kind with regard to knowledge and to fortune, and flattered himself with advances to be made in science, as with riches to be enjoyed in some distant period of his life. For the acquisition of knowledge he was indeed far better qualified than for that of riches; for he was naturally inquisitive and desirous of the conversation of those from whom any information was to be obtained, but by no means solicitous to improve those opportunities that were sometimes offered of raising his fortune; and he was remarkably retentive of his ideas, which, when once he was in possession of them, rarely forsook him; a quality which could never be communicated to his money.

While he was thus wearing out his life in expectation that the Queen would some time recollect her promise, he had recourse to the usual practice of writers, and published proposals for printing his works by subscription, to which he was encouraged by the success of many who had not a better right to the favour of the public; but whatever was the reason, he did not find the world equally inclined to favour him, and he observed with some discontent, that though he offered his works at half a guinea, he was able to procure but a small number in comparison with those who subscribed twice as much to Duck.

Nor was it without indignation that he saw his Proposals neglected by the Queen, who patronised Mr. Duck's with uncommon ardour, and incited a competition among those who attended the Court, who should most promote his interest, and who should first offer a subscription. This was a distinction to which Mr. Savage made no scruple of asserting that his birth, his misfortunes, and his genius gave him a fairer title, than could be pleaded by him on whom it was conferred.

Savage's applications were however not universally unsuccessful; for some of the nobility countenanced his design, encouraged his Proposals, and subscribed with great liberality. He related of the Duke of Chandos particularly, that, upon receiving his Proposals, he sent him ten guineas.

But the money which his subscriptions afforded him was not less volatile than that which he received from his other schemes; whenever a subscription was paid him he went to a tavern, and as money so collected is necessarily received in small sums, he never was able to send his poems to the press, but for many years continued his solicitation, and squandered whatever he obtained.

This project of printing his works was frequently revived, and as his Proposals grew obsolete, new ones were printed with fresher dates. To form schemes for the publication was one of his favourite amusements, nor was he ever more at ease than when with any friend who readily fell in with his schemes, he was adjusting the print, forming the advertisements, and regulating the dispersion of his new edition, which he really intended some time to publish, and which, as long experience had shewn him the impossibility of printing the volume together, he at last determined to divide into weekly or monthly numbers, that the profits of the first might supply the expences of the next.

Thus he spent his time in mean expedients and tormenting suspense, living for the greatest part in fear of prosecutions from his creditors, and consequently skulking in obscure parts of the town, of which he was no stranger to the remotest corners. But wherever he came his address secured him friends, whom his necessities soon alienated, so that he had perhaps a more numerous acquaintance than any man ever before attained, there being scarcely any person eminent on any account to whom he was not known, or whose character he was not in some degree able to delineate.

To the acquisition of this extensive acquaintance every circumstance of his life contributed. He excelled in the arts of conversation, and therefore willingly practised them: He had seldom any home, or even a lodging in which he could be private, and therefore was driven into public houses for the common conveniences of life, and supports of nature. He was always ready to comply with every invitation, having no employment to withhold him, and often no money to provide for himself; and by dining with one company, he never failed of obtaining an introduction into another.

Thus dissipated was his life, and thus casual his subsistence; yet did not the distraction of his views hinder him from reflection, nor the uncertainty of his condition depress his gaiety. When he had wandered about without any fortunate adventure, by which he was led into a tavern, he sometimes retired into the fields, and was able to employ his mind in study to amuse it with pleasing imaginations; and seldom appeared to be melancholy, but when some sudden misfortune had just fallen upon him, and even then in a few moments he would disentangle himself from his perplexity, adopt the subject of conversation, and apply his mind wholly to the objects that others presented to it.

This life, unhappy as it may be already imagined, was yet imbitter'd in 1738, with new calamities. The death of the Queen deprived him of all the prospects of preferment with which he had so long entertained his imagination; and as Sir Robert Walpole had before given him reason to believe that he never intended the performance of his promise, he was now abandoned again to fortune.

He was, however at that time, supported by a friend; and as it was not his custom to look out for distant calamities, or to feel any other pain than that which forced itself upon his senses, he was not much afflicted at his loss, and perhaps comforted himself that his pension would be now continued without the annual tribute of a panegyric.

Another expectation contributed likewise to support him; he had taken a resolution to write a second tragedy upon the story of Sir Thomas Overbury, in which he preserved a few lines of his former play; but made a total alteration of the plan, added new incidents, and introduced new characters; so that it was a new tragedy, not a revival of the former.

Many of his friends blamed him for not making choice of another subject; but in vindication of himself, he asserted, that it was not easy to find a better; and that he thought it his interest to extinguish the memory of the first tragedy, which he could only do by writing one less defective upon the same story; by which he should entirely defeat the artifice of the booksellers, who after the death of any author of reputation, are always industrious to swell his works, by uniting his worst productions with his best.

In the execution of this scheme however, he proceeded but slowly, and probably only employed himself upon it when he could find no other amusement; but he pleased himself with counting the profits, and perhaps imagined, that the theatrical reputation which he was about to acquire, would be equivalent to all that he had lost by the death of his patroness.

He did not in confidence of his approaching riches neglect the measures proper to secure the continuance of his pension, though some of his favourers thought him culpable for omitting to write on her death; but on her birth day next year, he gave a proof of the solidity of his judgment, and the power of his genius. He knew that the track of elegy had been so long beaten, that it was impossible to travel in it without treading in the footsteps of those who had gone before him; and that therefore it was necessary that he might distinguish himself from the herd of encomiasts, to find out some new walk of funeral panegyric.

This difficult task he performed in such a manner, that his poem may be justly ranked among the best pieces that the death of princes has produced. By transferring the mention of her death to her birth day, he has formed a happy combination of topics which any other man would have thought it very difficult to connect in one view; but which he has united in such a manner, that the relation between them appears natural; and it may be justly said that what no other man would have thought on, it now appears scarcely possible for any man to miss.[6]

The beauty of this peculiar combination of images is so masterly, that it is sufficient to set this poem above censure; and therefore it is not necessary to mention many other delicate touches which may be found in it, and which would deservedly be admired in any other performance.

To these proofs of his genius may be added, from the same poem, an instance of his prudence, an excellence for which he was not so often distinguished; he does not forget[7] to remind the King in the most delicate and artful manner of continuing his pension.

With regard to the success of this address he was for some time in suspense; but was in no great degree sollicitous about it; and continued his labour upon his new tragedy with great tranquillity, till the friend, who had for a considerable time supported him, removing his family to another place, took occasion to dismiss him. It then became necessary to enquire more diligently what was determined in his affair, having reason to suspect that no great favour was intended him, because he had not received his pension at the usual time.

It is said, that he did not take those methods of retrieving his interest which were most likely to succeed; and some of those who were employed in the Exchequer, cautioned him against too much violence in his proceedings; but Mr. Savage who seldom regulated his conduct by the advice of others, gave way to his passion, and demanded of Sir Robert Walpole, at his levee, the reason of the distinction that was made between him and the other pensioners of the Queen, with a degree of roughness which perhaps determined him to withdraw what had been only delayed.

Whatever was the crime of which he was accused or suspected, and whatever influence was imployed against him, he received soon after an account that took from him all hopes of regaining his pension; and he had now no prospect of subsistence but from his play, and he knew no way of living for the time required to finish it.

So peculiar were the misfortunes of this man, deprived of an estate and title by a particular law, exposed and abandoned by a mother, defrauded by a mother of a fortune which his father had allotted him, he enter'd the world without a friend; and though his abilities forced themselves into esteem and reputation, he was never able to obtain any real advantage, and whatever prospects arose, were always intercepted as he began to approach them. The King's intentions in his favour were frustrated; his Dedication to the Prince, whose generosity on every other occasion was eminent, procured him no reward; Sir Robert Walpole who valued himself upon keeping his promise to others, broke it to him without regret; and the bounty of the Queen was, after her death, withdrawn from him, and from him only.

Such were his misfortunes, which yet he bore not only with decency, but with cheerfulness, nor was his gaiety clouded even by his last disappointments, though he was in a short time reduced to the lowest degree of distress; and often wanted both lodging and food. At this time, he gave another instance of the insurmountable obstinacy of his spirit; his cloaths were worn out, and he received notice that at a coffee-house some cloaths and linen were left for him; the person who sent them, did not, I believe, inform him to whom he was to be obliged, that he might spare the perplexity of acknowledging the benefit; but though the offer was so far generous, it was made with some neglect of ceremonies, which Mr. Savage so much resented, that he refused the present, and declined to enter the house, till the cloaths that had been designed for him were taken away.

His distress was now publickly known, and his friends, therefore, thought it proper to concert some measures for his relief; and one of them wrote a letter to him, in which he expressed his concern *for the miserable withdrawing of his pension;* and gave him hopes that in a short time, he should find himself supplied with a competence, *without any dependence on those little creatures which we are pleased to call the great.*

The scheme proposed for this happy and independent subsistence, was, that he should retire into Wales, and receive an allowance of fifty pounds a year, to be raised by a subscription, on which he was to live privately in a cheap place, without aspiring any more to affluence, or having any farther care of reputation.

This offer Mr. Savage gladly accepted, tho' with intentions very different from those of his friends; for they proposed, that he should continue an exile from London for ever, and spend all the remaining part of his life at Swansea; but he designed only to take the opportunity, which their scheme offered him, of retreating for a short time, that he might prepare his play for the stage, and his other works for the press, and then to return to London to exhibit his tragedy, and live upon the profits of his own labour.

With regard to his Works, he proposed very great improvements, which would have required much time, or great application; and when he had finish'd them, he designed to do justice to his subscribers, by publishing them according to his Proposals.

As he was ready to entertain himself with future pleasures, he had planned out a scheme of life for the country, of which he had no knowledge but from pastorals and songs. He imagined that he should be transported to scenes of flow'ry felicity, like those which one poet has reflected to another, and had projected a perpetual round of innocent pleasures, of which he suspected no interruption from pride, or ignorance, or brutality.

With these expectations he was so enchanted, that when he was once gently reproach'd by a friend for submitting to live upon a subscription, and advised rather by a resolute exertion of his abilities to support himself, he could not bear to debar himself from the happiness which was to be found in the calm of a cottage, or lose the opportunity of listening without intermission, to the melody of the nightingale, which he believ'd was to be heard from every bramble, and which he did not fail to mention as a very important part of the happiness of a country life.

While this scheme was ripening, his friends directed him to take a lodging in the liberties of the Fleet, that he might be secure from his creditors, and sent him every Monday a guinea, which he commonly spent before the next morning, and trusted, after his usual manner, the remaining part of the week to the bounty of fortune.

He now began very sensibly to feel the miseries of dependence: Those by whom he was to be supported, began to prescribe to him with an air of authority, which he knew not how decently to resent, nor patiently to bear; and he soon discovered from the conduct of most of his subscribers, that he was yet in the hands of *little creatures*.

Of the insolence that he was obliged to suffer, he gave many instances, of which none appeared to raise his indignation to a greater height, than the method which was taken of furnishing him with cloaths. Instead of consulting him and allowing him to send to a taylor his orders for what they thought proper to allow him, they proposed to send for a taylor to take his measure, and then to consult how they should equip him.

This treatment was not very delicate, nor was it such as Savage's humanity would have suggested to him on a like occasion; but it had scarcely deserved mention, had it not, by affecting him in an uncommon degree, shewn the peculiarity of his character. Upon hearing the design that was formed, he came to the lodging of a friend with the most violent agonies of rage; and being asked what it could be that gave him such disturbance, he replied with the utmost vehemence of indignation, "That they had sent for a taylor to measure him."

How the affair ended, was never enquired, for fear of renewing his uneasiness. It is probable that, upon recollection, he submitted with a good grace to what he could not avoid, and that he discovered no resentment where he had no power.

He was, however, not humbled to implicit and universal compliance; for when the gentleman, who had first informed him of the design to support him by a subscription, attempted to procure a reconciliation with the Lord Tyrconnel, he could by no means be prevailed upon to comply with the measures that were proposed.

A letter was written for him to Sir William Lemon, to prevail upon him to interpose his good offices with Lord Tyrconnel, in which he solicited Sir William's assistance, *for a man who really needed it as much as any man could well do;* and informed him, that he was retiring *for ever to a place where he should no more trouble his relations, friends, or enemies;* he confessed, that his *passion* had *betrayed* him to some conduct, with regard to Lord Tyrconnel, *for which he could not but heartily ask his pardon;* and as he imagined Lord Tyrconnel's passion might be yet so high, that he would not *receive a letter from him,* begg'd that Sir William would endeavour to soften him; and expressed his hopes, that he would comply with his request, and that *so small a relation would not harden his heart against him.*

That any man should presume to dictate a letter to him, was not very agreeable to Mr. Savage; and therefore he was, before he had opened it, not much inclined to approve it. But when he read it, he found it contained sentiments entirely opposite to his own, and, as he asserted, to the truth, and therefore instead of copying it, wrote his friend a letter full of masculine resentment and warm expostulations. He very justly observed, that the style was too supplicatory, and the representation too abject, and that he ought at least to have made him complain with *the dignity of a gentleman in distress.* He declared that he would not write the paragraph in which he was to ask Lord Tyrconnel's pardon; for *he despised his pardon, and therefore could not heartily, and would not hypocritically ask it.* He remarked, that his friend made a very unreasonable distinction between himself and him; for, says he, when you mention men of high rank *in your own character,* they are *those little creatures whom we are pleased to call the great;* but when you address them *in mine,* no servility is sufficiently humble. He then with great propriety explained the ill consequences might be expected from such a letter, which his relations would print in their own defence, and which would for ever be produced as a full answer to all that he should allege against them; for he always intended to publish a minute account of the treatment which he had received. It is to be remembered to the honour of the gentleman by whom this letter was drawn up, that he yielded to Mr. Savage's reasons, and agreed that it ought to be suppressed.

After many alterations and delays, a subscription was at length raised which did not amount to fifty pounds a year, though twenty were paid by one gentleman; such was the generosity of mankind, that what had been done by a player without solicitation, could not now be effected by application and interest; and Savage had a great number to court and to obey for a pension less than that which Mrs. Oldfield paid him without exacting any servilities.

Mr. Savage however was satisfied, and willing to retire, and was convinced that the allowance, though scanty, would be more than sufficient for him, being now determined to commence a rigid oeconomist, and to live according to the exactest rules of frugality; for nothing was in his opinion more contemptible than a man, who, when he knew his income, exceeded it, and yet he confessed that instances of such folly, were too common, and lamented, that some men were not to be trusted with their own money.

Full of these salutary resolutions, he left London, in July 1739, having taken leave with great tenderness of his friends, and parted from the author of this narrative with tears in his eyes. He was furnished with fifteen guineas, and informed, that they would be sufficient, not only for the expence of his journey, but for his support in Wales for some time; and that there remained but little more of the first collection. He promised a strict adherence to his maxims of parsimony, and went away in the stage coach; nor did his friends expect to hear from him, till he informed them of his arrival at Swansea.

But when they least expected, arrived a letter dated the fourteenth day after his departure, in which he sent them word, that he was yet upon the road, and without money; and that he therefore could not proceed without a remittance. They then sent him the money that was in their hands, with which he was enabled to reach Bristol, from whence he was to go to Swansea by water.

At Bristol he found an embargo laid upon the shipping, so that he could not immediately obtain a passage; and being therefore obliged to stay there some time, he, with his usual felicity, ingratiated himself with many of the principal inhabitants, was invited to their houses, distinguished at their publick feasts, and treated with a regard that gratify'd his vanity, and therefore easily engaged his affection.

He began very early after his retirement to complain of the conduct of his friends in London, and irritated many of them so much by his letters, that they withdrew, however honourably, their contributions; and it is believed, that little more was paid him than the twenty pounds a year, which were allowed him by the gentleman who proposed the subscription.

After some stay at Bristol, he retired to Swansea, the place *originally* proposed for his residence, where he lived about a year very much dissatisfied with the diminution of his salary; but contracted, as in other places, acquaintance with those who were most distinguished in that country, among whom he has celebrated Mr. Powel and Mrs. Jones, by some verses which he inserted in the *Gentleman's Magazine*.

Here he completed his tragedy, of which two acts were wanting when he left London, and was desirous of coming to town to bring it upon the stage. This design was very warmly opposed, and he was advised by his chief benefactor to put it into the hands of Mr. Thomson and Mr. Mallet, that it might be fitted for the stage, and to allow his friends to receive the profits, out of which an annual pension should be paid him.

This proposal he rejected with the utmost contempt. He was by no means convinced that the judgment of those to whom he was required to submit, was superior to his own. He was now determined, as he expressed it, to be *no longer kept in leading-strings,* and had no elevated idea of *his bounty,* who proposed to *pension him out of the profits of his own labours.*

He attempted in Wales to promote a subscription for his Works, and had once hopes of success; but in a short time afterwards, formed a resolution of leaving that part of the country, to which he thought it not reasonable to be confined, for the gratification of those, who having promised him a liberal income, had no sooner banished him to a remote corner, than they reduced his allowance to a salary scarcely equal to the necessities of life.

His resentment of this treatment, which, in his own opinion, at least, he had not deserved, was such that he broke off all correspondence with most of his contributors, and appeared to consider them as persecutors and oppressors, and in the latter part of his life, declared, that their conduct toward him, since his departure from London, *had been perfidiousness improving on perfidiousness, and inhumanity on inhumanity.*

It is not to be supposed, that the necessities of Mr. Savage did not sometimes incite him to satirical exaggerations of the behaviour of those by whom he thought himself reduced to them. But it must be granted, that the diminution of his allowance was a great hardship, and, that those who withdrew their subscription from a man, who, upon the faith of their promise, had gone into a kind of banishment, and abandoned all those by whom he had been before relieved in his distresses, will find it no easy task to vindicate their conduct.

It may be alleged, and, perhaps, justly, that he was petulant and contemptuous, that he more frequently reproached his subscribers for not giving him more, than thanked them for what he received; but it is to be remembered, that this conduct, and this is the worst charge that can be drawn up against him, did them no real injury; and that it, therefore, ought rather to have been pitied than resented, at least, the resentment that it might provoke ought to have been generous and manly; epithets which his conduct will hardly deserve, that starves the man whom he has persuaded to put himself into his power.

It might have been reasonably demanded by Savage, that they should, before they had taken away what they promised, have replaced him in his former state, that they should have taken no advantages from the situation to which the appearance of their kindness had reduced him, and that he should have been re-called to London, before he was abandoned. He might justly represent, that he ought to have been considered as a lion in the toils, and demand to be released before the dogs should be loosed upon him.

He endeavoured, indeed, to release himself, and with an intent to return to London, went to Bristol, where a repetition of the kindness which he had formerly found, invited him to stay. He was not only caressed and treated, but had a collection made for him of about thirty pounds, with which it had been happy if he had immediately departed for London; but his negligence did not suffer him to consider, that such proofs of kindness were not often to be expected, and that this ardour of benevolence was in a great degree, the effect of novelty, and might, probably, be every day less; and, therefore, he took no care to improve the happy time, but was encouraged by one favour to hope for another, till at length generosity was exhausted, and officiousness wearied.

Another part of his misconduct was the practice of prolonging his visits, to unseasonable hours, and disconcerting all the families into which he was admitted. This was an error in a place of commerce which all the charms of his conversation could not compensate; for what trader would purchase such airy satisfaction by the loss of solid gain, which must be the consequence of midnight merriment, as those hours which were gained at night, were generally lost in the morning?

Thus Mr. Savage, after the curiosity of the inhabitants was gratified, found the number of his friends daily decreasing, perhaps without suspecting for what reason their conduct was altered, for he still continued to harrass, with his nocturnal intrusions, those that yet countenanced him, and admitted him to their houses.

But he did not spend all the time of his residence at Bristol, in visits or at taverns; for he sometimes returned to his studies, and began several considerable designs. When he felt an inclination to write, he always retired from the knowledge of his friends, and lay hid in an obscure part of the suburbs, till he found himself again desirous of company, to which it is likely that intervals of absence made him more welcome.

He was always full of his design of returning to London to bring his tragedy upon the stage; but having neglected to depart with the money that was raised for him, he could not afterwards procure a sum sufficient to defray the expences of his journey; nor, perhaps, would a fresh supply have had any other effect, than, by putting immediate pleasures in his power, to have driven the thoughts of his journey out of his mind.

While he was thus spending the day in contriving a scheme for the morrow, distress stole upon him by imperceptible degrees. His conduct had already wearied some of those who were at first enamoured of his conversation; but he might, perhaps, still have devolved to others, whom he might have entertained with equal success, had not the decay of his cloaths made it no longer consistent with their vanity to admit him to their tables, or to associate with him in publick places. He now began to find every man from home at whose house he called; and was, therefore, no longer able to procure the necessaries of life, but wandered about the town slighted and neglected, in quest of a dinner, which he did not always obtain.

To complete his misery, he was persued by the officers for small debts which he had contracted; and was, therefore, obliged to withdraw from the small number of friends from whom he had still reason to hope for favours. His custom was to lye in bed the greatest part of the day, and to go out in the dark with the utmost privacy, and after having paid his visit, return again before morning to his lodging, which was in the garret of an obscure inn.

Being thus excluded on one hand, and confined on the other, he suffered the utmost extremities of poverty, and often fasted so long, that he was seized with faintness, and had lost his appetite, not being able to bear the smell of meat, 'till the action of his stomach was restored by a cordial.

In this distress he received a remittance of five pounds from London, with which he provided himself a decent coat, and determined to go to London, but unhappily spent his money at a favourite tavern. Thus was he again confined to Bristol, where he was every day hunted by bailiffs. In this exigence he once more found a friend, who sheltered him in his house, though at the usual inconveniences with which his company was attended; for he could neither be persuaded to go to bed in the night, nor to rise in the day.

It is observable, that in these various scenes of misery, he was always disengaged and cheerful; he at some times persued his studies, and at others continued or enlarged his epistolary correspondence, nor was he ever so far dejected as to endeavour to procure an encrease of his allowance, by any other methods than accusations and reproaches.

He had now no longer any hopes of assistance from his friends at Bristol, who as merchants, and by consequence sufficiently studious of profit, cannot be supposed to have look'd with much compassion upon negligence and extravagance, or to think any excellence equivalent to a fault of such consequence as neglect of oeconomy. It is natural to imagine, that many of those who would have relieved his real wants, were discouraged from the exertion of their benevolence, by observation of the use which was made of their favours, and conviction that relief would only be momentary, and that the same necessity would quickly return.

At last he quitted the house of his friend, and returned to his lodging at the inn, still intending to set out in a few days for London, but on the tenth of January 1742–3, having been at supper with two of his friends, he was at his return to his lodgings arrested for a debt of about eight pounds, which he owed at a coffee-house, and conducted to the house of a sheriff's officer. The account which he gives of this misfortune in a letter to one of the gentlemen with whom he had supped, is too remarkable to be omitted.

"It was not a little unfortunate for me, that I spent yesterday's evening with you; because the hour hindered me from entering on my new lodging; however, I have now got one; but such an one, as I believe nobody would chuse.

"I was arrested at the suit of Mrs. Read, just as I was going up stairs to bed, at Mr. Bowyer's; but taken in so private a manner, that I believe nobody at the White Lyon is apprised of it. Tho' I let the officers know the strength (or rather weakness of my pocket) yet they treated me with the utmost civility, and even when they conducted me to confinement, 'twas in such a manner, that I verily believe I could have escaped, which I would rather be ruined than have done; notwithstanding the whole amount of my finances was but three pence halfpenny.

"In the first place I must insist, that you will industriously conceal this from Mrs. S——s; because I would not have her good nature suffer that pain, which, I know, she would be apt to feel on this occasion.

"Next I conjure you, dear Sir, by all the ties of friendship, by no means to have one uneasy thought on my account; but to have the same pleasantry of countenance and unruffled serenity of mind, which (God be praised!) I have in this, and have had in a much severer calamity. Furthermore, I charge you, if you value my friendship as truly as I do yours, *not* to utter, or even harbour the least resentment against Mrs. Read. I believe she has ruin'd me, but I freely forgive her; and (tho' I will never more have any intimacy with her) would, at a due distance, rather do her an act of good, than ill will. Lastly, (pardon the expression) I *absolutely command* you not to offer me any pecuniary assistance, nor to attempt getting me any from any one of your friends. At another time, or on any other occasion, you may, dear friend, be well assured, I would rather write to you in the submissive stile of a request, than that of a peremptory command.

"However, that my truly valuable friend may not think I am too proud to ask a favour, let me entreat you to let me have your boy to attend me for this day, not only for the sake of saving me the expence of porters; but for the delivery of some letters to people, whose names I would not have known to strangers.

"The civil treatment I have thus far met from those, whose prisoner I am, makes me thankful to the Almighty, that, tho' He has thought fit to visit me (on my birth-night) with affliction; yet (such is His great goodness!) my affliction is not without alleviating circumstances. I murmur not, but am all resignation to the *divine will.* As to the world, I hope that I shall be endued by heaven with that presence of mind, that serene dignity in misfortune, that constitutes the character of a true nobleman; a dignity far beyond that of coronets; a nobility arising from the just principles of philosophy, refined and exalted, by those of Christianity."

He continued five days at the officer's, in hopes that he should be able to procure bail, and avoid the necessity of going to prison. The state in which he passed his time, and the treatment which he received, are very justly expressed by him in a letter which he wrote to a friend; "The whole day," *says he*, "has been employed in various people's filling my head with their foolish chimerical systems, which has obliged me coolly (as far as nature will admit) to digest, and accommodate myself to, every different person's way of thinking; hurried from one wild system to another, 'till it has quite made a chaos of my imagination, and nothing done—promised—disappointed—order'd to send every hour, from one part of the town to the other."——

When his friends, who had hitherto caressed and applauded, found that to give bail and pay the debt was the same, they all refused to preserve him from a prison, at the expence of eight pounds; and therefore after having been for some time at the officer's house, *at an immense expence*, as he observes in his letter, he was at length removed to Newgate.

This expence he was enabled to support, by the generosity of Mr. Nash at Bath, who upon receiving from him an account of his condition, immediately sent him five guineas, and promised to promote his subscription at Bath, with all his interest.

By his removal to Newgate, he obtained at least a freedom from suspense, and rest from the disturbing vicissitudes of hope and disappointment; he now found that his friends were only companions, who were willing to share his gaiety, but not to partake of his misfortunes; and therefore he no longer expected any assistance from them.

It must however be observed of one gentleman, that he offered to release him by paying the debt, but that Mr. Savage would not consent, I suppose, because he thought he had been before too burthensome to him.

He was offered by some of his friends, that a collection should be made for his enlargement, but he *treated the proposal*, and declared,[8] *that he should again treat it, with disdain. As to writing any mendicant letters, he had too high a spirit, and determined only to write to some Ministers of State, to try to regain his pension.*

He continued to complain[9] of those that had sent him into the country, and objected to them, that he had *lost the profits of his play which had been finished three years,* and in another letter declares his resolution to publish a pamphlet, that the world might know how *he had been used.*

This pamphlet was never written, for he in a very short time recover'd his usual tranquillity, and chearfully applied himself to more inoffensive studies. He indeed steadily declared, that he was promised an yearly allowance of fifty pounds, and never received half the sum, but he seemed to resign himself to that as well as to other misfortunes, and lose the remembrance of it in his amusements, and employments.

The chearfulness with which he bore his confinement, appears from the following letter which he wrote Jan. 30th, to one of his friends in London.

> I now write to you from my confinement in Newgate, where I have been ever since Monday last was sev'n-night; and where I enjoy myself with much more tranquillity than I have known for upwards of a twelve-month past; having a room entirely to myself, and persuing the amusement of my poetical studies, uninterrupted and agreeable to my mind. I thank the Almighty, I am now all collected in myself, and tho' my person is in confinement, my mind can expatiate on ample and useful subjects, with all the freedom imaginable. I am now more conversant with the Nine than ever; and if, instead of a Newgate bird, I may be allowed to be a bird of the muses, I assure you, Sir, I sing very freely in my cage; sometimes indeed in the plaintive notes of the nightingale; but, at others, in the chearful strains of the lark.——

In another letter he observes, that he ranges from one subject to another without confining himself to any particular task, and that he was employed one week upon one attempt, and the next upon another.

Surely the fortitude of this man deserves, at least, to be mentioned with applause, and whatever faults may be imputed to him, the virtue of *suffering well* cannot be denied him. The two powers which, in the opinion of Epictetus, constituted a wise man, are those of *bearing* and *forbearing,* which it cannot indeed be affirmed to have been equally possessed by Savage, and indeed the want of one obliged him very *frequently* to practise the other.

He was treated by Mr. Dagg, the keeper of the prison, with great humanity; was supported by him at his own table without any certainty of recompense, had a room to himself, to which he could at any time retire from all disturbance, was allowed to stand at the door of the prison, and sometimes taken out into the fields; so that he suffered fewer hardships in the prison, than he had been accustomed to undergo in the greatest part of his life.

The keeper did not confine his benevolence to a gentle execution of his office, but made some overtures to the creditor for his release, but without effect; and continued, during the whole time of his imprisonment to treat him with the utmost tenderness and civility.

Virtue is undoubtedly most laudable in that state which makes it most difficult; and therefore the humanity of a goaler, certainly deserves this publick attestation; and the man whose heart has not been hardened by such an employment, may be justly proposed as a pattern of benevolence. If an inscription was once engraved to the *honest toll-gatherer,* less honours ought not to be paid *to the tender goaler.*

Mr. Savage very frequently received visits, and sometimes presents from his acquaintances, but they did not amount to a subsistence, for the greater part of which he was indebted to the generosity of this keeper; but these favours, however they might endear to him the particular persons, from whom he received them, were very far from impressing upon his mind any advantageous ideas of the people of Bristol, and therefore he thought he could not more properly employ himself in prison, than in writing the following poem.

London and Bristol[1] *delineated*

Two sea-port cities mark Britannia's fame,
And these from commerce different honours claim.
What different honours shall the muses pay,
While one inspires and one untunes the lay?

Now silver Isis bright'ning flows along,
Echoing from Oxford's shore each classic song;
Then weds with Tame; and these, O London, see
Swelling with naval pride, the pride of thee!
Wide deep unsullied Thames meand'ring glides
And bears thy wealth on mild majestic tides.
Thy ships, with gilded palaces that vie,
In glitt'ring pomp, strike wond'ring China's eye;
And thence returning bear, in splendid state,
To Britain's merchants, India's eastern freight.
India, her treasures from her western shores,
Due at thy feet, a willing tribute pours;
Thy warring navies distant nations awe,
And bid the world obey thy righteous law.
Thus shine thy manly sons of lib'ral mind;
Thy Change deep-busied, yet as courts refin'd;
Councils, like senates that enforce debate
With fluent eloquence and reason's weight.
Whose patriot virtue, lawless pow'r controuls;
Their British emulating Roman souls.
Of these the worthiest still selected stand,
Still lead the Senate, and still save the land:
Social, not selfish, here, O learning trace
Thy friends, the lovers of all human race!

In a dark bottom sunk, O Bristol now,
With native malice, lift thy low'ring brow!
Then as some hell-born sprite, in mortal guise,
Borrows the shape of goodness and belies,
All fair, all smug to yon proud hall invite,
To feast all strangers ape an air polite!
From Cambria drain'd, or England's western coast,
Not elegant yet costly banquets boast!
Revere, or seem the stranger to revere;
Praise, fawn, profess, be all things but sincere;
Insidious now, our bosom secrets steal,
And these with sly sarcastic sneer reveal.
Present we meet thy sneaking treach'rous smiles;
The harmless absent still thy sneer reviles;

Such as in thee all parts superior find;
The sneer that marks the fool and knave combin'd.
When melting pity wou'd afford relief,
The ruthless sneer that insult adds to grief.
What friendship can'st thou boast? what honours claim?
To thee each stranger owes an injur'd name.
What smiles thy sons must in their foes excite?
Thy sons to whom all discord is delight;
From whom eternal mutual railing flows;
Who in each others crimes, their own expose;
Thy sons, tho' crafty, deaf to wisdom's call;
Despising all men and despis'd by all.
Sons, while thy cliffs a ditch-like river laves,
Rude as thy rocks, and muddy as thy waves;
Of thoughts as narrow as of words immense;
As full of turbulence as void of sense:
Thee, thee what senatorial souls adorn?
Thy natives sure wou'd prove a senate's scorn.
Do strangers deign to serve thee? what their praise?
Their gen'rous services thy murmurs raise.
What fiend malign, that o'er thy air presides,
Around from breast to breast inherent glides,
And, as he glides, there scatters in a trice
The lurking seeds of ev'ry rank device?
Let foreign youths to thy indentures run!
Each, each will prove, in thy adopted son,
Proud, pert and dull—Tho' brilliant once from schools,
Will scorn all learning's as all virtue's rules;
And, tho' by nature friendly, honest, brave,
Turn a sly, selfish, simp'ring, sharping knave.
Boast petty-courts, where 'stead of fluent ease;
Of cited precedents and learned pleas;
'Stead of sage council in the dubious cause,
Attorneys chatt'ring wild, burlesque the laws.
So shameless quacks, who doctor's rights invade,
Of jargon and of poison form a trade.
So canting coblers, while from tubs they teach,
Buffoon the Gospel they pretend to preach.
Boast petty courts, whence rules new rigour draw;

Unknown to nature's and to statute law;
Quirks that explain all saving rights away,
To give th' attorney and the catch-poll prey.
Is there where law too rig'rous may descend?
Or charity her kindly hand extend?
Thy courts, that shut when pity wou'd redress,
Spontaneous open to inflict distress.
Try misdemeanours!—all thy wiles employ,
Not to chastise the offender but destroy;
Bid the large lawless fine his fate foretell;
Bid it beyond his crime and fortune swell.
Cut off from service due to kindred blood
To private welfare and to public good,
Pitied by all, but thee, he sentenc'd lies;
Imprison'd languishes, imprison'd dies,

* * * * * * * * * * * * * *

Boast swarming vessels, whose plaebeian state
Owes not to merchants but mechanics freight.
Boast nought but pedlar fleets—in war's alarms,
Unknown to glory, as unknown to arms.
Boast thy base[2] Tolsey, and thy turn-spit dogs;
Thy[3] hallier's horses and thy human hogs;
Upstarts and mushrooms, proud, relentless hearts;
Thou blank of sciences! Thou dearth of arts!
Such foes as learning once was doom'd to see;
Huns, Goths, and Vandals were but types of thee.
    Proceed, great Bristol, in all-righteous ways,
And let one justice heighten yet thy praise;
Still spare the catamite and swinge the whore,
And be, whate'er Gomorrah was before.

When he had brought this poem to its present state, which, without considering the chasm, is not perfect, he wrote to London an account of his design, and informed his friend, that he was determined to print it with his name; but enjoined him not to communicate his intention to his Bristol acquaintance. The gentleman surprised at his resolution, endeavoured to dissuade him from publishing it, at least, from prefixing his name, and declared, that he could not reconcile the injunction of secrecy with his resolution to own it at its first appearance. To this Mr. Savage returned an answer agreeable to his character in the following terms.

"I received yours this morning and not without a little surprize at the contents. To answer a question with a question, you ask me concerning London and Bristol, *why will I add* delineated? Why did Mr. Woolaston add the same word to his religion of nature? I suppose that it was his will and pleasure to add it in his case; and it is mine to do so in my own. You are pleased to tell me, that you understand not, why secrecy is injoin'd, and yet I intend to set my name to it. My answer is—I have my private reasons; which I am not obliged to explain to any one. You doubt, my friend Mr. S—— would not approve of it—And what is it to me whether he does or not? Do you imagine, that Mr. S—— is to dictate to me? If any man, who calls himself my friend, should assume such an air, I would spurn at his friendship with contempt. You say, I seem to think so by not letting him know it—And suppose I do, what then? Perhaps I can give reasons for that disapprobation, very foreign from what you would imagine. You go on in saying, suppose, I should not put my name to it—My answer is, that I will not suppose any such thing, being determined to the contrary; neither, Sir, would I have you suppose, that I applied to you for want of another press: Nor would I have you imagine, that I owe Mr. S—— obligations which I do not."

Such was his imprudence and such his obstinate adherence to his own resolutions, however absurd. A prisoner! supported by charity! and, whatever insults he might have received during the latter part of his stay in Bristol, once caressed, esteemed, and presented with a liberal collection, he could forget on a sudden his danger, and his obligations, to gratify the petulance of his wit, or the eagerness of his resentment, and publish a satire by which he might reasonably expect, that he should alienate those who then supported him, and provoke those whom he could neither resist nor escape.

This resolution, from the execution of which, it is probable, that only his death could have hindered him, is sufficient to show, how much he disregarded all considerations that opposed his present passions, and how readily he hazarded all future advantages for any immediate gratifications. Whatever was his predominant inclination, neither hope nor fear hinder'd him from complying with it, nor had opposition any other effect than to heighten his ardour and irritate his vehemence.

This performance was however laid aside, while he was employed in soliciting assistance from several great persons, and one interruption succeeding another hinder'd him from supplying the chasm, and perhaps from retouching the other parts, which he can hardly be imagined to have finished, in his own opinion; for it is very unequal, and some of the lines are rather inserted to rhyme to others than to support or improve the sense; but the first and last parts are worked up with great spirit and elegance.

His time was spent in the prison for the most part in study, or in receiving visits; but sometimes he descended to lower amusements, and diverted himself in the kitchen with the conversation of the criminals; for it was not pleasing to him to be much without company, and though he was very capable of a judicious choice, he was often contented with the first that offered; for this he was sometimes reproved by his friends who found him surrounded with felons; but the reproof was on that as on other occasions thrown away; he continued to gratify himself, and to set very little value on the opinion of others.

But here, as in every other scene of his life, he made use of such opportunities as occur'd of benefiting those who were more miserable than himself, and was always ready to perform any offices of humanity to his fellow prisoners.

He had now ceased from corresponding with any of his subscribers except one, who yet continued to remit him the twenty pounds a year which he had promised him, and by whom it was expected, that he would have been in a very short time enlarged, because he had directed the keeper to enquire after the state of his debts.

However he took care to enter his name according to the forms of the court, that the creditor might be obliged to make him some allowance, if he was continued a prisoner, and when on that occasion he appeared in the hall was treated with very unusual respect.

But the resentment of the city was afterwards raised by some accounts that had been spread of the satire, and he was informed that some of the merchants intended to pay the allowance which the law required, and to detain him a prisoner at their own expence. This he treated as an empty menace, and perhaps might have hasten'd the publication, only to shew how much he was superior to their insults, had not all his schemes been suddenly destroyed.

When he had been six months in prison he received from one of his friends in whose kindness he had the greatest confidence, and on whose assistance he chiefly depended, a letter that contained a charge of very atrocious ingratitude, drawn up in such terms as sudden resentment dictated. Mr. Savage returned a very solemn protestation of his innocence, but however appeared much disturbed at the accusation. Some days afterwards he was seized with a pain in his back and side, which as it was not violent was not suspected to be dangerous; but growing daily more languid and dejected, on the 25th of July he confined himself to his room, and a fever seized his spirits. The symptoms grew every day more formidable, but his condition did not enable him to procure any assistance. The last time that the keeper saw him was on July the 31st, when Savage seeing him at his bed-side said, with an uncommon earnestness, *I have something to say to you, Sir,* but after a pause, moved his hand in a melancholy manner, and finding himself unable to recollect what he was going to communicate, said *'Tis gone.* The keeper soon after left him, and the next morning he died. He was buried in the church-yard of St. Peter, at the expence of the keeper.

Such were the life and death of Richard Savage, a man equally distinguished by his virtues and vices, and at once remarkable for his weaknesses and abilities.

He was of a middle stature, of a thin habit of body, a long visage, coarse features, and melancholy aspect; of a grave and manly deportment, a solemn dignity of mien, but which upon a nearer acquaintance softened into an engaging easiness of manners. His walk was slow, and his voice tremulous and mournful. He was easily excited to smiles, but very seldom provoked to laughter.

His mind was in an uncommon degree vigorous and active. His judgment was accurate, his apprehension quick, and his memory so tenacious, that he was frequently observed to know what he had learned from others in a short time better than those by whom he was informed, and could frequently recollect incidents, with all their combination of circumstances, which few would have regarded at the present time; but which the quickness of his apprehension impressed upon him. He had the peculiar felicity, that his attention never deserted him; he was present to every object, and regardful of the most trifling occurrences. He had the art of escaping from his own reflections and accommodating himself to every new scene.

To this quality is to be imputed the extent of his knowledge compared with the small time which he spent in visible endeavours to acquire it. He mingled in cursory conversation with the same steadiness of attention as others apply to a lecture, and, amidst the appearance of thoughtless gayety, lost no new idea that was started, nor any hint that could be improved. He had therefore made in coffee-houses the same proficiency as others in studies; and it is remarkable, that the writings of a man of little education and little reading have an air of learning scarcely to be found in any other performances, but which perhaps as often obscures as embellishes them.

His judgment was eminently exact both with regard to writings and to men. The knowledge of life was indeed his chief attainment, and it is not without some satisfaction, that I can produce the suffrage of Savage in favour of human nature, of which he never appeared to entertain such odious ideas, as some who perhaps had neither his judgment nor experience have published, either in ostentation of their sagacity, vindication of their crimes, or gratification of their malice.

His method of life particularly qualified him for conversation, of which he knew how to practise all the graces. He was never vehement or loud, but at once modest and easy, open and respectful, his language was vivacious and elegant, and equally happy upon grave or humorous subjects. He was generally censured for not knowing when to retire, but that was not the defect of his judgment, but of his fortune; when he left his company he was frequently to spend the remaining part of the night in the street, or at least was abandoned to gloomy reflections, which it is not strange that he delayed as long as he could, and sometimes forgot that he gave others pain to avoid it himself.

It cannot be said, that he made use of his abilities for the direction of his own conduct; an irregular and dissipated manner of life had made him the slave of every passion that happened to be excited by the presence of its object, and that slavery to his passions reciprocally produced a life irregular and dissipated. He was not master of his own emotions, nor could promise any thing for the next day.

With regard to his oeconomy, nothing can be added to the relation of his life: he appeared to think himself born to be supported by others, and dispensed from all necessity of providing for himself; he therefore never prosecuted any scheme of advantage, nor endeavoured even to secure the profits which his writings might have afforded him.

His temper was in consequence of the dominion of his passions uncertain and capricious; he was easily engaged, and easily disgusted; but he is accused of retaining his hatred more tenaciously than his benevolence.

He was compassionate both by nature and principle, and always ready to perform offices of humanity; but when he was provoked, and very small offences were sufficient to provoke him, he would prosecute his revenge with the utmost acrimony till his passion had subsided.

His friendship was therefore of little value; for though he was zealous in the support or vindication of those whom he loved, yet it was always dangerous to trust him, because he considered himself as discharged by the first quarrel, from all ties of honour or gratitude; and would betray those secrets which in the warmth of confidence had been imparted to him. This practice drew upon him an universal accusation of ingratitude; nor can it be denied that he was very ready to set himself free from the load of an obligation; for he could not bear to conceive himself in a state of dependence, his pride being equally powerful with his other passions, and appearing in the form of insolence at one time and of vanity at another. Vanity the most innocent species of pride, was most frequently predominant: he could not easily leave off when he had once began to mention himself or his works, nor ever read his verses without stealing his eyes from the page, to discover in the faces of his audience, how they were affected with any favourite passage.

A kinder name than that of vanity ought to be given to the delicacy with which he was always careful to separate his own merit from every other man's; and to reject that praise to which he had no claim. He did not forget, in mentioning his performances, to mark every line that had been suggested or amended, and was so accurate as to relate that he owed *three words* in *The Wanderer,* to the advice of his friends.

His veracity was questioned but with little reason; his accounts, tho' not indeed always the same, were generally consistent. When he loved any man, he suppress'd all his faults, and when he had been offended by him, concealed all his virtues: but his characters were generally true, so far as he proceeded; tho' it cannot be denied that his partiality might have sometimes the effect of falsehood.

In cases indifferent he was zealous for virtue, truth and justice; he knew very well the necessity of goodness to the present and future happiness of mankind; nor is there perhaps any writer, who has less endeavoured to please by flattering the appetites or perverting the judgment.

As an author, therefore, and he now ceases to influence mankind in any other character, if one piece which he had resolved to suppress be excepted, he has very little to fear from the strictest moral or religious censure. And though he may not be altogether secure against the objections of the critic, it must however be acknowledged, that his works are the productions of a genius truly poetical; and, what many writers who have been more lavishly applauded cannot boast, that they have an original air, which has no resemblance to any foregoing writer; that the versification and sentiments have a cast peculiar to themselves, which no man can imitate with success, because what was nature in Savage would in another be affectation. It must be confessed that his descriptions are striking, his images animated, his fictions justly imagined, and his allegories artfully persued; that his diction is elevated, though sometimes forced, and his numbers sonorous and majestick, though frequently sluggish and encumbered. Of his stile the general fault is harshness, and its general excellence is dignity; of his sentiments the prevailing beauty is sublimity, and uniformity the prevailing defect.

For his life, or for his writings, none who candidly consider his fortune, will think an apology either necessary or difficult. If he was not always sufficiently instructed in his subject, his knowledge was at least greater than could have been attained by others in the same state. If his works were sometimes unfinished, accuracy cannot reasonably be exacted from a man oppressed with want, which he has no hope of relieving but by a speedy publication. The insolence and resentment of which he is accused, were not easily to be avoided by a great mind, irritated by perpetual hardships and constrained hourly to return the spurns of contempt, and repress the insolence of prosperity; and vanity may surely readily be pardoned in him, to whom life afforded no other comforts than barren praises, and the consciousness of deserving them.

Those are no proper judges of his conduct who have slumber'd away their time on the down of affluence, nor will any wise man presume to say, "Had I been in Savage's condition, I should have lived, or written, better than Savage."

This relation will not be wholly without its use, if those, who languish under any part of his sufferings, shall be enabled to fortify their patience by reflecting that they feel only those afflictions from which the abilities of Savage did not exempt him; or those, who in confidence of superior capacities or attainments disregard the common maxims of life, shall be reminded that nothing will supply the want of prudence, and that negligence and irregularity, long continued, will make knowledge useless, wit ridiculous, and genius contemptible.

NOTES

(between pp. 5-12)

1. This year was made remarkable by the dissolution of a marriage solemnized in the face of the Church. *Salmon's Review.*

The following protest is registered in the books of the House of Lords.

Dissentient.

Because we conceive that this is the first Bill of that nature that hath passed, where there was not a divorce first obtained in the Spiritual Court; which we look upon as an ill precedent, and may be of dangerous consequence in the future.

HALIFAX. ROCHESTER.

[All notes to the *Life of Savage* are Johnson's unless otherwise indicated.]

2. Savage's Preface to his Miscellany.
3. Preface to Savage's Miscellanies.

4. *Plain Dealer*. See Appendix [to the *Plain Dealer*].
5. Jacob's Lives of Dramatic Poets.
6. This play was printed first in 8vo, and afterwards in 12mo, the fifth edition.
7. *Plain Dealer*.
8. As it is a loss to mankind, when any good action is forgotten, I shall insert another instance of Mr. Wilk's generosity, very little known. Mr. Smith, a gentleman educated at Dublin, being hindered by an impediment in his pronunciation from engaging in Orders, for which his friends designed him, left his own country, and came to London in quest of employment, but found his solicitations fruitless and his necessities every day more pressing. In this distress he wrote a tragedy, and offered it to the players, by whom it was rejected. Thus were his last hopes defeated, and he had no other prospect than of the most deplorable poverty. But Mr. Wilks thought his performance, though not perfect, at least worthy of some reward, and therefore offered him a Benefit. This favour he improved with so much diligence, that the house afforded him a considerable sum, with which he went to Leyden, applied himself to the study of physic, and prosecuted his design with so much diligence and success, that when Dr. Boerhaave was desired by the Czarina to recommend proper persons to introduce into Russia the practice and study of physic, Dr. Smith was one of those whom he selected. He had a considerable pension settled on him at his arrival, and is now one of the chief physicians at the Russian Court.
9. This I write upon the credit of the author of his Life, which was published 1727.

(between pp. 14-17)

1. In 1724.
2. He inscribed to him a short poem, called *The Friend,* printed in his Miscellanies, in which he addresses him with the utmost ardour of affection.

   O lov'd, Hillarius! thou by Heav'n design'd
   To charm, to mend, and to instruct mankind:
   To whom my hopes, fears, joys, and sorrows tend,
   Thou brother, father, nearer yet—thou friend——
   —Kind are my wrongs, I thence thy friendship own,
   What state could bless, were I to thee unknown?
   ——While shun'd, obscur'd, or thwarted and expos'd,
   By friends abandon'd, and by foes enclos'd.
   Thy guardian counsel softens ev'ry care,
   To ease sooths anguish, and to hope, despair.
3. To. A. Hill, Esq., with the *Tragedy of Sir Thomas Overbury.*

   As the soul strip'd of mortal clay
       Shews all divinely fair,
   And boundless roves the Milky Way,
       And views sweet prospects there.
   This hero clog'd with drossy lines
       By thee new vigour tries;
   As thy correcting hand refines
       Bright scenes around him rise.
   Thy touch brings the wish'd stone to pass,
       So sought, so long foretold;

It turns polluted lead and brass
At once to purest gold.

4. In a full world our author lives alone,
Unhappy, and by consequence unknown;
Yet amidst sorrow he disdains complaint,
Nor languid in the race of life grows faint:
He swims, unyielding, against fortune's stream,
Nor to his private sufferings stoops his theme.

5. To —— Tryste, Esq; of Herefordshire.

6. The *Plain Dealer* was a periodical paper written by Mr. Hill and Mr. Bond, whom Mr. Savage called the two contending powers of light and darkness. They wrote by turns each six essays, and the character of the work was observed regularly to rise in Mr. Hill's weeks, and fall in Mr. Bond's.

7. Hopeless, abandon'd, aimless, and oppress'd,
Lost to delight, and, ev'ry way, distress'd;
Cross his cold bed, in wild disorder, thrown,
Thus sigh'd Alexis, friendless, and alone——
Why do I breathe?——What joy can being give?
When she, who gave me life, forgets I live!
Feels not these wintry blasts;——nor heeds my smart;
But shuts me from the shelter of her heart!
Saw me expos'd to want! to shame! to scorn!
To ills!——which make it *misery*, to be *born!*
Cast me, regardless, on the world's bleak wild;
And bade me be a wretch, while yet a child!
Where can he hope for pity, peace, or rest,
Who moves no softness in a mother's breast?
Custom, law, reason, *all!* my cause forsake,
And Nature *sleeps*, to keep my woes *awake!*
Crimes, which the *cruel* scarce believe can be,
The *kind* are guilty of, to ruin *me.*
Ev'n she, who bore me, blasts me with her hate,
And, *meant* my *fortune, makes* herself my *fate.*
Yet has this sweet neglecter of my woes,
The softest, tend'rest breast, that *pity* knows!
Her eyes shed mercy, wheresoe'er they shine;
And her soul *melts* at ev'ry woe——but *mine.*
Sure then! some secret fate, for guilt unwill'd,
Some sentence pre-ordain'd to be fulfill'd!
Plung'd me, thus deep, in sorrow's searching flood;
And wash'd me from the mem'ry of her blood.
But, Oh! whatever cause has mov'd her hate,
Let me but sigh, in silence, at my fate;
The God, *within*, perhaps may touch her breast;
And, when she *pities*, who can be distress'd?

8. The names of those who so generously contributed to his relief, having been mentioned in a former account, ought not to be omitted here. They were the Dutchess of Cleveland, Lady Cheyney, Lady Castlemain, Lady Gower, Lady Lechmere, the Dutchess Dowager, and Dutchess of Rutland. Lady Strafford, the Countess Dowager of Warwick, Mrs.

Mary Floyer, Mrs. Sofuel Noel, Duke of Rutland, Lord Gainsborough, Lord Milsington, Mr. John Savage.

9. This Preface is as follows:

Crudelis mater magis, an puer improbus ille?
Improbus ille puer, crudelis tu quoque mater. VIRG.

My readers, I am afraid, when they observe Richard Savage join'd so close, and so constantly, to *son of the late Earl Rivers,* will impute to a ridiculous vanity, what is the effect of an unhappy necessity, which my hard fortune has thrown me under——I am to be pardoned for adhering a little tenaciously to my father, because my mother will allow me to be no-body; and has almost reduced me, among heavier afflictions, to that uncommon kind of want, which the Indians of America complained of at our first settling among them; when they came to beg *names* of the English, because (said they) we are poor men of ourselves, and have none we can lay claim to.

The good nature of those, to whom I have not the honour to be known, would forgive me the ludicrous turn of this beginning, if they knew but how little reason I have to be merry——It was my misfortune to be son of the above-mentioned Earl, by the late Countess of Macclesfield, (now widow of Colonel Henry Bret,) whose divorce, on occasion of the amour which I was a consequence of, has left something on record, which I take to be very remarkable; and it is this: Certain of our great judges, in their *temporal* decisions, act with a *spiritual* regard to *Levitical divinity;* and in particular to the Ten Commandments: Two of which seem in my case, to have visibly influenced their opinions——*Thou shalt not commit adultery,* pointed fullest on my mother: But, as to *The Lord's visiting the sins of the fathers upon the children,* it was considered as what could regard *me* only: And for that reason, I suppose, it had been inconsistent with the rules of sanctity, to assign provision out of my mother's return'd estate, for support of an infant sinner.

Thus, while *legally* the son of one Earl, and *naturally* of another, I am, *nominally,* no-body's son at all: For the lady having given me *too much father,* thought it but an equivalent deduction, to leave me *no mother,* by way of balance——So I am sported into the world, a kind of shuttle-cock, between law and nature——If law had not beaten me back, by the stroke of an Act, on purpose, I had not been *above wit,* by the privilege of a man of quality: Nay, I might have preserved into the bargain, the lives of Duke Hamilton and Lord Mohun, whose dispute arose from the estate of that Earl of Macclesfield, whom (but for the mentioned Act) I must have *called father*——And, if nature had not struck me off, with a stranger blow than law did, the other Earl, who was most *emphatically* my father, could never have been told, I was *dead,* when he was about to enable me, by his *will,* to have lived to some purpose. An unaccountable severity of a mother! whom I was then not old enough to have deserved it from: And by which I am a single unhappy instance, among that nobleman's natural children; and thrown, friendless on the world, without means of supporting *myself;* and without authority to apply to those, whose duty I know it is to support me.

Thus however ill qualified I am to *live by my wits,* I have the best plea in the world for attempting it; since it is too apparent, that I was *born to it*——Having wearied my judgment with fruitless endeavours to be happy, I gave the reins to my fancy, that I might learn, at least, to be *easy.*

But I cease a while to speak of *myself,* that I may say something of my Miscellany——I was furnished, by the verses of my friends, with *wit* enough to deserve a subscription; but I wanted another much more profitable quality, which should have emboldened me to solicite it (another of my wants, that, I hope, may be imputed to my mother!) I had met with little encouragement, but for the endeavours of some few gentlemen, in my behalf, who were generous enough to consider my ill fortune, as a merit that intitled me to their notice.

Among these I am particularly indebted to the author of the *Plain Dealers,* who was pleased, in two of his papers (which I intreat his pardon, for reprinting before my Miscellany) to point out my unhappy story to the world, with so touching a humanity, and so good an effect, that many persons of quality, of all ranks, and of both sexes, distinguished themselves with the promptness he had hinted to the noble minded; and not staying till they were applied to, sent me the honour of their subscriptions, in the most liberal and handsom manner, for encouragement of my undertaking.

I ought here to acknowledge several favours from Mr. Hill, whose writings are a shining ornament of this Miscellany: but I wave detaining my readers, and beg leave to refer them to a copy of verses called the *Friend,* which I have taken the liberty to address to that gentleman.

To return to the lady, my mother——Had the celebrated Mr. Locke been acquainted with her example, it had certainly appeared in his *chapter* against innate practical principles; because it would have completed his instances of enormities: Some of which, though not exactly in the order that he mentions them, are as follow——*Have there not been* (says he) *whole nations, and those of the most civilized people, amongst whom, the exposing their children, to perish by want or wild beasts, has been a practice as little condemned or scrupled as the begetting them?* Were I inclinable to be serious, I could easily prove that I have not been more gently dealt with by Mrs. Bret; but if this is any way foreign to my case, I shall find a nearer example in the whimsical one that ensues.

It is familiar (says the afore-cited author) *among the Mengrelians, a people professing Christianity, to bury their children alive without scruple*——There are indeed sundry sects of Christians, and I have often wondered which could be my *mamma's,* but now I find she piously professes and practises Christianity after the manner of the Mengrelians; she industriously obscured me, when my fortune depended on my being known, and, in that sense, she may be said to have buried me alive; and sure, like a Mengrelian, she must have committed the action without scruple; for she is a woman of spirit, and can see the consequence without remorse——*The Caribbees* (continues my author) *were wont to castrate their children in order to fat and eat them*——Here indeed I can draw no parallel; for to speak justice of the lady, she never contributed ought to have me pampered, but always promoted my being starved: Nor did she, even in my infancy, betray fondness enough to be suspected of a design to devour me; but, on the contrary, not enduring me ever to approach her, offered a bribe to have me shipped off, in an odd manner, to one of the plantations—When I was about fifteen her affection began to awake, and had I but known my interest, I had been handsomly provided for. In short I was solicited to be bound apprentice to a very honest and reputable occupation—a *shoemaker;* an offer which I undutifully rejected. I was, in fine, unwilling to understand her in a literal sense, and hoped, that, like the prophets of old, she might have hinted her mind in a kind of parable, or proverbial way of speaking; as thus—That one time or other I might, on due application, have the honour of *taking the length of her foot.*

Mr. Locke mentions another set of people that dispatch their children, if a pretended astrologer declares them to have unhappy stars——Perhaps my *mamma* has procured some *cunning man* to calculate my nativity; or having had some ominous dream, which preceded my birth, the dire event may have appeared to her in the dark and dreary bottom of a China cup, where coffee-stains are often consulted for prophecies, and held as infallible as were the leaves of the ancient sybils——To be partly serious: I am rather willing to wrong her judgment, by suspecting it to be tainted a little with the tenets of superstition, than suppose she can be mistress of a seared conscience, and act on no principle at all.

(between pp. 17-29)

1. This the following extract from it will prove.

—"Since our country has been honour'd with the glory of your wit, as elevated and immortal as your soul, it no longer remains a doubt whether your sex have strength of mind in proportion to their sweetness. There is something in your verses as distinguished as your air——They are as strong as truth, as deep as reason, as clear as innocence, and as smooth as beauty ——They contain a nameless and peculiar mixture of force and grace, which is at once so movingly serene, and so majestically lovely, that it is too amiable to appear any where but in your eyes, and in your writings.

"As fortune is not more my enemy than I am the enemy of flattery, I know not how I can forbear this application to your Ladyship, because there is scarce a possibility that I should say more than I believe, when I am speaking of your excellence."——

2. Mr. Savage's Life.
3. Written by Mr. Beckingham and another gentleman.
4. The satire from which the following lines are extracted was called by Mr. Savage, *An Epistle on Authors:* It was never printed intire, but several fragments were inserted by him in the *Magazine*, after his retirement into the country.

Were all like *Yorke* of delicate address,
Strength to discern, and sweetness to express;
Learn'd, just, polite, born ev'ry heart to gain;
Like Cummins mild, like[a] Fortescue humane;
All eloquent of truth, divinely known;
So deep, so clear, all science is his own.
How far unlike such worthies, once a drudge,
From flound'ring in low causes, rose a *judge.*
Form'd to make pleaders laugh, his *nonsense* thunders,
And, on low juries, breathes contagious blunders.
His brothers blush, because no blush he knows,
Nor e'er[b] *one uncorrupted finger shows.*
See, drunk with power, the *Circuit Lord* exprest!
Full, in his eye, his betters stand confest;

[a] The Hon. William Fortescue, Esq; now Master of the Rolls.
[b] When Page one uncorrupted finger shows.
D. of Wharton.

Whose wealth, birth, virtue, from a tongue so loose,
'Scape not provincial, vile, buffoon abuse.
Still to what circuit is assign'd his name,
There, swift before him, flies the warner Fame.
Contest stops short, consent yields every cause
To cost, delay, endures them and withdraws.
But how 'scape Pris'ners? To their trial chain'd,
All, all shall stand condemn'd, who stand arraign'd.
Dire Guilt, which else would detestation cause,
Pre-judg'd with insult, wond'rous pity draws.
But 'scapes ev'n Innocence his harsh harangue?
Alas——ev'n Innocence itself must hang;
Must hang to please him, when of spleen possest:
Must hang to bring forth an abortive jest.
Why liv'd he not ere Star-Chambers had fail'd,
When fine, tax, censure, all, but law, prevail'd;
Or law, subservient to some murd'rous will,
Became a precedent to murder still?
Yet ev'n when patriots did for traytors bleed,
Was e'er the jobb to such a slave decreed;
Whose savage mind wants sophist art to draw,
O'er murder'd virtue, specious veils of law?

Gentleman's Magazine, Sept. 1741.

5. In one of his letters he stiles it, a *fatal quarrel, but too well known.*
6. Is chance a guilt, that my disast'rous heart,
For mischief never meant, must ever smart?
Can self-defence be sin?—Ah! plead no more;
What though no purpos'd malice stain'd thee o'er;
Had heav'n befriended thy unhappy side,
Thou hadst not been provok'd, or then hadst dy'd.
Far be the guilt of home-shed blood from all
On whom, unsought, embroiling dangers fall.
Still the pale Dead revives and lives to me,
To me, through pity's eye, condemn'd to see.
Remembrance veils his rage, but swells his fate,
Griev'd I forgive, and am grown cool too late.
Young and unthoughtful then, who knows one day
What rip'ning virtues might have made their way?
He might perhaps his country's friend have prov'd,
Been gen'rous, happy, candid and belov'd;
He might have sav'd some worth now doom'd to fall,
And I perchance in him have *murder'd* all.

Bastard.

7. The first edition reads "If the," in error. Eds.
8. *To the right honourable the Earl of Middlesex.*

My Lord,

That elegant taste in poetry, which is hereditary to your Lordship, together with that particular regard, with which you honour the author to whom these papers relate, make me imagine this collection will not be unpleasing to you. And I may presume to say, the pieces themselves are such as are not unworthy your Lordship's patronage, my own part in it excepted. I speak only of the *Author to be let,* having no title to any other, not even the small ones out of the journals. May I be permitted to declare (to the end I may seem not quite so unworthy of your Lordship's favour, as some writers of my *age* and circumstances) that I never was concerned in any journals. I ever thought the exorbitant liberty, which most of those papers take with their superiors, unjustifiable in any rank of men; but detestable in such who do it merely for hire, and without even the bad excuse of *passion* and *resentment*. On the contrary, being once inclined, upon some advantageous proposals, to enter into a [a]paper of another kind, I immediately desisted, on finding admitted into it (though as the publisher told me purely by an accident) two or three lines reflecting on a *great minister*. Were my life ever so unhappy, it shall not be stained with a conduct, which my birth at least (though neither my *education* nor *good fortune*) should set me above, much less with any ingratitude to that noble person, to whose intercession (next to his Majesty's goodness) I owe in a great measure that *life itself*.

——*Nec si miserum Fortuna Sinonem*
Finxit, vanum etiam mendacemque improba finget.

I believe your Lordship will pardon this digression, or any other which keeps me from the stile, you so much hate, of dedication.

I will not pretend to display those rising virtues in your Lordship, which the next age will certainly know without my help, but rather relate (what else it will as certainly be ignorant of) the history of these papers, and the occasion which produced the *War of the Dunces,* (for so it has been commonly called) which begun in the year 1727, and ended in 1730.

When Dr. Swift and Mr. Pope thought it proper, for reasons specified in the Preface to their Miscellanies, to publish such little pieces of theirs as had casually got abroad, there was added to them the treatise of the *Bathos, or the Art of Sinking in Poetry*. It happened that in one chapter of this piece, the several species of bad poets were ranged in classes, to which were prefixed almost all the letters of the alphabet (the greatest part of them at random) but such was the number of poets eminent in *that art,* that some one or other took every letter to himself: All fell into so violent a fury, that for half a year, or more, the common news-papers (in most of which they had some property, as being *hired writers*) were filled with the most abusive falshoods and scurrilities they could possibly devise. A liberty no way to be wondered at in those people, and in those papers, that, for many years during the uncontrolled liberty of the press, had aspersed almost all the great *characters* of the age; and this with impunity, their own *persons* and *names* being utterly secret and obscure.

This gave Mr. Pope the thought, that he had now some opportunity of doing good, by detecting and dragging into light these common enemies of mankind; since to *invalidate* this universal slander, it sufficed to shew what contemptible men were the authors of it. He was not without hopes, that by manifesting the dulness of those who had only malice to recommend them, either the booksellers would not find their account in employing them, or the men themselves when discovered, want courage to proceed in so unlawful an occupation. This it was that gave birth to the *Dunciad,* and he thought it an happiness, that by the late flood of slander on himself, he had acquired such a peculiar right over their *names* as was necessary to this design.

---

[a] The paper here meant, was probably the *Grubstreet-Journal,* which Mr. Savage was once invited to undertake, but which he declined, whether for the reason here mentioned is not certain.

On the 12th of March 1729, at St. James's, that poem was presented to the *King* and *Queen* (who had before been pleased to read it) by the right honourable Sir Robert Walpole: And some days after the whole impression was taken and dispersed by several noblemen and persons of the first distinction.

It is certainly a true observation, that no people are so impatient of censure as those who are the greatest slanderers: Which was wonderfully exemplified on this occasion. On the day the book was first vended, a crowd of authors besieged the shop; entreaties, advices, threats of law, and battery, nay cries of treason were all employed to hinder the coming out of the *Dunciad:* On the other side the booksellers and hawkers made as great efforts to procure it: What could a few poor authors do against so great a majority as the publick? There was no stopping a torrent with a finger, so out it came.

Many ludicrous circumstances attended it: The dunces (for by this name they were called) held weekly clubs, to consult of hostilities against the author; one wrote a letter to a great Minister, assuring him Mr. Pope was the greatest enemy the Government had; and another brought his image in clay, to execute him in effigy; with which sad sort of satisfactions the gentlemen were a little comforted.

Some false editions of the book having an owl in their frontispiece, the true one, to distinguish it, fixed in its stead an ass laden with authors. Then another surreptitious one being printed with the same ass, the new edition in octavo returned for distinction to the owl again. Hence arose a great contest of booksellers against booksellers, and advertisements against advertisements; some recommending the *edition of the owl,* and others the *edition of the ass;* by which names they came to be distinguished, to the great honour also of the gentlemen of the *Dunciad.*

Your Lordship will not think these particulars altogether unentertaining; nor are they impertinent, since they clear some passages in the following collection. The whole cannot but be of some use, to shew the *different spirit* with which good and bad authors have ever *acted,* as well as *written;* and to evince a truth, a greater than which was never advanced, that——

Each bad author is as bad a friend.

However, the imperfection of this collection cannot but be owned, as long as it wants that poem with which you, my lord, have honoured the author of the *Dunciad;* but which I durst not presume to add in your absence. As it is, may it please your Lordship to accept of it, as a distant testimony, with what respect and zeal I am,

My Lord,
your most obedient
and devoted servant,
R. SAVAGE.

9. This epigram was, I believe, never published.

Should Dennis publish you had stabb'd your brother,
Lampoon'd your Monarch, or debauch'd your mother;
Say what revenge on Dennis can be had,
Too dull for laughter, for reply too mad?
On one so poor you cannot take the law,
On one so old your sword you scorn to draw:

Uncag'd, then let the harmless monster rage,
Secure in dulness, madness, want, and age.

(between pp. 30-35)

1. 1729.
2. False pride! what vices on our conduct steal
From the world's eye one frailty to conceal.
Ye cruel mothers—soft! these words command—
So near should *cruelty* and *mother* stand?
Can the fond goat, or tender fleecy dam
Howl like the wolf to tear the kid or lamb?
Yes, there are mothers——there I fear'd his aim,
And conscious trembl'd at the coming name:
Then with a sigh his issuing words oppos'd,
Straight with a falling tear his speech he clos'd;
That tenderness which ties of blood deny,
Nature repaid me from a stranger's eye.
Pale grow my cheeks——
3. Of his descriptions this specimen may be offered.

Now, from yon range of rocks, strong rays rebound,
Doubling the day on flow'ry plains around:
Kingcups beneath far-striking colours glance,
Bright as th' etherial glows the green expanse.
Gems of the field!——The topez charms the sight,
Like these, effulging yellow streams of light.
From the same rocks fall rills with soften'd force,
Meet in yon mead, and well a river's source.
Through her clear channel shine her finny shoals,
O'er sands like gold the liquid crystal rolls.
Dim'd in yon coarser moor her charms decay,
And shape through rustling reeds a ruffled way.
Near willows short and bushy shadows throw:
Now lost she seems through nether tracts to flow;
Yet at yon point winds out in silver state,
Like virtue from a labyrinth of fate.
In length'ning rows prone from the mountains run
The flocks:—Their fleeces glist'ning in the sun;
Her streams they seek, and, 'twixt her neighb'ring trees,
Recline in various attitudes of ease:
Where the herds sip, the little scaly fry,
Swift from the shore, in scatt'ring myriads fly.
Each liv'ried cloud, that round th' horizon glows,
Shifts in odd scenes, like earth from whence it rose.
The bee hums wanton in yon jess'mine bower,
And circling settles, and despoils the flower.
Melodious there the plumy songsters meet,
And call charm'd Echo from her arch'd retreat.
Neat, polish'd mansions rise in prospect gay;
Time-batter'd tow'rs frown awful in decay:
The sun plays glitt'ring on the rocks and spires,
And the lawn lightens with reflected fires.

4. Who in the second canto is thus introduced;

Now grief and rage, by gath'ring sighs suprest,
Swell my full heart, and heave my lab'ring breast!
With struggling starts each vital string they strain,
And strike the tott'ring fabric of my brain!
O'er my sunk spirits frowns a vap'ry scene,
Woe's dark retreat! the madding maze of Spleen!
A deep, damp gloom o'erspreads the murky cell;
Here pining Thoughts, and secret Terrors dwell!
Here learn the great unreal wants to feign!
Unpleasing truths here mortify the vain!
Here Learning, blinded first, and then beguil'd,
Looks dark as Ignorance, as Frenzy wild!
Here first Credulity on Reason won!
And here *false* Zeal mysterious rants begun!
Here Love impearls each moment with a tear,
And Superstition owes to Spleen her fear!
——Here the lone hour, a blank of life, displays,
Till now bad thoughts a fiend more active raise;
A fiend in evil moments ever nigh!
Death in her hand, and frenzy in her eye!
Her eye all red, and sunk! A robe she wore,
With life's calamities embroider'd o'er.
A mirror in one hand collective shows,
Varied, and multiplied, that group of woes.
This endless foe to gen'rous toil and pain
Lolls on a couch for ease; but lolls in vain.
She muses o'er her woe-embroider'd vest,
And self-abhorrence heightens in her breast.
To shun her care, the force of sleep she tries,
Still wakes her mind, though slumbers doze her eyes:
She dreams, starts, rises, stalks from place to place,
With restless, thoughtful, interrupted pace:
Now eyes the sun, and curses ev'ry ray,
Now the green ground, where colour fades away.
Dim spectres dance! Again her eyes she rears;
Then from the blood-shot ball wipes purpled tears;
She presses hard her brow, with mischief fraught,
Her brow half bursts with agony of thought!
From me (she cries) pale wretch thy comfort claim,
Born of despair, and Suicide my name!

5. These three rebels are thus described.

Of these were three by different motives fir'd,
Ambition one, and one revenge inspir'd.
The third, O mammon, was thy meaner slave;
Thou idol seldom of the great and brave.
Florio, whose life was one continued feast,
His wealth diminish'd, and his debts encreas'd,
Vain pomp and equipage his low desires,
Who ne'er to intellectual bliss aspires;
He, to repair by vice what vice has broke,
Durst with bold treasons judgment's road provoke.
His strength of mind, by lux'ry half dissolv'd,

Ill brooks the woe where deep he stands involv'd.
——His genius flies; reflects he now on prayer?
Alas! bad spirits turn those thoughts to air.
What shall he next? What strait relinquish breath,
To bar a public, just and shameful death?
Rash, horrid thought! yet now afraid to live,
Murd'rous he strikes; may Heav'n the deed forgive!
——Why had he thus false spirit to rebel?
And why not fortitude to suffer well?
——Where no kind lips the hallow'd dirge resound,
Far from the compass of yon sacred ground;
Full in the center of three meeting ways,
Stak'd through he lies——Warn'd let the wicked gaze!
Near yonder fane where mis'ry sleeps in peace,
Whose spire fast-lessens, as these shades encrease,
Left to the north, whence oft brew'd tempests roll,
Tempests, dire emblems, Cosmo, of thy soul!
There! mark that Cosmo much for guile renown'd!
His grave by unbid plants of poison crown'd.
When out of pow'r, through him the public good,
So strong his factious tribe, suspended stood.
In power, vindictive actions were his aim,
And patriots perish'd by th' ungenerous flame.
If the best cause he in the senate chose,
Ev'n right in him from some wrong motive rose.
The bad he loath'd, and would the weak despise!
Yet courted for dark ends, and shun'd the wise.
When ill his purpose, eloquent his strain,
His malice had a look and voice humane:
His smile the signal of some vile intent,
A private ponyard, or empoison'd scent;
Proud, yet to popular applause a slave;
No friend he honour'd, and no foe forgave.
His boons unfrequent, or unjust to need,
The hire of guilt, of infamy the meed;
But if they chanc'd on learned worth to fall,
Bounty in him was ostentation all.
No true benevolence his thought sublimes,
His noblest actions are illustrious crimes.
——Cosmo, as death draws nigh, no more conceals
That storm of passions, which his nature feels;
He feels much fear, more anger, and most pride;
But pride and anger make all fear subside.
Dauntless he meets at length untimely fate;
A desp'rate spirit! rather fierce, than great.
Darking he glides along the dreary coast,
A sullen, wand'ring, self-tormenting ghost.
——Where veiny marble dignifies the ground,
With emblem fair in sculpture rising round,
Just where a crossing, length'ning isle we find,
Full east; whence God returns to judge mankind.
Once lov'd Horatio sleeps, a mind elate!

Lamented shade, ambition was thy fate!
Ev'n angels, wond'ring, oft his worth survey'd;
Behold a man like one of us! they said.
Straight heard the Furies, and with envy glar'd,
And to precipitate his fall prepar'd:
First Av'rice came. In vain self-love she press'd;
The poor he pitied still, and still redress'd:
Learning was his, and knowledge to commend,
Of arts a patron, and of want a friend.
Next came Revenge: But her essay, how vain?
Nor hate nor envy in his heart remain:
No previous malice could his mind engage,
Malice the mother of vindictive rage.
No——from his life his foes might learn to live;
He held it still a triumph to forgive.
At length Ambition urg'd his country's weal,
Assuming the fair look of public Zeal;
Still in his breast so gen'rous glow'd the flame,
The vice, when there, a virtue half became.
His pitying eye saw millions in distress,
He deem'd it God-like to have pow'r to bless;
Thus, when unguarded, treason stain'd him o'er,
And virtue and content were then no more.
But when to death by vig'rous justice doom'd,
His genuine spirit saint-like state resum'd.
Oft from soft penitence distill'd a tear;
Oft hope in heav'nly mercy lighten'd fear;
Oft would a drop from struggling nature fall,
And then a smile of patience brighten all.

Canto V.

6. Fain would my verse, Tyrconnel, boast thy name,
Brownlow at once my subject, and my fame:
O could that spirit which thy bosom warms,
Whose strength surprises, and whose goodness charms.
Thy various worth—could that inspire my lays,
Envy should smile, and censure learn to praise:
Yet though unequal to a soul like thine,
A gen'rous soul approaching to divine;
While bless'd beneath such patronage I write,
Great my attempt, though hazardous my flight.

7. His expression in one of his letters, was, that Lord T——l *had involved his estate, and therefore poorly sought an occasion to quarrel with him.*

8. Part of this poem had the honour of your Lordship's perusal when in manuscript, and it was no small pride to me when it met with approbation. —My intention is to embrace this opportunity of throwing out sentiments that relate to your Lordship's goodness and generosity, which give me leave to say I have lately experienced.

That *I live,* my Lord, is a proof, that dependance upon your Lordship and the present Ministry is an assurance of success. I am persuaded distress in many other instances affects your soul with a compassion that always shews itself in a manner most humane and active, that to forgive injuries, and confer benefits, is your delight, and that to deserve your friendship is to deserve the countenance of the best of men. To be admitted to the honour of your Lordship's conversation (permit me to speak but justice) is to be elegantly introduced into the most instructive as well as entertaining parts of literature: It is to be furnished with the finest observations upon human nature, and to receive from the most unassuming, sweet, and winning candour, the worthiest and most polite maxims—such as are always inforced by the actions of your own life.—If my future morals and writings should gain any approbation from men of parts and probity, I must acknowledge all to be the product of your Lordship's goodness.—

9. Of the numbers and sentiments the following lines will afford a specimen.

Where Thames with pride beholds Augusta's charms,
And either India pours into her arms,—
High thron'd appears the laughter-loving dame—
Goddess of Mirth——
    O'er the gay world the sweet inspirer reigns,
Spleen flies, and elegance her pomp sustains;
Thee, goddess, thee the fair and young obey,
Wealth, wit, and music, all confess thy sway.—
    The goddess summons each illustrious name,
Bids the gay talk, and forms th' amusive game,
She whose fair throne is fix'd in human souls,
From joy to joy her eye delighted rolls:
But where, she cry'd, is she, my fav'rite she,
Of all my race the dearest far to me—
Whose life's the source of each refin'd delight,
She said, but no Belinda glads her sight—
In kind low murmurs all the loss deplore,
Belinda droops, and pleasure is no more.
    The goddess silent paus'd in museful air,
But Mirth, like Virtue, cannot long despair,—
Strait wafted on the tepid breeze she flies,
Where Bath's ascending turrets meet her eyes,
She flies, her elder sister Health to find,
She finds her on a mountain's brow reclin'd,
Around her birds in earliest consort sing,
Her cheek the semblance of the kindling spring.—
Loose to the wind her verdant vestments flow,
Her limbs yet recent from the springs below:
Thereof she bathes, then peaceful sits secure,
Where ev'ry breath is fragrant, fresh and pure.—
    Hail, sister, hail, the kindred goddess cries,
No common suppliant stands before your eyes—
Strength, vigour, wit, depriv'd of thee decline,
Each finer sense that forms delight is thine—
Bright suns by thee diffuse a brighter blaze,
And the fresh green a fresher green displays—
Such thy vast pow'r—the Deity replies,
Mirth never asks a boon which Health denies;
Our mingled gifts transcend imperial wealth,
Health strengthens Mirth, and Mirth inspirits Health.

(between pp. 40-76)

1. In gayer hours, when high my fancy ran,

The muse, exulting, thus her lay began.
Blest be the Bastard's birth! thro' wondrous ways,
He shines eccentrick like a comet's blaze.
No sickly fruit of faint compliance he;
He! stampt in nature's mint with extasy!
He lives to build, not boast, a gen'rous race:
No tenth transmitter of a foolish face.
His daring hope, no sire's example bounds;
His first-born lights no prejudice confounds.
He, kindling, from within, requires no flame,
He glories, in a bastard's glowing name.
—Loos'd to the world's wide range—enjoin'd no aim;
Prescrib'd no duty, and assign'd no name:
Nature's unbounded son he stands alone,
His heart unbiass'd, and his mind his own.
——O mother, yet no mother!—'tis to you,
My thanks for such distinguish'd claims are due.
——What had I lost, if conjugally kind,
By nature hating, yet by vows confin'd,
——You had *faint-drawn* me with a form alone,
A lawful lump of life by force your own!
——I had been born your dull domestick heir;
Load of your life and motive of your care;
Perhaps been poorly rich, and meanly great;
The slave of pomp, a cypher in the state;
Lordly neglectful of a worth unknown,
And slumb'ring in a *seat*, by *chance* my own.
——Thus unprophetic, lately uninspir'd,
I sung; gay, flatt'ring hope my fancy fir'd;
Inly secure, thro' conscious scorn of ill;
Nor taught by wisdom how to balance will.
——But now expos'd and shrinking from distress,
I fly to shelter while the tempests press.

After the mention of the death of Sinclair, he goes on thus:

—Where shall my hope find rest?—No mother's care
Shielded my infant innocence with pray'r:
No father's guardian hand my youth maintain'd,
Call'd forth my virtues, and from vice restrain'd.

2. A short satire was likewise published in the same paper, in which were the following lines:

For cruel murder doom'd to hempen death,
Savage, by royal grace, prolong'd his breath.
Well might you think, he spent his *future* years
In prayer, and fasting and repentant tears.
—But, O vain hope!——the truly Savage cries,
"Priests, and their slavish doctrines, I despise.
Shall I——————
Who, by free thinking to free action fir'd,
In midnight brawls a deathless name acquir'd,
Now stoop to *learn* of *ecclesiastic men*?——

——No arm'd with rhime, at priests I'll take my aim,
Though prudence bids me murder but their fame."
Weekly Miscellany.

An answer was published in the *Gentleman's Magazine,* written by an unknown hand, from which the following lines are selected:

Transform'd by thoughtless rage, and midnight wine,
From malice free, and push'd without *design;*
In equal brawl if Savage lung'd a thrust,
And brought the youth a victim to the dust:
So strong the hand of accident appears,
The royal hand from guilt and vengeance clears.
Instead of wasting "*all thy future years,*
Savage in pray'r and vain repentant tears;"
Exert thy pen to mend a vicious age,
To curb the priest, and sink his High-Church rage;
To shew what frauds the holy vestments hide,
The nests of av'rice, lust, and pedant pride.
Then change the scene, let merit brightly shine,
And round the patriot twist the wreath divine;
The heav'nly guide deliver down to fame;
In well-tun'd lays transmit a Foster's name.
Touch every passion with harmonious art,
Exalt the genius, and correct the heart.
Thus future times shall royal grace extol;
Thus polish'd lines thy present fame enrol.
——But grant——————
——Maliciously that Savage plung'd the *steel,*
And made the youth its shining vengeance feel;
My soul abhors the act, the man detests,
But more the bigotry in priestly breasts.
Gentleman's Magazine, May 1735.

3. The Poet's Dependence on a Statesman, which was published in the *Gentleman's Magazine,* (Vol. VI. p. 225.) and contained among others the following passages.

Some seem to hint, and others proof will bring,
That, from neglect, my num'rous hardships spring.
"Seek the *great man,*" they cry——'tis then decreed,
In *him* if I court *fortune,* I succeed.
What friends to second? Who, for *me,* should sue,
Have int'rests, partial to *themselves,* in view.
They own my matchless fate compassion draws,
They all wish well, lament, but drop my cause.
——Say, shall I turn where *lucre* points my views;
At first desert my friends, at length abuse?
But, on less terms, in *promise* he complies;
Years bury years, and hopes on hopes arise;
I trust, am trusted on my fairy gain;
And woes on woes attend an endless train.
Be posts dispos'd at will!——I have, for these,
No gold to plead, no impudence to teaze.
All secret service from my soul I hate;

All dark intrigues of pleasure, or of state.
——Where these are not what claim to me belongs;
Though mine the *muse* and *virtue, birth* and *wrongs?*
Where lives the *statesman*, so in *honour* clear,
To give where he has nought to hope, nor fear?
No!—there to seek, is but to find fresh pain:
The promise broke, renew'd and broke again;
To be, as humour deigns, receiv'd, refus'd;
By turns affronted, and by turns amus'd;
To lose that time, which worthier thoughts require;
To lose that health, which should those thoughts inspire;
To starve on hope; or, like camelions, fare
On *ministerial faith*, which means but air.
—A scene *will* shew—(all-righteous vision haste)
The meek exalted, and the proud debas'd!——
Oh! to be there!—to tread that friendly shore;
Where *falsehood*, *pride* and *statesmen* are no more!

4. From these the following lines are selected as an instance rather of his impartiality than genius.

Materials which belief in gazettes claim,
Loose strung, run gingling into hist'ry's name.
Thick as Egyptian clouds of raining flies;
As thick as worms where man corrupting lies;
As pests obscene that haunt the ruin'd pile;
As monsters flound'ring in the muddy Nile;
Minutes, memoirs, views and reviews appear,
Where slander darkens each recorded year.
In a past reign is fam'd some am'rous league;
Some ring, or letter, now reveals th' intrigue;
Queens with their minions work unseemly things;
And boys grow dukes, when catamites to kings?
Does a prince die? What poisons they surmise?
No royal mortal sure by nature dies.
Is a prince born? What birth more base believ'd?
Or, what's more strange, his mother ne'er conceiv'd!
Thus slander popular o'er truth prevails,
And easy minds imbibe romantic tales.
Some usurp names——an English *garreteer*,
From *minutes* forg'd, is *Monsieur Menager*.
——Where *hear-say knowledge* sits on public names,
And bold *conjecture* or extols, or blames,
Spring *party libels;* from whose ashes dead,
A *monster*, misnam'd Hist'ry, lifts its head.
Contending factions croud to hear its roar!
But when once heard, it dies to noise no more.
From these no answer, no applause from those,
O'er half they simper, and o'er half they doze.
So when in senate, with egregious pate,
Perks up, Sir —— in some deep debate;
He hems, looks wise, tunes then his lab'ring throat,
To prove black white, postpone or palm the vote;
In sly contempt, some, *hear him! hear him!* cry;

Some yawn, some sneer; none second, none reply.
    But dare such miscreants now rush abroad,
By blanket, cane, pump, pillory, unaw'd?
Dare they imp falshood thus, and plume her wings,
From present characters, and recent things?
Yes, what untruths? Or truths in what disguise?
What Boyers, and what Oldmixons arise?
What *facts* from all but *them* and *slander* screen'd?
Here meets a *council,* no where else conven'd.
There, from *originals,* come, thick as spawn,
Letters ne'er wrote, memorials never drawn;
To *secret conf'rence,* never held, they yoke
Treaties ne'er plann'd, and speeches never spoke.
From, Oldmixon, thy brow, too well we know,
Like *sin* from Satan's, far and wide they go.
    In vain may St. John safe in conscience sit,
In vain with truth confute, contemn with wit:
Confute, contemn, amid selected friends;
There sinks the justice, there the satire ends.
Here through a *cent'ry* scarce such leaves unclose,
From mold and dust the slander sacred grows.
Now none reply where all despise the page;
But will dumb scorn deceive no future age?

Gentleman's Magazine, Sept. 1741

5. Learn, future natives of this promis'd land,
What your fore-fathers ow'd my saving hand!
Learn, when *despair* such sudden bliss shall see,
Such bliss must shine from *Oglethorpe* or [a]*me!*
Do you the neighb'ring, blameless Indian aid,
Culture what he neglects, not his invade;
Dare not, oh! dare not, with ambitious view,
Force or demand subjection, never due.
Let by *my* specious name no *tyrants* rise,
And cry, while they enslave, they civilize!
Why must I Afric's sable children see
Vended for slaves, though form'd by nature free,
The nameless tortures cruel minds invent,
Those to subject, whom nature equal meant?
If these you dare, albeit unjust success
Empow'rs you now unpunish'd to oppress,
Revolving empire you and yours may doom;
Rome all subdued, yet Vandals vanquish'd Rome:
Yes, empire may revolve, give them the day,
And yoke may yoke, and blood may blood repay.

6. To exhibit a specimen of the beauties of this poem, the following passages are selected.

Oft has the muse, on this distinguish'd day,
Tun'd to glad harmony the vernal lay;
But, O lamented change! The lay must flow

---

[a] Publick spirit.

From grateful rapture now, to grateful woe.
She, to this day, who joyous lustre gave,
Descends for ever to the silent grave.
She born at once to charm us and to mend,
Of human race the pattern and the friend.
——And, thou, bright Princess! seated now on high,
Next one, the fairest daughter of the sky,
Whose warm-felt love is to all beings known,
Thy sister Charity! next her thy throne;
See at thy tomb the virtues weeping lie!
There in dumb sorrow seem the arts to die.
So were the sun o'er other orbs to blaze,
And from our world, like thee, withdraw his rays,
No more to visit where he warm'd before,
All life must cease, and nature be no more.
Yet shall the *Muse* a heav'nly height essay,
Beyond the weakness mix'd with mortal clay;
Beyond the loss, which, tho' she bleeds to see,
Tho' ne'er to be redeem'd the loss of thee;
Beyond ev'n this, she hails with joyous lay,
Thy better birth, thy first true natal day;
A day, that sees thee born, beyond the tomb,
To endless health, to youth's eternal bloom.
Born to the mighty dead, the souls sublime
Of ev'ry famous age, and ev'ry clime,
To goodness fixed by truth's unvarying laws;
To bliss that knows no period, knows no pause——
Save when thine eye, from yonder pure serene,
Sheds a soft ray on this our gloomy scene.

7. ——Deign one look more! Ah! See thy consort dear!
Wishing all hearts, except his own, to cheer.
Lo! still he bids thy wonted bounties flow
To weeping families of worth and woe.
He stops all tears, however fast they rise,
Save those, that still must fall from grateful eyes:
And spite of griefs, that so usurp his mind,
Still watches o'er the welfare of mankind.

8. In a letter after his confinement.
9. Letter Jan. 15.

(between pp. 77-80)

1. The author preferr'd this title to that *of* London *and* Bristol *compared;* which, when he began the piece, he intended to prefix to it.
2. A place where the merchants used to meet to transact their affairs before the Exchange was erected. See *Gentleman's Magazine*. Vol. XIII. p. 496.
3. *Halliers* are the persons who drive or own the sledges, which are here used instead of carts.

Published in a handsome quarto on January 9, 1749, The Vanity of Human Wishes *was Johnson's first work to bear his name. Unlike* London, *his earlier imitation of Juvenal, no second separate edition was required. Johnson revised the poem for inclusion in the most popular anthology of the century, Dodsley's* Collection of Poems, *IV (1755), and took the occasion to make his most famous alteration, "garret" to "patron" (l. 160) in a satiric bow to Chesterfield's neglect of the* Dictionary. *Reprinted from the first edition.*

The Vanity of Human Wishes

The Tenth Satire of Juvenal, Imitated

[a]Let observation with extensive view,
Survey mankind, from China to Peru;
Remark each anxious toil, each eager strife,
And watch the busy scenes of crouded life;
Then say how hope and fear, desire and hate, 5
O'erspread with snares the clouded maze of fate,
Where wav'ring man, betray'd by vent'rous pride,
To tread the dreary paths without a guide;
As treach'rous phantoms in the mist delude,
Shuns fancied ills, or chases airy good. 10
How rarely reason guides the stubborn choice,
Rules the bold hand, or prompts the suppliant voice,
How nations sink, by darling schemes oppress'd,

[1] Superior letter *a* indicates Johnson's reference to the corresponding lines in Juvenal. These references are listed at the end of the selection, pages 116-17.

When vengeance listens to the fool's request.
Fate wings with ev'ry wish th' afflictive dart, 15
Each gift of nature, and each grace of art,
With fatal heat impetuous courage glows,
With fatal sweetness elocution flows,
Impeachment stops the speaker's pow'rful breath,
And restless fire precipitates on death. 20
[b]But scarce observ'd the knowing and the bold,
Fall in the gen'ral massacre of gold;
Wide-wasting pest! that rages unconfin'd,
And crouds with crimes the records of mankind,
For gold his sword the hireling ruffian draws, 25
For gold the hireling judge distorts the laws;
Wealth heap'd on wealth, nor truth nor safety buys,
The dangers gather as the treasures rise.
Let hist'ry tell where rival kings command,
And dubious title shakes the madded land, 30
When statutes glean the refuse of the sword,
How much more safe the vassal than the lord,
Low sculks the hind beneath the rage of pow'r,
And leaves the bonny traytor in the Tow'r,
Untouch'd his cottage, and his slumbers sound, 35
Tho' confiscation's vulturs clang around.
The needy traveller, serene and gay,
Walks the wild heath, and sings his toil away.
Does envy seize thee? crush th' upbraiding joy,
Encrease his riches and his peace destroy, 40
New fears in dire vicissitude invade,
The rustling brake alarms, and quiv'ring shade,
Nor light nor darkness bring his pain relief,
One shews the plunder, and one hides the thief.
[c]Yet still the gen'ral cry the skies assails 45
And gain and grandeur load the tainted gales;
Few know the toiling statesman's fear or care,
Th' insidious rival and the gaping heir.
[d]Once more, Democritus, arise on earth,

---

[34] *bonny traytor:* a general reference to the Scots lords beheaded after the Jacobite rebellion of 1745.

With chearful wisdom and instructive mirth, 50
See motley life in modern trappings dress'd,
And feed with varied fools th' eternal jest:
Thou who couldst laugh where want enchain'd caprice,
Toil crush'd conceit, and man was of a piece;
Where wealth unlov'd without a mourner dy'd; 55
And scarce a sycophant was fed by pride;
Where ne'er was known the form of mock debate,
Or seen a new-made mayor's unwieldy state;
Where change of fav'rites made no change of laws,
And senates heard before they judg'd a cause; 60
How wouldst thou shake at Britain's modish tribe,
Dart the quick taunt, and edge the piercing gibe?
Attentive truth and nature to descry,
And pierce each scene with philosophic eye.
To thee were solemn toys or empty shew, 65
The robes of pleasure and the veils of woe:
All aid the farce, and all thy mirth maintain,
Whose joys are causeless, or whose griefs are vain.
  Such was the scorn that fill'd the sage's mind,
Renew'd at ev'ry glance on humankind; 70
How just that scorn ere yet thy voice declare,
Search every state, and canvass ev'ry pray'r.
  [e]Unnumber'd suppliants croud Preferment's gate,
Athirst for wealth, and burning to be great;
Delusive Fortune hears th' incessant call, 75
They mount, they shine, evaporate, and fall.
On ev'ry stage the foes of peace attend,
Hate dogs their flight, and insult mocks their end.
Love ends with hope, the sinking statesman's door
Pours in the morning worshiper no more; 80
For growing names the weekly scribbler lies,
To growing wealth the dedicator flies,
From every room descends the painted face,
That hung the bright Palladium of the place,
And smoak'd in kitchens, or in auctions sold, 85
To better features yields the frame of gold;
For now no more we trace in ev'ry line
Heroic worth, benevolence divine:

The form distorted justifies the fall,
And detestation rids th' indignant wall. 90
But will not Britain hear the last appeal,
Sign her foes doom, or guard her fav'rites zeal;
Through Freedom's sons no more remonstrance rings,
Degrading nobles and controuling kings;
Our supple tribes repress their patriot throats, 95
And ask no questions but the price of votes;
With weekly libels and septennial ale,
Their wish is full to riot and to rail.
In full-blown dignity, see Wolsey stand,
Law in his voice, and fortune in his hand: 100
To him the church, the realm, their pow'rs consign,
Thro' him the rays of regal bounty shine,
Turn'd by his nod the stream of honour flows,
His smile alone security bestows:
Still to new heights his restless wishes tow'r, 105
Claim leads to claim, and pow'r advances pow'r;
Till conquest unresisted ceas'd to please,
And rights submitted, left him none to seize.
At length his sov'reign frowns—the train of state
Mark the keen glance, and watch the sign to hate. 110
Where-e'er he turns he meets a stranger's eye,
His suppliants scorn him, and his followers fly;
Now drops at once the pride of aweful state,
The golden canopy, the glitt'ring plate,
The regal palace, the luxurious board, 115
The liv'ried army, and the menial lord.
With age, with cares, with maladies oppress'd,
He seeks the refuge of monastic rest.
Grief aids disease, remember'd folly stings,
And his last sighs reproach the faith of kings. 120
Speak thou, whose thoughts at humble peace repine,
Shall Wolsey's wealth, with Wolsey's end be thine?
Or liv'st thou now, with safer pride content,
The richest landlord on the banks of Trent?
For why did Wolsey by the steeps of fate, 125

---

125 *steeps:* misprinted "steps" in the first edition.

On weak foundations raise th' enormous weight?
Why but to sink beneath misfortune's blow,
With louder ruin to the gulphs below?
[f]What gave great Villiers to th' assassin's knife,
And fix'd disease on Harley's closing life? 130
What murder'd Wentworth, and what exil'd Hyde,
By kings protected and to kings ally'd?
What but their wish indulg'd in courts to shine,
And pow'r too great to keep or to resign?
[g]When first the college rolls receive his name, 135
The young enthusiast quits his ease for fame;
Resistless burns the fever of renown,
Caught from the strong contagion of the gown;
O'er Bodley's dome his future labours spread,
And Bacon's mansion trembles o'er his head; 140
Are these thy views? proceed, illustrious youth,
And virtue guard thee to the throne of Truth,
Yet should thy soul indulge the gen'rous heat,
Till captive Science yields her last retreat;
Should Reason guide thee with her brightest ray, 145
And pour on misty Doubt resistless day;
Should no false kindness lure to loose delight,
Nor Praise relax, nor Difficulty fright;
Should tempting Novelty thy cell refrain,
And Sloth's bland opiates shed their fumes in vain; 150
Should Beauty blunt on fops her fatal dart,
Nor claim the triumph of a letter'd heart;
Should no disease thy torpid veins invade,
Nor Melancholy's phantoms haunt thy shade;
Yet hope not life from grief or danger free, 155
Nor think the doom of man revers'd for thee:

---

[129] *Villiers:* first Duke of Buckingham, assassinated in 1628.

[130] *Harley:* Swift's friend, the Earl of Oxford.

[131] *Wentworth:* Earl of Strafford, executed in 1641; *Hyde:* Earl of Clarendon, banished in 1667.

[139] *Bodley's dome:* the Bodleian Library; "dome" in the old sense of "building."

[140] *Bacon's mansion:* the gatehouse, now demolished, at Folly Bridge in Oxford. In 1755 Johnson added this note: "There is a tradition, that the study of friar Bacon, built on an arch over the bridge, will fall, when a man greater than Bacon shall pass under it."

Deign on the passing world to turn thine eyes,
And pause awhile from learning to be wise;
There mark what ills the scholar's life assail,
Toil, envy, want, the garret, and the jail. 160
See nations slowly wise, and meanly just,
To buried merit raise the tardy bust.
If dreams yet flatter, once again attend,
Hear Lydiat's life, and Galileo's end.
  Nor deem, when learning her lost prize bestows 165
The glitt'ring eminence exempt from foes;
See when the vulgar 'scap'd, despis'd or aw'd,
Rebellion's vengeful talons seize on Laud.
From meaner minds, tho' smaller fines content
The plunder'd palace or sequester'd rent; 170
Mark'd out by dangerous parts he meets the shock,
And fatal Learning leads him to the block:
Around his tomb let Art and Genius weep,
But hear his death, ye blockheads, hear and sleep.
  [h]The festal blazes, the triumphal show, 175
The ravish'd standard, and the captive foe,
The senate's thanks, the gazette's pompous tale,
With force resistless o'er the brave prevail.
Such bribes the rapid Greek o'er Asia whirl'd,
For such the steady Romans shook the world; 180
For such in distant lands the Britons shine,
And stain with blood the Danube or the Rhine;
This pow'r has praise, that virtue scarce can warm,
Till fame supplies the universal charm.
Yet Reason frowns on War's unequal game, 185
Where wasted nations raise a single name,
And mortgag'd states their grandsires wreaths regret
From age to age in everlasting debt;
Wreaths which at last the dear-bought right convey
To rust on medals, or on stones decay. 190
  [i]On what foundation stands the warrior's pride?

---

[160] *garret:* after Johnson's experience with Chesterfield and the *Dictionary,* he replaced "garret" with "patron."

[164] Thomas Lydiat (1572–1646), a needy mathematician of Oxford.

[168] Archbishop Laud was executed by the Puritans in 1645, though not because of his learning.

How just his hopes let Swedish Charles decide;
A frame of adamant, a soul of fire,
No dangers fright him, and no labours tire;
O'er love, o'er force, extends his wide domain, 195
Unconquer'd lord of pleasure and of pain;
No joys to him pacific scepters yield,
War sounds the trump, he rushes to the field;
Behold surrounding kings their pow'r combine,
And one capitulate, and one resign; 200
Peace courts his hand, but spreads her charms in vain;
"Think nothing gain'd," he cries, "till nought remain,
On Moscow's walls till Gothic standards fly,
And all is mine beneath the polar sky."
The march begins in military state, 205
And nations on his eye suspended wait;
Stern Famine guards the solitary coast,
And Winter barricades the realms of Frost;
He comes, nor want nor cold his course delay;——
Hide, blushing Glory, hide Pultowa's day: 210
The vanquish'd hero leaves his broken bands,
And shews his miseries in distant lands;
Condemn'd a needy supplicant to wait,
While ladies interpose, and slaves debate.
But did not Chance at length her error mend? 215
Did no subverted empire mark his end?
Did rival monarchs give the fatal wound?
Or hostile millions press him to the ground?
His fall was destin'd to a barren strand,
A petty fortress, and a dubious hand; 220
He left the name, at which the world grew pale,
To point a moral, or adorn a tale.
[j]All times their scenes of pompous woes afford,
From Persia's tyrant to Bavaria's lord.
In gay hostility, and barb'rous pride, 225
With half mankind embattled at his side,

---

[192] Charles XII, defeated by Peter the Great at Pultowa (l. 210), was killed in the attack on Frederikshald, Norway, in 1718.

[224] *Bavaria's lord:* Charles Albert, Elector of Bavaria, crowned emperor as Charles VII in 1742, died discredited in 1745.

Great Xerxes comes to seize the certain prey,
And starves exhausted regions in his way;
Attendant Flatt'ry counts his myriads o'er,
Till counted myriads sooth his pride no more; 230
Fresh praise is try'd till madness fires his mind,
The waves he lashes, and enchains the wind;
New pow'rs are claim'd, new pow'rs are still bestow'd,
Till rude resistance lops the spreading god;
The daring Greeks deride the martial shew, 235
And heap their vallies with the gaudy foe;
Th' insulted sea with humbler thoughts he gains,
A single skiff to speed his flight remains;
Th' incumber'd oar scarce leaves the dreaded coast
Through purple billows and a floating host. 240

The bold Bavarian, in a luckless hour,
Tries the dread summits of Cesarean pow'r,
With unexpected legions bursts away,
And sees defenceless realms receive his sway;
Short sway! fair Austria spreads her mournful charms, 245
The Queen, the beauty, sets the world in arms;
From hill to hill the beacons rousing blaze
Spreads wide the hope of plunder and of praise;
The fierce Croatian, and the wild Hussar,
And all the sons of ravage croud the war; 250
The baffled prince in honour's flatt'ring bloom
Of hasty greatness finds the fatal doom,
His foes derision, and his subjects blame,
And steals to death from anguish and from shame.

[k]Enlarge my life with multitude of days, 255
In health, in sickness, thus the suppliant prays;
Hides from himself his state, and shuns to know,
That life protracted is protracted woe.
Time hovers o'er, impatient to destroy,
And shuts up all the passages of joy: 260
In vain their gifts the bounteous seasons pour,
The fruit autumnal, and the vernal flow'r,
With listless eyes the dotard views the store,

---

[245] *Fair Austria:* Maria Theresa.

He views, and wonders that they please no more;
Now pall the tastless meats, and joyless wines, 265
And Luxury with sighs her slave resigns.
Approach, ye minstrels, try the soothing strain,
And yield the tuneful lenitives of pain:
No sounds alas would touch th' impervious ear,
Though dancing mountains witness'd Orpheus near; 270
Nor lute nor lyre his feeble pow'rs attend,
Nor sweeter musick of a virtuous friend,
But everlasting dictates croud his tongue,
Perversely grave, or positively wrong.
The still returning tale, and ling'ring jest, 275
Perplex the fawning niece and pamper'd guest,
While growing hopes scarce awe the gath'ring sneer,
And scarce a legacy can bribe to hear;
The watchful guests still hint the last offence,
The daughter's petulance, the son's expence, 280
Improve his heady rage with treach'rous skill,
And mould his passions till they make his will.
Unnumber'd maladies each joint invade,
Lay siege to life and press the dire blockade;
But unextinguish'd av'rice still remains, 285
And dreaded losses aggravate his pains;
He turns, with anxious heart and cripled hands,
His bonds of debt, and mortgages of lands;
Or views his coffers with suspicious eyes,
Unlocks his gold, and counts it till he dies. 290
But grant, the virtues of a temp'rate prime
Bless with an age exempt from scorn or crime;
An age that melts in unperceiv'd decay,
And glides in modest innocence away;
Whose peaceful day Benevolence endears, 295
Whose night congratulating Conscience cheers;
The gen'ral fav'rite as the gen'ral friend:
Such age there is, and who could wish its end?
Yet ev'n on this her load Misfortune flings,
To press the weary minutes flagging wings: 300
New sorrow rises as the day returns,
A sister sickens, or a daughter mourns.

Now kindred Merit fills the sable bier,
Now lacerated Friendship claims a tear.
Year chases year, decay pursues decay, 305
Still drops some joy from with'ring life away;
New forms arise, and diff'rent views engage,
Superfluous lags the vet'ran on the stage,
Till pitying Nature signs the last release,
And bids afflicted worth retire to peace. 310
  But few there are whom hours like these await,
Who set unclouded in the gulphs of fate.
From Lydia's monarch should the search descend,
By Solon caution'd to regard his end,
In life's last scene what prodigies surprise, 315
Fears of the brave, and follies of the wise?
From Marlb'rough's eyes the streams of dotage flow,
And Swift expires a driv'ler and a show.
  [1]The teeming mother, anxious for her race,
Begs for each birth the fortune of a face: 320
Yet Vane could tell what ills from beauty spring;
And Sedley curs'd the form that pleas'd a king.
Ye nymphs of rosy lips and radiant eyes,
Whom pleasure keeps too busy to be wise,
Whom joys with soft varieties invite 325
By day the frolick, and the dance by night,
Who frown with vanity, who smile with art,
And ask the latest fashion of the heart,
What care, what rules your heedless charms shall save,
Each nymph your rival, and each youth your slave? 330
An envious breast with certain mischief glows,
And slaves, the maxim tells, are always foes.
Against your fame with fondness hate combines,
The rival batters, and the lover mines.
With distant voice neglected Virtue calls, 335
Less heard, and less the faint remonstrance falls;
Tir'd with contempt, she quits the slipp'ry reign,

---

313 *Lydia's monarch:* Croesus.

321 Anne Vane (1705–36), mistress of Frederick, Prince of Wales.

322 Catherine Sedley (1657–1717), mistress of the Duke of York, afterwards James II.

And Pride and Prudence take her seat in vain.
In croud at once, where none the pass defend,
The harmless Freedom, and the private Friend. 340
The guardians yield, by force superior ply'd;
By Int'rest, Prudence; and by Flatt'ry, Pride.
Here beauty falls betray'd, despis'd, distress'd,
And hissing Infamy proclaims the rest.
[m]Where then shall Hope and Fear their objects find? 345
Must dull Suspence corrupt the stagnant mind?
Must helpless man, in ignorance sedate,
Swim darkling down the current of his fate?
Must no dislike alarm, no wishes rise,
No cries attempt the mercies of the skies? 350
Enquirer, cease, petitions yet remain,
Which heav'n may hear, nor deem religion vain.
Still raise for good the supplicating voice,
But leave to heav'n the measure and the choice.
Safe in his pow'r, whose eyes discern afar 355
The secret ambush of a specious pray'r.
Implore his aid, in his decisions rest,
Secure whate'er he gives, he gives the best.
Yet with the sense of sacred presence prest,
When strong devotion fills thy glowing breast, 360
Pour forth thy fervours for a healthful mind,
Obedient passions, and a will resign'd;
For love, which scarce collective man can fill;
For patience sov'reign o'er transmuted ill;
For faith, that panting for a happier seat, 365
Thinks death kind Nature's signal of retreat:
These goods for man the laws of heav'n ordain,
These goods he grants, who grants the pow'r to gain;
With these celestial wisdom calms the mind,
And makes the happiness she does not find. 370

NOTES

a. Ver. 1–11.
b. Ver. 12–22.
c. Ver. 23–27.
d. Ver. 28–55.

e. Ver. 56–107.
f. Ver. 108–113.
g. Ver. 114–132.
h. Ver. 133–146.
i. Ver. 147–167.
j. Ver. 168–187.
k. Ver. 188–288.
l. Ver. 289–345.
m. Ver. 346–366.

In 1747, when Johnson addressed his Plan of a Dictionary of the English Language *to Lord Chesterfield, he was confident he could produce his work in three years. Eight years later the two huge folio volumes appeared. These years had taught Johnson a great deal about the nature of language—and of patrons. Both kinds of learning may be seen in his superb Preface, which is reprinted from the first edition, as are the selections from the* Dictionary *which follow.*

Preface to A Dictionary of the English Language

It is the fate of those who toil at the lower employments of life, to be rather driven by the fear of evil, than attracted by the prospect of good; to be exposed to censure, without hope of praise; to be disgraced by miscarriage, or punished for neglect, where success would have been without applause, and diligence without reward.

Among these unhappy mortals is the writer of dictionaries; whom mankind have considered, not as the pupil, but the slave of science, the pionier of literature, doomed only to remove rubbish and clear obstructions from the paths of Learning and Genius, who press forward to conquest and glory, without bestowing a smile on the humble drudge that facilitates their progress. Every other authour may aspire to praise; the lexicographer can only hope to escape reproach, and even this negative recompense has been yet granted to very few.

I have, notwithstanding this discouragement, attempted a dictionary of the English language, which, while it was employed in the cultivation of every species of literature, has itself been hitherto neglected, suffered to spread, under the direction of chance, into wild exuberance, resigned to the tyranny of time and fashion, and exposed to the corruptions of ignorance, and caprices of innovation.

When I took the first survey of my undertaking, I found our speech copious without order, and energetick without rules: wherever I turned my view, there was perplexity to be disentangled, and confusion to be regulated; choice was to be made out of boundless variety, without any established principle of selection; adulterations were to be detected, without a settled test of purity; and modes of expression to be rejected or received, without the suffrages of any writers of classical reputation or acknowledged authority.

Having therefore no assistance but from general grammar, I applied myself to the perusal of our writers; and noting whatever might be of use to ascertain or illustrate any word or phrase, accumulated in time the materials of a dictionary, which, by degrees, I reduced to method, establishing to myself, in the progress of the work, such rules as experience and analogy suggested to me; experience, which practice and observation were continually increasing; and analogy, which, though in some words obscure, was evident in others.

In adjusting the *orthography,* which has been to this time unsettled and fortuitous, I found it necessary to distinguish those irregularities that are inherent in our tongue, and perhaps coeval with it, from others which the ignorance or negligence of later writers has produced. Every language has its anomalies, which, though inconvenient, and in themselves once unnecessary, must be tolerated among the imperfections of human things, and which require only to be registred, that they may not be increased, and ascertained, that they may not be confounded: but every language has likewise its improprieties and absurdities, which it is the duty of the lexicographer to correct or proscribe.

As language was at its beginning merely oral, all words of necessary or common use were spoken before they were written; and while they were unfixed by any visible signs, must have been spoken with great diversity, as we now observe those who cannot read to catch sounds imperfectly, and utter them negligently. When this wild and barbarous jargon was first reduced to an alphabet, every penman endeavoured to express, as he could, the sounds which he was accustomed to pronounce or to receive, and vitiated in writing such words as were already vitiated in speech. The powers of the letters, when they were applied to a new language, must have been vague and unsettled, and therefore different hands would exhibit the same sound by different combinations.

From this uncertain pronunciation arise in a great part the various dialects of the same country, which will always be observed to grow fewer, and less different, as books are multiplied; and from this arbitrary representation of sounds by letters, proceeds that diversity of spelling observable in the Saxon remains, and I suppose in the first books of every nation, which perplexes or destroys analogy, and produces anomalous formations, which, being once incorporated, can never be afterward dismissed or reformed.

Of this kind are the derivatives *length* from *long*, *strength* from *strong*, *darling* from *dear*, *breadth* from *broad*, from *dry*, *drought*, and from *high*, *height*, which Milton, in zeal for analogy, writes *highth*; *Quid te exempta juvat spinis de pluribus una;*[1] to change all would be too much, and to change one is nothing.

This uncertainty is most frequent in the vowels, which are so capriciously pronounced, and so differently modified, by accident or affectation, not only in every province, but in every mouth, that to them, as is well known to etymologists, little regard is to be shewn in the deduction of one language from another.

Such defects are not errours in orthography, but spots of barbarity impressed so deep in the English language, that criticism can never wash them away; these, therefore, must be permitted to remain untouched: but many words have likewise been altered by accident, or depraved by ignorance, as the pronunciation of the vulgar has been weakly followed; and some still continue to be variously written, as authours differ in their care or skill: of these it was proper to enquire the true orthography, which I have always considered as depending on their derivation, and have therefore referred them to their original languages: thus I write *enchant*, *enchantment*, *enchanter*, after the French, and *incantation* after the Latin; thus *entire* is chosen rather than *intire*, because it passed to us not from the Latin *integer*, but from the French *entier*.

---

[1] "What good would it do to remove one out of many errors?" Horace, *Epistles*, 2.2.212.

Of many words it is difficult to say whether they were immediately received from the Latin or the French, since at the time when we had dominions in France, we had Latin service in our churches. It is, however, my opinion, that the French generally supplied us; for we have few Latin words, among the terms of domestick use, which are not French; but many French, which are very remote from Latin.

Even in words of which the derivation is apparent, I have been often obliged to sacrifice uniformity to custom; thus I write, in compliance with a numberless majority, *convey* and *inveigh, deceit* and *receipt, fancy* and *phantom;* sometimes the derivative varies from the primitive, as *explain* and *explanation, repeat* and *repetition.*

Some combinations of letters having the same power are used indifferently without any discoverable reason of choice, as in *choak, choke; soap, sope; fewel, fuel,* and many others; which I have sometimes inserted twice, that those who search for them under either form, may not search in vain.

In examining the orthography of any doubtful word, the mode of spelling by which it is inserted in the series of the dictionary, is to be considered as that to which I give, perhaps not often rashly, the preference. I have left, in the examples, to every authour his own practice unmolested, that the reader may balance suffrages, and judge between us: but this question is not always to be determined by reputed or by real learning; some men, intent upon greater things, have thought little on sounds and derivations; some, knowing in the ancient tongues, have neglected those in which our words are commonly to be sought. Thus Hammond writes *fecibleness* for *feasibleness,* because I suppose he imagined it derived immediately from the Latin; and some words, such as *dependant, dependent; dependance, dependence,* vary their final syllable, as one or other language is present to the writer.

In this part of the work, where caprice has long wantoned without controul, and vanity sought praise by petty reformation, I have endeavoured to proceed with a scholar's reverence for antiquity, and a grammarian's regard to the genius of our tongue. I have attempted few alterations, and among those few, perhaps the greater part is from the modern to the ancient practice; and I hope I may be allowed to recommend to those, whose thoughts have been, perhaps, employed too anxiously on verbal singularities, not to disturb, upon narrow views, or for minute propriety, the orthography of their fathers. It has been asserted, that for the law to be *known*, is of more importance than to be *right*. Change, says Hooker, is not made without inconvenience, even from worse to better. There is in constancy and stability a general and lasting advantage, which will always overbalance the slow improvements of gradual correction. Much less ought our written language to comply with the corruptions of oral utterance, or copy that which every variation of time or place makes different from itself, and imitate those changes, which will again be changed, while imitation is employed in observing them.

This recommendation of steadiness and uniformity does not proceed from an opinion, that particular combinations of letters have much influence on human happiness; or that truth may not be successfully taught by modes of spelling fanciful and erroneous: I am not yet so lost in lexicography, as to forget that *words are the daughters of earth, and that things are the sons of heaven.*[2] Language is only the instrument of science, and words are but the signs of ideas: I wish, however, that the instrument might be less apt to decay, and that signs might be permanent, like the things which they denote.

In settling the orthography, I have not wholly neglected the pronunciation, which I have directed, by printing an accent upon the acute or elevated syllable. It will sometimes be found, that the accent is placed by the authour quoted, on a different syllable from that marked in the alphabetical series; it is then to be understood, that custom has varied, or that the authour has, in my opinion, pronounced wrong. Short directions are sometimes given where the sound of letters is irregular; and if they are sometimes omitted, defect in such minute observations will be more easily excused, than superfluity.

In the investigation both of the orthography and signification of words, their *etymology* was necessarily to be considered, and they were therefore to be divided into primitives and derivatives. A primitive word, is that which can be traced no further to any English root; thus *circumspect, circumvent, circumstance, delude,*

---

[2] Paraphrased from a line in Samuel Madden's *Boulter's Monument,* a poem which Johnson was paid to revise before publication.

concave, and *complicate*, though compounds in the Latin, are to us primitives. Derivatives, are all those that can be referred to any word in English of greater simplicity.

The derivatives I have referred to their primitives, with an accuracy sometimes needless; for who does not see that *remoteness* comes from *remote*, *lovely* from *love*, *concavity* from *concave*, and *demonstrative* from *demonstrate*? but this grammatical exuberance the scheme of my work did not allow me to repress. It is of great importance in examining the general fabrick of a language, to trace one word from another, by noting the usual modes of derivation and inflection; and uniformity must be preserved in systematical works, though sometimes at the expence of particular propriety.

Among other derivatives I have been careful to insert and elucidate the anomalous plurals of nouns and preterites of verbs, which in the Teutonick dialects are very frequent, and, though familiar to those who have always used them, interrupt and embarrass the learners of our language.

The two languages from which our primitives have been derived are the Roman and Teutonick: under the Roman I comprehend the French and provincial tongues; and under the Teutonick range the Saxon, German, and all their kindred dialects. Most of our polysyllables are Roman, and our words of one syllable are very often Teutonick.

In assigning the Roman original, it has perhaps sometimes happened that I have mentioned only the Latin, when the word was borrowed from the French; and considering myself as employed only in the illustration of my own language, I have not been very careful to observe whether the Latin word be pure or barbarous, or the French elegant or obsolete.

For the Teutonick etymologies I am commonly indebted to Junius and Skinner,[3] the only names which I have forborn to quote when I copied their books; not that I might appropriate their labours or usurp their honours, but that I might spare a perpetual repetition by one general acknowledgment. Of these, whom I

---

[3] Francis Junius (d. 1677) author of *Etymologicum Anglicanum*, 1743; Stephen Skinner (d. 1667) author of *Etymologicon Linguae Anglicanae*, 1671.

ought not to mention but with the reverence due to instructors and benefactors, Junius appears to have excelled in extent of learning, and Skinner in rectitude of understanding. Junius was accurately skilled in all the northern languages, Skinner probably examined the ancient and remoter dialects only by occasional inspection into dictionaries; but the learning of Junius is often of no other use than to show him a track by which he may deviate from his purpose, to which Skinner always presses forward by the shortest way. Skinner is often ignorant, but never ridiculous: Junius is always full of knowledge; but his variety distracts his judgment, and his learning is very frequently disgraced by his absurdities.

The votaries of the northern muses will not perhaps easily restrain their indignation, when they find the name of Junius thus degraded by a disadvantageous comparison; but whatever reverence is due to his diligence, or his attainments, it can be no criminal degree of censoriousness to charge that etymologist with want of judgment, who can seriously derive *dream* from *drama*, because *life is a drama, and a drama is a dream;* and who declares with a tone of defiance, that no man can fail to derive *moan* from *μόνος, monos,* who considers that grief naturally loves to be alone.[4]

Our knowledge of the northern literature is so scanty, that of words undoubtedly Teutonick the original is not always to be found in any ancient language; and I have therefore inserted Dutch or German substitutes, which I consider not as radical but parallel, not as the parents, but sisters of the English.

The words which are represented as thus related by descent or cognation, do not always agree in sense; for it is incident to words, as to their authours, to degenerate from their ancestors, and to change their manners when they change their country. It is sufficient, in etymological enquiries, if the senses of kindred words be found such as may easily pass into each other, or such as may both be referred to one general idea.

The etymology, so far as it is yet known, was easily found in the volumes where it is particularly and professedly delivered; and, by proper attention to the rules of derivation, the orthogra-

[4] We have omitted a long footnote in which Johnson gives other examples of Junius's "etymological extravagance."

phy was soon adjusted. But to *collect* the *words* of our language was a task of greater difficulty: the deficiency of dictionaries was immediately apparent; and when they were exhausted, what was yet wanting must be sought by fortuitous and unguided excursions into books, and gleaned as industry should find, or chance should offer it, in the boundless chaos of a living speech. My search, however, has been either skilful or lucky; for I have much augmented the vocabulary.

As my design was a dictionary, common or appellative, I have omitted all words which have relation to proper names; such as *Arian, Socinian, Calvinist, Benedictine, Mahometan;* but have retained those of a more general nature, as *Heathen, Pagan.*

Of the terms of art I have received such as could be found either in books of science or technical dictionaries; and have often inserted, from philosophical writers, words which are supported perhaps only by a single authority, and which being not admitted into general use, stand yet as candidates or probationers, and must depend for their adoption on the suffrage of futurity.

The words which our authours have introduced by their knowledge of foreign languages, or ignorance of their own, by vanity or wantonness, by compliance with fashion, or lust of innovation, I have registred as they occurred, though commonly only to censure them, and warn others against the folly of naturalizing useless foreigners to the injury of the natives.

I have not rejected any by design, merely because they were unnecessary or exuberant; but have received those which by different writers have been differently formed, as *viscid,* and *viscidity, viscous,* and *viscosity.*

Compounded or double words I have seldom noted, except when they obtain a signification different from that which the components have in their simple state. Thus *highwayman, woodman,* and *horsecourser,* require an explication; but of *thieflike* or *coachdriver* no notice was needed, because the primitives contain the meaning of the compounds.

Words arbitrarily formed by a constant and settled analogy, like diminutive adjectives in *ish,* as *greenish, bluish,* adverbs in *ly,* as *dully, openly,* substantives in *ness,* as *vileness, faultiness,* were less diligently sought, and many sometimes have been omitted, when I had no authority that invited me to insert them; not that they are not genuine and regular offsprings of English roots, but because their relation to the primitive being always the same, their signification cannot be mistaken.

The verbal nouns in *ing*, such as the *keeping* of the *castle*, the *leading* of the *army*, are always neglected, or placed only to illustrate the sense of the verb, except when they signify things as well as actions, and have therefore a plural number, as *dwelling, living;* or have an absolute and abstract signification, as *colouring, painting, learning.*

The participles are likewise omitted, unless, by signifying rather qualities than action, they take the nature of adjectives; as a *thinking* man, a man of prudence; a *pacing* horse, a horse that can pace: these I have ventured to call *participial adjectives.* But neither are these always inserted, because they are commonly to be understood, without any danger of mistake, by consulting the verb.

Obsolete words are admitted, when they are found in authours not obsolete, or when they have any force or beauty that may deserve revival.

As composition is one of the chief characteristicks of a language, I have endeavoured to make some reparation for the universal negligence of my predecessors, by inserting great numbers of compounded words, as may be found under *after, fore, new, night, fair*, and many more. These, numerous as they are, might be multiplied, but that use and curiosity are here satisfied, and the frame of our language and modes of our combination amply discovered.

Of some forms of composition, such as that by which *re* is prefixed to note *repetition,* and *un* to signify *contrariety* or *privation,* all the examples cannot be accumulated, because the use of these particles, if not wholly arbitrary, is so little limited, that they are hourly affixed to new words as occasion requires, or is imagined to require them.

There is another kind of composition more frequent in our language than perhaps in any other, from which arises to foreigners the greatest difficulty. We modify the signification of many verbs by a particle subjoined; as to *come off*, to escape by a fetch; to *fall on,* to attack; to *fall off,* to apostatize; to *break off,* to stop abruptly; to *bear out,* to justify; to *fall in,* to comply; to *give over,* to cease; to *set off,* to embellish; to *set in,* to begin a continual tenour; to *set out,* to begin a course or journey; to *take off,* to copy; with innumerable expressions of the same kind, of which some appear wildly irregular, being so far distant from the sense of the simple words, that no sagacity will be able to trace the steps by which they arrived at the present use. These I have noted with great care; and though I cannot flatter myself that the collection is complete, I believe I have so far assisted the students of our language, that this kind of phraseology will be no longer insuperable; and the combinations of verbs and particles, by chance omitted, will be easily explained by comparison with those that may be found.

Many words yet stand supported only by the name of Bailey, Ainsworth, Philips,[5] or the contracted *Dict.* for *Dictionaries* subjoined: of these I am not always certain that they are read in any book but the works of lexicographers. Of such I have omitted many, because I had never read them; and many I have inserted, because they may perhaps exist, though they have escaped my notice: they are, however, to be yet considered as resting only upon the credit of former dictionaries. Others, which I considered as useful, or know to be proper, though I could not at present support them by authorities, I have suffered to stand upon my own attestation, claiming the same privilege with my predecessors of being sometimes credited without proof.

The words, thus selected and disposed, are grammatically considered; they are referred to the different parts of speech; traced, when they are irregularly inflected, through their various terminations; and illustrated by observations, not indeed of great or striking importance, separately considered, but necessary to the elucidation of our language, and hitherto neglected or forgotten by English grammarians.

That part of my work on which I expect malignity most frequently to fasten, is the *Explanation;* in which I cannot hope to

---

[5] Nathaniel Bailey (d. 1742) compiled the *English Dictionary,* 1721, which was Johnson's principal reference to check inclusion of words. Robert Ainsworth (d. 1743) was the author of a Latin *Thesaurus,* 1736. Edward Phillips published *A New World of English Words* in 1658.

satisfy those, who are perhaps not inclined to be pleased, since I have not always been able to satisfy myself. To interpret a language by itself is very difficult; many words cannot be explained by synonimes, because the idea signified by them has not more than one appellation; nor by paraphrase, because simple ideas cannot be described. When the nature of things is unknown, or the notion unsettled and indefinite, and various in various minds, the words by which such notions are conveyed, or such things denoted, will be ambiguous and perplexed. And such is the fate of hapless lexicography, that not only darkness, but light, impedes and distresses it; things may be not only too little, but too much known, to be happily illustrated. To explain, requires the use of terms less abstruse than that which is to be explained, and such terms cannot always be found; for as nothing can be proved but by supposing something intuitively known, and evident without proof, so nothing can be defined but by the use of words too plain to admit a definition.

Other words there are, of which the sense is too subtle and evanescent to be fixed in a paraphrase; such are all those which are by the grammarians termed *expletives,* and, in dead languages, are suffered to pass for empty sounds, of no other use than to fill a verse, or to modulate a period, but which are easily perceived in living tongues to have power and emphasis, though it be sometimes such as no other form of expression can convey.

My labour has likewise been much increased by a class of verbs too frequent in the English language, of which the signification is so loose and general, the use so vague and indeterminate, and the senses detorted so widely from the first idea, that it is hard to trace them through the maze of variation, to catch them on the brink of utter inanity, to circumscribe them by any limitations, or interpret them by any words of distinct and settled meaning: such are *bear, break, come, cast, full, get, give, do, put, set, go, run, make, take, turn, throw.* If of these the whole power is not accurately delivered, it must be remembered, that while our language is yet living, and variable by the caprice of every one that speaks it, these words are hourly shifting their relations, and can no more be ascertained in a dictionary, than a grove, in the agitation of a storm, can be accurately delineated from its picture in the water.

The particles are among all nations applied with so great latitude, that they are not easily reducible under any regular scheme of explication: this difficulty is not less, nor perhaps greater, in English, than in other languages. I have laboured them with diligence, I hope with success; such at least as can be expected in a task, which no man, however learned or sagacious, has yet been able to perform.

Some words there are which I cannot explain, because I do not understand them; these might have been omitted very often with little inconvenience, but I would not so far indulge my vanity as to decline this confession: for when Tully owns himself ignorant whether *lessus,* in the twelve tables, means a *funeral song,* or *mourning garment;* and Aristotle doubts whether οὔρευς[6] in the Iliad, signifies a *mule,* or *muleteer,* I may freely, without shame, leave some obscurities to happier industry, or future information.

The rigour of interpretative lexicography requires that *the explanation, and the word explained, should be always reciprocal;* this I have always endeavoured, but could not always attain. Words are seldom exactly synonimous; a new term was not introduced, but because the former was thought inadequate: names, therefore, have often many ideas, but few ideas have many names. It was then necessary to use the proximate word, for the deficiency of single terms can very seldom be supplied by circumlocution; nor is the inconvenience great of such mutilated interpretations, because the sense may easily be collected entire from the examples.

In every word of extensive use, it was requisite to mark the progress of its meaning, and show by what gradations of intermediate sense it has passed from its primitive to its remote and accidental signification; so that every foregoing explanation should tend to that which follows, and the series be regularly concatenated from the first notion to the last.

This is specious, but not always practicable; kindred senses may be so interwoven, that the perplexity cannot be disentangled, nor any reason be assigned why one should be ranged before the other. When the radical idea branches out into parallel ramifications, how can a consecutive series be formed of senses in their

[6] Read οὐρεύς; Aristotle, Poetics, 25.16. Ordinarily *mule,* the word is used by Homer for *guard.*

nature collateral? The shades of meaning sometimes pass imperceptibly into each other; so that though on one side they apparently differ, yet it is impossible to mark the point of contact. Ideas of the same race, though not exactly alike, are sometimes so little different, that no words can express the dissimilitude, though the mind easily perceives it, when they are exhibited together; and sometimes there is such a confusion of acceptations, that discernment is wearied, and distinction puzzled, and perseverance herself hurries to an end, by crouding together what she cannot separate.

These complaints of difficulty will, by those that have never considered words beyond their popular use, be thought only the jargon of a man willing to magnify his labours, and procure veneration to his studies by involution and obscurity. But every art is obscure to those that have not learned it: this uncertainty of terms, and commixture of ideas, is well known to those who have joined philosophy with grammar; and if I have not expressed them very clearly, it must be remembered that I am speaking of that which words are insufficient to explain.

The original sense of words is often driven out of use by their metaphorical acceptations, yet must be inserted for the sake of a regular origination. Thus I know not whether *ardour* is used for *material heat,* or whether *flagrant,* in English, ever signifies the same with *burning;* yet such are the primitive ideas of these words, which are therefore set first, though without examples, that the figurative senses may be commodiously deduced.

Such is the exuberance of signification which many words have obtained, that it was scarcely possible to collect all their senses; sometimes the meaning of derivatives must be sought in the mother term, and sometimes deficient explanations of the primitive may be supplied in the train of derivation. In any case of doubt or difficulty, it will be always proper to examine all the words of the same race; for some words are slightly passed over to avoid repetition, some admitted easier and clearer explanation than others, and all will be better understood, as they are considered in greater variety of structures and relations.

All the interpretations of words are not written with the same skill, or the same happiness: things equally easy in themselves, are not all equally easy to any single mind. Every writer of a long work commits errours, where there appears neither ambiguity to mislead, nor obscurity to confound him; and in a search like this, many felicities of expression will be casually overlooked, many convenient parallels will be forgotten, and many particulars will admit improvement from a mind utterly unequal to the whole performance.

But many seeming faults are to be imputed rather to the nature of the undertaking, than the negligence of the performer. Thus some explanations are unavoidably reciprocal or circular, as *hind, the female of the stag; stag, the male of the hind:* sometimes easier words are changed into harder, as *burial* into *sepulture* or *interment, drier* into *desiccative, dryness* into *siccity* or *aridity, fit* into *paroxysm;* for the easiest word, whatever it be, can never be translated into one more easy. But easiness and difficulty are merely relative, and if the present prevalence of our language should invite foreigners to this dictionary, many will be assisted by those words which now seem only to increase or produce obscurity. For this reason I have endeavoured frequently to join a Teutonick and Roman interpretation, as to *cheer* to *gladden,* or *exhilarate,* that every learner of English may be assisted by his own tongue.

The solution of all difficulties, and the supply of all defects, must be sought in the examples, subjoined to the various senses of each word, and ranged according to the time of their authours.

When first I collected these authorities, I was desirous that every quotation should be useful to some other end than the illustration of a word; I therefore extracted from philosophers principles of science; from historians remarkable facts; from chymists complete processes; from divines striking exhortations; and from poets beautiful descriptions. Such is design, while it is yet at a distance from execution. When the time called upon me to range this accumulation of elegance and wisdom into an alphabetical series, I soon discovered that the bulk of my volumes would fright away the student, and was forced to depart from my scheme of including all that was pleasing or useful in English literature, and reduce my transcripts very often to clusters of words, in which scarcely any meaning is retained; thus to the weariness of copying, I was condemned to add the vexation of expunging. Some passages I have yet spared, which may relieve the labour of verbal searches, and intersperse with verdure and flowers the dusty desarts of barren philology.

The examples, thus mutilated, are no longer to be considered as conveying the sentiments or doctrine of their authours; the word for the sake of which they are inserted, with all its appendant clauses, has been carefully preserved; but it may sometimes happen, by hasty detruncation, that the general tendency of the sentence may be changed: the divine may desert his tenets, or the philosopher his system.

Some of the examples have been taken from writers who were never mentioned as masters of elegance or models of stile; but words must be sought where they are used; and in what pages, eminent for purity, can terms of manufacture or agriculture be found? Many quotations serve no other purpose, than that of proving the bare existence of words, and are therefore selected with less scrupulousness than those which are to teach their structures and relations.

My purpose was to admit no testimony of living authours, that I might not be misled by partiality, and that none of my cotemporaries might have reason to complain; nor have I departed from this resolution, but when some performance of uncommon excellence excited my veneration, when my memory supplied me, from late books, with an example that was wanting, or when my heart, in the tenderness of friendship, solicited admission for a favourite name.

So far have I been from any care to grace my pages with modern decorations, that I have studiously endeavoured to collect examples and authorities from the writers before the restoration, whose works I regard as *the wells of English undefiled,* as the pure sources of genuine diction. Our language, for almost a century, has, by the concurrence of many causes, been gradually departing from its original Teutonick character, and deviating towards a Gallick structure and phraseology, from which it ought to be our endeavour to recal it, by making our ancient volumes the ground-work of stile, admitting among the additions of later times, only such as may supply real deficiencies, such as are readily adopted by the genius of our tongue, and incorporate easily with our native idioms.

But as every language has a time of rudeness antecedent to perfection, as well as of false refinement and declension, I have been cautious lest my zeal for antiquity might drive me into times too remote, and croud my book with words now no longer understood. I have fixed Sidney's work for the boundary, beyond which I make few excursions. From the authours which rose in the time of Elizabeth, a speech might be formed adequate to all the purposes of use and elegance. If the language of theology were extracted from Hooker and the translation of the Bible; the terms of natural knowledge from Bacon; the phrases of policy, war, and navigation from Raleigh; the dialect of poetry and fiction from Spenser and Sidney; and the diction of common life from Shakespeare, few ideas would be lost to mankind, for want of English words, in which they might be expressed.

It is not sufficient that a word is found, unless it be so combined as that its meaning is apparently determined by the tract and tenour of the sentence; such passages I have therefore chosen, and when it happened that any authour gave a definition of a term, or such an explanation as is equivalent to a definition, I have placed his authority as a supplement to my own, without regard to the chronological order, that is otherwise observed.

Some words, indeed, stand unsupported by any authority, but they are commonly derivative nouns or adverbs, formed from their primitives by regular and constant analogy, or names of things seldom occurring in books, or words of which I have reason to doubt the existence.

There is more danger of censure from the multiplicity than paucity of examples; authorities will sometimes seem to have been accumulated without necessity or use, and perhaps some will be found, which might, without loss, have been omitted. But a work of this kind is not hastily to be charged with superfluities: those quotations which to careless or unskilful perusers appear only to repeat the same sense, will often exhibit, to a more accurate examiner, diversities of signification, or, at least, afford different shades of the same meaning: one will shew the word applied to persons, another to things; one will express an ill, another a good, and a third a neutral sense; one will prove the expression genuine from an ancient authour; another will shew it elegant from a modern: a doubtful authority is corroborated by another of more credit; an ambiguous sentence is ascertained by a passage clear and determinate; the word, how often soever repeated, appears with new associates and in different combinations, and every quotation contributes something to the stability or enlargement of the language.

When words are used equivocally, I receive them in either sense; when they are metaphorical, I adopt them in their primitive acceptation.

I have sometimes, though rarely, yielded to the temptation of exhibiting a genealogy of sentiments, by shewing how one authour copied the thoughts and diction of another: such quotations are indeed little more than repetitions, which might justly be censured, did they not gratify the mind, by affording a kind of intellectual history.

The various syntactical structures occurring in the examples have been carefully noted; the licence or negligence with which many words have been hitherto used, has made our stile capricious and indeterminate; when the different combinations of the same word are exhibited together, the preference is readily given to propriety, and I have often endeavoured to direct the choice.

Thus have I laboured to settle the orthography, display the analogy, regulate the structures, and ascertain the signification of English words, to perform all the parts of a faithful lexicographer: but I have not always executed my own scheme, or satisfied my own expectations. The work, whatever proofs of diligence and attention it may exhibit, is yet capable of many improvements: the orthography which I recommend is still controvertible, the etymology which I adopt is uncertain, and perhaps frequently erroneous; the explanations are sometimes too much contracted, and sometimes too much diffused, the significations are distinguished rather with subtilty than skill, and the attention is harrassed with unnecessary minuteness.

The examples are too often injudiciously truncated, and perhaps sometimes, I hope very rarely, alleged in a mistaken sense; for in making this collection I trusted more to memory, than, in a state of disquiet and embarrassment, memory can contain, and purposed to supply at the review what was left incomplete in the first transcription.

Many terms appropriated to particular occupations, though necessary and significant, are undoubtedly omitted; and of the words most studiously considered and exemplified, many senses have escaped observation.

Yet these failures, however frequent, may admit extenuation and apology. To have attempted much is always laudable, even when the enterprize is above the strength that undertakes it: To rest below his own aim is incident to every one whose fancy is active, and whose views are comprehensive; nor is any man satisfied with himself because he has done much, but because he can conceive little. When first I engaged in this work, I resolved to leave neither words nor things unexamined, and pleased myself with a prospect of the hours which I should revel away in feasts of literature, the obscure recesses of northern learning, which I should enter and ransack, the treasures with which I expected every search into those neglected mines to reward my labour, and the triumph with which I should display my acquisitions to mankind. When I had thus enquired into the original of words, I resolved to show likewise my attention to things; to pierce deep into every science, to enquire the nature of every substance of which I inserted the name, to limit every idea by a definition strictly logical, and exhibit every production of art or nature in an accurate description, that my book might be in place of all other dictionaries whether appellative or technical. But these were the dreams of a poet doomed at last to wake a lexicographer. I soon found that it is too late to look for instruments, when the work calls for execution, and that whatever abilities I had brought to my task, with those I must finally perform it. To deliberate whenever I doubted, to enquire whenever I was ignorant, would have protracted the undertaking without end, and, perhaps, without much improvement; for I did not find by my first experiments, that what I had not of my own was easily to be obtained: I saw that one enquiry only gave occasion to another, that book referred to book, that to search was not always to find, and to find was not always to be informed; and that thus to persue perfection, was, like the first inhabitants of Arcadia, to chace the sun, which, when they had reached the hill where he seemed to rest, was still beheld at the same distance from them.

I then contracted my design, determining to confide in myself, and no longer to solicit auxiliaries, which produced more incumbrance than assistance: by this I obtained at least one advantage, that I set limits to my work, which would in time be finished, though not completed.

Despondency has never so far prevailed as to depress me to negligence; some faults will at last appear to be the effects of anxious diligence and persevering activity. The nice and subtle ramifications of meaning were not easily avoided by a mind intent upon accuracy, and convinced of the necessity of disentangling combinations, and separating similitudes. Many of the distinctions which to common readers appear useless and idle, will be found real and important by men versed in the school philosophy, without which no dictionary ever shall be accurately compiled, or skilfully examined.

Some senses however there are, which, though not the same, are yet so nearly allied, that they are often confounded. Most men think indistinctly, and therefore cannot speak with exactness; and consequently some examples might be indifferently put to either signification: this uncertainty is not to be imputed to me, who do not form, but register the language; who do not teach men how they should think, but relate how they have hitherto expressed their thoughts.

The imperfect sense of some examples I lamented, but could not remedy, and hope they will be compensated by innumerable passages selected with propriety, and preserved with exactness; some shining with sparks of imagination, and some replete with treasures of wisdom.

The orthography and etymology, though imperfect, are not imperfect for want of care, but because care will not always be successful, and recollection or information come too late for use.

That many terms of art and manufacture are omitted, must be frankly acknowledged; but for this defect I may boldly allege that it was unavoidable: I could not visit caverns to learn the miner's language, nor take a voyage to perfect my skill in the dialect of navigation, nor visit the warehouses of merchants, and shops of artificers, to gain the names of wares, tools and operations, of which no mention is found in books; what favourable accident, or easy enquiry brought within my reach, has not been neglected; but it had been a hopeless labour to glean up words, by courting living information, and contesting with the sullenness of one, and the roughness of another.

To furnish the academicians della Crusca[7] with words of this

[7] The Accademia della Crusca was founded in 1582 to purify and standardize the Italian langauge. Its *Vocabulario* was published in 1612.

kind, a series of comedies called *la Fiera*, or *the Fair*, was professedly written by Buonaroti; but I had no such assistant, and therefore was content to want what they must have wanted likewise, had they not luckily been so supplied.

Nor are all words which are not found in the vocabulary, to be lamented as omissions. Of the laborious and mercantile part of the people, the diction is in a great measure casual and mutable; many of their terms are formed for some temporary or local convenience, and though current at certain times and places, are in others utterly unknown. This fugitive cant, which is always in a state of increase or decay, cannot be regarded as any part of the durable materials of a language, and therefore must be suffered to perish with other things unworthy of preservation.

Care will sometimes betray to the appearance of negligence. He that is catching opportunities which seldom occur, will suffer those to pass by unregarded, which he expects hourly to return; he that is searching for rare and remote things, will neglect those that are obvious and familiar: thus many of the most common and cursory words have been inserted with little illustration, because in gathering the authorities, I forbore to copy those which I thought likely to occur whenever they were wanted. It is remarkable that, in reviewing my collection, I found the word *sea* unexemplified.

Thus it happens, that in things difficult there is danger from ignorance, and in things easy from confidence; the mind, afraid of greatness, and disdainful of littleness, hastily withdraws herself from painful searches, and passes with scornful rapidity over tasks not adequate to her powers, sometimes too secure for caution, and again too anxious for vigorous effort; sometimes idle in a plain path, and sometimes distracted in labyrinths, and dissipated by different intentions.

A large work is difficult because it is large, even though all its parts might singly be performed with facility; where there are many things to be done, each must be allowed its share of time and labour, in the proportion only which it bears to the whole; nor can it be expected, that the stones which form the dome of a temple, should be squared and polished like the diamond of a ring.

Of the event of this work, for which, having laboured it with so much application, I cannot but have some degree of parental fondness, it is natural to form conjectures. Those who have been persuaded to think well of my design, require that it should fix our language, and put a stop to those alterations which time and chance have hitherto been suffered to make in it without opposition. With this consequence I will confess that I flattered myself for a while; but now begin to fear that I have indulged expectation which neither reason nor experience can justify. When we see men grow old and die at a certain time one after another, from century to century, we laugh at the elixir that promises to prolong life to a thousand years; and with equal justice may the lexicographer be derided, who being able to produce no example of a nation that has preserved their words and phrases from mutability, shall imagine that his dictionary can embalm his language, and secure it from corruption and decay, that it is in his power to change sublunary nature, or clear the world at once from folly, vanity, and affectation.

With this hope, however, academies have been instituted, to guard the avenues of their languages, to retain fugitives, and repulse intruders; but their vigilance and activity have hitherto been vain; sounds are too volatile and subtile for legal restraints; to enchain syllables, and to lash the wind, are equally the undertakings of pride, unwilling to measure its desires by its strength. The French language has visibly changed under the inspection of the academy; the stile of Amelot's translation of father Paul is observed by Le Courayer to be *un peu passé;* and no Italian will maintain, that the diction of any modern writer is not perceptibly different from that of Boccace, Machiavel, or Caro.[8]

Total and sudden transformations of a language seldom happen; conquests and migrations are now very rare: but there are other causes of change, which, though slow in their operation, and invisible in their progress, are perhaps as much superiour to human resistance, as the revolutions of the sky, or intumescence of the tide. Commerce, however necessary, however lucrative, as it depraves the manners, corrupts the language; they that have fre-

[8] Le Courayer made a French translation of Father Paolo Sarpi's *History of the Council of Trent* in 1736; Amelot had made an earlier one in 1683. The first edition of the dictionary of the French Academy appeared in 1694. Boccaccio (d. 1375), Machiavelli (d. 1527), and the poet Annibale Caro (d. 1566) were too early to benefit from the dictionary published by the Accademia della Crusca in 1612.

quent intercourse with strangers, to whom they endeavour to accommodate themselves, must in time learn a mingled dialect, like the jargon which serves the traffickers on the Mediterranean and Indian coasts. This will not always be confined to the exchange, the warehouse, or the port, but will be communicated by degrees to other ranks of the people, and be at last incorporated with the current speech.

There are likewise internal causes equally forcible. The language most likely to continue long without alteration, would be that of a nation raised a little, and but a little, above barbarity, secluded from strangers, and totally employed in procuring the conveniencies of life; either without books, or, like some of the Mahometan countries, with very few: men thus busied and unlearned, having only such words as common use requires, would perhaps long continue to express the same notions by the same signs. But no such constancy can be expected in a people polished by arts, and classed by subordination, where one part of the community is sustained and accommodated by the labour of the other. Those who have much leisure to think, will always be enlarging the stock of ideas, and every increase of knowledge, whether real or fancied, will produce new words, or combinations of words. When the mind is unchained from necessity, it will range after convenience; when it is left at large in the fields of speculation, it will shift opinions; as any custom is disused, the words that expressed it must perish with it; as any opinion grows popular, it will innovate speech in the same proportion as it alters practice.

As by the cultivation of various sciences, a language is amplified, it will be more furnished with words deflected from their original sense; the geometrician will talk of a courtier's zenith, or the excentrick virtue of a wild hero, and the physician of sanguine expectations and phlegmatick delays. Copiousness of speech will give opportunities to capricious choice, by which some words will be preferred, and others degraded; vicissitudes of fashion will enforce the use of new, or extend the signification of known terms. The tropes of poetry will make hourly encroachments, and the metaphorical will become the current sense: pronunciation will be varied by levity or ignorance, and the pen must at length comply with the tongue; illiterate writers will at one time or other, by publick infatuation, rise into renown, who, not knowing the original import of words, will use them with colloquial licentiousness, confound distinction, and forget propriety. As politeness increases, some expressions will be considered as too gross and vulgar for the delicate, others as too formal and ceremonious for the gay and airy; new phrases are therefore adopted, which must, for the same reasons, be in time dismissed. Swift, in his petty treatise on the English language, allows that new words must sometimes be introduced, but proposes that none should be suffered to become obsolete. But what makes a word obsolete, more than general agreement to forbear it? and how shall it be continued, when it conveys an offensive idea, or recalled again into the mouths of mankind, when it has once by disuse become unfamiliar, and by unfamiliarity unpleasing.

There is another cause of alteration more prevalent than any other, which yet in the present state of the world cannot be obviated. A mixture of two languages will produce a third distinct from both, and they will always be mixed, where the chief part of education, and the most conspicuous accomplishment, is skill in ancient or in foreign tongues. He that has long cultivated another language, will find its words and combinations croud upon his memory; and haste and negligence, refinement and affectation, will obtrude borrowed terms and exotick expressions.

The great pest of speech is frequency of translation. No book was ever turned from one language into another, without imparting something of its native idiom; this is the most mischievous and comprehensive innovation; single words may enter by thousands, and the fabrick of the tongue continue the same, but new phraseology changes much at once; it alters not the single stones of the building, but the order of the columns. If an academy should be established for the cultivation of our stile, which I, who can never wish to see dependance multiplied, hope the spirit of English liberty will hinder or destroy, let them, instead of compiling grammars and dictionaries, endeavour, with all their influence, to stop the licence of translatours, whose idleness and ignorance, if it be suffered to proceed, will reduce us to babble a dialect of France.

If the changes that we fear be thus irresistible, what remains but to acquiesce with silence, as in the other insurmountable distresses of humanity? it remains that we retard what we cannot repel, that we palliate what we cannot cure. Life may be lengthened by care, though death cannot be ultimately defeated: tongues, like governments, have a natural tendency to degeneration; we have long preserved our constitution, let us make some struggles for our language.

In hope of giving longevity to that which its own nature forbids to be immortal, I have devoted this book, the labour of years, to the honour of my country, that we may no longer yield the palm of philology, to the nations of the continent. The chief glory of every people arises from its authours: whether I shall add any thing by my own writings to the reputation of English literature, must be left to time: much of my life has been lost under the pressures of disease; much has been trifled away; and much has always been spent in provision for the day that was passing over me; but I shall not think my employment useless or ignoble, if by my assistance foreign nations, and distant ages, gain access to the propagators of knowledge, and understand the teachers of truth; if my labours afford light to the repositories of science, and add celebrity to Bacon, to Hooker, to Milton, and to Boyle.

When I am animated by this wish, I look with pleasure on my book, however defective, and deliver it to the world with the spirit of a man that has endeavoured well. That it will immediately become popular I have not promised to myself: a few wild blunders, and risible absurdities, from which no work of such multiplicity was ever free, may for a time furnish folly with laughter, and harden ignorance in contempt; but useful diligence will at last prevail, and there never can be wanting some who distinguish desert; who will consider that no dictionary of a living tongue ever can be perfect, since while it is hastening to publication, some words are budding, and some falling away; that a whole life cannot be spent upon syntax and etymology, and that even a whole life would not be sufficient; that he, whose design includes whatever language can express, must often speak of what he does not understand; that a writer will sometimes be hurried by eagerness to the end, and sometimes faint with weariness under a task, which Scaliger compares to the labours of the anvil and the mine; that what is obvious is not always known, and what is known is not always present; that sudden fits of inadvertency will surprize vigilance, slight avocations will seduce attention, and casual eclipses of the mind will darken learning; and that the writer shall often in vain trace his memory at the moment of need, for that which yesterday he knew with intuitive readiness, and which will come uncalled into his thoughts tomorrow.

In this work, when it shall be found that much is omitted, let it not be forgotten that much likewise is performed; and though no book was ever spared out of tenderness to the authour, and the world is little solicitous to know whence proceeded the faults of that which it condemns; yet it may gratify curiosity to inform it, that the *English Dictionary* was written with little assistance of the learned, and without any patronage of the great; not in the soft obscurities of retirement, or under the shelter of academick bowers, but amidst inconvenience and distraction, in sickness and in sorrow: and it may repress the triumph of malignant criticism to observe, that if our language is not here fully displayed, I have only failed in an attempt which no human powers have hitherto completed. If the lexicons of ancient tongues, now immutably fixed, and comprised in a few volumes, be yet, after the toil of successive ages, inadequate and delusive; if the aggregated knowledge, and co-operating diligence of the Italian academicians, did not secure them from the censure of Beni, if the embodied criticks of France, when fifty years had been spent upon their work, were obliged to change its oeconomy, and give their second edition another form, I may surely be contented without the praise of perfection, which, if I could obtain, in this gloom of solitude, what would it avail me? I have protracted my work till most of those whom I wished to please, have sunk into the grave, and success and miscarriage are empty sounds: I therefore dismiss it with frigid tranquillity, having little to fear or hope from censure or from praise.

Selections from the *Dictionary*

advi'ce. (4) Intelligence; as, the merchants received *advice* of their loss. This sense is somewhat low, and chiefly commercial.

agoni'stes. A prize-fighter; one that contends at any public solemnity for a prize. Milton has so stiled his tragedy, because Sampson was called out to divert the Philistines with feats of strength.

to ail. (4) It is remarkable, that this word is never used but with some indefinite term, or the word *nothing;* as, *What ails* him? *What* does he *ail?* He *ails something:* he *ails nothing. Something ails* him; *nothing ails* him. Thus we never say, a fever *ails* him, or he *ails* a fever, or use definite terms with this verb.

to ake. (2) It is frequently applied, in an improper sense, to the heart; as, *the heart akes;* to imply grief or fear. Shakespeare has used it, still more licentiously, of the soul.

alamo'de. According to the fashion: a low word. It is used likewise by shopkeepers for a kind of thin silken manufacture.

a'lias. A Latin word, signifying otherwise; often used in the trials of criminals, whose danger has obliged them to change their names; as, Simpson *alias* Smith, *alias* Baker; that is, *otherwise* Smith, *otherwise* Baker.

alliga'tor. The crocodile. This name is chiefly used for the crocodile of America, between which, and that of Africa, naturalists have laid down this difference, that one moves the upper, and the other the lower jaw; but this is now known

---

advice. (4) I.e., the fourth definition of this word.

to be chimerical, the lower jaw being equally moved by both.

amba'ssadress. (2) In ludicrous language, a woman sent on a message.

ambide'xter. (2) A man who is equally ready to act on either side, in party disputes. This sense is ludicrous.

anthropophagi'nian. A ludicrous word, formed by Shakespeare from *anthropophagi,* for the sake of a formidable sound.

aphrodisi'acal, aphrodisi'ack. Relating to the venereal disease.

appro'val. Approbation: a word not much used.

awa'y. (6) It is often used with a verb; as, to *drink away* an estate; to *idle away* a manor; that is, to drink or idle till an estate or manor is gone.

bear-garden. A word used in familiar or low phrase for *rude* or *turbulent;* as, a *bear-garden* fellow; that is, a man rude enough to be a proper frequenter of the bear-garden. *Bear-garden sport,* is used for gross inelegant entertainment.

beast. (3) A brutal savage man, a man acting in any manner unworthy of a reasonable creature.

bee. (1) The animal that makes honey, remarkable for its industry and art.

belda'm. (1) An old woman; generally a term of contempt, marking the last degree of old age, with all its faults and miseries.

be'llibone. A woman excelling both in beauty and goodness. A word now out of use.

to bethu'mp. To beat; to lay blows upon; a ludicrous word.

to bewa're. (2) It is observable, that it is only used in such forms of speech as admit the word *be:* thus we say, *he may beware, let him beware, he will beware;* but not, *he did beware,* or *he has been ware.*

bi'lingsgate. (A cant word, borrowed from *Bilingsgate* in London, a place where there is always a croud of low people, and frequent brawls and foul language.) Ribaldry; foul language.

blush. (3) Sudden appearance; a signification that seems barbarous, yet used by good writers.

bo'mbast. (This word seems to be derived from Bombastius, one of the names of Paracelsus; a man remarkable for sounding professions, and unintelligible language.) Fustian; big words, without meaning.

bo'oby. (A word of no certain etymology; Henshaw thinks it a corruption of *bull-beef* ridiculously; Skinner imagines it to be derived from *bobo,* foolish, Span. Junius finds *bowbard* to be an old Scottish word for a *coward,* a *contemptible fellow;* from which he naturally deduces *booby;* but the original of *bowbard* is not known.) A dull, heavy, stupid fellow; a lubber.

bo'okish. Given to books; acquainted only with books. It is generally used contemptuously.

bookle'arned. Versed in books, or literature: a term implying some slight contempt.

bu'lly. (Skinner derives this word from *burly,* as a corruption in the pronunciation; which is very probably right: or from *bulky,* or *bull-eyed;* which are less probable. May it not come from *bull,* the pope's letter, implying the insolence of those who came invested with authority from the papal court?) A noisy, blustering, quarrelling fellow: it is generally taken for a man that has only the appearance of courage.

bum. (1) The buttocks; the part on which we sit.

bu'mpkin. (This word is of uncertain etymology; Henshaw derives it from *pumpkin,* a kind of worthless gourd, or melon. This seems harsh. *Bump* is used amongst us for a knob, or lump; may not *bumpkin* be much the same with *clodpate, loggerhead, block,* and *blockhead.*) An awkward heavy rustick; a country lout.

bu'tterfly. A beautiful insect, so named because it first appears at the beginning of the season for butter.

cant. (3) A whining pretension to goodness, in formal and affected terms.

ca'nter. A term of reproach for hypocrites, who talk formally of religion, without obeying it.

ca'rpet. (4) *Carpet* is used, proverbially, for a state of ease and luxury; as a *carpet knight,* a knight that has never known the field, and has recommended himself only at table.

(5) To be on the *carpet,* is the subject of consideration; an affair in hand.

cat. A domestick animal that catches mice, commonly reckoned by naturalists the lowest order of the leonine species.

chi'cken. (3) A term for a young girl.

chiru'rgeon. One that cures ailments, not by internal medicines, but outward applications. It is now generally pronounced, and by many written, *surgeon.*

chit. (1) A child; a baby. Generally used of young persons in contempt.

chop-house. A mean house of entertainment, where provision ready dressed is sold.

cit. An inhabitant of a city, in an ill sense. A pert low townsman; a pragmatical trader.

cli'cker. A low word for the servant of a salesman, who stands at the door to invite customers.

cliente'le. The condition or office of a client. A word scarcely used.

to coax. To wheedle; to flatter; to humour. A low word.

to co'lour. To blush. A low word, only used in conversation.

co'nfident. (5) Bold to a vice; elated with false opinion of his own excellencies; impudent.

conu'ndrum. A low jest; a quibble; a mean conceit: a cant word.

cough. A convulsion of the lungs, vellicated by some sharp serosity. It is pronounced *coff.*

cream. (1) The unctuous or oily part of milk, which, when it is cold, floats on the top, and is changed by the agitation of the churn into butter; the flower of milk.

cu'ckoo. (1) A bird which appears in the spring; and is said to suck the eggs of other birds, and lay her own to be hatched in their place; from which practice, it was usual to alarm a husband at the approach of an adulterer by calling *cuckoo,* which, by mistake, was in time applied to the husband. This bird is remarkable for the uniformity of his note, from which his name in most tongues seems to have been formed.

cu'dden, cu'ddy. (Without etymology.) A clown; a stupid rustick; a low dolt: a low bad word.

cu'lprit. (About this word there is great dispute. It is used by the judge at criminal trials, who, when the prisoner declares himself not guilty, and puts himself upon his trial, answers; *Culprit, God send thee a good deliverance.* It is likely that it is a corruption of *Qu'il paroit, May it so appear,* the wish of the judge being that the prisoner may be found innocent.) A man arraigned before his judge.

to cu'rtail. (*curto,* Latin. It was anciently written *curtal,* which perhaps is more proper; but dogs that had their tails cut, being called *curtal* dogs, the word was vulgarly conceived to mean originally *to cut the tail,* and was in time written according to that notion.) (1) To cut off; to cut short; to shorten.

cu'stard. A kind of sweetmeat made by boiling eggs with milk and sugar, 'till the whole thickens into a mass. It is a food much used in city feasts.

a dab. (4) (In low language.) An artist; a man expert at something. This is not used in writing.

da'pper. Little and active; lively without bulk. It is usually spoken in contempt.

da'rkling. (A participle, as it seems, from *darkle,* which yet I have never found.) Being in the dark; being without light: a word merely poetical.

dedica'tion. (2) A servile address to a patron.

dedica'tor. One who inscribes his work to a patron with compliment and servility.

deflora'tion. (2) A selection of that which is most valuable.

demu're. (2) Grave; affectedly modest: it is now generally taken in a sense of contempt.

den. (1) A cavern or hollow running horizontally, or with a small obliquity, under ground; distinct from a hole, which runs down perpendicularly.

dese'rver. A man who merits rewards. It is used, I think, only in a good sense.

de'spot. An absolute prince; one that governs with unlimited authority. This word is not in use, except as applied to some Dacian prince; as, the *despot* of Servia.

devote'e. One erroneously or superstitiously religious; a bigot.

di'ckens. A kind of adverbial exclamation, importing, as it seems, much the same with the *devil;* but I know not whence derived.

To disannu'l. (*dis* and *annul.* This word is formed contrary to analogy by those who not knowing the meaning of the word *annul,* intended to form a negative sense by the needless use

---

dedication. Johnson wrote only two dedications for his own books, his first, and, significantly, the *Plan of a Dictionary,* to Lord Chesterfield. But after he had written this definition, he wrote about twenty dedications for other people, none "servile."

of the negative particle. It ought therefore to be rejected as ungrammatical and barbarous.) To annul; to deprive of authority; to vacate; to make null; to make void; to nullify.

di'sard. A prattler; a boasting talker. This word is inserted both by Skinner and Junius; but I do not remember it.

disciplina'rian. (2) A follower of the presbyterian sect, so called from their perpetual clamour about discipline.

to disgui'se. (4) To deform by liquor: a low term.

to disse'ver. (*dis* and *sever*. In this word the particle *dis* makes no change in the signification, and therefore the word, though supported by great authorities, ought to be ejected from our language.) To part in two; to break; to divide; to sunder; to separate; to disunite.

ditch. (2) Any long narrow receptacle of water: used sometimes of a small river in contempt.

dog. (1) A domestick animal remarkably various in his species; comprising the mastiff, the spaniel, the buldog, the greyhound, the hound, the terrier, the curr, with many others. The larger sort are used as a guard; the less for sports.

(6) *Dog* is a particle added to any thing to mark meanness, or degeneracy, or worthlessness; as *dog* rose.

dose. (3) It is often used of the utmost quantity of strong liquor that a man can swallow. He has his *dose*, that is, he can carry off no more.

dug. (1) A pap; a nipple; a teat: spoken of beasts, or in malice or contempt of human beings.

(2) It seems to have been used formerly of the breast without reproach.

dull. (8) Not exhilarating; not delightful; as, *to make dictionaries is* dull *work*.

eame. Uncle: a word still used in the wilder parts of Staffordshire.

eme'rgence, eme'rgency. (4) Pressing necessity. A sense not proper.

enthu'siasm. (1) A vain belief of private revelation; a vain confidence of divine favour or communication.

e'ssay. (2) A loose sally of the mind; an irregular indigested piece; not a regular and orderly composition.

---

disannul. The ungrammatical barbarians quoted by Johnson are Hooker, Bacon, Herbert, and Sandys.

eame. Johnson was born in the Athens of Staffordshire, Lichfield.

exci'se. A hateful tax levied upon commodities, and adjudged not by the common judges of property, but wretches hired by those to whom excise is paid.

eyese'rvant. A servant that works only while watched.

fa'ngle. Silly attempt; trifling scheme. It is never used, or rarely, but in contempt with the epithet *new;* as, *new fangles, new fangleness.*

fasti'dious. Disdainful; squeamish; delicate to a vice; insolently nice.

fa'vourite. (2) One chosen as a companion by his superiour; a mean wretch whose whole business is by any means to please.

fib. (A cant word among children.) A lye; a falsehood.

to fidge, to fi'dget. (A cant word.) To move nimbly and irregularly. It implies in Scotland agitation.

fi'tchat, fi'tchew. A stinking little beast, that robs the henroost and warren. Skinner calls him the *stinking ferret;* but he is much larger, at least as some provinces distinguish them, in which the polecat is termed a *fitchat,* and the *stinking ferret* a stoat.

fitz. A son. Only used in law and genealogy: as *Fitzherbert,* the son of Herbert; *Fitzthomas,* the son of Thomas; *Fitzroy,* the son of the king. It is commonly used of illegitimate children.

flippa'nt. (A word of no great authority, probably derived from *flip-flap.*) (1) Nimble; moveable. It is used only of the act of speech.

flirta'tion. A quick sprightly motion. A cant word among women.

to flit. (2) To remove; to migrate. In Scotland it is still used for removing from one place to another at quarter-day, or the usual term.

flush. (2) Affluent; abounding. A cant word.

foo'tlicker. A slave; an humble fawner; one who licks the foot.

fo'pdoodle. A fool; an insignificant wretch.

freethi'nker. A libertine; a contemner of religion.

fri'ghtful. (2) A cant word among women for any thing unpleasing.

fume'tte. A word introduced by cooks, and the pupils of cooks, for the stink of meat.

fun. (A low cant word.) Sport; high merriment; frolicksome delight.

---

excise. Johnson's father had had trouble with the commissioners of excise, in the conduct of his business as a bookseller and maker of parchment.

fuss. (A low cant word.) A tumult; a bustle.

ga'mbler. (A cant word, I suppose, for *game,* or *gamester.*) A knave whose practice it is to invite the unwary to game and cheat them.

gang. A number herding together; a troop; a company; a tribe; a herd. It is seldom used but in contempt or abhorrence.

gaol. A prison; a place of confinement. It is always pronounced and too often written *jail,* and sometimes *goal.*

gazette'er. (2) It was lately a term of the utmost infamy, being usually applied to wretches who were hired to vindicate the court.

to gi'ggle. To laugh idly; to titter; to grin with merry levity. It is retained in Scotland.

goat. A ruminant animal that seems a middle species between deer and sheep.

gob. A small quantity. A low word.

to go'spel. To fill with sentiments of religion. This word in Shakespeare, in whom alone I have found it, is used, though so venerable in itself, with some degree of irony: I suppose from the gospellers, who had long been held in contempt.

go'speller. A name of the followers of Wicklif, who first attempted a reformation from popery, given them by the Papists in reproach, from their professing to follow and preach only the gospel.

gra'vy. The serous juice that runs from flesh not much dried by the fire.

to grease. (2) To bribe; to corrupt with presents.

gru'bstreet. Originally the name of a street in Moorfields in London, much inhabited by writers of small histories, dictionaries, and temporary poems; whence any mean production is called grubstreet.

> Χαῖρ' Ἰθάκη μετ' ἄεθλα μετ' ἄλγεα πικρὰ
> Ἀσπασίως τεὸν οὖδας ἱκάνομαι.

half-seas over. A proverbial expression for any one far advanced. It is commonly used of one half drunk.

ha'tchet-face. An ugly face; such, I suppose, as might be hewn out of a block by a hatchet.

---

grubstreet. Johnson never lived in Grub Street, but he salutes that home of poor writers like himself with the quotation: "Hail, Ithaca! After toil and bitter woe, I am glad to reach your soil" (*Greek Anthology,* IX. 458).

to hiss. To utter a noise like that of a serpent and some other animals. It is remarkable, that this word cannot be pronounced without making the noise which it signifies.

hop. (3) A place where meaner people dance.

ho'peful. (2) Full of hope; full of expectation of success. This sense is now almost confined to Scotland, though it is analogical, and found in good writers.

ho'rrid. (2) Shocking; offensive; unpleasing: in womens cant.

horse. (1) A neighing quadruped, used in war, and draught and carriage.

hu'swife. (1) A bad manager; a sorry woman. It is common to use *housewife* in a good, and *huswife* or *hussy* in a bad sense.

ice. (3) To break the ice. To make the first opening to any attempt.

immate'rial. (2) Unimportant; without weight; impertinent; without relation. This sense has crept into the conversation and writings of barbarians; but ought to be utterly rejected.

ink. The black liquor with which men write.

irre'gular. (3) Not being according to the laws of virtue. A soft word for *vitious*.

itch. (1) A cutaneous disease extremely contagious, which overspreads the body with small pustules filled with a thin serum, and raised as microscopes have discovered by a small animal. It is cured by sulphur.

ja'ilbird. One who has been in a jail.

je'opardy. Hazard; danger; peril. A word not now in use.

job. (A low word now much in use, of which I cannot tell the etymology.) (1) A low mean lucrative busy affair.

ju'ncate. (3) A furtive or private entertainment. It is now improperly written *junket* in this sense, which alone remains much in use.

to knu'ckle. To submit: I suppose from an odd custom of striking the under side of the table with the knuckles, in confession of an argumental defeat.

lack. (1) Want; need; failure.

(2) *Lack*, whether noun or verb, is now almost obsolete.

la'ntern jaws. A term used of a thin visage, such as if a candle were burning in the mouth might transmit the light.

lass. A girl; a maid; a young woman: used now only of mean girls.

lead. Guidance; first place: a low despicable word.

le'sser. A barbarous corruption of *less,* formed by the vulgar from the habit of terminating comparatives in *er;* afterwards adopted by poets, and then by writers of prose.

lexico'grapher. A writer of dictionaries; a harmless drudge, that busies himself in tracing the original, and detailing the signification of words.

lich. A dead carcase; whence *lichwake,* the time or act of watching by the dead; *lichgate,* the gate through which the dead are carried to the grave; *Lichfield,* the field of the dead, a city in Staffordshire, so named from martyred christians. *Salve magna parens. Lichwake* is still retained in Scotland in the same sense.

li'ngo. Language; tongue; speech. A low cant word.

li'on. The fiercest and most magnanimous of fourfooted beasts.

lipla'bour. Action of the lips without concurrence of the mind; words without sentiments.

load. (3) As much drink as one can bear.

to loll. (Of this word the etymology is not known. Perhaps it might be contemptuously derived from *lollard,* a name of great reproach before the reformation; of whom one tenet was, that all trades not necessary to life are unlawful.) (1) To lean idly; to rest lazily against any thing.

lunch, lu'ncheon. As much food as one's hand can hold.

magazi'ne. (2) Of late this word has signified a miscellaneous pamphlet, from a periodical miscellany named the *Gentleman's Magazine,* by Edward Cave.

ma'udlin. (*Maudlin* is the corrupt appellation of *Magdelen,* who being drawn by painters with swoln eyes, and disordered look, a drunken countenance, seems to have been so named from a ludicrous resemblance to the picture of *Magdelen.*) Drunk; fuddled.

meeting-house. Place where Dissenters assemble to worship.

me'rrythought. A forked bone on the body of fowls; so called be-

---

lich. Johnson's salutation to his birthplace, his "great parent," is, as with many of his most personal remarks, "veiled in the obscurity of a learned language."

magazine. Johnson had edited the *Gentleman's Magazine* under Cave, the founder and publisher of the first general magazine in English. Cave had died recently, and this reference memorializes a long-time friend.

cause boys and girls pull in play at the two sides, the longest part broken off betokening priority of marriage.

me'thodist. (2) One of a new kind of puritans lately arisen, so called from their profession to live by rules and in constant method.

mo'nsieur. A term of reproach for a Frenchman.

mould. (1) A kind of concretion on the top or outside of things kept, motionless and damp; now discovered by microscopes to be perfect plants.

to mu'cker. To scramble for money; to hoard up; to get or save meanly: a word used by Chaucer, and still retained in conversation.

mum. (Of this word I know not the original: it may be observed, that when it is pronounced it leaves the lips closed.) A word denoting prohibition to speak, or resolution not to speak; silence; hush.

mu'shroom. (2) An upstart; a wretch risen from the dunghill; a director of a company.

ne'twork. Any thing reticulated or decussated, at equal distances, with interstices between the intersections.

oats. A grain, which in England is generally given to horses, but in Scotland supports the people.

ode. A poem written to be sung to musick; a lyrick poem; the ode is either of the greater or less kind. The less is characterised by sweetness and ease; the greater by sublimity, rapture, and quickness of transition.

to owe. (5) A practice has long prevailed among writers, to use *owing*, the active participle of *owe*, in a passive sense, for *owed* or *due*. Of this impropriety Bolinbroke was aware, and, having no quick sense of the force of English words, has used *due*, in the sense of consequence or imputation, which by other writers is only used of *debt*. We say, the money is *due* to me; Bolinbroke says, the effect is *due* to the cause.

pailma'il. (This is commonly written pellmell; nor do I know which of the two is right.) Violent, boisterous.

pamphletee'r. A scribbler of small books.

pa'ramour. (1) A lover or wooer.

(2) A mistress. It is obsolete in both senses, though not inelegant or unmusical.

pa'rasite. One that frequents rich tables, and earns his welcome by flattery.

pa'stern. (1) The knee of an horse.

pat. Fit; convenient; exactly suitable either as to time or place. This is a low word, and should not be used but in burlesque writings.

pa'triot. One whose ruling passion is the love of his country.

pa'tron. (1) One who countenances, supports or protects. Commonly a wretch who supports with insolence, and is paid with flattery.

pe'dant. (2) A man vain of low knowledge; a man awkwardly ostentatious of his literature.

pe'nguin. (1) A bird. This bird was found with this name, as is supposed, by the first discoverers of America; and *penguin* signifying in Welsh a white head, and the head of this fowl being white, it has been imagined, that America was peopled from Wales; whence *Hudibras:*

British Indians nam'd from *penguins.*

Grew gives another account of the name, deriving it from *pinguis,* Lat. *fat;* but is, I believe, mistaken.

pe'nsion. An allowance made to any one without an equivalent. In England it is generally understood to mean pay given to a state hireling for treason to his country.

pe'nsioner. (2) A slave of state hired by a stipend to obey his master.

picktha'nk. An officious fellow, who does what he is not desired; a whispering parasite.

pi'rate. (2) Any robber; particularly a bookseller who seizes the copies of other men.

to pla'cate. To appease; to reconcile. This word is used in Scotland.

po'sse. An armed power; from *posse comitatus,* the power of the shires. A low word.

---

pastern. (1) In fact, part of the foot of a horse. When a lady asked Johnson how he came to define the word in this way, he answered, "Ignorance, Madam, pure ignorance." But he didn't bother to correct his definition until eighteen years later.

patriot. The fourth edition adds: "It is sometimes used for a factious disturber of the government."

preca'rious. Dependent; uncertain, because depending on the will of another; held by courtesy; changeable or alienable at the pleasure of another. No word is more unskilfully used than this with its derivatives. It is used for *uncertain* in all its senses; but it only means uncertain, as dependent on others; thus there are authors who mention the *precariousness* of an *account*, of the *weather*, of a *die*.

to prejudi'ce. (3) To injure; to hurt; to diminish; to impair; to be detrimental to. This sense, as in the noun, is often improperly extended to meanings that have no relation to the original sense; who can read with patience of an ingredient that *prejudices* a medicine?

presbyte'rian. An abettor of presbytery or calvinistical discipline.

prig. (A cant word derived perhaps from *prick*, as he *pricks* up, he is *pert;* or from *prickeared*, an epithet of reproach bestowed upon the presbyterian teachers.) A pert, conceited, saucy, pragmatical, little fellow.

pro. For; in defence of; *pro* and *con*, for *pro* and *contra*, for and against. Despicable cant.

pro'ceed. Produce: as, *the* proceeds *of an estate. Clarissa.* Not an imitable word, though much used in law writings.

pu'nster. A quibbler; a low wit who endeavours at reputation by double meaning.

pu'rist. One superstitiously nice in the use of words.

pu'ritan. A sectary pretending to eminent purity of religion.

to refu'nd. (3) Swift has somewhere the absurd phrase, *to* refund *himself*, for to *reimburse*.

reli'gionist. A bigot to any religious persuasion.

to restri'ct. To limit; to confine. A word scarce English.

reti'culated. Made of network; formed with interstitial vacuities.

rhino'ceros. A vast beast in the East Indies armed with a horn in his front.

to rise. (1) To change a jacent or recumbent, to an erect posture.

to roll. (1) To be moved by the successive application of all parts of the surface to the ground.

---

refund. "The printer has a demand . . . to be fully refunded, both for his disgraces, his losses, and the apparent danger of his life." Swift, letter to Bishop Hort, May 12, 1736, cited by *O.E.D.*

ruse. Cunning; artifice; little stratagem; trick; wile; fraud; deceit. A French word neither elegant nor necessary.

sa'tire. A poem in which wickedness or folly is censured. Proper *satire* is distinguished, by the generality of the reflections, from a *lampoon* which is aimed against a particular person; but they are too frequently confounded.

sco'rpion. (1) A reptile much resembling a small lobster, but that his tail ends in a point with a very venomous sting.

se'nsible. (8) In low conversation it has sometimes the sense of reasonable; judicious; wise.

sha'bby. (A word that has crept into conversation and low writing; but ought not to be admitted into the language.) Mean; paltry.

sheep. (1) The animal that bears wool: remarkable for its usefulness and innocence.

shre'wmouse. A mouse of which the bite is generally supposed venomous, and to which vulgar tradition assigns such malignity, that she is said to lame the foot over which she runs. I am informed that all these reports are calumnious, and that her feet and teeth are equally harmless with those of any other little mouse. Our ancestors however looked on her with such terrour, that they are supposed to have given her name to a scolding woman, whom for her venom they call a *shrew*.

slim. (A cant word as it seems, and therefore not to be used.) Slender; thin of shape.

smu'ggler. A wretch, who, in defiance of justice and the laws, imports or exports goods either contraband or without payment of the customs.

snake. A serpent of the oviparous kind, distinguished from a viper. The snake's bite is harmless. *Snake* in poetry is a general name for a viper.

to sneeze. To emit wind audibly by the nose.

so'nnet. (1) A short poem consisting of fourteen lines, of which the rhymes are adjusted by a particular rule. It is not very suitable to the English language, and has not been used by any man of eminence since Milton.

soup. Strong decoction of flesh for the table.

spa'niel. (2) A low, mean, sneaking fellow; a courtier; a dedicator; a pensioner; a dependant; a placeman.

spick and span. (This word I should not have expected to have found authorised by a polite writer. *Span-new* is used by Chaucer, and is supposed to come from *spannan,* to stretch, Sax. *expandere,* Lat. whence *span. Span-new* is therefore originally used of cloath new extended or dressed at the clothiers, and *spick and span* is newly extended on the *spikes* or tenters: it is however a low word.) Quite new; now first used.

sta'teswoman. A woman who meddles with publick affairs. In contempt.

sto'ckjobber. A low wretch who gets money by buying and selling shares in the funds.

stu'rdy. (1) Hardy; stout; brutal; obstinate. It is always used of men with some disagreeable idea of coarseness or rudeness.

suds. (1) A lixivium of soap and water.

(2) To be in the suds. A familiar phrase for being in any difficulty.

swe'arer. A wretch who obtests the great name wantonly and profanely.

tail. (1) That which terminates the animal behind; the continuation of the vertebrae of the back hanging loose behind.

tale. (1) A narrative; a story. Commonly a slight or petty account of some trifling or fabulous incident: as, *a* tale *of a tub.*

tar. A sailor; a seaman in contempt.

ta'wdry. Meanly shewy; splendid without cost; fine without grace; shewy without elegance. It is used both of things and of persons wearing them.

ti'ny. Little; small; puny. A burlesque word.

toad. An animal resembling a frog; but the frog leaps, the toad crawls: the toad is accounted venomous, I believe truly.

too. (1) Over and above; overmuch; more than enough. It is used to augment the signification of an adjective or adverb to a vicious degree.

to'ry. (A cant term, derived, I suppose, from an Irish word signifying a savage.) One who adheres to the antient constitution of the state, and the apostolical hierarchy of the church of England, opposed to a whig.

---

tale. Johnson told Boswell that he thought *A Tale of a Tub* too brilliant to have been written by Swift.

tra'desman. A shopkeeper. A merchant is called a *trader,* but not a tradesman; and it seems distinguished in Shakespeare from a man that labours with his hands.

to traipse. (A low word, I believe, without any etymology.) To walk in a careless or sluttish manner.

tu'rtle. It is used among sailors and gluttons for a tortoise.

to unphilo'sophize. To degrade from the character of a philosopher. A word made by Pope.

ve'rdant. Green. This word is so lately naturalized, that Skinner could find it only in a dictionary.

vi'sion. (4) A dream; something shewn in a dream. A dream happens to a sleeping, a vision may happen to a waking man. A dream is supposed natural, a vision miraculous; but they are confounded.

viz. (This word is *videlicet,* written with a contraction.) To wit; that is. A barbarous form of an unnecessary word.

to voluntee'r. To go for a soldier. A cant word.

whig. (2) The name of a faction.

wi'tticism. A mean attempt at wit.

to worm. (2) To deprive a dog of something, nobody knows what, under his tongue, which is said to prevent him, nobody knows why, from running mad.

would. (8) It has the signification of I wish, or I pray; this, I believe, is improper; and formed by a gradual corruption of the phrase, *would God;* which originally imputed, *that God would, might God will, might God decree;* from this phrase ill understood came, *would to God;* thence, *I would to God:* And thence *I would,* or elliptically, *would* come to signify, *I wish:* and so it is used even in good authours, but ought not to be imitated.

ye'llowboy. A gold coin. A very low word.

you'ngster, you'nker. A young person. In contempt.

---

turtle. A curious example of Johnson's conservatism: the better classes would speak of "tortoise steak or soup"; vulgarians like sailors or gluttons would talk of "turtle soup."

The Rambler *followed in the tradition of Addison and Steele's* Tatler *and* Spectator. *It was an anonymous, separately published folio of three leaves, appearing on Tuesdays and Saturdays from March 20, 1750, to March 14, 1752. Johnson added a table of contents and translations of the mottoes at the end of the first edition. Even before the end of the original run, Edinburgh and London reprints in small volumes had begun to appear, and about ten more reprints followed during his lifetime. Now reprinted from the first edition.*

The Rambler

No. 4. Saturday, March 31, 1750

Simul et jucunda et idonea dicere Vitae.
HOR. [*Ars. Poet.* 334.]

And join both profit and delight in one.
CREECH.

The works of fiction, with which the present generation seems more particularly delighted, are such as exhibit life in its true state, diversified only by the accidents that daily happen in the world, and influenced by those passions and qualities which are really to be found in conversing with mankind.

This kind of writing may be termed not improperly the comedy of romance, and is to be conducted nearly by the rules of comic poetry. Its province is to bring about natural events by easy means, and to keep up curiosity without the help of wonder; it is therefore precluded from the machines and expedients of the heroic romance, and can neither employ giants to snatch away a lady from the nuptial rites, nor knights to bring her back from captivity; it can neither bewilder its personages in desarts, nor lodge them in imaginary castles.

I remember a remark made by Scaliger upon Pontanus, that all his writings are filled with images, and that if you take from him his lillies and his roses, his satyrs and his dryads, he will have nothing left that can be called poetry. In like manner, almost all the fictions of the last age will vanish, if you deprive them of a hermit and a wood, a battle and a shipwreck.

Why this wild strain of imagination found reception so long, in polite and learned ages, it is not easy to conceive; but we cannot wonder, that, while readers could be procured, the authors were willing to continue it: For when a man had, by practice, gained some fluency of language, he had no farther care than to retire to his closet, to let loose his invention, and heat his mind with incredibilities; and a book was produced without fear of criticism, without the toil of study, without knowledge of nature, or acquaintance with life.

The task of our present writers is very different; it requires, together with that learning which is to be gained from books, that experience which can never be attained by solitary diligence, but must arise from general converse, and accurate observation of the living world. Their performances have, as Horace expresses it, *plus oneris quantum veniae minus,* little indulgence, and therefore more difficulty. They are engaged in portraits of which every one knows the original, and can therefore detect any deviation from exactness of resemblance. Other writings are safe, except from the malice of learning; but these are in danger from every common reader; as the slipper ill executed was censured by a shoemaker who happened to stop in his way at the Venus of Apelles.

But the danger of not being approved as just copyers of human manners, is not the most important apprehension that an author of this sort ought to have before him. These books are written chiefly to the young, the ignorant, and the idle, to whom they serve as lectures of conduct, and introductions into life. They are the entertainment of minds unfurnished with ideas, and therefore easily susceptible of impressions; not fixed by principles, and therefore easily following the current of fancy; not informed by experience, and consequently open to every false suggestion and partial account.

That the highest degree of reverence should be paid to youth, and that nothing indecent or unseemly should be suffered to approach their eyes or ears, are precepts extorted by sense and virtue from an ancient writer by no means eminent for chastity of thought. The same kind, tho' not the same degree of caution, is required in every thing which is laid before them, to secure them from unjust prejudices, perverse opinions, and improper combinations of images.

In the romances formerly written every transaction and sentiment was so remote from all that passes among men, that the reader was in very little danger of making any applications to himself; the virtues and crimes were equally beyond his sphere of activity; and he amused himself with heroes and with traitors, deliverers and persecutors, as with beings of another species, whose actions were regulated upon motives of their own, and who had neither faults nor excellencies in common with himself.

But when an adventurer is levelled with the rest of the world, and acts in such scenes of the universal drama, as may be the lot of any other man, young spectators fix their eyes upon him with closer attention, and hope by observing his behaviour and success to regulate their own practices, when they shall be engaged in the like part.

For this reason these familiar histories may perhaps be made of greater use than the solemnities of professed morality, and convey the knowledge of vice and virtue with more efficacy than axioms and definitions. But if the power of example is so great, as to take possession of the memory by a kind of violence, and produce effects almost without the intervention of the will, care ought to be taken that, when the choice is unrestrained, the best examples only should be exhibited; and that which is likely to operate so strongly, should not be mischievous or uncertain in its effects.

The chief advantages which these fictions have over real life is, that their authors are at liberty, tho' not to invent, yet to select objects, and to cull from the mass of mankind, those individuals upon which the attention ought most to be employ'd; as a diamond, though it cannot be made, may be polished by art, and placed in such a situation, as to display that lustre which before was buried among common stones.

It is justly considered as the greatest excellency of art, to imitate nature; but it is necessary to distinguish those parts of nature, which are most proper for imitation: Greater care is still required in representing life, which is so often discoloured by passion, or deformed by wickedness. If the world be promiscuously described, I cannot see of what use it can be to read the account; or why it may not be as safe to turn the eye immediately upon mankind, as upon a mirrour which shows all that presents itself without discrimination.

It is therefore not a sufficient vindication of a character, that it is drawn as it appears; for many characters ought never to be drawn; nor of a narrative, that the train of events is agreeable to observation and experience; for that observation which is called knowledge of the world, will be found much more frequently to make men cunning than good. The purpose of these writings is surely not only to show mankind, but to provide that they may be seen hereafter with less hazard; to teach the means of avoiding the snares which are laid by *treachery* for *innocence,* without infusing any wish for that superiority with which the betrayer flatters his vanity; to give the power of counteracting fraud without the temptation to practise it; to initiate youth by mock encounters in the art of necessary defence, and to increase prudence without impairing virtue.

Many writers for the sake of following nature, so mingle good and bad qualities in their principal personages, that they are both equally conspicuous; and as we accompany them through their adventures with delight, and are led by degrees to interest ourselves in their favour, we lose the abhorrence of their faults, because they do not hinder our pleasure, or, perhaps, regard them with some kindness for being united with so much merit.

There have been men indeed splendidly wicked, whose endowments throw a brightness on their crimes, and whom scarce any villainy made perfectly detestable, because they never could be wholly divested of their excellencies; but such have been in all ages the great corrupters of the world, and their resemblance ought no more to be preserved, than the art of murdering without pain.

Some have advanced, without due attention to the consequences of this notion, that certain virtues have their correspondent faults, and therefore to exhibit either apart is to deviate from probability.

Thus men are observed by Swift to be grateful in the same degree as they are resentful. This principle, with others of the same kind, supposes man to act from a brute impulse, and pursue a certain degree of inclination, without any choice of the object; for, otherwise, though it should be allow'd that gratitude and resentment arise from the same constitution of the passions, it follows not that they will be equally indulged when reason is consulted; and unless that consequence be admitted, this sagacious maxim becomes an empty sound, without any relation to practice or to life.

Nor is it evident, that even the first motions to these effects are always in the same proportion. For pride, which produces quickness of resentment, will frequently obstruct gratitude, by an unwillingness to admit that inferiority which obligation necessarily implies; and it is surely very unlikely, that he who cannot think he receives a favour will ever acknowledge it.

It is of the utmost importance to mankind, that positions of this tendency should be laid open and confuted; for while men consider good and evil as springing from the same root, they will spare the one for the sake of the other, and in judging, if not of others at least of themselves, will be apt to estimate their virtues by their vices. To this fatal error all those will contribute, who confound the colours of right and wrong, and instead of helping to settle their boundaries, mix them with so much art, that no common mind is able to disunite them.

In narratives, where historical veracity has no place, I cannot discover why there should not be exhibited the most perfect idea of virtue; of virtue not angelical, nor above probability; for what we cannot credit we shall never imitate; but of the highest and purest kind that humanity can reach, which, when exercised in such trials as the various revolutions of things shall bring upon it, may, by conquering some calamities, and enduring others, teach us what we may hope, and what we can perform. Vice, for vice is necessary to be shewn, should always disgust; nor should the graces of gaiety, or the dignity of courage, be so united with it, as to reconcile it to the mind. Wherever it appears, it should raise hatred by the malignity of its practices; and contempt, by the meanness of its stratagems; for while it is supported by either parts or spirit, it will be seldom heartily abhorred. The Roman tyrant was content to be hated, if he was but feared; and there are thousands of the readers of romances willing to be thought wicked, if they may be allowed to be wits. It is therefore to be always inculcated, that virtue is the highest proof of a superior understanding, and the only solid basis of greatness; and that vice is the natural consequence of narrow thoughts; that it begins in mistake, and ends in ignominy.

No. 18. Saturday, May 19, 1750

Illic matre carentibus
Privignis mulier temperat innocens,
Nec dotata regit virum
Conjux, nec nitido fidit adultero;
Dos est magna parentium
Virtus, et metuens alterius tori
Certo foedere castitas. Hor. [*Odes,* III.xxiv.17.]

Not there the guiltless stepdame knows
The baleful draught for orphans to compose;
No wife high portion'd rules her spouse,
Or trusts her essenc'd lover's faithless vows:
The lovers there for dowry claim
The father's virtue, and the spotless fame,
Which dares not break the nuptial tie.

Francis.

There is no observation more frequently made by such as employ themselves in surveying the conduct of mankind, than that marriage, though the dictate of nature, and the institution of providence, is yet very often the cause of misery, and that those who enter into that state can seldom forbear to express their repentance of the folly, and their envy of those, whom either chance, or caution, has withheld from it.

This general unhappiness has given occasion to many sage maxims among the serious, and many smart remarks among the gay; the moralist and the writer of epigrams have equally shown their abilities upon it; some have lamented, and some have ridiculed it; but as the faculty of writing has been, in all ages, chiefly a masculine endowment, the reproach of making the world miserable has been almost always thrown upon the women, and the grave and the merry have equally thought themselves at liberty to conclude either with declamatory complaints, or satyrical censures of female folly or fickleness, ambition or cruelty, extravagance or lust.

Led by such a number of examples, and incited by my share in the common interest, I have sometimes ventured to consider this universal grievance, having endeavoured to divest my heart of all partiality, and place myself as a kind of neutral being between the sexes, whose clamours, if we attend only to the world passing before us, being equally loud, and vented on both sides with all the vehemence of distress, all the apparent confidence of justice, and all the indignation of injured virtue, seem therefore entitled to equal regard. The men have, indeed, by their superiority of writing, been able to collect the evidence of many ages, and raise prejudices in their favour by the venerable testimonies of philosophers, historians and poets. But the pleas of the ladies appeal to passions of more forcible operation than the reverence of antiquity; if they have not so great names on their side, they have stronger arguments; it is to little purpose that Socrates, or Euripides, are produced against the sighs of softness, and the tears of beauty. The most frigid and inexorable judge would, at least, stand suspended between equal powers, as Lucan was perplexed in the determination of the cause, where the deities were on one side, and Cato on the other.

But I, who have long studied the severest and most abstracted philosophy, have now, in the cool maturity of life, arrived to such command over my passions, that I can hear the vociferations of either sex, without catching any of the fire from those that utter them. For I have found, by long experience, that a man will sometimes rage at his wife, when in reality his mistress has offended him; and a lady complain of the cruelty of her husband, when she has no other enemy than bad cards. I do not suffer myself now to be any longer imposed upon by oaths on one side, or fits on the other; nor, when the husband retires to punch, and the lady to citron water, am I always confident that they are driven to it by their miseries; since I have sometimes reason to believe, that they purpose not so much to sooth their sorrows, as to animate their fury. But how little credit soever may be given to particular accusations, the general accumulation of the charge shews, with too much evidence, that married persons are not very often advanced in felicity; and, therefore, it may be no improper enquiry to examine at what avenues so many evils have made their way into the world. With this purpose, I have reviewed the lives of many of my friends, who have been least successful in connubial contracts, and attentively considered by what motives they were incited to marry, and by what principles they regulated their choice.

One of the first of my acquaintances that resolved to quit the unsettled thoughtless condition of a batchelor was Prudentius; a man of slow parts, but not without knowledge, or judgment, in things which he had leisure to consider gradually before he determined them. Whenever we met at a tavern, it was his province to settle the scheme of our entertainment, contract with the cook, and inform us when we had called for wine to the sum originally proposed. This grave considerer found, by deep meditation, that a man was no loser by marrying early, even though he contented himself with a less fortune; for estimating the exact worth of annuities, he found that, considering the constant diminution of the value of life, with the probable fall of the interest of money, it was not worse to have ten thousand pounds at the age of two and twenty years, than a much larger fortune at thirty; for many opportunities, says he, occur of improving money, which if a man misses, he may not afterwards recover.

Full of these reflections he threw his eyes about him, not in search of beauty, or elegance, or dignity, or understanding, but of a woman with ten thousand pounds. Such a woman, in a wealthy part of the kingdom, it was not very difficult to find; and by artful management with her father, whose ambition was to make his daughter a gentlewoman, my friend got her, as he boasted to us in confidence two days after his marriage, for a settlement of seventy three pounds a year less than her fortune might have claimed, and less than he would himself have given, if the fools had been but wise enough to conduct their bargain.

Thus, at once delighted with the superiority of his parts, and the augmentation of his fortune, he carried Furia to his own house, in which he never afterwards enjoyed one hour of happiness. For Furia was a wretch of mean intellects, violent passions, a strong voice, and low education, without any sense of happiness but that which consisted in eating, and counting money. Furia was a scold. They agreed in the desire of wealth, but with this difference, that Prudentius was for growing rich by gain, Furia by parsimony. Prudentius would venture his money with the chances very much in his favour; but Furia very wisely observed, that what they had was, while they had it, *their own,* thought all traffick too great a hazard, and was for putting it out at low interest, upon good security. Prudentius ventured, however, to insure a ship, at a very unreasonable price, but happening to lose his money, was so tormented with the clamours of his wife, that he never durst try a second experiment. He has now grovelled seven and forty years under Furia's direction, who has never mentioned him, since his bad luck, by any other name than that of *the insurer.*

The next that married from our society was Florentius. He happened to see Zephyretta in a chariot at a horse-race, danced with her at night, and was confirmed in his first ardour; waited on her next morning, and declared himself her lover. Florentius had not knowledge enough of the world, to distinguish between the flutter of coquetry, and the sprightliness of wit, or between the smile of allurement, and that of chearfulness. He was soon waked from his rapture by conviction that his pleasure was but the pleasure of a day. Zephyretta had in four and twenty hours spent her stock of repartee, gone round the circle of her airs, and had nothing remaining for him but childish insipidity, or for herself, but the practice of the same artifices upon new men; by which she is every day bringing contempt upon them both.

Melissus was a man of parts, capable of enjoying, and of improving life. He had passed through the various scenes of gayety with that indifference and possession of himself, natural to men who have something higher and nobler in their prospect. He retired to spend the summer in a village little frequented, where happening to lodge in the same house with Ianthe, he was unavoidably drawn to some acquaintance, which her wit and politeness soon invited him to improve. Having no opportunity of any other company, they were always together; and, as they owed their pleasures to each other, they began to forget that any pleasure was enjoyed before their meeting. Melissus from being delighted with her company, quickly began to be uneasy in her absence, and being sufficiently convinced of the merit of her understanding, and finding, as he imagined, such a conformity of temper as declared them formed for each other, he addressed her as a lover, after no very long courtship obtained her for his wife, and brought her next winter to town in triumph.

Now began their infelicity. Melissus had only seen her in one scene, where there was no variety of objects to produce the proper excitements to contrary desires. They had both loved solitude and reflection, where there was nothing but solitude and reflection to be loved. But, when they came into publick life, Ianthe discovered those passions which accident rather than hypocrisy had hitherto concealed. She was, indeed, not without the power of thinking, for that he would have detected, but was wholly without the exertion of that power, when either gayety, or splendour, played on her imagination. She was expensive in her diversions, vehement in her passions, insatiate of pleasure however dangerous to her reputation, and eager of applause by whomsoever it could be given. This was the wife which Melissus the philosopher found in his retirement, and from whom he expected an associate in his studies, and an assistant to his virtues.

Prosapius, upon the death of his younger brother, that the family might not be extinct, married his housekeeper, and has ever since been complaining to his friends, that mean notions are instilled into his children, that he is ashamed to sit at his own table, and that his house is uneasy to him for want of suitable companions.

Avaro, master of a very large estate, took a woman of bad reputation, recommended to him by a rich uncle, who made that marriage the condition on which he should be his heir. Avaro now wonders to perceive his own fortune, his wife's, and his uncle's, insufficient to give him that happiness, which is to be found only with a woman of virtue.

I intend to treat in more papers on this important article of life, to recount the reasons, which influenced not on[ly] others among my friends, but likewise some ladies whom I have known, in the choice of an inseparable companion, and give account of other causes which have disappointed the hope of lovers, I shall, therefore, make no reflexion upon these histories, except that all whom I have mentioned failed to obtain happiness, for want of considering that marriage is the strictest tye of perpetual friendship;

that there can be no friendship without confidence, and no confidence without integrity; and that he, therefore, must expect to be wretched, who pays to beauty, riches, or politeness, that regard which only virtue and piety can justly claim.

No. 21. Tuesday, May 29, 1750

Terra salutiferas herbas, eademque nocentes,
Nutrit; et urticae proxima saepe rosa est.
OVID. [*Remedia Amoris,* 45.]

Our bane and physick the same earth bestows,
And near the noisome nettle blooms the rose.

Every man is prompted by the love of himself to imagine, that he possesses some peculiar qualities superior, either in kind or in degree, to those which he sees allotted to the rest of the world; and whatever apparent disadvantages he may suffer in the comparison with others, he has some invisible distinctions, some latent reserve of excellence, which he throws into the balance, and by which he generally fancies that it is turned in his favour.

The studious and speculative part of mankind have always seemed to consider their fraternity, as placed in a state of opposition to those, who are engaged in the tumult of public business; and have pleased themselves, from age to age, with celebrating the felicity of their own condition, and with recounting the perplexity of politics, the dangers of greatness, the anxieties of ambition, and the miseries of riches.

Among the numerous topics of declamation, that their industry has discovered on this subject, there is none which they press with greater efforts, or on which they have more copiously laid out their reason and their imagination, than the instability of high stations, and the uncertainty with which those profits and honours are possessed, that must be acquired with so much hazard, vigilance and labour.

This they appear to consider as an irrefragable argument against the choice of the statesman and the warrior; to this weapon they have always recourse in their rhetorical attacks, and swell with all the confidence of victory, thus furnished by the Muses with the arms which never can be blunted, and which no art or strength of their adversaries can elude or resist.

It was well known by experience to the nations which employed elephants in war, that, though by the terror of their bulk, and the violence of their impression, they often threw the enemy into disorder, yet there was always danger in the use of them, very nearly equivalent to the advantage; for, if their first charge could be supported, they were easily driven back upon their confederates, they broke through the troops behind them, and made no less havock in the precipitation of their retreat, than in the fury of their onset.

I know not whether those, who have so vehemently urged the inconveniences and dangers of an active life, have not made use of arguments that may be retorted with equal force upon themselves; and whether the happiness of a candidate for literary fame be not subject to the same uncertainty, with that of him who governs provinces, or commands armies, presides in the senate, or dictates in the cabinet.

That eminence of learning is not to be gained without labour, at least equal to that which any other kind of greatness can require, will scarcely be denied by those who mean to elevate the character of a scholar; since they cannot but know, that every human acquisition is valuable in proportion to the difficulty implied in its attainment. And that those, who have gained the esteem and veneration of the world, by their knowledge or their genius, are by no means exempt from the solicitude which any other kind of dignity produces, may be conjectured from the innumerable artifices which they make use of to degrade a superior, to repress a rival, or obstruct a follower; artifices so gross and so mean, as to be an evident proof, how easily a man may excel in many kinds of learning, without being either more wise or more virtuous than those, whose ignorance he pities or despises.

Nothing therefore remains, by which the student can gratify his desire of appearing to have built his happiness on a more firm basis than his antagonist, except the security with which literary honours may be enjoyed. The garlands gained by the heroes of literature must be gathered from summits equally difficult to climb with those that bear the civic or triumphal wreaths, they must be worn with equal envy, and guarded with equal care from those hands that are always employed in efforts to tear them away; the only remaining hope is, that their verdure is more lasting, and that they are less likely to fade by time, or less obnoxious to the blasts of accident.

Even this hope will receive very little encouragement from the examination of literary history, or observation of the fate of scholars in the present age. If we look back into past times, we find innumerable names of authors once in high reputation, sung perhaps by the beautiful, quoted by the witty, and commented by the grave; but of whom we now know only that they once existed. If we consider the distribution of literary fame in our own time, we shall find it a possession of very uncertain tenure; sometimes bestowed by a sudden caprice of the public, and again transferred to a new favourite, for no other reason than that he is new; sometimes refused to long labour and eminent desert, and sometimes granted to very slight pretensions; lost sometimes by security and negligence, and sometimes by too diligent endeavours to retain it.

A successful author is equally in danger of the diminution of his fame, whether he continues or ceases to write. The regard of the public is not to be kept but by tribute, and the remembrance of past service will quickly languish, unless some new performance sometimes revives it. Yet in every new attempt there is new hazard, and there are few who do not, at some unlucky time, injure their own characters by attempting to enlarge them.

There are many possible causes of the inequality which we may so frequently observe in the performances of the same man, from the influence of which no ability or industry is sufficiently secured, and which have so often sullied the splendour of genius, that the wit, as well as the conqueror, may be properly cautioned not to indulge his pride with too early triumphs, but to defer to the end of life his estimate of happiness.

———————*Ultima semper*
Expectanda dies homini, dicique beatus
Ante obitum nemo supremaque funera debet
[OVID. *Metamorphoses,* III. 135.]

But no frail man, however great or high,
Can be concluded blest before he die.
ADDISON.

Among the motives which urge an author to undertakings that injure his reputation, one of the most frequent is scarcely to be mentioned; because it is not to be counted among his follies, but his miseries. It very often happens that the works of learning or of wit are performed at the direction of those by whom they are to be rewarded; the writer therefore has not always the choice of his subject, but is compelled to accept any task which is thrown before him, without much consideration of his own convenience, and without time to prepare himself for the execution by previous studies.

But miscarriages of this kind are likewise frequently the consequences of that acquaintance with the great, which is generally considered as one of the chief privileges of literature and genius. A man, who has once learned to think himself exalted by familiarity with those, whom nothing but their birth, or their fortunes, or such stations as are seldom gained by moral excellence, set above him, will not be long without submitting his understanding to their conduct, and suffering them to prescribe the course of his studies, and employ him for their own purposes either of diversion or interest. His desire of pleasing those whose favour he has weakly made necessary to himself, will not suffer him always to consider how little he is qualified for the work imposed, his vanity will not allow him to confess his deficiencies, or that cowardice, which always encroaches fast upon such as spend their lives in the company of persons higher than themselves, leaves them not resolution to assert the liberty of choice.

But though we suppose that a man has fortune to avoid the necessity of dependance, and spirit to repel the usurpations of patronage, yet he may easily, by writing long, happen to write ill. There is a general succession of effects, in which contraries are produced by periodical vicissitudes; labour and care are rewarded with success, success produces confidence, confidence relaxes industry, and negligence ruins that reputation which diligence had raised.

He that happens not to be lulled by praise into supineness, may be animated by it to undertakings above his strength, or incited to fancy himself alike qualified for every kind of composition, and able to comply with the public taste through all its variations. From some opinion like this, many men have engaged, at an advanced age, in attempts which they had not time to complete, and, after a few weak efforts, sunk into the grave with vexation to see the rising generation gain ground upon them. That judgment which appears often so penetrating, when it is employed upon the works of others, very often fails when it is applied to performances, where interest or passion can exert their power. We are blinded in examining our own labours by innumerable prejudices. Our juvenile compositions please us, because they bring to our minds the remembrance of youth; our later performances we are ready to esteem, because we are unwilling to think that we have made no improvement; what flows easily from the pen charms us, because we read with pleasure that which flatters our opinion of our own powers; what was composed with great struggles of the mind we are unwilling to reject, because we cannot bear that so much labour should be fruitless. But the reader has none of these prepossessions, and only wonders that the author is so unlike himself, without considering that the same soil will, with different culture, afford different products.

No. 31. Tuesday, July 3, 1750

Non ego mendosos ausim defendere mores
Falsaque pro vitiis arma tenere meis.
OVID. [*Amores,* II.iv.1.]

Corrupted manners I shall ne'er defend;
Nor, falsely witty, for my faults contend. ELPHINSTON.

Though the fallibility of man's reason, and the narrowness of his knowledge, be very generally and liberally confessed, yet if an enquiry be made into the conduct of those who so willingly admit the weakness of human nature, there will appear some reason for imagining that this acknowledgment is not altogether sincere, at least, that most make it with a tacit reserve in favour of themselves, and that with whatever ease they give up the claims of their neighbours, they are desirous of being thought exempt from faults in their own conduct, and from error in their opinions.

The certain and obstinate opposition, which we may observe

made to confutation, however clear, and to reproof however tender, is an undoubted argument, that some dormant privilege is thought to be attacked; for as no man can lose what he neither possesses, nor imagines himself to possess, nor be defrauded of that to which he has no right, it is reasonable to suppose that those who break out into fury at the first attacks of contradiction, or the slightest touches of censure, conceive some injury offered to their honour, some antient immunity violated, or some natural prerogative invaded; to be mistaken, if they thought themselves liable to mistake, could not be considered by them as either shameful or wonderful, and they would not surely receive with so much emotion intelligence which could only inform them of that which they knew before, or struggle with so much earnestness against a force that deprives them of nothing to which they thought themselves entitled.

It is related of one of the philosophers, that when an account was brought him of his son's death, he received it only with this reflection, *I knew that my son was subject to death.* He that is convinced of an error, if he had the same knowledge of his own weakness, would, instead of yielding to resentment and indignation, and artifice and malignity, only regard such oversights as the appendages of humanity, and pacify himself with considering that he had always known man to be a fallible being.

If it be true that most of our passions are excited by the novelty of the objects, there is little reason for doubting that to be considered as subject to fallacies of ratiocination, or imperfection of knowledge, is to a very great part of mankind entirely new; for it is impossible to enter any place of general resort, or fall into any company where there is not some regular and established subordination, without finding rage and vehemence produced only by difference of sentiments about things often very trifling, and in which neither of the disputants have any other interest than what proceeds from their mutual unwillingness to give way to any suggestion that may bring upon them the disgrace of being wrong.

I have heard of men that, having advanced some erroneous doctrines in philosophy, have refused to see the experiments by which they were confuted; and the observation of every day will give new proofs with how much industry subterfuges and evasions are sought to decline the pressure of resistless arguments, how often the state of the question is altered, how often the antagonist is wilfully misrepresented, and in how much perplexity the clearest positions are involved by those whom they happen to obstruct in the extension of a pleasing hypothesis.

Of all mortals in every age, none seem to have been more infected with this species of vanity, than the race of writers, whose reputation arising solely from their understanding, has given them a very delicate sensibility of any violence attempted on their literary honour. It is often not unpleasing to remark with what solicitude men of acknowledged abilities will endeavour to palliate absurdities and reconcile contradictions, only to obviate criticisms to which all human performances must ever be exposed, and from which they can never suffer, but when they teach the world by a vain and ridiculous impatience to think them of importance.

Dryden, whose warmth of mind and haste of composition very frequently hurried him into inaccuracies, heard himself sometimes exposed to ridicule for having said in one of his tragedies,

I follow fate, which does too fast pursue.

That no man could at once follow and be followed was, it may be thought, too plain to be long disputed; and the truth is, that Dryden was apparently betrayed into the blunder by the double meaning of the word *fate*, to which in the former part of the verse he had annexed the idea of *fortune*, and in the latter that of *death;* so that the sense only was, *Though persued by* death, *I will not resign myself to despair, but will follow* fortune, *and do and suffer what is appointed.* This however was not completely expressed, and Dryden being determined not to give any way to his critics, never confessed that he had been surprised by an ambiguity; but finding luckily in Virgil an account of a man moving in a circle with this expression,——*Et se sequitur fugitque*—— "Here," says he, "is the passage in imitation of which I wrote the line that my critics were pleased to condemn as nonsense, not but I may sometimes write nonsense, though they have not the fortune to find it."

Every one sees the folly of such mean doublings to escape the persuit of criticism; nor is there a single reader of this poet, who would not have paid him greater veneration, had he shewn consciousness enough of his own superiority to set such cavils at defiance, and owned that he sometimes slipped into errors by the tumult of his imagination, and the multitude of his ideas.

It is however happy when this temper discovers itself only in little things, which may be right or wrong without any influence on the virtue or happiness of mankind; and we may, with very little inquietude, see a man persist in a project, which he himself reckons to be impracticable, live in an inconvenient house because it was contrived by himself, or wear a coat of a particular cut, in hopes by perseverance to bring it into fashion. These are indeed follies, but they are only follies, and, however wild or ridiculous, can very little affect others.

But such pride, once indulged, too frequently operates upon more important objects, and inclines men not only to vindicate their errors, but their vices; to persist in practices which their own hearts condemn, only lest they should seem to feel reproaches, or be made wiser by the advice of others; or to search for sophisms tending to the confusion of all principles, and the evacuation of all duties, that they may not appear to act what they are not able to defend.

Let every man, who finds vanity so far predominant, as to betray him to the danger of this last period of corruption, pause a moment to consider what will be the consequences of the plea which he is about to offer for that to which he knows himself not led at first by reason, but impelled by the violence of desire, surprized by the suddenness of passion, or seduced by the soft approaches of temptation, and by imperceptible gradations of guilt. Let him consider what he is going to commit by forcing his understanding to patronise those appetites, which it is its chief business to hinder and reform.

The cause of virtue requires so little art to defend it, and good and evil, when they have been once shewn, are so easily distinguished, that such apologists very seldom gain over any new pro´selytes to their party, nor have their fallacies power to deceive any but those whose desires have clouded their discernment, and therefore all that the best faculties thus employed can gain, is, that they may persuade the hearers that the man is hopeless whom they only thought vitious, that corruption has passed from his manners to his principles, that all endeavours for his recovery are without prospect of advantage, and that nothing remains but to avoid him as infectious, or to chase him as destructive.

But if it be supposed that he may impose on his audience by partial representations of consequences, intricate deductions of remote causes, or perplexed combinations of ideas which having various relations appear different as viewed on different sides; that he may sometimes puzzle the weak and well-meaning, and now and then seduce, by the admiration of his abilities, a young mind still fluctuating in unsettled notions, and neither fortified by instruction nor enlightened by experience; yet what must be the event of such a triumph? A man cannot spend all this life in frolick: age, or disease, or solitude will bring some hours of serious consideration, and it will then afford no comfort to think, that he has extended the dominion of vice, that he has loaded himself with the crimes of others, and can never know the extent of his own wickedness, or make reparation for the mischief that he has caused. There is not perhaps in all the stores of ideal anguish, a thought more painful, than the consciousness of having propagated corruption by vitiating the mind, of having not only drawn others from the paths of virtue, but blocked up the way by which they should return, of having blinded them to every beauty but the paint of pleasure, and deafened them to every call but the alluring voice of the syrens of destruction.

There is yet another danger in this practice: men who cannot deceive others, are very often successful in deceiving themselves; they weave their sophistry till they are themselves entangled, and repeat their positions till they credit them; by often contending they grow sincere in the cause, and by long wishing for demonstrative arguments they at last bring themselves to fancy that they have found them. They are then at the uttermost verge of wickedness, and may die without having that light rekindled in their minds, which their own pride and contumacy have extinguished.

The men who can be charged with fewest failings, either with respect to abilities or virtue, are generally most ready to confess them; for not to dwell on things of solemn and awful consideration, the humility of confessors, the tears of saints, and the terrors of persons eminent for piety and innocence, it is well known that Caesar wrote an account of the errors committed by him in his wars of Gaul, and that Hippocrates, a name perhaps in rational estimation greater than Caesar, warned posterity against a mistake into which he had fallen: *So much,* observes Celsus, *does the open and artless confession of an error become a man conscious that he has enough remaining to support his character.*

As all error is meanness, it is incumbent on every man who consults his own dignity, to retract it as soon as he discovers it, without fearing any censure so much as that of his own mind. As justice requires that all injuries should be repaired, it is the duty of him who has seduced others by bad practices, or false notions, to endeavour that such as have adopted his errors should know his retraction, and that those who have learned vice by his example, should by his example be taught amendment.

No. 60. Saturday, October 13, 1750

—Quid sit pulchrum, quid turpe, quid utile, quid non,
Plenius et melius Chrysippo et Crantore dicit.
Hor. [*Epistles,* 1.2.3.]

Whose works the beautiful and base contain,
Of vice and virtue more instructive rules,
Than all the sober sages of the schools. Francis.

All joy or sorrow for the happiness or calamities of others is produced by an act of the imagination, that realises the event however fictitious, or approximates it however remote, by placing us, for a time, in the condition of him whose fortune we contemplate; so that we feel, while the deception lasts, whatever motions would be excited by the same good or evil happening to ourselves.

Our passions are therefore more strongly moved, in proportion as we can more readily adopt the pains or pleasures proposed to our minds, by recognising them as once our own, or considering them as naturally incident to our state of life. It is not easy for the most artful writer to give us an interest in happiness or misery, which we think ourselves never likely to feel, and with which we have never yet been made acquainted. Histories of the downfall of kingdoms, and revolutions of empires are read with great tranquillity; the imperial tragedy pleases common auditors only by its pomp of ornament, and grandeur of ideas; and the man whose faculties have been engrossed by business, and whose heart never fluttered but at the rise or fall of stocks, wonders how the attention can be seized, or the affections agitated by a tale of love.

Those parallel circumstances, and kindred images to which we readily conform our minds, are, above all other writings, to be found in narratives of the lives of particular persons; and there seems therefore no species of writing more worthy of cultivation than biography, since none can be more delightful, or more useful, none can more certainly enchain the heart by irresistible interest, or more widely diffuse instruction to every diversity of condition.

The general and rapid narratives of history, which involve a thousand fortunes in the business of a day, and complicate innumerable incidents in one great transaction, afford few lessons applicable to private life, which derives its comforts and its wretchedness from the right or wrong management of things, that nothing but their frequency makes considerable, *Parva si non fiunt quotidie*, says Pliny, and which can have no place in those relations which never descend below the consultation of senates, the motions of armies, and the schemes of conspirators.

I have often thought that there has rarely passed a life of which a judicious and faithful narrative would not be useful. For, not only every man has in the mighty mass of the world great numbers in the same condition with himself, to whom his mistakes and miscarriages, escapes and expedients would be of immediate and apparent use; but there is such an uniformity in the life of man, if it be considered apart from adventitious and separable decorations and disguises, that there is scarce any possibility of good or ill, but is common to humankind. A great part of the time of those who are placed at the greatest distance by fortune, or by temper, must unavoidably pass in the same manner; and though, when the claims of nature are satisfied, caprice, and vanity, and accident, begin to produce discriminations, and peculiarities, yet the eye is not very heedful, or quick, which cannot discover the same causes still terminating their influence in the same effects, though sometimes accelerated, sometimes retarded, or perplexed by multiplied combinations. We are all prompted by the same motives, all deceived by the same fallacies, all animated by hope, obstructed by danger, entangled by desire, and seduced by pleasure.

It is frequently objected to relations of particular lives, that they are not distinguished by any striking or wonderful vicissitudes. The scholar who passes his life among his books, the merchant who conducted only his own affairs, the priest whose sphere of action was not extended beyond that of his duty, are considered as no proper objects of publick regard, however they might have excelled in their several stations, whatever might have been their learning, integrity, and piety. But this notion arises from false measures of excellence and dignity, and must be eradicated by considering, that, in the eye of uncorrupted reason, what is of most use is of most value.

It is, indeed, not improper to take honest advantages of prejudice, and to gain attention by a great name; but the business of the biographer is often to pass slightly over those performances and incidents, which produce vulgar greatness, to lead the thoughts into domestick privacies, and display the minute details of daily life, where exterior appendages are cast aside, and men excel each other only by prudence, and by virtue. The life of Thuanus is, with great propriety, said by its author to have been written, that it might lay open to posterity the private and familiar character of that man, *cujus ingenium et candorem ex ipsius scriptis sunt olim semper mirati*, whose candour and genius his writings will to the end of time preserve in admiration.

There are many invisible circumstances, which whether we read as enquirers after natural or moral knowledge, whether we intend to enlarge our science, or encrease our virtue, are more important than publick occurrences. Thus Salust, the great master, has not forgot, in his account of Catiline, to remark that *his walk was now quick, and again slow,* as an indication of a mind revolving something with violent commotion. Thus the story of Melancthon affords a striking lecture on the value of time, by informing us that when he made an appointment, he expected not only the hour, but the minute to be fixed, that life might not run out in the idleness of suspense; and all the plans and enterprizes of De Wit are now of less importance to the world, than that part of his personal character which represents him as careful of his health, and negligent of his life.

But biography has often been allotted to writers who seem very little acquainted with the nature of their task, or very negligent about the performance. They rarely afford any other account than might be collected from publick papers, and imagine themselves writing a life when they exhibit a chronological series of actions or preferments; and so little regard the manners or behaviour of their heroes, that more knowledge may be gained of a man's real character, by a short conversation with one of his servants, than from a formal and studied narrative, begun with his pedigree, and ended with his funeral.

If now and then they condescend to inform the world of particular facts, they are not always so happy as to select those which are of most importance. I know not well what advantage posterity can receive from the only circumstance by which Tickell has distinguished Addison from the rest of mankind, the irregularity of his pulse: nor can I think myself overpaid for the time spent in reading the life of Malherb, by being enabled to relate, after the learned biographer, that Malherb had two predominant opinions; one, that the looseness of a single woman might destroy all the boast of ancient descent; the other, that the French beggers made use very improperly and barbarously of the phrase *noble gentleman,* because either word included the sense of both.

There are, indeed, some natural reasons why these narratives are often written by such as were not likely to give much instruction or delight, and why most accounts of particular persons are barren and useless. If a life be delayed till all interest and envy are at an end, and all motives to calumny or flattery are suppressed, we may hope for impartiality, but must expect little intelligence; for the incidents which give excellence to biography are of a volatile and evanescent kind, such as soon escape the memory, and are rarely transmitted by tradition. We know how few can portray a living acquaintance, except by his most prominent and observable particularities, and the grosser features of his mind; and it may be easily imagined how much of this little knowledge may be lost in imparting it, and how soon a succession of copies will lose all resemblance of the original.

If the biographer writes from personal knowledge, and makes haste to gratify the publick curiosity, there is danger lest his interest, his fear, his gratitude, or his tenderness, overpower his fidelity, and tempt him to conceal, if not to invent. There are many who think it an act of piety to hide the faults or failings of their friends, even when they can no longer suffer by their detection; we therefore see whole ranks of characters adorned with uniform panegyrick, and not to be known from one another, but by extrinsick and casual circumstances. "Let me remember," says Hale, "when I find myself inclined to pity a criminal, that there is likewise a pity due to the country." If there is a regard due to the memory of the dead, there is yet more respect to be paid to knowledge, to virtue, and to truth.

No. 144. Saturday, August 3, 1751

——————Daphnidis arcum
Fregisti et calamos: quae tu, perverse Menalca,
Et cum vidisti puero donata, dolebas;
Et si non aliqua nocuisses, mortuus esses.

VIRG. [*Eclogues*, III.12.]

The bow of Daphnis and the shafts you broke;
When the fair boy receiv'd the gift of right;
And but for mischief, you had dy'd for spite. DRYDEN.

It is impossible to mingle in any conversation without observing the difficulty with which a new name makes its way into the world. The first appearance of any excellence unites multitudes against it, unexpected opposition rises up on every side, the celebrated and the obscure join in the confederacy, subtilty furnishes arms to impudence, and invention leads on credulity.

The strength and unanimity of this alliance is not easily conceived. It might be expected that no man should suffer his heart to be enflamed with malice, but by injuries, that none should busy himself in contesting the pretensions of another, but where some right of his own was involved in the question, and that at least hostilities commenced without cause, should quickly cease, that the armies of malignity should soon disperse, when no common interest could be found to hold them together, and that the attack upon a rising character should be left entirely to those who had something to hope or fear from the event.

The hazards of those that aspire to eminence would be much diminished if they had none but acknowledged rivals to encounter. Their enemies would then be few, and, what is of yet greater importance, would be known. But what caution is sufficient to ward off the blows of invisible assailants, or what force can stand against unintermitted violence, and a continual succession of enemies? Yet such is the state of the world, that no sooner can any man emerge from the crowd, and fix the eyes of the publick upon him, than he stands as a mark to the arrows of lurking calumny, and receives, in the tumult of hostility, from distant and from nameless hands, wounds not always easy to be cured.

It is indeed probable that the first onset against the candidates for renown, is originally incited by those who imagine themselves in danger of suffering by their success, but when war is once declared, volunteers flock to the standard, multitudes follow the camp only for want of employment, and flying squadrons are dispersed to every part, so pleased with an opportunity of mischief, that they toil without prospect of praise, and pillage without hope of profit.

When any man has endeavoured to deserve distinction, he may easily convince himself how long his claim is likely to remain unacknowledged, by wandering for a few days from one place of resort to another. He will be surprised to hear himself censured where he could not expect to have been named; he will find himself persecuted with the utmost acrimony of malice, by those whom he never could have offended, and perhaps may be invited to an association against himself, or appealed to as a witness of his own infamy.

As there are commonly to be found in the service of envy men of every diversity of temper and degree of understanding, calumny is diffused by every art and method of propagation. Nothing is too gross or too refined, too cruel or too trifling to be practised; very little regard is had to the rules of honourable hostility, but every weapon is accounted lawful, and those that cannot make a thrust at life are content to keep themselves in play with petty malevolence, to teaze with feeble blows and impotent disturbance.

But as the industry of observation has divided the most miscellaneous and confused assemblages into proper classes, and ranged the insects of the summer, that torment us with their drones or stings, by their several tribes; the persecutors of merit notwithstanding their number may be likewise commodiously distinguished into Roarers, Whisperers and Moderators.

The Roarer is an enemy rather terrible than dangerous; he has commonly no other qualifications for a champion of controversy than a hardened front and strong voice. He seldom has so much desire to confute as to silence, he depends, therefore, rather upon vociferation than argument, and has very little care to adjust one part of his accusation to another, to preserve decency in his language or probability in his narratives. He has always a store of reproachful epithets and contemptuous appellations, ready to be produced as occasion may require, which by constant use he pours out with resistless volubility. If the wealth of a trader is mentioned, he without hesitation devotes him to bankruptcy; if the beauty and elegance of a lady be commended, he wonders how the town can fall in love with rustick deformity; if a new performance of a rising genius happens to be celebrated, he pronounces the writer a hopeless ideot, without knowledge of books or life, and without the understanding by which it must be acquired. His exaggerations are generally without effect upon those whom he compels to hear them, and though it will sometimes happen that the timorous are awed by his violence, and that the credulous mistake his confidence for knowledge, yet the opinions which he endeavours to suppress commonly recover their former strength, as the trees that bend to the tempest erect themselves again when its force is past.

The Whisperer is more dangerous. He easily gains attention by a soft address, and excites curiosity by an air of importance. As secrets are not to be made cheap by promiscuous publication, he calls a select audience about him, and gratifies their vanity with an appearance of trust by communicating his intelligence in a low voice. Of the trader he can tell that though he seems to manage a very extensive commerce, talks in high terms of the funds, and has a counting-house crowded with clerks and porters, yet his wealth is not equal to his reputation; he has lately suffered much by the miscarriage of an expensive project, and had a greater share than is publickly acknowledged in the rich ship that perished by the storm. Of the beauty he has little to say, but that they who see her in a morning do not discover all the graces which are admired in the park. Of the writer he can tell with great certainty, that, though the excellence of the work be incontestable, he can justly claim but a small part of the reputation;

that he owed most of the shining images and elevated sentiments to the kindness of a secret friend, and that the accuracy and equality of the stile was produced by the successive correction of the chief criticks of the age.

Every man is pleased with imagining that he knows something not yet commonly divulged, and therefore secret history easily gains credit, but it is for the most part believed only while it is circulated in whispers, and when once it comes to be openly told is openly confuted.

The most pernicious enemy is the man of Moderation. Without any interest in the question, or any motive but honest curiosity this impartial and zealous enquirer after truth, is ready to hear whatever can be urged on either side, and always disposed to kind interpretations and favourable opinions. He has indeed heard the trader's affairs reported with great variation, and after a diligent comparison of the evidence, concludes it most probable that the splendid superstructure of business and credit being originally built upon a narrow basis, has lately been found to totter, but between dilatory payment and bankruptcy there is a great distance; many merchants have supported themselves by expedients for a time, without any final injury to their creditors; what is lost by one adventure may be recovered by another, and no man however prudent, can secure himself against the failure of correspondents. He believes that a young lady pleased with admiration, and desirous to make perfect what is already excellent, may heighten some of her charms by artificial improvements, but surely most of her beauties must be genuine, and who can say that he is wholly what he endeavours to appear? The author he knows to be a man of application, and though perhaps he does not sparkle with the fire of Homer, yet he has the judgment to discover his own deficiencies, and to supply them by the help of others; and in his opinion modesty is a quality so amiable and so rare that [it] ought to find a patron wherever it appears, and may justly be preferred by the publick suffrage to petulant wit and ostentatious literature.

He who thus discovers failings with unwillingness, and extenuates the faults which cannot be denied, puts an end at once to doubt or vindication; his hearers repose upon his candour and veracity, and admit the charge without allowing the excuse.

Such are the arts by which the envious, the idle, the peevish, and the thoughtless obstruct that worth which they cannot equal, and by artifices thus easy, thus sordid, and thus detestable is industry defeated, beauty blasted, and genius depressed.

No. 208. Saturday, March 14, 1752

Ἡράκλειτος ἐγώ· τί με ὦ κάτω ἕλκετ' ἄμουσοι;
Οὐχ ὑμῖν ἐπόνουν, τοῖς δέ μ' ἐπισταμένοις.
Εἷς ἐμοὶ ἄνθρωπος τρισμύριοι· οἱ δ' ἀνάριθμοι
Οὐδείς· ταῦτ αὐδῶ καὶ παρὰ Περσεφόνῃ.

Diog. Laert. [IX. 1. 16.]

Begone ye blockheads, Heraclitus cries,
And leave my labours to the learn'd and wise:
By wit, by knowledge, studious to be read,
I scorn the multitude, alive and dead.

Time, which puts an end to all human pleasures and sorrows, has likewise concluded the labours of the *Rambler*. Having supported for two years the anxious employment of a periodical writer, and multiplied my essays to six volumes, I have now determined to desist.

What are the reasons of this resolution, it is of little importance to declare, since no justification is necessary when no objection is made. I am far from supposing, that the cessation of my performances will raise any inquiry; for I have never been much a favourite of the publick, nor can boast that, in the progress of my undertaking, I have been animated by the rewards of the liberal, the caresses of the great, or the praises of the eminent.

I have, however, no intention to gratify pride by submission, or malice by lamentation, nor think it reasonable to complain of neglect from those whose attention I never solicited. If I have not been distinguished by the distributers of literary honours, I have seldom descended to any of the arts by which favour is obtained. I have seen the meteors of fashion rise and fall, without any attempt to add a moment to their duration; I have never complied with temporary curiosity, nor furnished my readers with abilities to discuss the topic of the day; I have seldom exemplified my assertions by living characters from my papers; therefore no man could hope either censures of his enemies, or praises of himself, and they only could be expected to peruse them, whose passions left them leisure for the contemplation of abstracted truth, and whom virtue could please by her native dignity, without the assistance of modish ornaments.

To some, however, I am indebted for encouragement, and to others for assistance; the number of my friends was never great, but they have been such as would not suffer me to think I was writing in vain, and I therefore felt very little uneasiness at the want of popularity.

As my obligations have not been frequent, my acknowledgements may be soon dispatched. I can restore to all my correspondents their productions, with very little diminution of the bulk of my volumes, tho' not without the loss of some pieces to which particular honours have been paid.

The parts, from which I can claim no other praise than that of having given them an opportunity of appearing, are the four billets in the tenth paper, the second letter in the fifteenth; the thirtieth, the forty-fourth, the ninety-seventh, and the hundredth papers; and the second letter in the hundred and seventh.

Having thus deprived myself of many excuses, which candor might have admitted for the inequality of my compositions, being no longer able to allege the necessity of gratifying my correspondents, the importunity with which publication was solicited, or the obstinacy with which correction was rejected, I must now remain accountable for all my faults, and submit without subterfuge to the censures of criticism; which, however, I shall not endeavour to soften by a formal deprecation, or to overbear by the influence of a patron; for the supplications of an author never yet reprieved him a moment from oblivion; and, though greatness has sometimes sheltered guilt, it can afford no protection to ignorance or dulness. Having hitherto attempted only the propagation of truth, I will not at last violate it by the confession of terrors which I do not feel: Having laboured to maintain the dignity of virtue, I will not now degrade it by the meanness of dedication.

The seeming vanity with which I have sometimes spoken of myself, would perhaps require an apology, were it not extenuated by the example of all those who have published essays before me, and by the privilege which a nameless writer has been hitherto allowed. "A mask," says Castiglione, "confers a right of acting and speaking with less restraint, even when the wearer is known to the whole company." He that is discovered without his own consent, may claim some indulgence, and cannot be rigorously called to justify those sallies or frolicks which his disguise is a proof that he wishes to conceal.

But I have been cautious lest this offence should be very frequently or grossly committed; for as one of the philosophers directs us to live with a friend, as with one that is sometime to become an enemy, I have always thought it the duty of an anonymous author to write, as if he expected to be hereafter known.

I am willing to flatter myself with hopes, that, by collecting these papers, I am not preparing for my future life either shame or repentance. That they are all happily imagined, or accurately polished; that the same sentiment will not sometimes recur, or the same form of expression be too frequently repeated, I have not confidence in my abilities sufficient to promise. He that condemns himself to compose on a stated day, will often bring to his task, an attention dissipated, a memory overwhelmed, an imagination embarrassed, a mind distracted with anxieties, and a body languishing with disease: He will sometimes labour on a barren topic, till it is too late to change it; and sometimes, in the ardour of invention, diffuse his thoughts into wild exuberance, which the pressing hour of publication will not suffer judgment to examine or reduce.

Whatever shall be the final sentence of mankind, I have at least endeavoured to deserve their kindness; I have laboured to refine our language to grammatical purity, and to clear it from colloquial barbarisms, licentious idioms, and irregular combinations. Something, perhaps, I have added to the elegance of its construction, and something to the harmony of its cadence. When common words were less pleasing to the ear, or less distinct in their signification, I have familiarized the terms of philosophy, by applying them to known objects and popular ideas, but have rarely admitted any word, not authorized by former writers; for I believe, that whoever knows the English tongue in its present extent, will be able to express all his thoughts without farther help from other nations.

As it has been always my principal design to inculcate wisdom or piety, I have allotted few papers to the idle sports of wild imagination; and though some, perhaps, may be found, of which the highest excellence is harmless merriment, yet scarcely any man will be so steadily serious, as not rather to complain, that the severity of dictatorial instruction is too seldom relieved, and that he is driven by the sternness of philosophy to more chearful and airy companions.

Next to the excursions of fancy are the disquisitions of criticism, which, in my opinion, is to be ranked only among the subordinate and instrumental arts. The common practice of arbitrary decision and general exclamation, I have carefully avoided. I have asserted nothing without a reason; and have established all my principles of judgment on unalterable and evident truth.

In the pictures of life I have never been so studious of novelty or surprize, as to depart wholly from all resemblance; a fault which some writers, deservedly celebrated, frequently commit, only that they may raise, as the occasion requires, either mirth or abhorrence. Some enlargement may be allowed to declamation, and some exaggeration to burlesque; but as they deviate farther from life, they are less useful, because their lessons will fail of application. The mind of the reader is carried away from the contemplation of his own manners; he finds in himself no likeness to the phantom before him, and though he laughs or rages, he is not reformed.

The essays professedly serious, if I have been able to execute my own intentions, will be found exactly conformable to the precepts of Christianity, without any accommodation to the licentiousness and levity of the present age. I therefore look back on this part of my work with pleasure, which no blame or praise of man shall diminish or augment; I shall never envy the honours which wit and learning obtain in any other cause, if I can be numbered among the writers, who have given ardour to virtue, and confidence to truth.

Αὐτῶν ἐκ μακάρων ἀντάξιος εἴη ἀμοιβή.

[Dionysius, *Periegesis,* 1186.]

Celestial pow'rs! that piety regard,
From you my labours wait their last reward.

First published in The Literary Magazine, *which Johnson was editing, in No. IV, July 15–August 15, 1756, this article is representative of Johnson's attitude toward the Seven Years' War, and particularly of his opinions of the relations between the American colonists and the Indians.*

Observations on the Present State of Affairs

The time is now come in which every Englishman expects to be informed of the national affairs, and in which he has a right to have that expectation gratified. For whatever may be urged by ministers, or those whom vanity or interest make the followers of ministers, concerning the necessity of confidence in our governors, and the presumption of prying with profane eyes into the recesses of policy, it is evident, that this reverence can be claimed only by counsels yet unexecuted, and projects suspended in deliberation. But when a design has ended in miscarriage or success, when every eye and every ear is witness to general discontent, or general satisfaction, it is then a proper time to disentangle confusion and illustrate obscurity; to shew by what causes every event was produced, and in what effects it is likely to terminate; to lay down with distinct particularity, what rumour always huddles in general exclamations, or perplexes by undigested narratives; to shew whence happiness or calamity is derived, and whence it may be expected, and honestly to lay before the people what inquiry can gather of the past, and conjecture can estimate of the future.

The general subject of the present war is sufficiently known. It is allowed on both sides, that hostilities began in America, and that the French and English quarrelled about the boundaries of their settlements, about grounds and rivers to which, I am afraid, neither can shew any other right than that of power, and which neither can occupy but by usurpation, and the dispossession of the natural lords and original inhabitants. Such is the contest that no honest man can heartily wish success to either party.

It may indeed be alleged, that the Indians have granted large tracts of land both to one and to the other; but these grants can add little to the validity of our titles, till it be experienced how they were obtained: for if they were extorted by violence, or induced by fraud; by threats, which the miseries of other nations had shewn not to be vain, or by promises of which no performance was ever intended, what are they but new modes of usurpation, but new instances of cruelty and treachery?

And indeed what but false hope, or resistless terror can prevail upon a weaker nation to invite a stronger into their country, to give their lands to strangers whom no affinity of manners, or similitude of opinion, can be said to recommend, to permit them to build towns from which the natives are excluded, to raise fortresses by which they are intimidated, to settle themselves with such strength, that they cannot afterwards be expelled, but are for ever to remain the masters of the original inhabitants, the dictators of their conduct, and the arbiters of their fate?

When we see men acting thus against the precepts of reason, and the instincts of nature, we cannot hesitate to determine, that by some means or other they were debarred from choice; that they were lured or frighted into compliance; that they either granted only what they found impossible to keep, or expected advantages upon the faith of their new inmates, which there was no purpose to confer upon them. It cannot be said, that the Indians originally invited us to their coasts; we went uncalled and unexpected to nations who had no imagination that the earth contained any inhabitants so distant and so different from themselves. We astonished them with our ships, with our arms, and with our general superiority. They yielded to us as to beings of another and higher race, sent among them from some unknown regions, with power which naked Indians could not resist, and which they were therefore, by every act of humility, to propitiate, that they, who could so easily destroy, might be induced to spare.

To this influence, and to this only, are to be attributed all the cessions and submissions of the Indian princes, if indeed any such cessions were ever made, of which we have no witness but those who claim from them, and there is no great malignity in suspecting, that those who have robbed have also lied.

Some colonies indeed have been established more peaceably than others. The utmost extremity of wrong has not always been practised; but those that have settled in the new world on the fairest terms, have no other merit than that of a scrivener[1] who ruins in silence over a plunderer that seizes by force; all have taken what had other owners, and all have had recourse to arms, rather than quit the prey on which they had fastened.

The American dispute between the French and us is therefore only the quarrel of two robbers for the spoils of a passenger, but, as robbers have terms of confederacy, which they are obliged to observe as members of the gang, so the English and French may have relative rights, and do injustice to each other, while both are injuring the Indians. And such, indeed, is the present contest: they have parted the northern continent of America between them, and are now disputing about their boundaries, and each is endeavouring the destruction of the other by the help of the Indians, whose interest it is that both should be destroyed.

Both nations clamour with great vehemence about infraction of limits, violation of treaties, open usurpation, insidious artifices, and breach of faith. The English rail at the perfidious French, and the French at the encroaching English; they quote treaties on each side, charge each other with aspiring to universal monarchy, and complain on either part of the insecurity of possession near such turbulent neighbours.

Through this mist of controversy it can raise no wonder, that the truth is not easily discovered. When a quarrel has been long carried on between individuals, it is often very hard to tell by whom it was begun. Every fact is darkened by distance, by interest, and by multitudes. Information is not easily procured from far; those whom the truth will not favour, will not step voluntarily forth to tell it; and where there are many agents, it is easy for every single action to be concealed.

---

[1] scrivener: "One whose business is to place money at interest." Johnson's *Dictionary*.

All these causes concur to the obscurity of the question, by whom were hostilities in America commenced? Perhaps there never can be remembered a time in which hostilities had ceased. Two powerful colonies enflamed with immemorial rivalry, and placed out of the superintendence of the mother nations, were not likely to be long at rest. Some opposition was always going forward, some mischief was every day done or meditated, and the borderers were always better pleased with what they could snatch from their neighbours, than what they had of their own.

In this disposition to reciprocal invasion a cause of dispute never could be wanting. The forests and desarts of America are without land-marks, and therefore cannot be particularly specified in stipulations; the appellations of those wide extended regions have in every mouth a different meaning, and are understood on either side as inclination happens to contract or extend them. Who has yet pretended to define how much of America is included in Brazil, Mexico, or Peru? It is almost as easy to divide the Atlantic ocean by a line, as clearly to ascertain the limits of those uncultivated, uninhabitable, unmeasured regions.

It is likewise to be considered, that contracts concerning boundaries are often left vague and indefinite without necessity, by the desire of each party, to interpret the ambiguity to its own advantage when a fit opportunity shall be found. In forming stipulations, the commissaries are often ignorant, and often negligent; they are sometimes weary with debate, and contract a tedious discussion into general terms, or refer it to a former treaty, which was never understood. The weaker part is always afraid of requiring explanations, and the stronger always has an interest in leaving the question undecided: thus it will happen without great caution on either side, that after long treaties solemnly ratified, the rights that had been disputed are still equally open to controversy.

In America it may easily be supposed, that there are tracts of land not yet claimed by either party, and therefore mentioned in no treaties, which yet one or the other may be afterwards inclined to occupy; but to these vacant and unsettled countries each nation may pretend, as each conceives itself intitled to all that is not expressly granted to the other.

Here then is a perpetual ground of contest, every enlargement of the possessions of either will be considered as something taken from the other, and each will endeavour to regain what had never been claimed, but that the other occupied it.

Thus obscure in its original is the American contest. It is difficult to find the first invader, or to tell where invasion properly begins; but I suppose it is not to be doubted, that after the last war, when the French had made peace with such apparent superiority, they naturally began to treat us with less respect in distant parts of the world, and to consider us as a people from whom they had nothing to fear, and who could no longer presume to contravene their designs, or to check their progress.

The power of doing wrong with impunity seldom waits long for the will, and it is reasonable to believe, that in America the French would avow their purpose of aggrandising themselves with at least as little reserve as in Europe. We may therefore readily believe, that they were unquiet neighbours, and had no great regard to right which they believed us no longer able to enforce.

That in forming a line of forts behind our colonies, if in no other part of their attempt, they had acted against the general intention, if not against the literal terms of treaties, can scarcely be denied; for it never can be supposed, that we intended to be inclosed between the sea and the French garrisons, or preclude ourselves from extending our plantations backwards to any length that our convenience should require.

With dominion is conferred every thing that can secure dominion. He that has the coast, has likewise the sea to a certain distance; he that possesses a fortress, has the right of prohibiting another fortress to be built within the command of its cannon. When therefore we planted the coast of North-America we supposed the possession of the inland region granted to an indefinite extent, and every nation that settled in that part of the world, seems, by the permission of every other nation, to have made the same supposition in its own favour.

Here then, perhaps, it will be safest to fix the justice of our cause; here we are apparently and indisputably injured, and this injury may, according to the practice of nations, be justly resented. Whether we have not in return made some incroachments upon them, must be left doubtful, till our practices on the Ohio shall be stated and vindicated. There are no two nations confining on each other, between whom a war may not always be kindled with plausible pretences on either part, as there is always passing between them a reciprocation of injuries and fluctuation of incroachments.

From the conclusion of the last peace perpetual complaints of the supplantations and invasions of the French have been sent to Europe from our colonies, and transmitted to our ministers at Paris, where good words were sometimes given us, and the practices of the American commanders were sometimes disowned; but no redress was ever obtained, nor is it probable that any prohibition was sent to America. We were still amused with such doubtful promises as those who are afraid of war are ready to interpret in their own favour, and the French pushed forward their line of fortresses, and seemed to resolve that before our complaints were finally dismissed, all remedy should be hopeless.

We, likewise, endeavour'd at the same time to form a barrier against the Canadians by sending a colony to New-Scotland, a cold uncomfortable tract of ground, of which we had long the nominal possession before we really began to occupy it. To this those were invited whom the cessation of war deprived of employment, and made burdensome to their country, and settlers were allured thither by many fallacious descriptions of fertile vallies and clear skies. What effects these pictures of American happiness had upon my countrymen I was never informed, but I suppose very few sought provision in those frozen regions, whom guilt or poverty did not drive from their native country. About the boundaries of this new colony there were some disputes; but as there was nothing yet worth a contest, the power of the French was not much exerted on that side; some disturbance was however given and some skirmishes ensued. But perhaps being peopled chiefly with soldiers, who would rather live by plunder than by agriculture, and who consider war as their best trade, New-Scotland would be more obstinately defended than some settlements of far greater value, and the French are too well informed of their own interest, to provoke hostility for no advantage, or to select that country for invasion, where they must hazard much, and can win little. They therefore pressed on southward behind our ancient and wealthy settlements, and built fort after fort at such distances that they might conveniently relieve one another, invade our colonies with sudden incursions, and retire to places of safety before our people could unite to oppose them.

This design of the French has been long formed, and long known, both in America and Europe, and might at first have been easily repressed had force been used instead of expostulation. When the English attempted a settlement upon the Island of St. Lucia, the French, whether justly or not, considering it as neutral and forbidden to be occupied by either nation, immediately landed upon it, and destroyed the houses, wasted the plantations, and drove or carried away the inhabitants. This was done in the time of peace, when mutual professions of friendship were daily exchanged by the two courts, and was not considered as any violation of treaties, nor was any more than a very soft remonstrance made on our part.

The French therefore taught us how to act, but an Hanoverian quarrel with the house of Austria for some time induced us to court, at any expence, the alliance of a nation whose very situation makes them our enemies. We suffered them to destroy our settlements, and to advance their own, which we had an equal right to attack. The time however came at last, when we ventured to quarrel with Spain, and then France no longer suffered the appearance of peace to subsist between us, but armed in defence of her ally.

The events of the war are well known, we pleased ourselves with a victory at Dettingen, where we left our wounded men to the care of our enemies, but our army was broken at Fontenoy and Val; and though after the disgrace which we suffered in the Mediterranean we had some naval success, and an accidental dearth made peace necessary for the French, yet they prescribed the conditions, obliged us to give hostages, and acted as conquerors, though as conquerors of moderation.

In this war the Americans distinguished themselves in a manner unknown and unexpected. The New English raised an army, and under the command of Pepperel took Cape-Breton, with the assistance of the fleet. This is the most important fortress in America. We pleased ourselves so much with the acquisition, that we could not think of restoring it, and among the arguments used to inflame the people against Charles Stuart, it was very clamorously urged, that if he gained the kingdom, he would give Cape-Breton back to the French.

The French however had a more easy expedient to regain Cape-

Breton than by exalting Charles Stuart to the English throne, they took in their turn Fort St. George, and had our East-India company wholly in their power, whom they restored at the peace to their former possessions, that they may continue to export our silver.

Cape-Breton therefore was restored, and the French were re-established in America, with equal power and greater spirit, having lost nothing by the war which they had before gained.

To the general reputation of their arms, and that habitual superiority which they derive from it, they owe their power in America, rather than to any real strength, or circumstances of advantage. Their numbers are yet not great; their trade, though daily improved, is not very extensive; their country is barren, their fortresses, though numerous, are weak, and rather shelters from wild beasts, or savage nations, than places built for defence against bombs or cannons. Cape-Breton has been found not to be impregnable; nor, if we consider the state of the places possessed by the two nations in America, is there any reason upon which the French should have presumed to molest us; but that they thought our spirit so broken that we durst not resist them, and in this opinion our long forbearance easily confirmed them.

We forgot, or rather avoided to think, that what we delayed to do must be done at last, and done with more difficulty, as it was delayed longer; that while we were complaining, and they were eluding, or answering our complaints, fort was rising upon fort, and one invasion made a precedent for another.

This confidence of the French is exalted by some real advantages. If they possess in those countries less than we, they have more to gain, and less to hazard; if they are less numerous, they are better united.

The French compose one body with one head. They have all the same interest, and agree to pursue it by the same means. They are subject to a governor commission'd by an absolute monarch, and participating the authority of his master. Designs are therefore formed without debate, and executed without impediment. They have yet more martial than mercantile ambition, and seldom suffer their military schemes to be entangled with collateral projects of gain: they have no wish but for conquest, of which they justly consider riches as the consequence.

Some advantages they will always have as invaders. They make war at the hazard of their enemies: the contest being carried on in our territories we must lose more by a victory than they will suffer by a defeat. They will subsist, while they stay, upon our plantations, and perhaps destroy them when they can stay no longer. If we pursue them and carry the war into their dominions, our difficulties will encrease every step as we advance, for we shall leave plenty behind us, and find nothing in Canada, but lakes and forests barren and trackless, our enemies will shut themselves up in their forts, against which it is difficult to bring cannon through so rough a country, and which if they are provided with good magazines will soon starve those who besiege them.

All these are the natural effects of their government, and situation; they are accidentally more formidable as they are less happy. But the favour of the Indians which they enjoy, with very few exceptions, among all the nations of the northern continent, we ought to consider with other thoughts; this favour we might have enjoyed, if we had been careful to deserve it. The French by having these savage nations on their side, are always supplied with spies, and guides, and with auxiliaries, like the Tartars to the Turks or the Hussars to the Germans, of no great use against troops ranged in order of battle, but very well qualified to maintain a war among woods and rivulets, where much mischief may be done by unexpected onsets, and safety be obtained by quick retreats. They can waste a colony by sudden inroads, surprise the straggling planters, frighten the inhabitants into towns, hinder the cultivation of lands, and starve those whom they are not able to conquer.

Unlike The Rambler, The Idler *appeared in a weekly newspaper,* The Universal Chronicle, *as the first piece of the eight pages. The first* Idler *appeared in the second number, April 8, 1758, and the rest followed to No. 104, April 5, 1760. They were reprinted in two small volumes in 1761, and again in 1767; in both instances Johnson suppressed No. 22, perhaps because of its violence. Reprinted from* The Universal Chronicle, *with the original numbering.*

The Idler

No. 22. Saturday, September 9, 1758

Many naturalists are of opinion, that the animals which we commonly consider as mute, have the power of imparting their thoughts to one another. That they can express general sensations is very certain; every being that can utter sounds, has a different voice for pleasure and for pain. The hound informs his fellows when he scents his game; the hen calls her chickens to their food by her cluck, and drives them from danger by her scream.

Birds have the greatest variety of notes; they have indeed a variety, which seems almost sufficient to make a speech adequate to the purposes of a life, which is regulated by instinct, and can admit little change or improvement. To the cries of birds, curiosity or superstition has been always attentive, many have studied the language of the feathered tribes, and some have boasted that they understood it.

The most skilful or most confident interpreters of the silvan dialogues have been commonly found among the philosophers of the East, in a country where the calmness of the air, and the mildness of the seasons, allow the student to pass a great part of the year in groves and bowers. But what may be done in one place by peculiar opportunities, may be performed in another by peculiar diligence. A shepherd of Bohemia has, by long abode in the forests, enabled himself to understand the voice of birds, at least he relates with great confidence a story of which the credibility may be considered by the learned.

"As I was sitting, (said he) within a hollow rock, and watching my sheep that fed in the valley, I heard two vultures interchangeably crying on the summit of the cliff. Both voices were earnest and deliberate. My curiosity prevailed over my care of the flock; I climbed slowly and silently from crag to crag, concealed among the shrubs, till I found a cavity where I might sit and listen without suffering, or giving disturbance.

"I soon perceived, that my labour would be well repaid; for an old vulture was sitting on a naked prominence, with her young about her, whom she was instructing in the arts of a vulture's life, and preparing, by the last lecture, for their final dismission to the mountains and the skies.

" 'My children,' said the old vulture, 'you will the less want my instructions because you have had my practice before your eyes; you have seen me snatch from the farm the houshold fowl, you have seen me seize the leveret in the bush, and the kid in the pasture, you know how to fix your talons, and how to balance your flight when you are laden with your prey. But you remember the taste of more delicious food; I have often regaled you with the flesh of man.' 'Tell us,' said the young vultures, 'where man may be found, and how he may be known; his flesh is surely the natural food of a vulture. Why have you never brought a man in your talons to the nest?' 'He is too bulky,' said the mother; 'when we find a man, we can only tear away his flesh and leave his bones upon the ground.' 'Since man is so big,' said the young ones, 'how do you kill him. You are afraid of the wolf and of the bear, by what power are vultures superior to man, is man more defenseless than a sheep?' 'We have not the strength of man,' returned the mother, 'and I am sometimes in doubt whether we have the subtilty; and the vultures would seldom feast upon his flesh, had not nature, that devoted him to our uses, infused into him a strange ferocity, which I have never observed in any other being that feeds upon the earth. Two herds of men will often meet and shake the earth with noise, and fill the air with fire. When you hear noise and see fire which flashes along the ground, hasten to the place with your swiftest wing, for men are surely destroying one another; you will then find the ground smoaking with blood and covered with carcasses, of which many are dismembered and mangled for the convenience of the vulture.' 'But when men have killed their prey,' said the pupil, 'why do they not eat it? When the wolf has killed a sheep he suffers not the vulture to touch it till he has satisfied himself. Is not man another kind of wolf?' 'Man,' said the mother, 'is the only beast who kills that which he does not devour, and this quality makes him so much a benefactor to our species.' 'If men kill our prey and lay it in our way,' said the young one, 'what need shall we have of labouring for ourselves.' 'Because man will, sometimes,' replied the mother, 'remain for a long time quiet in his den. The old vultures will tell you when you are to watch his motions. When you see men in great numbers moving close together, like a flight of storks, you may conclude that they are hunting, and that you will soon revel in human blood.' 'But still,' said the young one, 'I would gladly know the reason of this mutual slaughter. I could never kill what I could not eat.' 'My child,' said the mother, 'this is a question which I cannot answer, tho' I am reckoned the most subtile bird of the mountain. When I was young I used frequently to visit the ayry of an old vulture who dwelt upon the Carpathian rocks; he had made many observations; he knew the places that afforded prey round his habitation, as far in every direction as the strongest wing can fly between the rising and setting of the summer sun; he had fed year after year on the entrails of men. His opinion was, that men had only the appearance of animal life, being really vegetables with a power of motion; and that as the boughs of an oak are dashed together by the storm, that swine may fatten upon the falling acorns, so men are by some unaccountable power driven one against another, till they lose their motion, that vultures may be fed. Others think they have observed something of contrivance and policy among these mischievous beings, and those that hover more closely round them, pretend, that there is, in every herd, one that gives directions to the rest, and seems to be more eminently delighted with a wide carnage. What it is that intitles him to such pre-eminence we know not;

he is seldom the biggest or the swiftest, but he shews by his eagerness and diligence that he is, more than any of the others, a friend to vultures.' "

No. 23. Saturday, September 16, 1758

To the Idler

Sir,

As I was passing lately under one of the gates of this city, I was struck with horror by a rueful cry, which summoned me *to remember the poor debtors.*

The wisdom and justice of the English laws are, by Englishmen at least, loudly celebrated; but scarcely the most zealous admirers of our institutions can think that law wise, which, when men are capable of work, obliges them to beg; or just, which exposes the liberty of one to the passions of another.

The prosperity of a people is proportionate to the number of hands and minds usefully employed. To the community sedition is a fever, corruption is a gangrene, and idleness an atrophy. Whatever body, and whatever society, wastes more than it acquires, must gradually decay; and every being that continues to be fed, and ceases to labour, takes away something from the public stock.

The confinement, therefore, of any man in the sloth and darkness of a prison, is a loss to the nation, and no gain to the creditor. For of the multitudes who are pining in those cells of misery, a very small part is suspected of any fraudulent act by which they retain what belongs to others. The rest are imprisoned by the wantonness of pride, the malignity of revenge, or the acrimony of disappointed expectation.

If those who thus rigorously exercise the power, which the law has put into their hands, be asked, why they continue to imprison those whom they know to be unable to pay them: One will answer, that his debtor once lived better than himself; another, that his wife looked above her neighbours, and his children went in silk cloaths to the dancing school; and another, that he pretended to be a joker and a wit. Some will reply, that if they were in debt they should meet with the same treatment; some, that they owe no more than they can pay, and need therefore give no account of their actions. Some will confess their resolution, that their debtors shall rot in jail; and some will discover, that they hope, by cruelty, to wring the payment from their friends.

The end of all civil regulations is to secure private happiness from private malignity; to keep individuals from the power of one another; but this end is apparently neglected, when a man, irritated with loss, is allowed to be the judge of his own cause, and to assign the punishment of his own pain; when the distinction between guilt and unhappiness, between casualty and design, is intrusted to eyes blind with interest, to understandings depraved by resentment.

Since poverty is punished among us as a crime, it ought at least to be treated with the same lenity as other crimes; the offender ought not to languish, at the will of him whom he has offended, but to be allowed some appeal to the justice of his country. There can be no reason, why any debtor should be imprisoned, but that he may be compelled to payment; and a term should therefore be fixed, in which the creditor should exhibit his accusation of concealed property. If such property can be discovered, let it be given to the creditor; if the charge is not offered, or cannot be proved, let the prisoner be dismissed.

Those who made the laws have apparently supposed, that every deficiency of payment is the crime of the debtor. But the truth is, that the creditor always shares the act, and often more than shares the guilt of improper trust. It seldom happens that any man imprisons another but for debts which he suffered to be contracted, in hope of advantage to himself, and for bargains in which he proportioned his profit to his own opinion of the hazard; and there is no reason, why one should punish the other, for a contract in which both concurred.

Many of the inhabitants of prisons may justly complain of harder treatment. He that once owes more than he can pay, is often obliged to bribe his creditor to patience, by encreasing his debt. Worse and worse commodities, at a higher and higher price, are forced upon him; he is impoverished by compulsive traffick, and at last overwhelmed, in the common receptacles of misery, by debts, which, without his own consent, were accumulated on his head. To the relief of such distress, and to the redress of such misery, no other objection can be made, but that by such easy dissolution of debts, fraud will be left without punishment, and imprudence without awe, and that when insolvency shall become no longer punishable, credit will cease.

The motive to credit, is the hope of advantage. Commerce can never be at a stop, while one man wants what another can supply; and credit will never be denied, while it is likely to be repaid with profit. He that trusts one whom he designs to sue, is criminal by the act of trust; the cessation of such insidious traffick is to be desired, and no reason can be given, why a change of the law should impair any other.

We see nation trade with nation, where no payment can be compelled. Mutual convenience produces mutual confidence, and the merchants continue to satisfy the demands of each other, though they have nothing to dread but the loss of trade.

It is vain to continue an institution, which experience shews to be ineffectual. We have now imprisoned one generation of debtors after another, but we do not find that their numbers lessen. We have now learned, that rashness and imprudence will not be deterred from taking credit; let us try whether fraud and avarice may be more easily restrained from giving it.

I am, Sir, &c.

No. 61. Saturday, June 9, 1759

Criticism is a study by which men grow important and formidable at a very small expence. The power of invention has been conferred by nature upon few, and the labour of learning those sciences which may, by mere labour, be obtained, is too great to be willingly endured; but every man can exert such judgment as he has upon the works of others, and he whom nature has made weak and idleness keeps ignorant, may yet support his vanity by the name of a critick.

I hope it will give comfort to great numbers who are passing thro' the world in obscurity, when I inform them how easily distinction may be obtained. All the other powers of literature are coy and haughty, they must be long courted, and at last are not always gained; but criticism is a goddess easy of access and forward of advance, who will meet the slow and encourage the timorous; the want of meaning she supplies with words, and the want of spirit with malignity.

This profession has one recommendation peculiar to itself, that it gives vent to malignity without real mischief. No genius was ever blasted by the breath of criticks. The poison, which, if confined, would have burst the heart, fumes away in empty hisses, and malice is set at ease with very little danger to merit. The critick is the only man whose triumph is without another's pain, and whose greatness does not rise upon another's ruin.

To a study at once so easy and so reputable, so malicious, and so harmless, it cannot be necessary to invite my readers by a long or laboured exhortation; it is sufficient, since all would be criticks if they could, to shew by one eminent example that all can be criticks if they will.

Dick Minim, after the common course of puerile studies, in which he was no great proficient, was put apprentice to a brewer, with whom he had lived two years, when his uncle died in the city, and left him a large fortune in the stocks. Dick had for six months before used the company of the lower players, of whom he had learned to scorn a trade, and being now at liberty to follow his genius, he resolved to be a man of wit and humour. That he might be properly initiated in his new character, he frequented the coffee-houses near the theatres, where he listned very diligently day after day to those who talked of language and sentiments, and unities and catastrophes, till by slow degrees he began to think that he understood something of the stage, and hoped in time to talk himself.

But he did not trust so much to natural sagacity as wholly to neglect the help of books. When the theatres were shut, he retired to Richmond with a few select writers, whose opinion he impressed upon his memory by unwearied diligence; and when he returned with other wits to the town, was able to tell in very proper phrases that the chief business of art is to copy nature; that a perfect writer is not to be expected, because genius decays as judgment increases; that the great art is the art of blotting, and that according to the rule of Horace every piece should be kept nine years.

Of the great authors he now began to display the characters, laying down as an universal position that all had beauties and defects. His opinion was, that Shakespeare committing himself wholly to the impulse of nature wanted that correctness which learning would have given him; and that Johnson, trusting to learning, did not sufficiently cast his eye on nature. He blamed the stanza of Spenser, and could not bear the hexameters of Sidney. Denham and Waller he held the first reformers of English numbers, and thought that if Waller could have obtained the strength of Denham, or Denham the sweetness of Waller, there had been nothing wanting to compleat a poet. He often expressed his commiseration of Dryden's poverty, and his indignation at the age which suffered him to write for bread; he repeated with rapture the first lines of *All for Love,* but wondered at the corruption of taste which could bear any thing so unnatural as rhyming tragedies. In Otway he found uncommon powers of moving the passions, but was disgusted by his general negligence, and blamed him for making a conspirator his hero. He never concluded his disquisition without remarking how happily the sound of the clock is made to alarm the audience. Southerne would have been his favourite, but that he mixes comic with tragic scenes, intercepts the natural course of the passions, and fills the mind with a mild confusion of mirth and melancholy. The versification of Rowe he thought too melodious for the stage, and too little varied in different passions. He made it the great fault of Congreve, that all his persons were wits, and that he always wrote with more art than nature. He considered *Cato* rather as a poem than a play, and allowed Addison to be the complete master of allegory and grave humour, but paid no great deference to him as a critic. He thought the chief merit of Prior was in his easy tales and lighter poems, though he allowed that his *Solomon* had many noble sentiments elegantly expressed. In Swift he discovered an inimitable vein of irony, and an easiness which all would hope and few would attain. Pope he was inclined to degrade from a poet to a versifier, and thought his numbers rather luscious than sweet. He often lamented the neglect of *Phaedra and Hippolitus,* and wished to see the stage under better regulations.

These assertions passed commonly uncontradicted, and if now and then an opponent started up, he was quickly repressed by the suffrages of the company, and Minim went away from every dispute with elation of heart, and encrease of confidence.

He now grew conscious of his abilities, and began to talk of the present state of dramatic poetry, wondered what was become of the comick genius which supplied our ancestors with wit and pleasantry, and why no writer could be found that durst now venture beyond a farce. He saw no reason for thinking that the vein of humour was exhausted, since we live in a country where liberty suffers every character to spread itself to its utmost bulk, and which therefore produces more originals than all the rest of the world together. Of tragedy he concluded business to be the soul, and yet often hinted that love predominates too much upon the modern stage.

He was now an acknowledged critick, and had his own seat in the coffee-house, and headed a party in the pit. Minim has more vanity than ill-nature, and seldom desires to do much mischief; he will, perhaps, murmur a little in the ear of him that sits next him, but endeavours to influence the audience to favour, by clapping, when an actor exclaims *ye Gods,* or laments the misery of his country.

By degrees he was admitted to rehearsals, and many of his friends are of opinion, that our present poets are indebted to him for their happiest thoughts; by his contrivance the bell was rung twice in *Barbarossa,* and by his persuasion the author of *Cleone* concluded his play without a couplet; for what can be more absurd, said Minim, than that part of a play should be rhymed, and part written in blank verse? and by what acquisition of faculties is the speaker who never could find rhymes before, enabled to rhyme at the conclusion of an act?

He is the great investigator of hidden beauties, and is particularly delighted when he finds *the sound an echo to the sense.* He has read all our poets with particular attention to this delicacy of versification, and wonders at the supineness with which their works have been hitherto perused, so that no man has found the sound of a drum in this distich,

> When pulpit, drum ecclesiastic,
> Was beat with fist instead of a stick;

and that the wonderful lines upon honour and a bubble have hitherto passed without notice,

Honour is like the glassy bubble,
Which costs philosophers such trouble,
Where one part crack'd, the whole does fly,
And wits are crack'd to find out why.

In these verses, says Minim, we have two striking accommodations of the sound to the sense. It is impossible to utter the two lines emphatically without an act like that which they describe; *bubble* and *trouble* causing a momentary inflation of the cheeks by the retention of the breath which is afterwards forcibly emitted as in the practice of *blowing bubbles*. But the greatest excellence is in the third line which is *cracked* in the middle to express a crack, and then shivers into monosyllables. Yet has [this] diamond lain neglected with common stones, and among the innumerable admirers of *Hudibrass* the observation of this superlative passage has been reserved for the sagacity of Minim.

No. 62. Saturday, June 16, 1759

Mr. Minim had now advanced himself to the zenith of critical reputation; when he was in the pit, every eye in the boxes was fixed upon him, when he entered his coffee-house, he was surrounded by circles of candidates who passed their noviciate of literature under his tuition; his opinion was asked by all who had no opinion of their own, and yet loved to debate and decide, and no composition was supposed to pass in safety to posterity, till it had been secured by Minim's approbation.

Minim professes great admiration of the wisdom and munificence, by which the academies are formed on the continent, and often wishes for some standard of taste, for some tribunal, to which merit might appeal from caprice, prejudice, and malignity. He has formed a plan for an academy of criticism, where every work of imagination may be read before it is printed, and which shall authoritatively direct the theatres what pieces to receive or reject, to exclude or to revive.

Such an institution would, in Dick's opinion, spread the fame of English literature over Europe, and make London the metropolis of elegance and politeness, the place to which the learned and ingenious of all countries would repair for instruction and improvement, and where nothing would any longer be applauded or endured that was not conformed to the nicest rules, and finished with the highest elegance.

Till some happy conjunction of the planets shall dispose our princes or ministers to make themselves immortal by such an academy, Minim contents himself to preside four nights in a week in a critical society selected by himself, where he is heard without contradiction, and whence his judgment is disseminated through the great vulgar and the small.

When he is placed in the chair of criticism, he declares loudly for the noble simplicity of our ancestors, in opposition to the petty refinements, and ornamental luxuriance. Sometimes he is sunk in despair, and perceives false delicacy daily gaining ground, and sometimes brightens his countenance with a gleam of hope, and predicts the revival of the true sublime. He then fulminates his loudest censures against the monkish barbarity of rhime; wonders how beings that pretend to reason can be pleased with one line always ending like another; tells how unjustly and unnaturally sense is sacrificed to sound, how often the best thoughts are mangled by the necessity of confining or extending them to the dimensions of a couplet, and rejoices that genius has in our days shaken off the shackles which had encumbered it so long. Yet he allows that rhyme may sometimes be borne, if the lines be often broken, and the pauses judiciously diversified.

From blank verse he makes an easy transition to Milton, whom he produces as an example of the slow advance of lasting reputation. Milton is the only writer whose books Minim can read for ever without weariness. What cause it is that exempts this pleasure from satiety he has long and diligently enquired, and believes it to consist in the perpetual variation of the numbers, by which the ear is gratified, and the attention awakened. The lines that are commonly thought rugged and unmusical he conceives to have been written to temper the melodious luxury of the rest, or to express things by a proper cadence: for he scarcely finds a verse that has not this favourite beauty; he declares that he could shiver in a hothouse when he reads that

the ground
Burns frore, and cold performs th' effect of fire;

and that when Milton bewails his blindness, the verse

So thick a drop serene has quench'd these orbs,

has, he knows not how, something that strikes him with an obscure sensation like that which he fancies would be felt from the sound of darkness.

Minim is not so confident of his rules of judgment as not very eagerly to catch new light from the name of the author. He is commonly so prudent as to spare those whom he cannot resist, unless, as will sometimes happen, he finds the public combined against them. But a new pretender to fame he is strongly inclined to censure, till his own honour requires that he commend him. 'Till he knows the success of a new production, he intrenches himself in general terms; there are some new thoughts, and beautiful passages, but there is likewise much which he would have advised the author to expunge. He has several favourite epithets, of which he has never settled the meaning, but which are very commodiously applied to books which he has not read, or cannot understand. One is *manly,* another is *dry,* another *stiff,* and another *flimzy;* sometimes he discovers delicacy of stile, and sometimes meets with *strange expressions.*

He is never so great, or so happy, as when a youth of promising parts is brought to receive his advice for the prosecution of his studies. He then puts on a very serious air; he advises the pupil to read none but the best authors, and when he finds one congenial to his own mind, to study his beauties, to avoid his faults, and, when he sits down to write, to consider how his favourite author would think at the present time on the present occasion. He directs him to catch those moments when he finds his thoughts expanded, and his genius exalted, but to take care lest his imagination hurry him beyond the bounds of nature. He holds diligence the mother of success, yet enjoins him, with great earnestness, not to read more than he can digest, and not to confuse his mind by pursuing studies of contrary tendencies. He tells him, that every man has his genius, and that Cicero could never be a poet. The boy retires illuminated, resolves to follow his genius, and to think how Milton would have thought; and Minim feasts upon his own beneficence till another day brings another pupil.

Printed anonymously in the first number of The British Magazine, *edited by Smollett (January 1760, pp. 37–39). In the same issue,* Idler *No. 89 was reprinted, "by permission of the author, whose great genius and extensive learning may be justly numbered among the most shining ornaments of the present age." This is quite unexpected praise from Smollett, who a few months earlier had called Johnson "that great CHAM of literature." Reprinted, without revision, at the end of the third edition of* The Idler, *1767.*

The Bravery of the English Common Soldiers

By those who have compared the military genius of the English with that of the French nation, it is remarked, that *the French officers will always lead, if the soldiers will follow;* and that *the English soldiers will always follow, if their officers will lead.*

In all pointed sentences some degree of accuracy must be sacrificed to conciseness; and, in this comparison, our officers seem to lose what our soldiers gain. I know not any reason for supposing that the English officers are less willing than the French to lead; but it is, I think, universally allowed, that the English soldiers are more willing to follow. Our nation may boast, beyond any other people in the world, of a kind of epidemick bravery, diffused equally through all its ranks. We can shew a peasantry of heroes, and fill our armies with clowns, whose courage may vie with that of their general.

There may be some pleasure in tracing the causes of this plebeian magnanimity. The qualities which commonly make an army formidable, are long habits of regularity, great exactness of discipline, and great confidence in the commander. Regularity may, in time, produce a kind of mechanical obedience to signals and commands, like that which the perverse Cartesians impute to animals: discipline may impress such an awe upon the mind, that any danger shall be less dreaded than the danger of punishment; and confidence in the wisdom or fortune of the general, may induce the soldiers to follow him blindly to the most dangerous enterprize.

What may be done by discipline and regularity, may be seen in the troops of the Russian empress, and Prussian monarch. We find that they may be broken without confusion, and repulsed without flight.

But the English troops have none of these requisites, in any eminent degree. Regularity is by no means part of their character: they are rarely exercised, and therefore shew very little dexterity in their evolutions as bodies of men, or in the manual use of their weapons as individuals: they neither are thought by others, nor by themselves, more active or exact than their enemies, and therefore derive none of their courage from such imaginary superiority.

The manner in which they are dispersed in quarters over the country, during times of peace, naturally produces laxity of discipline: they are very little in sight of their officers; and, when they are not engaged in the slight duty of the guard, are suffered to live every man his own way.

The equality of English privileges, the impartiality of our laws, the freedom of our tenures, and the prosperity of our trade, dispose us very little to reverence of superiours. It is not to any great esteem of the officers that the English soldier is indebted for his spirit in the hour of battle; for perhaps it does not often happen that he thinks much better of his leader than of himself. The French Count,[1] who has lately published the *Art of War,* remarks how much soldiers are animated, when they see all their dangers shared by those who were born to be their masters, and whom they consider as beings of a different rank. The Englishman despises such motives of courage: he was born without a master;

---

[1] Maurice, Comte de Saxe (1696–1750), Marshal of France, author of *Rêveries, ou Mémoires sur l'art de la Guerre* (1756–58), an important work in the history of warfare, though described by Carlyle as "a strange military farrago, dictated, as I should think, under opium."

and looks not on any man, however dignified by lace or titles, as deriving from nature any claims to his respect, or inheriting any qualities superior to his own.

There are some, perhaps, who would imagine that every Englishman fights better than the subjects of absolute governments, because he has more to defend. But what has the English more than the French soldier? Property they are both commonly without. Liberty is, to the lowest rank of every nation, little more than the choice of working or starving; and this choice is, I suppose, equally allowed in every country. The English soldier seldom has his head very full of the constitution; nor has there been, for more than a century, any war that put the property or liberty of a single Englishman in danger.

Whence then is the courage of the English vulgar? It proceeds, in my opinion, from that dissolution of dependance which obliges every man to regard his own character. While every man is fed by his own hands, he has no need of any servile arts: he may always have wages for his labour; and is no less necessary to his employer, than his employer is to him. While he looks for no protection from others, he is naturally roused to be his own protector; and having nothing to abate his esteem of himself, he consequently aspires to the esteem of others. Thus every man that crowds our streets is a man of honour, disdainful of obligation, impatient of reproach, and desirous of extending his reputation among those of his own rank; and as courage is in most frequent use, the fame of courage is most eagerly persued. From this neglect of subordination I do not deny that some inconveniences may from time to time proceed: the power of the law does not always sufficiently supply the want of reverence, or maintain the proper distinction between different ranks: but good and evil will grow up in this world together; and they who complain, in peace, of the insolence of the populace, must remember, that their insolence in peace is bravery in war.

Joseph Knight, a Negro who had been kidnapped as a child, was sold to a Scottish gentleman, who gave him sixpence a week. After marriage he found this inadequate and left. His case was brought to the Court of Session, which freed him. Johnson dictated the following argument to Boswell on September 23, 1777, for the use of Knight's counsel (Life, *III. 202-3*).

Freeing a Negro Slave

It must be agreed that in most ages many countries have had part of their inhabitants in a state of slavery; yet it may be doubted whether slavery can ever be supposed the natural condition of man. It is impossible not to conceive that men in their original state were equal; and very difficult to imagine how one would be subjected to another but by violent compulsion. An individual may, indeed, forfeit his liberty by a crime; but he cannot by that crime forfeit the liberty of his children. What is true of a criminal seems true likewise of a captive. A man may accept life from a conquering enemy on condition of perpetual servitude; but it is very doubtful whether he can entail that servitude on his descendants; for no man can stipulate without commission for another. The condition which he himself accepts, his son or grandson perhaps would have rejected. If we should admit, what perhaps may with more reason be denied, that there are certain relations between man and man which may make slavery necessary and just, yet it can never be proved that he who is now suing for his freedom ever stood in any of those relations. He is certainly subject by no law, but that of violence, to his present master; who pretends no claim to his obedience, but that he bought him from a merchant of slaves, whose right to sell him never was examined. It is said that, according to the constitutions of Jamaica, he was legally enslaved; these constitutions are merely positive; and apparently injurious to the rights of mankind, because whoever is exposed to sale is condemned to slavery without appeal; by whatever fraud or violence he might have been originally brought into the merchant's power. In our own time Princes have been sold, by wretches to whose care they were entrusted, that they might have an European education; but when once they were brought to a market in the plantations, little would avail either their dignity or their wrongs. The laws of Jamaica afford a Negro no redress. His colour is considered as a sufficient testimony against him. It is to be lamented that moral right should ever give way to political convenience. But if temptations of interest are sometimes too strong for human virtue, let us at least retain a virtue where there is no temptation to quit it. In the present case there is apparent right on one side, and no convenience on the other. Inhabitants of this island can neither gain riches nor power by taking away the liberty of any part of the human species. The sum of the argument is this:—No man is by nature the property of another: The defendant is, therefore, by nature free: The rights of nature must be some way forfeited before they can be justly taken away: That the defendant has by any act forfeited the rights of nature we require to be proved; and if no proof of such forfeiture can be given, we doubt not but the justice of the court will declare him free.

Rasselas appeared anonymously in two small volumes in April 1759 as The Prince of Abissinia. (The first page of the text of each volume is headed "The History of Rasselas, Prince of Abissinia," and that is the title ordinarily used.) A second edition followed at once, and by 1773 an edition had been printed in the American colonies, as well as translations into Dutch, French, German, and Italian. It is Johnson's most famous work. Reprinted from the first edition.

The History of Rasselas

Prince of Abissinia

I

DESCRIPTION OF A PALACE IN A VALLEY

Ye who listen with credulity to the whispers of fancy, and pursue with eagerness the phantoms of hope; who expect that age will perform the promises of youth, and that the deficiencies of the present day will be supplied by the morrow; attend to the history of Rasselas[1] prince of Abissinia.

Rasselas was the fourth son of the mighty emperour, in whose dominions the Father of waters begins his course; whose bounty pours down the streams of plenty, and scatters over half the world the harvests of Egypt.

According to the custom which has descended from age to age among the monarchs of the torrid zone, he[2] was confined in a private palace, with the other sons and daughters of Abissinian royalty, till the order of succession should call him to the throne.

---

[1] Rasselas: "Ratz" is explained as "viceroy" in Johnson's translation of Lobo's *Abyssinia*, 1735, p. 48.

[2] he: *changed to* Rasselas *in the second edition; hereafter such changes are marked* 2.

The place, which the wisdom or policy of antiquity had destined for the residence of the Abissinian princes, was a spacious valley in the kingdom of Amhara, surrounded on every side by mountains, of which the summits overhang the middle part. The only passage, by which it could be entered, was a cavern that passed under a rock, of which it has long been disputed whether it was the work of nature or of human industry. The outlet of the cavern was concealed by a thick wood, and the mouth which opened into the valley was closed with gates of iron, forged by the artificers of ancient days, so massy that no man could, without the help of engines, open or shut them.

From the mountains on every side, rivulets descended that filled all the valley with verdure and fertility, and formed a lake in the middle inhabited by fish of every species, and frequented by every fowl whom nature has taught to dip the wing in water. This lake discharged its superfluities by a stream which entered a dark cleft of the mountain on the northern side, and fell with dreadful noise from precipice to precipice till it was heard no more.

The sides of the mountains were covered with trees, the banks of the brooks were diversified with flowers; every blast shook spices from the rocks, and every month dropped fruits upon the ground. All animals that bite the grass, or brouse the shrub, whether wild or tame, wandered in this extensive circuit, secured from beasts of prey by the mountains which confined them. On one part were flocks and herds feeding in the pastures, on another all the beasts of chase frisking in the lawns; the spritely kid was bounding on the rocks, the subtle monkey frolicking in the trees, and the solemn elephant reposing in the shade. All the diversities of the world were brought together, the blessings of nature were collected, and its evils extracted and excluded.

The valley, wide and fruitful, supplied its inhabitants with the necessaries of life, and all delights and superfluities were added at the annual visit which the emperour paid his children, when the iron gate was opened to the sound of musick; and during eight days every one that resided in the valley was required to propose whatever might contribute to make seclusion pleasant, to fill up the vacancies of attention, and lessen the tediousness of time. Every desire was immediately granted. All the artificers of pleasure were called to gladden the festivity; the musicians exerted the power of harmony, and the dancers shewed their activity before the princes, in hope that they should pass their lives in this blisful captivity, to which these only were admitted whose performance was thought able to add novelty to luxury. Such was the appearance of security and delight which this retirement afforded, that they to whom it was new always desired that it might be perpetual; and as those, on whom the iron gate had once closed, were never suffered to return, the effect of longer experience could not be known. Thus every year produced new schemes of delight, and new competitors for imprisonment.

The palace stood on an eminence raised about thirty paces above the surface of the lake. It was divided into many squares or courts, built with greater or less magnificence according to the rank of those for whom they were designed. The roofs were turned into arches of massy stone joined with a cement that grew harder by time, and the building stood from century to century, deriding the solstitial rains and equinoctial hurricanes, without need of reparation.

This house, which was so large as to be fully known to none but some ancient officers who successively inherited the secrets of the place, was built as if suspicion herself had dictated the plan. To every room there was an open and secret passage, every square had a communication with the rest, either from the upper stories by private galleries, or by subterranean passages from the lower apartments. Many of the columns had unsuspected cavities, in which successive[3] monarchs reposited their treasures. They then closed up the opening with marble, which was never to be removed but in the utmost exigencies of the kingdom; and recorded their accumulations in a book which was itself concealed in a tower not entered but by the emperour, attended by the prince who stood next in succession.

II

THE DISCONTENT OF RASSELAS IN THE HAPPY VALLEY

Here the sons and daughters of Abissinia lived only to know the soft vicissitudes of pleasure and repose, attended by all that were

[3] successive monarchs: a long race of monarchs had 2

skilful to delight, and gratified with whatever the senses can enjoy. They wandered in gardens of fragrance, and slept in the fortresses of security. Every art was practised to make them pleased with their own condition. The sages who instructed them, told them of nothing but the miseries of publick life, and described all beyond the mountains as regions of calamity, where discord was always raging, and where man preyed upon man.

To heighten their opinion of their own felicity, they were daily entertained with songs, the subject of which was the *happy valley*. Their appetites were excited by frequent enumerations of different enjoyments, and revelry and merriment was the business of every hour from the dawn of morning to the close of even.

These methods were generally successful; few of the princes had ever wished to enlarge their bounds, but passed their lives in full conviction that they had all within their reach that art or nature could bestow, and pitied those whom fate had excluded from this seat of tranquility, as the sport of chance, and the slaves of misery.

Thus they rose in the morning, and lay down at night, pleased with each other and with themselves, all but Rasselas, who, in the twenty-sixth year of his age, began to withdraw himself from their pastimes and assemblies, and to delight in solitary walks and silent meditation. He often sat before tables covered with luxury, and forgot to taste the dainties that were placed before him: he rose abruptly in the midst of the song, and hastily retired beyond the sound of musick. His attendants observed the change and endeavoured to renew his love of pleasure: he neglected their endeavours,[4] repulsed their invitations, and spent day after day on the banks of rivulets sheltered with trees, where he sometimes listened to the birds in the branches, sometimes observed the fish playing in the stream, and anon cast his eyes upon the pastures and mountains filled with animals, of which some were biting the herbage, and some sleeping among the bushes.

This singularity of his humour made him much observed. One of the Sages, in whose conversation he had formerly delighted, followed him secretly, in hope of discovering the cause of his disquiet. Rasselas, who knew not that any one was near him,

---

[4] endeavours: officiousness 2, avoiding the repetition of the word.

having for some time fixed his eyes upon the goats that were brousing among the rocks, began to compare their condition with his own.

"What," said he, "makes the difference between man and all the rest of the animal creation? Every beast that strays beside me has the same corporal necessities with myself; he is hungry and crops the grass, he is thirsty and drinks the stream, his thirst and hunger are appeased, he is satisfied and sleeps; he rises again and is hungry, he is again fed and is at rest. I am hungry and thirsty like him, but when thirst and hunger cease I am not at rest; I am, like him, pained with want, but am not, like him, satisfied with fulness. The intermediate hours are tedious and gloomy; I long again to be hungry that I may again quicken my attention. The birds peck the berries or the corn, and fly away to the groves where they sit in seeming happiness on the branches, and waste their lives in tuning one unvaried series of sounds. I likewise can call the lutanist and the singer, but the sounds that pleased me yesterday weary me to day, and will grow yet more wearisome to morrow. I can discover within me no power of perception which is not glutted with its proper pleasure, yet I do not feel myself delighted. Man has surely some latent sense for which this place affords no gratification, or he has some desires distinct from sense which must be satisfied before he can be happy."

After this he lifted up his head, and seeing the moon rising, walked towards the palace. As he passed through the fields, and saw the animals around him, "Ye," said he, "are happy, and need not envy me that walk thus among you, burthened with myself; nor do I, ye gentle beings, envy your felicity; for it is not the felicity of man. I have many distresses from which ye are free; I fear pain when I do not feel it; I sometimes shrink at evils recollected, and sometimes start at evils anticipated: surely the equity of providence has ballanced peculiar sufferings with peculiar enjoyments."

With observations like these the prince amused himself as he returned, uttering them with a plaintive voice, yet with a look that discovered him to feel some complacence in his own perspicacity, and to receive some solace of the miseries of life, from consciousness of the delicacy with which he felt, and the eloquence with which he bewailed them. He mingled cheerfully in the diversions of the evening, and all rejoiced to find that his heart was lightened.

III

THE WANTS OF HIM THAT WANTS NOTHING

On the next day his old instructor, imagining that he had now made himself acquainted with his disease of mind, was in hope of curing it by counsel, and officiously sought an opportunity of conference, which the prince, having long considered him as one whose intellects were exhausted, was not very willing to afford: "Why," said he, "does this man thus intrude upon me; shall I be never suffered to forget those lectures which pleased only while they were new, and to become new again must be forgotten?" He then walked into the wood, and composed himself to his usual meditations; when, before his thoughts had taken any settled form, he perceived his persuer at his side, and was at first prompted by his impatience to go hastily away; but, being unwilling to offend a man whom he had once reverenced and still loved, he invited him to sit down with him on the bank.

The old man, thus encouraged, began to lament the change which had been lately observed in the prince, and to enquire why he so often retired from the pleasures of the palace, to loneliness and silence. "I fly from pleasure," said the prince, "because pleasure has ceased to please; I am lonely because I am miserable, and am unwilling to cloud with my presence the happiness of others." "You, Sir," said the sage, "are the first who has complained of misery in the *happy valley*. I hope to convince you that your complaints have no real cause. You are here in full possession of all that the emperour of Abissinia can bestow; here is neither labour to be endured nor danger to be dreaded, yet here is all that labour or danger can procure.[5] Look around and tell me which of your wants is without supply: if you want nothing, how are you unhappy?"

"That I want nothing," said the prince, "or that I know not what I want, is the cause of my complaint; if I had any known want, I

[5] procure: procure or purchase 2, completing the third member of a triplet.

should have a certain wish; that wish would excite endeavour, and I should not then repine to see the sun move so slowly towards the western mountain, or lament when the day breaks and sleep will no longer hide me from myself. When I see the kids and the lambs chasing one another, I fancy that I should be happy if I had something to persue. But, possessing all that I can want, I find one day and one hour exactly like another, except that the latter is still more tedious than the former. Let your experience inform me how the day may now seem as short as in my childhood, while nature was yet fresh, and every moment shewed me what I never had observed before. I have already enjoyed too much; give me something to desire."

The old man was surprised at this new species of affliction, and knew not what to reply, yet was unwilling to be silent. "Sir," said he, "if you had seen the miseries of the world, you would know how to value your present state." "Now," said the prince, "you have given me something to desire; I shall long to see the miseries of the world, since the sight of them is necessary to happiness."

IV

THE PRINCE CONTINUES TO GRIEVE AND MUSE

At this time the sound of musick proclaimed the hour of repast, and the conversation was concluded. The old man went away sufficiently discontented to find that his reasonings had produced the only conclusion which they were intended to prevent. But in the decline of life shame and grief are of short duration; whether it be that we bear easily what we have born long, or that, finding ourselves in age less regarded, we less regard others; or, that we look with slight regard upon afflictions, to which we know that the hand of death is about to put an end.

The prince, whose views were extended to a wider space, could not speedily quiet his emotions. He had been before terrified at the length of life which nature promised him, because he considered that in a long time much must be endured; he now rejoiced in his youth, because in many years much might be done.

This first beam of hope, that had been ever darted into his mind, rekindled youth in his cheeks, and doubled the lustre of his eyes. He was fired with the desire of doing something, though he knew not yet with distinctness, either end or means.

He was now no longer gloomy and unsocial; but, considering himself as master of a secret stock of happiness, which he could enjoy only by concealing it, he affected to be busy in all schemes of diversion, and endeavoured to make others pleased with the state of which he himself was weary. But pleasures never can be so multiplied or continued, as not to leave much of life unemployed; there were many hours, both of the night and day, which he could spend without suspicion in solitary thought. The load of life was much lightened: he went eagerly into the assemblies, because he supposed the frequency of his presence necessary to the success of his purposes; he retired gladly to privacy, because he had now a subject of thought.

His chief amusement was to picture to himself that world which he had never seen; to place himself in various conditions; to be entangled in imaginary difficulties, and to be engaged in wild adventures: but his benevolence always terminated his projects in the relief of distress, the detection of fraud, the defeat of oppression, and the diffusion of happiness.

Thus passed twenty months of the life of Rasselas. He busied himself so intensely in visionary bustle, that he forgot his real solitude; and, amidst hourly preparations for the various incidents of human affairs, neglected to consider by what means he should mingle with mankind.

One day, as he was sitting on a bank, he feigned to himself an orphan virgin robbed of her little portion by a treacherous lover, and crying after him for restitution and redress. So strongly was the image impressed upon his mind, that he started up in the maid's defence, and run forward to seize the plunderer with all the eagerness of real persuit. Fear naturally quickens the flight of guilt. Rasselas could not catch the fugitive with his utmost efforts; but, resolving to weary, by perseverance, him whom he could not surpass in speed, he pressed on till the foot of the mountain stopped his course.

Here he recollected himself, and smiled at his own useless impetuosity. Then raising his eyes to the mountain, "This," said he, "is the fatal obstacle that hinders at once the enjoyment of pleasure, and the exercise of virtue. How long is it that my hopes and wishes have flown beyond this boundary of my life, which yet I never have attempted to surmount!"

Struck with this reflection, he sat down to muse, and remembered, that since he first resolved to escape from his confinement, the sun had passed twice over him in his annual course. He now felt a degree of regret with which he had never been before acquainted. He considered how much might have been done in the time which had passed, and left nothing real behind it. He compared twenty months with the life of man. "In life," said he, "is not to be counted the ignorance of infancy, or imbecility of age. We are long before we are able to think, and we soon cease from the power of acting. The true period of human existence may be reasonably estimated as forty years, of which I have mused away the four and twentieth part. What I have lost was certain, for I have certainly possessed it; but of twenty months to come who can assure me?"

The consciousness of his own folly pierced him deeply, and he was long before he could be reconciled to himself. "The rest of my time," said he, "has been lost by the crime or folly of my ancestors, and the absurd institutions of my country; I remember it with disgust, but[6] without remorse: but the months that have passed since new light darted into my soul, since I formed a scheme of reasonable felicity, have been squandered by my own fault. I have lost that which can never be restored: I have seen the sun rise and set for twenty months, an idle gazer on the light of heaven: In this time the birds have left the nest of their mother, and committed themselves to the woods and to the skies: the kid has forsaken the teat, and learned by degrees to climb the rocks in quest of independant sustenance. I only have made no advances, but am still helpless and ignorant. The moon, by more than twenty changes, admonished me of the flux of life; the stream that rolled before my feet upbraided my inactivity. I sat feasting on intellectual luxury, regardless alike of the examples of the earth, and the instructions of the planets. Twenty months are past, who shall restore them!"

These sorrowful meditations fastened upon his mind; he past four months in resolving to lose no more time in idle resolves,

[6] but: yet 2

and was awakened to more vigorous exertion by hearing a maid, who had broken a porcelain cup, remark, that what cannot be repaired is not to be regretted.

This was obvious; and Rasselas reproached himself that he had not discovered it, having not known, or not considered, how many useful hints are obtained by chance, and how often the mind, hurried by her own ardour to distant views, neglects the truths that lie open before her. He, for a few hours, regretted his regret, and from that time bent his whole mind upon the means of escaping from the valley of happiness.

V

THE PRINCE MEDITATES HIS ESCAPE

He now found that it would be very difficult to effect that which it was very easy to suppose effected. When he looked round about him, he saw himself confined by the bars of nature which had never yet been broken, and by the gate, through which none that once had passed it were ever able to return. He was now impatient as an eagle in a grate. He passed week after week in clambering the mountains, to see if there was any aperture which the bushes might conceal, but found all the summits inaccessible by their prominence. The iron gate he despaired to open; for it was not only secured with all the power of art, but was always watched by successive sentinels, and was by its position exposed to the perpetual observation of all the inhabitants.

He then examined the cavern through which the waters of the lake were discharged; and, looking down at a time when the sun shone strongly upon its mouth, he discovered it to be full of broken rocks, which, though they permitted the stream to flow through many narrow passages, would stop any body of solid bulk. He returned discouraged and dejected; but, having now known the blessing of hope, resolved never to despair.

In these fruitless searches he spent ten months. The time, however, passed cheerfully away: in the morning he rose with new hope, in the evening applauded his own diligence, and in the night slept sound after his fatigue. He met a thousand amusements which beguiled his labour, and diversified his thoughts. He discerned the various instincts of animals, and properties of plants, and found the place replete with wonders, of which he purposed to solace himself with the contemplation, if he should never be able to accomplish his flight; rejoicing that his endeavours, though yet unsuccessful, had supplied him with a source of inexhaustible enquiry.

But his original curiosity was not yet abated; he resolved to obtain some knowledge of the ways of men. His wish still continued, but his hope grew less. He ceased to survey any longer the walls of his prison, and spared to search by new toils for interstices which he knew could not be found, yet determined to keep his design always in view, and lay hold on any expedient that time should offer.

VI

A DISSERTATION ON THE ART OF FLYING

Among the artists that had been allured into the happy valley, to labour for the accommodation and pleasure of its inhabitants, was a man eminent for his knowledge of the mechanick powers, who had contrived many engines both of use and recreation. By a wheel, which the stream turned, he forced the water into a tower, whence it was distributed to all the apartments of the palace. He erected a pavillion in the garden, around which he kept the air always cool by artificial showers. One of the groves, appropriated to the ladies, was ventilated by fans, to which the rivulet that run through it gave a constant motion; and instruments of soft musick were placed at proper distances, of which some played by the impulse of the wind, and some by the power of the stream.

This artist was sometimes visited by Rasselas, who was pleased with every kind of knowledge, imagining that the time would come when all his acquisitions should be of use to him in the open world. He came one day to amuse himself in his usual manner, and found the master busy in building a sailing chariot: he saw that the design was practicable upon a level surface, and with expressions of great esteem solicited its completion. The workman was pleased to find himself so much regarded by the prince, and resolved to gain yet higher honours. "Sir," said he, "you have seen but a small part of what the mechanick sciences can perform. I have been long of opinion, that, instead of the tardy conveyance of ships and chariots, man might use the swifter migration of wings; that the fields of air are open to knowledge, and that only ignorance and idleness need crawl upon the ground."

This hint rekindled the prince's desire of passing the mountains; and[7] having seen what the mechanist had already performed, he was willing to fancy that he could do more; yet resolved to enquire further before he suffered hope to afflict him by disappointment. "I am afraid," said he to the artist, "that your imagination prevails over your skill, and that you now tell me rather what you wish than what you know. Every animal has his element assigned him; the birds have the air, and man and beasts the earth." "So," replied the mechanist, "fishes have the water, in which yet beasts can swim by nature, and men by art. He that can swim needs not despair to fly: to swim is to fly in a grosser fluid, and to fly is to swim in a subtler. We are only to proportion our power of resistance to the different density of the matter through which we are to pass. You will be necessarily upborn by the air, if you can renew any impulse upon it, faster than the air can recede from the pressure."

"But the exercise of swimming," said the prince, "is very laborious; the strongest limbs are soon wearied; I am afraid the act of flying will be yet more violent, and wings will be of no great use, unless we can fly further than we can swim."

"The labour of rising from the ground," said the artist, "will be great, as we see it in the heavier domestick fowls; but, as we mount higher, the earth's attraction, and the body's gravity, will be gradually diminished, till we shall arrive at a region where the man will float in the air without any tendency to fall: no care will then be necessary, but to move forwards, which the gentlest impulse will effect. You, Sir, whose curiosity is so extensive, will easily conceive with what pleasure a philosopher, furnished with wings, and hovering in the sky, would see the earth, and all its inhabitants, rolling beneath him, and presenting to him successively, by its diurnal motion, all the countries within the same

---

[7] and having: having 2

parallel. How must it amuse the pendent spectator to see the moving scene of land and ocean, cities and desarts! To survey with equal security the marts of trade, and the fields of battle; mountains infested by barbarians, and fruitful regions gladdened by plenty, and lulled by peace! How easily shall we then trace the Nile through all his passage; pass over to distant regions, and examine the face of nature from one extremity of the earth to the other!"

"All this," said the prince, "is much to be desired, but I am afraid that no man will be able to breathe in these regions of speculation and tranquility. I have been told, that respiration is difficult upon lofty mountains, yet from these precipices, though so high as to produce great tenuity of the air, it is very easy to fall: and[8] I suspect, that from any height, where life can be supported, there may be danger of too quick descent."

"Nothing," replied the artist, "will ever be attempted, if all possible objections must be first overcome. If you will favour my project I will try the first flight at my own hazard. I have considered the structure of all volant animals, and find the folding continuity of the bat's wings most easily accommodated to the human form. Upon this model I shall begin my task to morrow, and in a year expect to tower into the air beyond the malice or pursuit of man. But I will work only on this condition, that the art shall not be divulged, and that you shall not require me to make wings for any but ourselves."

"Why," said Rasselas, "should you envy others so great an advantage? All skill ought to be exerted for universal good; every man has owed much to others, and ought to repay the kindness that he has received."

"If men were all virtuous," returned the artist, "I should with great alacrity teach them all to fly. But what would be the security of the good, if the bad could at pleasure invade them from the sky? Against an army sailing through the clouds neither walls, nor mountains, nor seas, could afford any security. A flight of northern savages might hover in the wind, and light at once with irresistible violence upon the capital of a fruitful region that was rolling under them. Even this valley, the retreat of princes, the abode of

[8] and: therefore 2

happiness, might be violated by the sudden descent of some of the naked nations that swarm on the coast of the southern sea."

The prince promised secrecy, and waited for the performance, not wholly hopeless of success. He visited the work from time to time, observed its progress, and remarked the[9] ingenious contrivances to facilitate motion, and unite levity with strength. The artist was every day more certain that he should leave vultures and eagles behind him, and the contagion of his confidence seized upon the prince.

In a year the wings were finished, and, on a morning appointed, the maker appeared furnished for flight on a little promontory: he waved his pinions a while to gather air, then leaped from his stand, and in an instant dropped into the lake. His wings, which were of no use in the air, sustained him in the water, and the prince drew him to land, half dead with terrour and vexation.

VII

THE PRINCE FINDS A MAN OF LEARNING

The prince was not much afflicted by this disaster, having suffered himself to hope for a happier event, only because he had no other means of escape in view. He still persisted in his design to leave the happy valley by the first opportunity.

His imagination was now at a stand; he had no prospect of entering into the world; and, notwithstanding all his endeavours to support himself, discontent by degrees preyed upon him, and he began again to lose his thoughts in sadness, when the rainy season, which in these countries is periodical, made it inconvenient to wander in the woods.

The rain continued longer and with more violence than had been ever known: the clouds broke on the surrounding mountains, and the torrents streamed into the plain on every side, till the cavern was too narrow to discharge the water. The lake overflowed its banks, and all the level of the valley was covered with the inundation. The eminence, on which the palace was built, and some other spots of rising ground, were all that the eye could

[9] the: many 2

now discover. The herds and flocks left the pastures, and both the wild beasts and the tame retreated to the mountains.

This inundation confined all the princes to domestick amusements, and the attention of Rasselas was particularly seized by a poem, which Imlac recited,[1] upon the various conditions of humanity. He commanded the poet to attend him in his apartment, and recite his verses a second time; then entering into familiar talk, he thought himself happy in having found a man who knew the world so well, and could so skilfully paint the scenes of life. He asked a thousand questions about things, to which, though common to all other mortals, his confinement from childhood had kept him a stranger. The poet pitied his ignorance, and loved his curiosity, and entertained him from day to day with novelty and instruction, so that the prince regretted the necessity of sleep, and longed till the morning should renew his pleasure.

As they were sitting together, the prince commanded Imlac to relate his history, and to tell by what accident he was forced, or by what motive induced, to close his life in the happy valley. As he was going to begin his narrative, Rasselas was called to a concert, and obliged to restrain his curiosity till the evening.

VIII

THE HISTORY OF IMLAC

The close of the day is, in the regions of the torrid zone, the only season of diversion and entertainment, and it was therefore midnight before the musick ceased, and the princesses retired. Rasselas then called for his companion and required him to begin the story of his life.

"Sir," said Imlac, "my history will not be long: the life that is devoted to knowledge passes silently away, and is very little diversified by events. To talk in publick, to think in solitude, to read and to hear, to inquire, and answer inquiries, is the business of a scholar. He wanders about the world without pomp or terrour, and is neither known nor valued but by men like himself.

"I was born in the kingdom of Goiama, at no greater distance

[1] recited: rehearsed 2

from the fountain of the Nile. My father was a wealthy merchant, who traded between the inland countries of Africk and the ports of the red sea. He was honest, frugal and diligent, but of mean sentiments, and narrow comprehension: he desired only to be rich, and to conceal his riches, lest he should be spoiled by the governours of the province."

"Surely," said the prince, "my father must be negligent of his charge, if any man in his dominions dares take that which belongs to another. Does he not know that kings are accountable for injustice permitted as well as done? If I were emperour, not the meanest of my subjects should be oppressed with impunity. My blood boils when I am told that a merchant durst not enjoy his honest gains for fear of losing[2] by the rapacity of power. Name the governour who robbed the people, that I may declare his crimes to the emperour."

"Sir," said Imlac, "your ardour is the natural effect of virtue animated by youth: the time will come when you will acquit your father, and perhaps hear with less impatience of the governour. Oppression is, in the Abissinian dominions, neither frequent nor tolerated; but no form of government has been yet discovered, by which cruelty can be wholly prevented. Subordination supposes power on one part and subjection on the other; and if power be in the hands of men, it will sometimes be abused. The vigilance of the supreme magistrate may do much, but much will still remain undone. He can never know all the crimes that are committed, and can seldom punish all that he knows."

"This," said the prince, "I do not understand, but I had rather hear thee than dispute. Continue thy narration."

"My father," proceeded Imlac, "originally intended that I should have no other education, than such as might qualify me for commerce; and discovering in me great strength of memory, and quickness of apprehension, often declared his hope that I should be some time the richest man in Abissinia."

"Why," said the prince, "did thy father desire the increase of his wealth, when it was already greater than he durst discover or enjoy? I am unwilling to doubt thy veracity, yet inconsistencies cannot both be true."

---

[2] losing: losing them 2

"Inconsistencies," answered Imlac, "cannot both be right, but, imputed to man, they may both be true. Yet diversity is not inconsistency. My father might expect a time of greater security. However, some desire is necessary to keep life in motion, and he, whose real wants are supplied, must admit those of fancy."

"This," said the prince, "I can in some measure conceive. I repent that I interrupted thee."

"With this hope," proceeded Imlac, "he sent me to school; but when I had once found the delight of knowledge, and felt the pleasure of intelligence and the pride of invention, I began silently to despise riches, and determined to disappoint the purpose of my father, whose grossness of conception raised my pity. I was twenty years old before his tenderness would expose me to the fatigue of travel, in which time I had been instructed, by successive masters, in all the literature of my native country. As every hour taught me something new, I lived in a continual course of gratifications; but, as I advanced towards manhood, I lost much of the reverence with which I had been used to look on my instructors; because, when the lesson was ended, I did not find them wiser or better than common men.

"At length my father resolved to initiate me in commerce, and, opening one of his subterranean treasuries, counted out ten thousand pieces of gold. 'This, young man,' said he, 'is the stock with which you must negociate. I began with less than the fifth part, and you see how diligence and parsimony have increased it. This is your own to waste or to improve. If you squander it by negligence or caprice, you must wait for my death before you will be rich: if, in four years, you double your stock, we will thenceforward let subordination cease, and live together as friends and partners; for he shall always be equal with me, who is equally skilled in the art of growing rich.'

"We laid our money upon camels, concealed in bales of cheap goods, and travelled to the shore of the red sea. When I cast my eye on the expanse of waters my heart bounded like that of a prisoner escaped. I felt an unextinguishable curiosity kindle in my mind, and resolved to snatch this opportunity of seeing the manners of other nations, and of learning sciences unknown in Abissinia.

"I remembered that my father had obliged me to the improvement of my stock, not by a promise which I ought not to violate, but by a penalty which I was at liberty to incur; and therefore determined to gratify my predominant desire, and by drinking at the fountains of knowledge, to quench the thirst of curiosity.

"As I was supposed to trade without connexion with my father, it was easy for me to become acquainted with the master of a ship, and procure a passage to some other country. I had no motives of choice to regulate my voyage; it was sufficient for me that, wherever I wandered, I should see a country which I had not seen before. I therefore entered a ship bound for Surat, having left a letter for my father declaring my intention.

IX

THE HISTORY OF IMLAC CONTINUED

"When I first entered upon the world of waters, and lost sight of land, I looked round about me with pleasing terrour, and thinking my soul enlarged by the boundless prospect, imagined that I could gaze round for ever without satiety; but, in a short time, I grew weary of looking on barren uniformity, where I could only see again what I had already seen. I then descended into the ship, and doubted for a while whether all my future pleasures would not end like this in disgust and disappointment. Yet, surely, said I, the ocean and the land are very different; the only variety of water is rest and motion, but the earth has mountains and vallies, desarts and cities: it is inhabited by men of different customs and contrary opinions; and I may hope to find variety in life, though I should miss it in nature.

"With this hope[3] I quieted my mind, and amused myself during the voyage; sometimes by learning from the sailors the art of navigation, which I have never practised, and sometimes by forming schemes for my conduct in different situations, in not one of which I have been ever placed.

"I was almost weary of my naval amusements when we landed safely at Surat. I secured my money, and purchasing some commodities for show, joined myself to a caravan that was passing

[3] hope: thought 2

into the inland country. My companions, for some reason or other, conjecturing that I was rich, and, by my inquiries and admiration, finding that I was ignorant, considered me as a novice whom they had a right to cheat, and who was to learn at the usual expence the art of fraud. They exposed me to the theft of servants, and the exaction of officers, and saw me plundered upon false pretences, without any advantage to themselves, but that of rejoicing in the superiority of their own knowledge."

"Stop a moment," said the prince, "is there such depravity in man, as that he should injure another without benefit to himself? I can easily conceive that all are pleased with superiority; but your ignorance was merely accidental, which, being neither your crime nor your folly, could afford them no reason to applaud themselves; and the knowledge which they had, and which you wanted, they might as effectually have shewn by warning you,[4] as betraying you."

"Pride," said Imlac, "is seldom delicate, it will please itself with very mean advantages; and envy feels not its own happiness, but when it may be compared with the misery of others. They were my enemies because they thought[5] me rich, and my oppressors because they delighted to find me weak."

"Proceed," said the prince: "I doubt not of the facts which you relate, but imagine that you impute them to mistaken motives."

"In this company," said Imlac, "I arrived at Agra, the capital of Indostan, the city in which the great Mogul commonly resides. I applied myself to the language of the country, and in a few months was able to converse with the learned men; some of whom I found morose and reserved, and others easy and communicative; some were unwilling to teach another what they had with difficulty learned themselves; and some shewed that the end of their studies was to gain the dignity of instructing.

"To the tutor of the young princes I recommended myself so much, that I was presented to the emperour as a man of uncommon knowledge. The emperour asked me many questions concerning my country and my travels; and though I cannot now recollect any thing that he uttered above the power of a common

---

[4] warning you: warning 2
[5] thought: grieved to think 2

man, he dismissed me astonished at his wisdom, and enamoured of his goodness.

"My credit was now so high, that the merchants, with whom I had travelled, applied to me for recommendations to the ladies of the court. I was surprised at their confidence of solicitation, and gently reproached them with their practices on the road. They heard me with cold indifference, and shewed no tokens of shame or sorrow.

"They then urged their request with the offer of a bribe; but what I would not do for kindness I would not do for money; and refused them, not because they had injured me, but because I would not enable them to injure others; for I knew they would have made use of my credit to cheat those who should buy their wares.

"Having resided at Agra, till there was no more to be learned, I travelled into Persia, where I saw many remains of ancient magnificence, and observed many new accommodations[6] of life. The Persians are a nation eminently social, and their assemblies afforded me daily opportunities of remarking characters and manners, and of tracing human nature through all its variations.

"From Persia I passed into Arabia, where I saw a nation at once pastoral and warlike; who live without any settled habitation; whose only wealth is their flocks and herds; and who have yet carried on, through all ages, an hereditary war with all mankind, though they neither covet nor envy their possessions.

X

IMLAC'S HISTORY CONTINUED. A DISSERTATION UPON POETRY

"Wherever I went, I found that Poetry was considered as the highest learning, and regarded with a veneration somewhat approaching to that which man would pay to the Angelick Nature. And it yet fills me with wonder, that, in almost all countries, the most ancient poets are considered as the best: whether it be that every other kind of knowledge is an acquistion gradually attained, and poetry is a gift conferred at once; or that the first poetry of

[6] accommodations: "conveniencies." Johnson's *Dictionary*.

every nation surprised them as a novelty, and retained the credit by consent which it received by accident at first: or whether[7] the province of poetry is to describe Nature and Passion, which are always the same, and[8] the first writers took possession of the most striking objects for description, and the most probable occurrences for fiction, and left nothing to those that followed them, but transcription of the same events, and new combinations of the same images. Whatever be the reason, it is commonly observed that the early writers are in possession of nature, and their followers of art: that the first excel in strength and invention, and the latter in elegance and refinement.

"I was desirous to add my name to this illustrious fraternity. I read all the poets of Persia and Arabia, and was able to repeat by memory the volumes that are suspended in the mosque of Mecca. But I soon found that no man was ever great by imitation. My desire of excellence impelled me to transfer my attention to nature and to life. Nature was to be my subject, and men to be my auditors: I could never describe what I had not seen: I could not hope to move those with delight or terrour, whose interests and opinions I did not understand.

"Being now resolved to be a poet, I saw every thing with a new purpose; my sphere of attention was suddenly magnified: no kind of knowledge was to be overlooked. I ranged mountains and deserts for images and resemblances, and pictured upon my mind every tree of the forest and flower of the valley. I observed with equal care the crags of the rock and the pinnacles of the palace. Sometimes I wandered along the mazes of the rivulet, and sometimes watched the changes of the summer clouds. To a poet nothing can be useless. Whatever is beautiful, and whatever is dreadful, must be familiar to his imagination: he must be conversant with all that is awfully vast or elegantly little. The plants of the garden, the animals of the wood, the minerals of the earth, and meteors of the sky, must all concur to store his mind with inexhaustible variety: for every idea is useful for the inforcement or decoration of moral or religious truth; and he, who knows most, will have most power of diversifying his scenes, and of gratifying his reader with remote allusions and unexpected instruction.

---

[7] whether: whether, as 2
[8] same, and: same, 2

"All the appearances of nature I was therefore careful to study, and every country which I have surveyed has contributed something to my poetical powers."

"In so wide a survey," said the prince, "you must surely have left much unobserved. I have lived, till now, within the circuit of these mountains, and yet cannot walk abroad without the sight of something which I had never beheld before, or never heeded."

"The business of a poet," said Imlac, "is to examine, not the individual, but the species; to remark general properties and large appearances: he does not number the streaks of the tulip, or describe the different shades in the verdure of the forest. He is to exhibit in his portraits of nature such prominent and striking features, as recal the original to every mind; and must neglect the minuter discriminations, which one may have remarked, and another have neglected, for those characteristicks which are alike obvious to vigilance and carelessness.

"But the knowledge of nature is only half the task of a poet; he must be acquainted likewise with all the modes of life. His character requires that he estimate the happiness and misery of every condition; observe the power of all the passions in all their combinations, and trace the changes of the human mind as they are modified by various institutions and accidental influences of climate or custom, from the spriteliness of infancy to the despondence of decrepitude. He must divest himself of the prejudices of his age or country; he must consider right and wrong in their abstracted and invariable state; he must disregard present laws and opinions, and rise to general and transcendental truths, which will always be the same: he must therefore content himself with the slow progress of his name; contemn the applause of his own time, and commit his claims to the justice of posterity. He must write as the interpreter of nature, and the legislator of mankind, and consider himself as presiding over the thoughts and manners of successive[9] generations; as a being superiour to time and place. His labour is not yet at an end: he must know many languages and many sciences; and, that his stile may be worthy of his thoughts, must, by incessant practice, familiarize to himself every delicacy of speech and grace of harmony."

---

[9] successive: future 2

XI

IMLAC'S NARRATIVE CONTINUED. A HINT ON PILGRIMAGE

Imlac now felt the enthusiastic fit, and was proceeding to aggrandize his own profession, when the prince cried out, "Enough! Thou hast convinced me, that no human being can ever be a poet. Proceed now with thy narration."

"To be a poet," said Imlac, "is indeed very difficult." "So difficult," returned the prince, "that I will at present hear no more of his labours. Tell me whither you went when you had seen Persia."

"From Persia," said the poet, "I travelled through Syria, and for three years resided in Palestine, where I conversed with great numbers of the northern and western nations of Europe; the nations which are now in possession of all power and all knowledge; whose armies are irresistible, and whose fleets command the remotest parts of the globe. When I compared these men with the natives of our own kingdom, and those that surround us, they appeared almost another order of beings. In their countries it is difficult to wish for any thing that may not be obtained: a thousand arts, of which we never heard, are continually labouring for their convenience and pleasure; and whatever their own climate has denied them is supplied by their commerce."

"By what means," said the prince, "are the Europeans thus powerful? or why, since they can so easily visit Asia and Africa for trade or conquest, cannot the Asiaticks and Africans invade their coasts, plant colonies in their ports, and give laws to their natural princes? The same wind that carries them back would bring us thither."

"They are more powerful, Sir, than we," answered Imlac, "because they are wiser; knowledge will always predominate over ignorance, as man governs the other animals. But why their knowledge is more than ours, I know not what reason can be given, but the unsearchable will of the Supreme Being."

"When," said the prince with a sigh, "shall I be able to visit Palestine, and mingle with this mighty confluence of nations? Till that happy moment shall arrive, let me fill up the time with such representations as thou canst give me. I am not ignorant of the motive that assembles such numbers in that place, and cannot but consider it as the center of wisdom and piety, to which the best and wisest men of every land must be continually resorting."

"There are some nations," said Imlac, "that send few visitants to Palestine; for many numerous and learned sects in Europe, concur to censure pilgrimage as superstitious, or deride it as ridiculous."

"You know," said the prince, "how little my life has made me acquainted with diversity of opinions: it will be too long to hear the arguments on both sides; you, that have considered them, tell me the result."

"Pilgrimage," said Imlac, "like many other acts of piety, may be reasonable or superstitious, according to the principles upon which it is performed. Long journies in search of truth are not commanded. Truth, such as is necessary to the regulation of life, is always found where it is honestly sought. Change of place is no natural cause of the increase of piety, for it inevitably produces dissipation of mind. Yet, since men go every day to view the places[1] where great actions have been performed, and return with stronger impressions of the event, curiosity of the same kind may naturally dispose us to view that country whence our religion had its beginning; and I believe no man surveys those awful scenes without some confirmation of holy resolutions. That the Supreme Being may be more easily propitiated in one place than in another, is the dream of idle superstition; but that some places may operate upon our own minds in an uncommon manner, is an opinion which hourly experience will justify. He who supposes that his vices may be more successfully combated in Palestine, will, perhaps, find himself mistaken, yet he may go thither without folly: he who thinks they will be more freely pardoned, dishonours at once his reason and religion."

"These," said the prince, "are European distinctions. I will consider them another time. What have you found to be the effect of knowledge? Are those nations happier than we?"

"There is so much infelicity," said the poet, "in the world, that scarce any man has leisure from his own distresses to estimate the comparative happiness of others. Knowledge is certainly one of the means of pleasure, as is confessed by the natural desire which

[1] places: fields 2

every mind feels of increasing its ideas. Ignorance is mere privation, by which nothing can be produced: it is a vacuity in which the soul sits motionless and torpid for want of attraction; and, without knowing why, we always rejoice when we learn, and grieve when we forget. I am therefore inclined to conclude, that, if nothing counteracts the natural consequence of learning, we grow more happy as our minds take a wider range.

"In enumerating the particular comforts of life we shall find many advantages on the side of the Europeans. They cure wounds and diseases with which we languish and perish. We suffer inclemencies of weather which they can obviate. They have engines for the despatch of many laborious works, which we must perform by manual industry. There is such communication between distant places, that one friend can hardly be said to be absent from another. Their policy removes all publick inconveniencies: they have roads cut through their mountains, and bridges laid upon their rivers. And, if we descend to the privacies of life, their habitations are more commodious, and their possessions are more secure."

"They are surely happy," said the prince, "who have all these conveniencies, of which I envy none so much as the facility with which separated friends interchange their thoughts."

"The Europeans," answered Imlac, "are less unhappy than we, but they are not happy. Human life is every where a state in which much is to be endured, and little to be enjoyed."

XII

THE STORY OF IMLAC CONTINUED

"I am not yet willing," said the prince, "to suppose that happiness is so parsimoniously distributed to mortals; nor can believe but that, if I had the choice of life, I should be able to fill every day with pleasure. I would injure no man, and should provoke no resentment: I would relieve every distress, and should enjoy the benedictions of gratitude. I would choose my friends among the wise, and my wife among the virtuous; and therefore should be in no danger from treachery, or unkindness. My children should, by my care, be learned and pious, and would repay to my age what their childhood had received. What would dare to molest him who might call on every side to thousands enriched by his bounty, or assisted by his power? And why should not life glide quietly away in the soft reciprocation of protection and reverence? All this may be done without the help of European refinements, which appear by their effects to be rather specious than useful. Let us leave them and persue our journey."

"From Palestine," said Imlac, "I passed through many regions of Asia; in the more civilized kingdoms as a trader, and among the Barbarians of the mountains as a pilgrim. At last I began to long for my native country, that I might repose after my travels, and fatigues, in the places where I had spent my earliest years, and gladden my old companions with the recital of my adventures. Often did I figure to myself those, with whom I had sported away the gay hours of dawning life, sitting round me in its evening, wondering at my tales, and listening to my counsels.

"When this thought had taken possession of my mind, I considered every moment as wasted which did not bring me nearer to Abissinia. I hastened into Egypt, and, notwithstanding my impatience, was detained ten months in the contemplation of its ancient magnificence, and in enquiries after the remains of its ancient learning. I found in Cairo a mixture of all nations; some brought thither by the love of knowledge, some by the hope of gain, and many by the desire of living after their own manner without observation, and of lying hid in the obscurity of multitudes: for, in a city, populous as Cairo, it is possible to obtain at the same time the gratifications of society, and the secrecy of solitude.

"From Cairo I travelled to Suez, and embarked on the Red sea, passing along the coast till I arrived at the port from which I had departed twenty years before. Here I joined myself to a caravan and re-entered my native country.

"I now expected the caresses of my kinsmen, and the congratulations of my friends, and was not without hope that my father, whatever value he had set upon riches, would own with gladness and pride a son who was able to add to the felicity and honour of the nation. But I was soon convinced that my thoughts were vain. My father had been dead fourteen years, having divided his wealth among my brothers, who were removed to some other provinces. Of my companions the greater part was in the grave, of the rest some could with difficulty remember me, and some considered me as one corrupted by foreign manners.

"A man used to vicissitudes is not easily dejected. I forgot, after a time, my disappointment, and endeavoured to recommend myself to the nobles of the kingdom: they admitted me to their tables, heard my story, and dismissed me. I opened a school, and was prohibited to teach. I then resolved to sit down in the quiet of domestick life, and addressed a lady that was fond of my conversation, but rejected my suit, because my father was a merchant.

"Wearied at last with solicitation and repulses, I resolved to hide myself for ever from the world, and depend no longer on the opinion or caprice of others. I waited for the time when the gate of the *happy valley* should open, that I might bid farewell to hope and fear: the day came; my performance was distinguished with favour, and I resigned myself with joy to perpetual confinement."

"Hast thou here found happiness at last?" said Rasselas. "Tell me without reserve; art thou content with thy condition? or, dost thou wish to be again wandering and inquiring? All the inhabitants of this valley celebrate their lot, and, at the annual visit of the emperour, invite others to partake of their felicity."

"Great prince," said Imlac, "I shall speak the truth: I know not one of all your attendants who does not lament the hour when he entered this retreat. I am less unhappy than the rest, because I have a mind replete with images, which I can vary and combine at pleasure. I can amuse my solitude by the renovation of the knowledge which begins to fade from my memory, and with the[2] recollection of the accidents of my past life. Yet all this ends in the sorrowful consideration, that my acquirements are now useless, and that none of my pleasures can be again enjoyed. The rest, whose minds have no impression but of the present moment, are either corroded by malignant passions, or sit stupid in the gloom of perpetual vacancy."

"What passions can infest those," said the prince, "who have no rivals? We are in a place where impotence precludes malice, and where all envy is repressed by community of enjoyments."

"There may be community," said Imlac, "of material posses-

[2] with the: by 2

sions, but there can never be community of love or of esteem. It must happen that one will please more than another; he that knows himself despised will always be envious; and still more envious and malevolent, if he is condemned to live in the presence of those who despise him. The invitations, by which they allure others to a state which they feel to be wretched, proceed from the natural malignity of hopeless misery. They are weary of themselves, and of each other, and expect to find relief in new companions. They envy the liberty which their folly has forfeited, and would gladly see all mankind imprisoned like themselves.

"From this crime, however, I am wholly free. No man can say that he is wretched by my persuasion. I look with pity on the crowds who are annually soliciting admission to captivity, and wish that it were lawful for me to warn them of their danger."

"My dear Imlac," said the prince, "I will open to thee my whole heart, that[3] I have long meditated an escape from the happy valley. I have examined the mountains on every side, but find myself insuperably barred: teach me the way to break my prison; thou shalt be the companion of my flight, the guide of my rambles, the partner of my fortune, and my sole director in the *choice of life.*"

"Sir," answered the poet, "your escape will be difficult, and, perhaps, you may soon repent your curiosity. The world, which you figure to yourself smooth and quiet as the lake in the valley, you will find a sea foaming with tempests, and boiling with whirlpools: you will be sometimes overwhelmed by the waves of violence, and sometimes dashed against the rocks of treachery. Amidst wrongs and frauds, competitions and anxieties, you will wish a thousand times for these seats of quiet, and willingly quit hope to be free from fear."

"Do not seek to deter me from my purpose," said the prince: "I am impatient to see what thou hast seen; and, since thou art thyself weary of the valley, it is evident, that thy former state was better than this. Whatever be the consequence of my experiment, I am resolved to judge with my own eyes of the various conditions of men, and then to make deliberately my *choice of life.*"

[3] heart, that: heart. 2

"I am afraid," said Imlac, "you are hindered by stronger restraints than my persuasions; yet, if your determination is fixed, I do not counsel you to despair. Few things are impossible to diligence and skill."

XIII

RASSELAS DISCOVERS THE MEANS OF ESCAPE

The prince now dismissed his favourite to rest, but the narrative of wonders and novelties filled his mind with perturbation. He revolved all that he had heard, and prepared innumerable questions for the morning.

Much of his uneasiness was now removed. He had a friend to whom he could impart his thoughts, and whose experience could assist him in his designs. His heart was no longer condemned to swell with silent vexation. He thought that even the *happy valley* might be endured with such a companion, and that, if they could range the world together, he should have nothing further to desire.

In a few days the water was discharged, and the ground dried. The prince and Imlac then walked out together to converse without the notice of the rest. The prince, whose thoughts were always on the wing, as he passed by the gate, said, with a countenance of sorrow, "Why art thou so strong, and why is man so weak?"

"Man is not weak," answered his companion; "knowledge is more than equivalent to force. The master of mechanicks laughs at strength. I can burst the gate, but cannot do it secretly. Some other expedient must be tried."

As they were walking on the side of the mountain, they observed that the conies, which the rain had driven from their burrows, had taken shelter among the bushes, and formed holes behind them, tending upwards in an oblique line. "It has been the opinion of antiquity," said Imlac, "that human reason borrowed many arts from the instinct of animals; let us, therefore, not think ourselves degraded by learning from the coney. We may escape by piercing the mountain in the same direction. We will begin where the summit hangs over the middle part, and labour upward till we shall issue out beyond the prominence."

The eyes of the prince, when he heard this proposal, sparkled with joy. The execution was easy, and the success certain.

No time was now lost. They hastened early in the morning to chuse a place proper for their mine. They clambered with great fatigue among crags and brambles, and returned without having discovered any part that favoured their design. The second and the third day were spent in the same manner, and with the same frustration. But, on the fourth, they found a small cavern, concealed by a thicket, where they resolved to make their experiment.

Imlac procured instruments proper to hew stone and remove earth, and they fell to their work on the next day with more eagerness than vigour. They were presently exhausted by their efforts, and sat down to pant upon the grass. The prince, for a moment, appeared to be discouraged. "Sir," said his companion, "practice will enable us to continue our labour for a longer time; mark, however, how far we have advanced, and you will find that our toil will some time have an end. Great works are performed, not by strength, but perseverance: yonder palace was raised by single stones, yet you see its height and spaciousness. He that shall walk with vigour three hours a day will pass in seven years a space equal to the circumference of the globe."

They returned to their labour[4] day after day, and, in a short time, found a fissure in the rock, which enabled them to pass far with very little obstruction. This Rasselas considered as a good omen. "Do not disturb your mind," said Imlac, "with other hopes or fears than reason may suggest: if you are pleased with prognosticks of good, you will be terrified likewise with tokens of evil, and your whole life will be a prey to superstition. Whatever facilitates our work is more than an omen, it is a cause of success. This is one of those pleasing surprises which often happen to active resolution. Many things difficult to design prove easy to performance."

XIV

RASSELAS AND IMLAC RECEIVE AN UNEXPECTED VISIT

They had now wrought their way to the middle, and solaced their labour[5] with the approach of liberty, when the prince, coming

---

[4] labour: work 2
[5] labour: toil 2

down to refresh himself with air, found his sister Nekayah standing before the mouth of the cavity. He started and stood confused, afraid to tell his design, and yet hopeless to conceal it. A few moments determined him to repose on her fidelity, and secure her secrecy by a declaration without reserve.

"Do not imagine," said the princess, "that I came hither as a spy: I had often[6] observed from my window, that you and Imlac directed your walk every day towards the same point, but I did not suppose you had any better reason for the preference than a cooler shade, or more fragrant bank; nor followed you with any other design than to partake of your conversation. Since then not suspicion but fondness has detected you, let me not lose the advantage of my discovery. I am equally weary of confinement with yourself, and not less desirous of knowing what is done or suffered in the world. Permit me to fly with you from this tasteless tranquility, which will yet grow more loathsome when you have left me. You may deny me to accompany you, but cannot hinder me from following."

The prince, who loved Nekayah above his other sisters, had no inclination to refuse her request, and grieved that he had lost an opportunity of shewing his confidence by a voluntary communication. It was therefore agreed that she should leave the valley with them; and that, in the mean time, she should watch, lest any other straggler should, by chance or curiosity, follow them to the mountain.

At length their labour was at an end; they saw light beyond the prominence, and, issuing to the top of the mountain, beheld the Nile, yet a narrow current, wandering beneath them.

The prince looked round with rapture, anticipated all the pleasures of travel, and in thought was already transported beyond his father's dominions. Imlac, though very joyful at his escape, had less expectation of pleasure in the world, which he had before tried, and of which he had been weary.

Rasselas was so much delighted with a wider horizon, that he could not soon be persuaded to return into the valley. He informed his sister that the way was open, and that nothing now remained but to prepare for their departure.

---

[6] often: long 2

XV

THE PRINCE AND PRINCESS LEAVE THE VALLEY, AND SEE MANY WONDERS

The prince and princess had jewels sufficient to make them rich whenever they came into a place of commerce, which, by Imlac's direction, they hid in their cloaths, and, on the night of the next full moon, all left the valley. The princess was followed only by a single favourite, who did not know whither she was going.

They clambered through the cavity, and began to go down on the other side. The princess and her maid turned their eyes towards every part, and, seeing nothing to bound their prospect, considered themselves as in danger of being lost in a dreary vacuity. They stopped and trembled. "I am almost afraid," said the princess, "to begin a journey of which I cannot perceive an end, and to venture into this immense plain where I may be approached on every side by men whom I never saw." The prince felt nearly the same emotions, though he thought it more manly to conceal them.

Imlac smiled at their terrours, and encouraged them to proceed; but the princess continued irresolute till she had been imperceptibly drawn forward too far to return.

In the morning they found some shepherds in the field, who set milk and fruits before them. The princess wondered that she did not see a palace ready for her reception, and a table spread with delicacies; but, being faint and hungry, she drank the milk and eat the fruits, and thought them of a higher flavour than the products of the valley.

They travelled forward by easy journeys, being all unaccustomed to toil or difficulty, and knowing, that though they might be missed, they could not be persued. In a few days they came into a more populous region, where Imlac was diverted with the admiration which his companions expressed at the diversity of manners, stations and employments.

Their dress was such as might not bring upon them the suspicion of having any thing to conceal, yet the prince, wherever he came, expected to be obeyed, and the princess was frighted, because those that came into her presence did not prostrate themselves before her. Imlac was forced to observe them with great vigilance, lest they should betray their rank by their unusual behaviour, and detained them several weeks in the first village to accustom them to the sight of common mortals.

By degrees the royal wanderers were taught to understand that they had for a time laid aside their dignity, and were to expect only such regard as liberality and courtesy could procure. And Imlac, having, by many admonitions, prepared them to endure the tumults of a port, and the ruggedness of the commercial race, brought them down to the sea-coast.

The prince and his sister, to whom every thing was new, were gratified equally at all places, and therefore remained for some months at the port without any inclination to pass further. Imlac was content with their stay, because he did not think it safe to expose them, unpractised in the world, to the hazards of a foreign country.

At last he began to fear lest they should be discovered, and proposed to fix a day for their departure. They had no pretensions to judge for themselves, and referred the whole scheme to his direction. He therefore took passage in a ship to Suez; and, when the time came, with great difficulty prevailed on the princess to enter the vessel. They had a quick and prosperous voyage, and from Suez travelled by land to Cairo.

XVI

THEY ENTER CAIRO, AND FIND EVERY MAN HAPPY

As they approached the city, which filled the strangers with astonishment, "This," said Imlac to the prince, "is the place where travellers and merchants assemble from all the corners of the earth. You will here find men of every character, and every occupation. Commerce is here honourable: I will act as a merchant, and you shall live as strangers, who have no other end of travel than curiosity; it will soon be observed that we are rich; our reputation will procure us access to all whom we shall desire to know; you will see all the conditions of humanity, and enable yourself at leisure to make your *choice of life.*"

They now entered the town, stunned by the noise, and offended by the crowds. Instruction had not yet so prevailed over habit, but that they wondered to see themselves pass undistinguished along the street, and met by the lowest of the people without reverence or notice. The princess could not at first bear the thought of being levelled with the vulgar, and, for some days, continued in her chamber, where she was served by her favourite[7] as in the palace of the valley.

Imlac, who understood traffick, sold part of the jewels the next day, and hired a house, which he adorned with such magnificence, that he was immediately considered as a merchant of great wealth. His politeness attracted many acquaintance, and his generosity made him courted by many dependants. His table was crowded by men of every nation, who all admired his knowledge, and solicited his favour. His companions, not being able to mix in the conversation, could make no discovery of their ignorance or surprise, and were gradually initiated in the world as they gained knowledge of the language.

The prince had, by frequent lectures, been taught the use and nature of money; but the ladies could not, for a long time, comprehend what the merchants did with small pieces of gold and silver, or why things of so little use should be received as equivalent to the necessaries of life.

They studied the language two years, while Imlac was preparing to set before them the various ranks and conditions of mankind. He grew acquainted with all who had any thing uncommon in their fortune or conduct. He frequented the voluptuous and the frugal, the idle and the busy, the merchants and the men of learning.

The prince, being now able to converse with fluency, and having learned the caution necessary to be observed in his intercourse with strangers, began to accompany Imlac to places of resort, and to enter into all assemblies, that he might make his *choice of life*.

For some time he thought choice needless, because all appeared to him equally happy. Wherever he went he met gayety and kindness, and heard the song of joy, or the laugh of carelessness. He began to believe that the world overflowed with universal plenty,

---

[7] favourite: favourite Pekuah 2

and that nothing was withheld either from want or merit; that every hand showered liberality, and every heart melted with benevolence: "and who then," says he, "will be suffered to be wretched?"

Imlac permitted the pleasing delusion, and was unwilling to crush the hope of inexperience, till one day, having sat a while silent, "I know not," said the prince, "what can be the reason that I am more unhappy than any of our friends. I see them perpetually and unalterably chearful, but feel my own mind restless and uneasy. I am unsatisfied with those pleasures which I seem most to court; I live in the crowds of jollity, not so much to enjoy company as to shun myself, and am only loud and merry to conceal my sadness."

"Every man," said Imlac, "may, by examining his own mind, guess what passes in the minds of others: when you feel that your own gaiety is counterfeit, it may justly lead you to suspect that of your companions not to be sincere. Envy is commonly reciprocal. We are long before we are convinced that happiness is never to be found, and each believes it possessed by others, to keep alive the hope of obtaining it for himself. In the assembly, where you passed the last night, there appeared such spriteliness of air, and volatility of fancy, as might have suited beings of an higher order, formed to inhabit serener regions inaccessible to care or sorrow: yet, believe me, prince, there was not one who did not dread the moment when solitude should deliver him to the tyranny of reflection."

"This," said the prince, "may be true of others, since it is true of me; yet, whatever be the general infelicity of man, one condition is more happy than another, and wisdom surely directs us to take the least evil in the *choice of life*."

"The causes of good and evil," answered Imlac, "are so various and uncertain, so often entangled with each other, so diversified by various relations, and so much subject to accidents which cannot be foreseen, that he who would fix his condition upon incontestable reasons of preference, must live and die enquiring and deliberating."

"But surely," said Rasselas, "the wise men, to whom we listen with reverence and wonder, chose that mode of life for themselves which they thought most likely to make them happy."

"Very few," said the poet, "live by choice. Every man is placed in his present condition by causes which acted without his foresight, and with which he did not always willingly co-operate; and therefore you will rarely meet one who does not think the lot of his neighbour better than his own."

"I am pleased to think," said the prince, "that my birth has given me at least one advantage over others, by enabling me to determine for myself. I have here the world before me; I will review it at leisure: surely happiness is somewhere to be found."

XVII

THE PRINCE ASSOCIATES WITH YOUNG MEN OF SPIRIT AND GAIETY

Rasselas rose next day, and resolved to begin his experiments upon life. "Youth," cried he, "is the time of gladness: I will join myself to the young men, whose only business is to gratify their desires, and whose time is all spent in a succession of enjoyments."

To such societies he was readily admitted, but a few days brought him back weary and disgusted. Their mirth was without images, their laughter without motive; their pleasures were gross and sensual, in which the mind had no part; their conduct was at once wild and mean; they laughed at order and at law, but the frown of power dejected, and the eye of wisdom abashed them.

The prince soon concluded, that he should never be happy in a course of life of which he was ashamed. He thought it unsuitable to a reasonable being to act without a plan, and to be sad or chearful only by chance. "Happiness," said he, "must be something solid and permanent, without fear and without uncertainty."

But his young companions had gained so much of his regard by their frankness and courtesy, that he could not leave them without warning and remonstrance. "My friends," said he, "I have seriously considered our manners and our prospects, and find that we have mistaken our own interest. The first years of man must make provision for the last. He that never thinks never can be wise. Perpetual levity must end in ignorance; and intemperance, though it may fire the spirits for an hour, will make life short or miserable. Let us consider that youth is of no long duration, and that in maturer age, when the enchantments of fancy shall cease, and phantoms of delight dance no more about us, we shall have no comforts but the esteem of wise men, and the means of doing good. Let us, therefore, stop, while to stop is in our power: let us live as men who are sometime to grow old, and to whom it will be the most dreadful of all evils not to count their past years but by follies, and to be reminded of their former luxuriance of health only by the maladies which riot has produced."

They stared a while in silence one upon another, and, at last, drove him away by a general chorus of continued laughter.

The consciousness that his sentiments were just, and his intentions kind, was scarcely sufficient to support him against the horrour of derision. But he recovered his tranquility, and persued his search.

XVIII

THE PRINCE FINDS A WISE AND HAPPY MAN

As he was one day walking in the street, he saw a spacious building which all were, by the open doors, invited to enter: he followed the stream of people, and found it a hall or school of declamation, in which professors read lectures to their auditory. He fixed his eye upon a sage raised above the rest, who discoursed with great energy on the government of the passions. His look was venerable, his action graceful, his pronunciation clear, and his diction elegant. He shewed, with great strength of sentiment, and variety of illustration, that human nature is degraded and debased, when the lower faculties predominate over the higher; that when fancy, the parent of passion, usurps the dominion of the mind, nothing ensues but the natural effect of unlawful government, perturbation and confusion; that she betrays the fortresses of the intellect to rebels, and excites her children to sedition against reason their lawful sovereign. He compared reason to the sun, of which the light is constant, uniform, and lasting; and fancy to a meteor, of bright but transitory lustre, irregular in its motion, and delusive in its direction.

He then communicated the various precepts given from time

to time for the conquest of passion, and displayed the happiness of those who had obtained the important victory, after which man is no longer the slave of fear, nor the fool of hope; is no more emaciated by envy, inflamed by anger, emasculated by tenderness, or depressed by grief; but walks on calmly through the tumults or the privacies of life, as the sun persues alike his course through the calm or the stormy sky.

He enumerated many examples of heroes immovable by pain or pleasure, who looked with indifference on those modes or accidents to which the vulgar give the names of good and evil. He exhorted his hearers to lay aside their prejudices, and arm themselves against the shafts of malice or misfortune, by invulnerable patience; concluding, that this state only was happiness, and that this happiness was in every one's power.

Rasselas listened to him with the veneration due to the instructions of a superiour being, and, waiting for him at the door, humbly implored the liberty of visiting so great a master of true wisdom. The lecturer hesitated a moment, when Rasselas put a purse of gold into his hand, which he received with a mixture of joy and wonder.

"I have found," said the prince, at his return to Imlac, "a man who can teach all that is necessary to be known, who, from the unshaken throne of rational fortitude, looks down on the scenes of life changing beneath him. He speaks, and attention watches his lips. He reasons, and conviction closes his periods. This man shall be my future guide: I will learn his doctrines, and imitate his life."

"Be not too hasty," said Imlac, "to trust, or to admire, the teachers of morality: they discourse like angels, but they live like men."

Rasselas, who could not conceive how any man could reason so forcibly without feeling the cogency of his own arguments, paid his visit in a few days, and was denied admission. He had now learned the power of money, and made his way by a piece of gold to the inner apartment, where he found the philosopher in a room half darkened, with his eyes misty, and his face pale. "Sir," said he, "you are come at a time when all human friendship is useless; what I suffer cannot be remedied, what I have lost cannot be supplied. My daughter, my only daughter, from whose tenderness I expected all the comforts of my age, died last night of a fever. My views, my purposes, my hopes are at an end: I am now a lonely being disunited from society."

"Sir," said the prince, "mortality is an event by which a wise man can never be surprised: we know that death is always near, and it should therefore always be expected." "Young man," answered the philosopher, "you speak like one that has never felt the pangs of separation." "Have you then forgot the precepts," said Rasselas, "which you so powerfully enforced? Has wisdom no strength to arm the heart against calamity? Consider, that external things are naturally variable, but truth and reason are always the same." "What comfort," said the mourner, "can truth and reason afford me? of what effect are they now, but to tell me, that my daughter will not be restored?"

The prince, whose humanity would not suffer him to insult misery with reproof, went away convinced of the emptiness of rhetorical sound, and the inefficacy of polished periods and studied sentences.

XIX

A GLIMPSE OF PASTORAL LIFE

He was still eager upon the same enquiry; and, having heard of a hermit, that lived near the lowest cataract of the Nile, and filled the whole country with the fame of his sanctity, resolved to visit his retreat, and enquire whether that felicity, which publick life could not afford, was to be found in solitude; and whether a man, whose age and virtue made him venerable, could teach any peculiar art of shunning evils, or enduring them.

Imlac and the princess agreed to accompany him, and, after the necessary preparations, they began their journey. Their way lay through fields, where shepherds tended their flocks, and the lambs were playing upon the pasture. "This," said the poet, "is the life which has been often celebrated for its innocence and quiet: let us pass the heat of the day among the shepherds tents, and know whether all our searches are not to terminate in pastoral simplicity."

The proposal pleased them, and they induced the shepherds, by small presents and familiar questions, to tell their opinion of their own state: they were so rude and ignorant, so little able to compare the good with the evil of the occupation, and so indistinct in their narratives and descriptions, that very little could be learned from them. But it was evident that their hearts were cankered with discontent; that they considered themselves as condemned to labour for the luxury of the rich, and looked up with stupid malevolence toward those that were placed above them.

The princess pronounced with vehemence, that she would never suffer these envious savages to be her companions, and that she should not soon be desirous of seeing any more specimens of rustick happiness; but could not believe that all the accounts of primeval pleasures were fabulous, and was yet in doubt whether life had any thing that could be justly preferred to the placid gratifications of fields and woods. She hoped that the time would come, when, with a few virtuous and elegant companions, she should gather flowers planted by her own hand, fondle the lambs of her own ewe, and listen, without care, among brooks and breezes, to one of her maidens reading in the shade.

XX

THE DANGER OF PROSPERITY

On the next day they continued their journey, till the heat compelled them to look round for shelter. At a small distance they saw a thick wood, which they no sooner entered than they perceived that they were approaching the habitations of men. The shrubs were diligently cut away to open walks where the shades were darkest; the boughs of opposite trees were artificially interwoven; seats of flowery turf were raised in vacant spaces, and a rivulet, that wantoned along the side of a winding path, had its banks sometimes opened into small basons, and its stream sometimes obstructed by little mounds of stone heaped together to increase its murmurs.

They passed slowly through the wood, delighted with such unexpected accommodations, and entertained each other with conjecturing what, or who, he could be, that, in those rude and unfrequented regions, had leisure and art for such harmless luxury.

As they advanced, they heard the sound of musick, and saw youths and virgins dancing in the grove; and, going still further, beheld a stately palace built upon a hill surrounded with woods. The laws of eastern hospitality allowed them to enter, and the master welcomed them like a man liberal and wealthy.

He was skilful enough in appearances soon to discern that they were no common guests, and spread his table with magnificence. The eloquence of Imlac caught his attention, and the lofty courtesy of the princess excited his respect. When they offered to depart he entreated their stay, and was the next day still more unwilling to dismiss them than before. They were easily persuaded to stop, and civility grew up in time to freedom and confidence.

The prince now saw all the domesticks chearful, and all the face of nature smiling round the place, and could not forbear to hope that he should find here what he was seeking; but when he was congratulating the master upon his possessions, he answered with a sigh, "My condition has indeed the appearance of happiness, but appearances are delusive. My prosperity puts my life in danger; the Bassa of Egypt is my enemy, incensed only by my wealth and popularity. I have been hitherto protected against him by the princes of the country; but, as the favour of the great is uncertain, I know not how soon my defenders may be persuaded to share the plunder with the Bassa. I have sent my treasures into a distant country, and, upon the first alarm, am prepared to follow them. Then will my enemies riot in my mansion, and enjoy the gardens which I have planted."

They all joined in lamenting his danger, and deprecating his exile; and the princess was so much disturbed with the tumult of grief and indignation, that she retired to her apartment. They continued with their kind inviter a few days longer, and then went forward to find the hermit.

XXI

THE HAPPINESS OF SOLITUDE. THE HERMIT'S HISTORY

They came on the third day, by the direction of the peasants, to the hermit's cell: it was a cavern in the side of a mountain, overshadowed with palm-trees; at such a distance from the cataract, that nothing more was heard than a gentle uniform murmur, such as composed the mind to pensive meditation, especially when it was assisted by the wind whistling among the branches. The first rude essay of nature had been so much improved by human labour, that the cave contained several apartments, appropriated to different uses, and often afforded lodging to travellers, whom darkness or tempests happened to overtake.

The hermit sat on a bench at the door, to enjoy the coolness of the evening. On one side lay a book with pens and papers, on the other mechanical instruments of various kinds. As they approached him unregarded, the princess observed that he had not the countenance of a man that had found, or could teach, the way to happiness.

They saluted him with great respect, which he repaid like a man not unaccustomed to the forms of courts. "My children," said he, "if you have lost your way, you shall be willingly supplied with such conveniencies for the night as this cavern will afford. I have all that nature requires, and you will not expect delicacies in a hermit's cell."

They thanked him, and, entering, were pleased with the neatness and regularity of the place. The hermit set flesh and wine before them, though he fed only upon fruits and water. His discourse was chearful without levity, and pious without enthusiasm.[8] He soon gained the esteem of his guests, and the princess repented of her hasty censure.

At last Imlac began thus: "I do not now wonder that your reputation is so far extended; we have heard at Cairo of your wisdom, and came hither to implore your direction for this young man and maiden in the *choice of life.*"

"To him that lives well," answered the hermit, "every form of life is good; nor can I give any other rule for choice, than to remove from all apparent evil."

"He will remove most certainly from evil," said the prince, "who shall devote himself to that solitude which you have recommended by your example."

---

[8] enthusiasm: "A vain belief of private revelation; a vain confidence of divine favour or communication." Johnson's *Dictionary*.

"I have indeed lived fifteen years in solitude," said the hermit, "but have no desire that my example should gain any imitators. In my youth I professed arms, and was raised by degrees to the highest military rank. I have traversed wide countries at the head of my troops, and seen many battles and sieges. At last, being disgusted by the preferment of a younger officer, and finding my vigour[9] beginning to decay, I resolved to close my life in peace, having found the world full of snares, discord, and misery. I had once escaped from the persuit of the enemy by the shelter of this cavern, and therefore chose it for my final residence. I employed artificers to form it into chambers, and stored it with all that I was likely to want.

"For some time after my retreat, I rejoiced like a tempest-beaten sailor at his entrance into the harbour, being delighted with the sudden change of the noise and hurry of war, to stillness and repose. When the pleasure of novelty went away, I employed my hours in examining the plants which grow in the valley, and the minerals which I collected from the rocks. But that enquiry is now grown tasteless and irksome. I have been for some time unsettled and distracted: my mind is disturbed with a thousand perplexities of doubt, and vanities of imagination, which hourly prevail upon me, because I have no opportunities of relaxation or diversion. I am sometimes ashamed to think that I could not secure myself from vice, but by retiring from the practice[1] of virtue, and begin to suspect that I was rather impelled by resentment, than led by devotion, into solitude. My fancy riots in scenes of folly, and I lament that I have lost so much, and have gained so little. In solitude, if I escape the example of bad men, I want likewise the counsel and conversation of the good. I have been long comparing the evils with the advantages of society, and resolve to return into the world to morrow. The life of a solitary man will be certainly miserable, but not certainly devout."

They heard his resolution with surprise, but, after a short pause, offered to conduct him to Cairo. He dug up a considerable treasure which he had hid among the rocks, and accompanied them to the city, on which, as he approached it, he gazed with rapture.

[9] finding my vigour: feeling that my vigour was 2
[1] practice: exercise 2

XXII

THE HAPPINESS OF A LIFE LED ACCORDING TO NATURE

Rasselas went often to an assembly of learned men, who met at stated times to unbend their minds, and compare their opinions. Their manners were somewhat coarse, but their conversation was instructive, and their disputations acute, though sometimes too violent, and often continued till neither controvertist remembered upon what question they began. Some faults were almost general among them: every one was desirous to dictate to the rest, and every one was pleased to hear the genius or knowledge of another depreciated.

In this assembly Rasselas was relating his interview with the hermit, and the wonder with which he heard him censure a course of life which he had so deliberately chosen, and so laudably followed. The sentiments of the hearers were various. Some were of opinion, that the folly of his choice had been justly punished by condemnation to perpetual perseverance. One of the youngest among them, with great vehemence, pronounced him an hypocrite. Some talked of the right of society to the labour of individuals, and considered retirement as a desertion of duty. Others readily allowed, that there was a time when the claims of the publick were satisfied, and when a man might properly sequester himself, to review his life, and purify his heart.

One, who appeared more affected with the narrative than the rest, thought it likely, that the hermit would, in a few years, go back to his retreat, and, perhaps, if shame did not restrain, or death intercept him, return once more from his retreat into the world: "For the hope of happiness," says[2] he, "is so strongly impressed, that the longest experience is not able to efface it. Of the present state, whatever it be, we feel, and are forced to confess, the misery, yet, when the same state is again at a distance, imagination paints it as desirable. But the time will surely come, when desire will be no longer our torment, and no man shall be wretched but by his own fault."

"This," said a philosopher, who had heard him with tokens of

[2] says: said 2

great impatience, "is the present condition of a wise man. The time is already come, when none are wretched but by their own fault. Nothing is more idle, than to enquire after happiness, which nature has kindly placed within our reach. The way to be happy is to live according to nature, in obedience to that universal and unalterable law with which every heart is originally impressed; which is not written on it by precept, but engraven by destiny, not instilled by education, but infused at our nativity. He that lives according to nature will suffer nothing from the delusions of hope, or importunities of desire: he will receive and reject with equability of temper; and act or suffer as the reason of things shall alternately prescribe. Other men may amuse themselves with subtle definitions, or intricate raciocination. Let them learn to be wise by easier means: let them observe the hind of the forest, and the linnet of the grove: let them consider the life of animals, whose motions are regulated by instinct; they obey their guide and are happy. Let us therefore, at length, cease to dispute, and learn to live; throw away the incumbrance of precepts, which they who utter them with so much pride and pomp do not understand, and carry with us this simple and intelligible maxim, That deviation from nature is deviation from happiness."

When he had spoken, he looked round him with a placid air, and enjoyed the consciousness of his own beneficence. "Sir," said the prince, with great modesty, "as I, like all the rest of mankind, am desirous of felicity, my closest attention has been fixed upon your discourse: I doubt not the truth of a position which a man so learned has so confidently advanced. Let me only know what it is to live according to nature."

"When I find young men so humble and so docile," said the philosopher, "I can deny them no information which my studies have enabled me to afford. To live according to nature, is to act always with due regard to the fitness arising from the relations and qualities of causes and effects; to concur with the great and unchangeable scheme of universal felicity; to co-operate with the general disposition and tendency of the present system of things."

The prince soon found that this was one of the sages whom he should understand less as he heard him longer. He therefore bowed and was silent, and the philosopher, supposing him satisfied, and the rest vanquished, rose up and departed with the air of a man that had co-operated with the present system.

XXIII

THE PRINCE AND HIS SISTER DIVIDE BETWEEN THEM THE WORK OF OBSERVATION

Rasselas returned home full of reflexions, doubtful how to direct his future steps. Of the way to happiness he found the learned and simple equally ignorant; but, as he was yet young, he flattered himself that he had time remaining for more experiments, and further enquiries. He communicated to Imlac his observations and his doubts, but was answered by him with new doubts, and remarks that gave him no comfort. He therefore discoursed more frequently and freely with his sister, who had yet the same hope with himself, and always assisted him to give some reason why, though he had been hitherto frustrated, he might succeed at last.

"We have hitherto," said she, "known but little of the world: we have never yet been either great or mean. In our own country, though we had royalty, we had no power, and in this we have not yet seen the private recesses of domestick peace. Imlac favours not our search, lest we should in time find him mistaken. We will divide the task between us: you shall try what is to be found in the splendour of courts, and I will range the shades of humbler life. Perhaps command and authority may be the supreme blessings, as they afford most opportunities of doing good: or, perhaps, what this world can give may be found in the modest habitations of middle fortune; too low for great designs, and too high for penury and distress."

XXIV

THE PRINCE EXAMINES THE HAPPINESS OF HIGH STATIONS

Rasselas applauded the design, and appeared next day with a splendid retinue at the court of the Bassa. He was soon distinguished for his magnificence, and admitted, as a prince whose curiosity had brought him from distant countries, to an intimacy with the great officers, and frequent conversation with the Bassa himself.

He was at first inclined to believe, that the man must be pleased with his own condition, whom all approached with reverence, and heard with obedience, and who had the power to extend his edicts to a whole kingdom. "There can be no pleasure," said he, "equal to that of feeling at once the joy of thousands all made happy by wise administration. Yet, since, by the law of subordination, this sublime delight can be in one nation but the lot of one, it is surely reasonable to think that there is some satisfaction more popular and accessible, and that millions can hardly be subjected to the will of a single man, only to fill his particular breast with incommunicable content."

These thoughts were often in his mind, and he found no solution of the difficulty. But as presents and civilities gained him more familiarity, he found that almost every man that[3] stood high in employment hated all the rest, and was hated by them, and that their lives were a continual succession of plots and detections, stratagems and escapes, faction and treachery. Many of those, who surrounded the Bassa, were sent only to watch and report his conduct; every tongue was muttering censure, and every eye was searching for a fault.

At last the letters of revocation arrived, the Bassa was carried in chains to Constantinople, and his name was mentioned no more.

"What are we now to think of the prerogatives of power," said Rasselas to his sister; "is it without any efficacy to good? or, is the subordinate degree only dangerous, and the supreme safe and glorious? Is the Sultan the only happy man in his dominions? or, is the Sultan himself subject to the torments of suspicion, and the dread of enemies?"

In a short time the second Bassa was deposed. The Sultan, that had advanced him, was murdered by the Janisaries, and his successor had other views and different favourites.

XXV

THE PRINCESS PERSUES HER ENQUIRY WITH MORE DILIGENCE THAN SUCCESS

The princess, in the mean time, insinuated herself into many families; for there are few doors, through which liberality, joined with good humour, cannot find its way. The daughters of many houses were airy and chearful, but Nekayah had been too long

[3] that: who 2

accustomed to the conversation of Imlac and her brother to be much pleased with childish levity and prattle which had no meaning. She found their thoughts narrow, their wishes low, and their merriment often artificial. Their pleasures, poor as they were, could not be preserved pure, but were embittered by petty competitions and worthless emulation. They were always jealous of the beauty of each other; of a quality to which solicitude can add nothing, and from which detraction can take nothing away. Many were in love with triflers like themselves, and many fancied that they were in love when in truth they were only idle. Their affection was seldom fixed on sense or virtue, and therefore seldom ended but in vexation. Their grief, however, like their joy, was transient; every thing floated in their mind unconnected with the past or future, so that one desire easily gave way to another, as a second stone cast into the water effaces and confounds the circles of the first.

With these girls she played as with inoffensive animals, and found them proud of her countenance, and weary of her company.

But her purpose was to examine more deeply, and her affability easily persuaded the hearts that were swelling with sorrow to discharge their secrets in her ear: and those whom hope flattered, or prosperity delighted, often courted her to partake their pleasures.

The princess and her brother commonly met in the evening in a private summer-house on the bank of the Nile, and related to each other the occurrences of the day. As they were sitting together, the princess cast her eyes upon the river that flowed before her. "Answer," said she, "great father of waters, thou that rollest thy floods through eighty nations, to the invocations of the daughter of thy native king. Tell me if thou waterest, through all thy course, a single habitation from which thou dost not hear the murmurs of complaint?"

"You are then," said Rasselas, "not more successful in private houses than I have been in courts." "I have, since the last partition of our provinces," said the princess, "enabled myself to enter familiarly into many families, where there was the fairest show of prosperity and peace, and know not one house that is not haunted by some fiend[4] that destroys its quiet.

"I did not seek ease among the poor, because I concluded that

[4] fiend: fury 2

there it could not be found. But I saw many poor whom I had supposed to live in affluence. Poverty has, in large cities, very different appearances: it is often concealed in splendour, and often in extravagance. It is the care of a very great part of mankind to conceal their indigence from the rest: they support themselves by temporary expedients, and every day is lost in contriving for the morrow.

"This, however, was an evil, which, though frequent, I saw with less pain, because I could relieve it. Yet some have refused my bounties; more offended with my quickness to detect their wants, than pleased with my readiness to succour them: and others, whose exigencies compelled them to admit my kindness, have never been able to forgive their benefactress. Many, however, have been sincerely grateful without the ostentation of gratitude, or the hope of other favours."

XXVI

THE PRINCESS CONTINUES HER REMARKS UPON PRIVATE LIFE

Nekayah perceiving her brother's attention fixed, proceeded in her narrative.

"In families, where there is or is not poverty, there is commonly discord: if a kingdom be, as Imlac tells us, a great family, a family likewise is a little kingdom, torn with factions and exposed to revolutions. An unpractised observer expects the love of parents and children to be constant and equal; but this kindness seldom continues beyond the years of infancy: in a short time the children become rivals to their parents. Benefits are allayed[5] by reproaches, and gratitude debased by envy.

"Parents and children seldom act in concert: each child endeavours to appropriate the esteem or fondness of the parents, and the parents, with yet less temptation, betray each other to their children; thus some place their confidence in the father, and some in the mother, and, by degrees, the house is filled with artifices and feuds.

"The opinions of children and parents, of the young and the

[5] allayed: i.e., alloyed.

old, are naturally opposite, by the contrary effects of hope and despondence, of expectation and experience, without crime or folly on either side. The colours of life in youth and age appear different, as the face of nature in spring and winter. And how can children credit the assertions of parents, which their own eyes show them to be false?

"Few parents act in such a manner as much to enforce their maxims by the credit of their lives. The old man trusts wholly to slow contrivance and gradual progression: the youth expects to force his way by genius, vigour, and precipitance. The old man pays regard to riches, and the youth reverences virtue. The old man deifies prudence: the youth commits himself to magnanimity and chance. The young man, who intends no ill, believes that none is intended, and therefore acts with openness and candour: but his father, having suffered the injuries of fraud, is impelled to suspect, and too often allured to practice it. Age looks with anger on the temerity of youth, and youth with contempt on the scrupulosity of age. Thus parents and children, for the greatest part, live on to love less and less: and, if those whom nature has thus closely united are the torments of each other, where shall we look for tenderness and consolation?"

"Surely," said the prince, "you must have been unfortunate in your choice of acquaintance: I am unwilling to believe, that the most tender of all relations is thus impeded in its effects by natural necessity."

"Domestick discord," answered she, "is not inevitably and fatally necessary; but yet is not easily avoided. We seldom see that a whole family is virtuous: the good and evil cannot well agree; and the evil can yet less agree with one another: even the virtuous fall sometimes to variance, when their virtues are of different kinds, and tending to extremes. In general, those parents have most reverence who most deserve it: for he that lives well cannot be despised.

"Many other evils infest private life. Some are the slaves of servants whom they have trusted with their affairs. Some are kept in continual anxiety to the caprice of rich relations, whom they cannot please, and dare not offend. Some husbands are imperious, and some wives perverse: and, as it is always more easy to do evil than good, though the wisdom or virtue of one can very rarely make many happy, the folly or vice of one may often make many miserable."

"If such be the general effect of marriage," said the prince, "I shall, for the future, think it dangerous to connect my interest with that of another, lest I should be unhappy by my partner's fault."

"I have met," said the princess, "with many who live single for that reason; but I never found that their prudence ought to raise envy. They dream away their time without friendship, without fondness, and are driven to rid themselves of the day, for which they have no use, by childish amusements, or vicious delights. They act as beings under the constant sense of some known inferiority, that fills their minds with rancour, and their tongues with censure. They are peevish at home, and malevolent abroad; and, as the out-laws of human nature, make it their business and their pleasure to disturb that society which debars them from its privileges. To live without feeling or exciting sympathy, to be fortunate without adding to the felicity of others, or afflicted without tasting the balm of pity, is a state more gloomy than solitude: it is not retreat but exclusion from mankind. Marriage has many pains, but celibacy has no pleasures."

"What then is to be done?" said Rasselas; "the more we enquire, the less we can resolve. Surely he is most likely to please himself that has no other inclination to regard."

XXVII

DISQUISITION UPON GREATNESS

The conversation had a short pause. The prince, having considered his sister's observations, told her, that she had surveyed life with prejudice, and supposed misery where she did not find it. "Your narrative," says he, "throws yet a darker gloom upon the prospects of futurity: the predictions of Imlac were but faint sketches of the evils painted by Nekayah. I have been lately convinced that quiet is not the daughter of grandeur, or of power: that her presence is not to be bought by wealth, nor enforced by conquest. It is evident, that as any man acts in a wider compass, he must be more exposed to opposition from enmity or miscarriage from chance; whoever has many to please or to govern, must use the ministry of many agents, some of whom will be wicked, and some ignorant; by some he will be misled, and by others betrayed. If he gratifies one he will offend another: those that are not favoured will think themselves injured; and, since favours can be conferred but upon few, the greater number will be always discontented."

"The discontent," said the princess, "which is thus unreasonable, I hope that I shall always have spirit to despise, and you, power to repress."

"Discontent," answered Rasselas, "will not always be without reason under the most just or vigilant administration of publick affairs. None, however attentive, can always discover that merit which indigence or faction may happen to obscure; and none, however powerful, can always reward it. Yet, he that sees inferiour desert advanced above him, will naturally impute that preference to partiality or caprice; and, indeed, it can scarcely be hoped that any man, however magnanimous by nature, or exalted by condition, will be able to persist for ever in fixed and inexorable justice of distribution: he will sometimes indulge his own affections, and sometimes those of his favourites; he will permit some to please him who can never serve him; he will discover in those whom he loves qualities which in reality they do not possess; and to those, from whom he receives pleasure, he will in his turn endeavour to give it. Thus will recommendations sometimes prevail which were purchased by money, or by the more destructive bribery of flattery and servility.

"He that has much to do will do something wrong, and of that wrong must suffer the consequences; and, if it were possible that he should always act rightly, yet when such numbers are to judge of his conduct, the bad will censure and obstruct him by malevolence, and the good sometimes by mistake.

"The highest stations cannot therefore hope to be the abodes of happiness, which I would willingly believe to have fled from thrones and palaces to seats of humble privacy and placid obscurity. For what can hinder the satisfaction, or intercept the expectations, of him whose abilities are adequate to his employments, who sees with his own eyes the whole circuit of his influence, who chooses by his own knowledge all whom he trusts, and whom none are tempted to deceive by hope or fear? Surely he has nothing to do but to love and to be loved, to be virtuous and to be happy."

"Whether perfect happiness would be procured by perfect goodness," said Nekayah, "this world will never afford an opportunity of deciding. But this, at least, may be maintained, that we do not always find visible happiness in proportion to visible virtue. All natural and almost all political evils, are incident alike to the bad and good: they are confounded in the misery of a famine, and not much distinguished in the fury of a faction; they sink together in a tempest, and are driven together from their country by invaders. All that virtue can afford is quietness of conscience, a steady prospect of a happier state; this may enable us to endure calamity with patience; but remember that patience must suppose pain."

XXVIII

RASSELAS AND NEKAYAH CONTINUE THEIR CONVERSATION

"Dear princess," said Rasselas, "you fall into the common errours of exaggeratory declamation, by producing, in a familiar disquisition, examples of national calamities, and scenes of extensive misery, which are found in books rather than in the world, and which, as they are horrid, are ordained to be rare. Let us not imagine evils which we do not feel, nor injure life by misrepresentations. I cannot bear that querelous eloquence which threatens every city with a siege like that of Jerusalem, that makes famine attend on every flight of locusts, and suspends pestilence on the wing of every blast that issues from the south.

"On necessary and inevitable evils, which overwhelm kingdoms at once, all disputation is vain: when they happen they must be endured. But it is evident, that these bursts of universal distress are more dreaded than felt: thousands and ten thousands flourish in youth, and wither in age, without the knowledge of any other than domestick evils, and share the same pleasures and vexations whether their kings are mild or cruel, whether the armies of their country persue their enemies, or retreat before them. While courts are disturbed with intestine competitions, and ambassadours are negotiating in foreign countries, the smith still plies his anvil, and the husbandman drives his plow forward; the necessaries of life are required and obtained, and the successive business of the seasons continues to make its wonted revolutions.

"Let us cease to consider what, perhaps, may never happen, and what, when it shall happen, will laugh at human speculation. We will not endeavour to modify the motions of the elements, or to fix the destiny of kingdoms. It is our business to consider what beings like us may perform; each labouring for his own happiness, by promoting within his circle, however narrow, the happiness of others.

"Marriage is evidently the dictate of nature; men and women were made to be companions of each other, and therefore I cannot be persuaded but that marriage is one of the means of happiness."

"I know not," said the princess, "whether marriage be more than one of the innumerable modes of human misery. When I see and reckon the various forms of connubial infelicity, the unexpected causes of lasting discord, the diversities of temper, the oppositions of opinion, the rude collisions of contrary desire where both are urged by violent impulses, the obstinate contests of disagreeing virtues, where both are supported by consciousness of good intention, I am sometimes disposed to think with the severer casuists of most nations, that marriage is rather permitted than approved, and that none, but by the instigation of a passion too much indulged, entangle themselves with indissoluble compacts."

"You seem to forget," replied Rasselas, "that you have, even now, represented celibacy as less happy than marriage. Both conditions may be bad, but they cannot both be worst. Thus it happens when wrong opinions are entertained, that they mutually destroy each other, and leave the mind open to truth."

"I did not expect," answered the princess, "to hear that imputed to falshood which is the consequence only of frailty. To the mind, as to the eye, it is difficult to compare with exactness objects vast in their extent, and various in their parts. Where we see or conceive the whole at once we readily note the discriminations and decide the preference: but of two systems, of which neither can be surveyed by any human being in its full compass of magnitude and multiplicity of complication, where is the wonder, that judging of the whole by parts, I am affected by one or[6] the other as either presses on my memory or fancy? We differ from ourselves just as we differ from each other, when we see only part of the question, as in the multifarious relations of politicks and morality: but when we perceive the whole at once, as in numerical computations, all agree in one judgment, and none ever varies his opinion."

"Let us not add," said the prince, "to the other evils of life, the bitterness of controversy, nor endeavour to vie with each other in subtilties of argument. We are employed in a search, of which both are equally to enjoy the success, or suffer by the miscarriage. It is therefore fit that we assist each other. You surely conclude too hastily from the infelicity of marriage against its institution. Will not the misery of life prove equally that life cannot be the gift of heaven? The world must be peopled by marriage, or peopled without it."

"How the world is to be peopled," returned Nekayah, "is not my care, and needs not be yours. I see no danger that the present generation should omit to leave successors behind them: we are not now enquiring for the world, but for ourselves."

XXIX

THE DEBATE ON MARRIAGE CONTINUED

"The good of the whole," says Rasselas, "is the same with the good of all its parts. If marriage be best for mankind it must be evidently best for individuals, or a permanent and necessary duty must be the cause of evil, and some must be inevitably sacrificed to the convenience of others. In the estimate which you have made of the two states, it appears that the incommodities of a single life are, in a great measure, necessary and certain, but those of the conjugal state accidental and avoidable.

"I cannot forbear to flatter myself that prudence and benevolence will make marriage happy. The general folly of mankind is the cause of general complaint. What can be expected but dis-

[6] affected by one or: alternately affected by one and 2

appointment and repentance from a choice made in the immaturity of youth, in the ardour of desire, without judgment, without foresight, without enquiry after conformity of opinions, similarity of manners, rectitude of judgment, or purity of sentiment.

"Such is the common process of marriage. A youth and maiden meeting by chance, or brought together by artifice, exchange glances, reciprocate civilities, go home, and dream of one another. Having little to divert attention, or diversify thought, they find themselves uneasy when they are apart, and therefore conclude that they shall be happy together. They marry, and discover what nothing but voluntary blindness had before concealed; they wear out life in altercations, and charge nature with cruelty.

"From those early marriages proceeds likewise the rivalry of parents and children: the son is eager to enjoy the world before the father is willing to forsake it, and there is hardly room at once for two generations. The daughter begins to bloom before the mother can be content to fade, and neither can forbear to wish for the absence of the other.

"Surely all these evils may be avoided by that deliberation and delay which prudence prescribes to irrevocable choice. In the variety and jollity of youthful pleasures life may be well enough supported without the help of a partner. Longer time will increase experience, and wider views will allow better opportunities of enquiry and selection: one advantage, at least, will be certain; the parents will be visibly older than their children."

"What reason cannot collect," said Nekayah, "and what experiment has not yet taught, can be known only from the report of others. I have been told that late marriages are not eminently happy. This is a question too important to be neglected, and I have often proposed it to those, whose accuracy of remark, and comprehensiveness of knowledge, made their suffrages worthy of regard. They have generally determined, that it is dangerous for a man and woman to suspend their fate upon each other, at a time when opinions are fixed, and habits are established; when friendships have been contracted on both sides, when life has been planned into method, and the mind has long enjoyed the contemplation of its own prospects.

"It is scarcely possible that two travelling through the world under the conduct of chance, should have been both directed to the same path, and it will not often happen that either will quit the track which custom has made pleasing. When the desultory levity of youth has settled into regularity, it is soon succeeded by pride ashamed to yield, or obstinacy delighting to contend. And even though mutual esteem produces mutual desire to please, time itself, as it modifies unchangeably the external mien, determines likewise the direction of the passions, and gives an inflexible rigidity to the manners. Long customs are not easily broken: he that attempts to change the course of his own life, very often labours in vain; and how shall we do that for others which we are seldom able to do for ourselves?"

"But surely," interposed the prince, "you suppose the chief motive of choice forgotten or neglected. Whenever I shall seek a wife, it shall be my first question, whether she be willing to be led by reason?"

"Thus it is," said Nekayah, "that philosophers are deceived. There are a thousand familiar disputes which reason never can decide; questions that elude investigation, and make logick ridiculous; cases where something must be done, and where little can be said. Consider the state of mankind, and enquire how few can be supposed to act upon any occasions, whether small or great, with all the reasons of action present to their minds. Wretched would be the pair above all names of wretchedness, who should be doomed to adjust by reason every morning all the minute detail of a domestick day.

"Those who marry at an advanced age, will probably escape the encroachments of their children; but, in diminution of this advantage, they will be likely to leave them, ignorant and helpless, to a guardian's mercy: or, if that should not happen, they must at least go out of the world before they see those whom they love best either wise or great.

"From their children, if they have less to fear, they have less also to hope, and they lose, without equivalent, the joys of early love, and the convenience of uniting with manners pliant, and minds susceptible of new impressions, which might wear away their dissimilitudes by long cohabitation, as soft bodies, by continual attrition, conform their surfaces to each other.

"I believe it will be found that those who marry late are best pleased with their children, and those who marry early with their partners."

"The union of these two affections," said Rasselas, "would produce all that could be wished. Perhaps there is a time when marriage might unite them, a time neither too early for the father, nor too late for the husband."

"Every hour," answered the princess, "confirms my prejudice in favour of the position so often uttered by the mouth of Imlac, 'That nature sets her gifts on the right hand and on the left.' Those conditions, which flatter hope and attract desire, are so constituted, that, as we approach one, we recede from another. There are goods so opposed that we cannot seize both, but, by too much prudence, may pass between them at too great a distance to reach either. This is often the fate of long consideration; he does nothing who endeavours to do more than is allowed to humanity. Flatter not yourself with contrarieties of pleasure. Of the blessings set before you make your choice, and be content. No man can taste the fruits of autumn while he is delighting his scent with the flowers of the spring: no man can, at the same time, fill his cup from the source and from the mouth of the Nile."

XXX

IMLAC ENTERS, AND CHANGES THE CONVERSATION

Here Imlac entered, and interrupted them. His look was clouded with thought.[7] "Imlac," said Rasselas, "I have been taking from the princess the dismal history of private life, and am almost discouraged from further search."

"It seems to me," said Imlac, "that while you are making the choice of life, you neglect to live. You wander about a single city, which, however large and diversified, can now afford few novelties, and forget that you are in a country, famous among the earliest monarchies for the power and wisdom of its inhabitants; a country where the sciences first dawned that illuminate the world, and beyond which the arts cannot be traced of civil society or domestick life.

"The old Egyptians have left behind them monuments of industry and power before which all European magnificence is confessed to fade away. The ruins of their architecture are the

[7] His . . . thought: *omitted* 2

schools of modern builders, and from the wonders which time has spared we may conjecture, though uncertainly, what it has destroyed."

"My curiosity," said Rasselas, "does not very strongly lead me to survey piles of stone, or mounds of earth; my business is with man. I came hither not to measure fragments of temples, or trace choaked aqueducts, but to look upon the various scenes of the present world."

"The things that are now before us," said the princess, "necessarily require attention, and sufficiently deserve it.[8] What have I to do with the heroes or the monuments of ancient times? with times which never can return, and heroes, whose form of life was different from all that the present condition of mankind requires or allows."

"To know any thing," returned the poet, "we must know its effects; to see men we must see their works, that we may learn what reason has dictated, or passion has incited, and find what are the most powerful motives of action. To judge rightly of the present we must oppose it to the past; for all judgment is comparative, and of the future nothing can be known. The truth is, that no mind is much employed upon the present: recollection and anticipation fill up almost all our moments. Our passions are joy and grief, love and hatred, hope and fear. Of joy and grief the past is the object, and the future of hope and fear; even love and hatred respect the past, for the cause must have been before the effect.

"The present state of things is the consequence of the former, and it is natural to inquire what were the sources of the good that we enjoy, or of the evil that we suffer. If we act only for ourselves, to neglect the study of history is not prudent: if we are entrusted with the care of others, it is not just. Ignorance, when it is voluntary, is criminal; and he may properly be charged with evil who refused to learn how he might prevent it.

"There is no part of history so generally useful as that which relates the progress of the human mind, the gradual improvement of reason, the successive advances of science, the vicissitudes of

---

[8] necessarily require attention, and sufficiently deserve it: require attention, and deserve it 2

learning and ignorance, which are the light and darkness of thinking beings, the extinction and resuscitation of arts, and all the revolutions of the intellectual world. If accounts of battles and invasions are peculiarly the business of princes, the useful or elegant arts are not to be neglected; those who have kingdoms to govern have understandings to cultivate.

"Example is always more efficacious than precept. A soldier is formed in war, and a painter must copy pictures. In this, contemplative life has the advantage: great actions are seldom seen, but the labours of art are always at hand for those who desire to know what art has been able to perform.

"When the eye or the imagination is struck with any uncommon work the next transition of an active mind is to the means by which it was performed. Here begins the true use of such contemplation; we enlarge our comprehension by new ideas, and perhaps recover some art lost to mankind, or learn what is less perfectly known in our own country. At least we compare our own with former times, and either rejoice at our improvements, or, what is the first motion towards good, discover our defects."

"I am willing," said the prince, "to see all that can deserve my search." "And I," said the princess, "shall rejoice to learn something of the manners of antiquity."

"The most pompous monument of Egyptian greatness, and one of the most bulky works of manual industry," said Imlac, "are the pyramids; fabricks raised before the time of history, and of which the earliest narratives afford us only uncertain traditions. Of these the greatest is still standing, very little injured by time."

"Let us visit them to morrow," said Nekayah. "I have often heard of the pyramids, and shall not rest, till I have seen them within and without with my own eyes."

XXXI

THEY VISIT THE PYRAMIDS

The resolution being thus taken, they set out the next day. They laid tents upon their camels, being resolved to stay among the pyramids till their curiosity was fully satisfied. They travelled gently, turned aside to every thing remarkable, stopped from time to time and conversed with the inhabitants, and observed the various appearances of towns ruined and inhabited, of wild and cultivated nature.

When they came to the great pyramid they were astonished at the extent of the base, and the height of the top. Imlac explained to them the principles upon which the pyramidal form was chosen for a fabrick intended to co-extend its duration with that of the world: he showed that its gradual diminution gave it such stability, as defeated all the common attacks of the elements, and could scarcely be overthrown by earthquakes themselves, the least resistible of natural violence. A concussion that should shatter the pyramid would threaten the dissolution of the continent.

They measured all its dimensions, and pitched their tents at its foot. Next day they prepared to enter its interiour apartments, and having hired the common guides climbed up to the first passage, when the favourite of the princess, looking into the cavity, stepped back and trembled. "Pekuah," said the princess, "of what art thou afraid?" "Of the narrow entrance," answered the lady, "and of the dreadful gloom. I dare not enter a place which must surely be inhabited by unquiet souls. The original possessors of these dreadful vaults will start up before us, and, perhaps, shut us up[9] for ever." She spoke, and threw her arms round the neck of her mistress.

"If all your fear be of apparitions," said the prince, "I will promise you safety: there is no danger from the dead; he that is once buried will be seen no more."

"That the dead are seen no more," said Imlac, "I will not undertake to maintain against the concurrent and unvaried testimony of all ages, and of all nations. There is no people, rude or learned, among whom apparitions of the dead are not related and believed. This opinion, which, perhaps, prevails as far as human nature is diffused, could become universal only by its truth: those, that never heard of one another, would not have agreed in a tale which nothing but experience can make credible. That it is doubted by single cavillers can very little weaken the general evidence, and some who deny it with their tongues confess it by their fears.

---

[9] up: in 2

"Yet I do not mean to add new terrours to those which have already seized upon Pekuah. There can be no reason why spectres should haunt the pyramid more than other places, or why they should have power or will to hurt innocence and purity. Our entrance is no violation of their privileges; we can take nothing from them, how then can we offend them?"

"My dear Pekuah," said the princess, "I will always go before you, and Imlac shall follow you. Remember that you are the companion of the princess of Abissinia."

"If the princess is pleased that her servant should die," returned the lady, "let her command some death less dreadful than enclosure in this horrid cavern. You know I dare not disobey you: I must go if you command me; but, if I once enter, I never shall come back."

The princess saw that her fear was too strong for expostulation or reproof, and embracing her, told her that she should stay in the tent till their return. Pekuah was yet not satisfied, but entreated the princess not to persue so dreadful a purpose as that of entering the recesses of the pyramid. "Though I cannot teach courage," said Nekayah, "I must not learn cowardise; nor leave at last undone what I came hither only to do."

XXXII

THEY ENTER THE PYRAMID

Pekuah descended to the tents, and the rest entered the pyramid: they passed through the galleries, surveyed the vaults of marble, and examined the chest in which the body of the founder is supposed to have been reposited. They then sat down in one of the most spacious chambers to rest a while before they attempted to return.

"We have now," said Imlac, "gratified our minds with an exact view of the greatest work of man, except the wall of China.

"Of the wall it is very easy to assign the motives. It secured a wealthy and timorous nation from the incursions of Barbarians, whose unskilfulness in arts made it easier for them to supply their wants by rapine than by industry, and who from time to time poured in upon the habitations of peaceful commerce, as vultures descend upon domestick fowl. Their celerity and fierceness made the wall necessary, and their ignorance made it efficacious.

"But for the pyramids no reason has ever been given adequate to the cost and labour of the work. The narrowness of the chambers proves that it could afford no retreat from enemies, and treasures might have been reposited at far less expence with equal security. It seems to have been erected only in compliance with that hunger of imagination which preys incessantly upon life, and must be always appeased by some employment. Those who have already all that they can enjoy, must enlarge their desires. He that has built for use, till use is supplied, must begin to build for vanity, and extend his plan to the utmost power of human performance, that he may not be soon reduced to form another wish.

"I consider this mighty structure as a monument of the insufficiency of human enjoyments. A king, whose power is unlimited, and whose treasures surmount all real and imaginary wants, is compelled to solace, by the erection of a pyramid, the satiety of dominion and tastelessness of pleasures, and to amuse the tediousness of declining life, by seeing thousands labouring without end, and one stone, for no purpose, laid upon another. Whoever thou art, that, not content with a moderate condition, imaginest happiness in royal magnificence, and dreamest that command or riches can feed the appetite of novelty with successive[1] gratifications, survey the pyramids, and confess thy folly!"

XXXIII

THE PRINCESS MEETS WITH AN UNEXPECTED MISFORTUNE

They rose up, and returned through the cavity at which they had entered, and the princess prepared for her favourite a long narrative of dark labyrinths, and costly rooms, and of the different impressions which the varieties of the way had made upon her. But, when they came to their train, they found every one silent and dejected: the men discovered shame and fear in their countenances, and the women were weeping in the tents.

What had happened they did not try to conjecture, but imme-

---

[1] successive: perpetual 2

diately enquired. "You had scarcely entered into the pyramid," said one of the attendants, "when a troop of Arabs rushed upon us: we were too few to resist them, and too slow to escape. They were about to search the tents, set us on our camels, and drive us along before them, when the approach of some Turkish horsemen put them to flight; but they seized the lady Pekuah with her two maids, and carried them away: the Turks are now persuing them by our instigation, but I fear they will not be able to overtake them."

The princess was overpowered with surprise and grief. Rasselas, in the first heat of his resentment, ordered his servants to follow him, and prepared to persue the robbers with his sabre in his hand. "Sir," said Imlac, "what can you hope from violence or valour? the Arabs are mounted on horses trained to battle and retreat; we have only beasts of burthen. By leaving our present station we may lose the princess, but cannot hope to regain Pekuah."

In a short time the Turks returned, having not been able to reach the enemy. The princess burst out into new lamentations, and Rasselas could scarcely forbear to reproach them with cowardice; but Imlac was of opinion, that the escape of the Arabs was no addition to their misfortune, for, perhaps, they would have killed their captives rather than have resigned them.

XXXIV

THEY RETURN TO CAIRO WITHOUT PEKUAH

There was nothing to be hoped from longer stay. They returned to Cairo repenting of their curiosity, censuring the negligence of the government, lamenting their own rashness which had neglected to procure a guard, imagining many expedients by which the loss of Pekuah might have been prevented, and resolving to do something for her recovery, though none could find any thing proper to be done.

Nekayah retired to her chamber, where her women attempted to comfort her, by telling her that all had their troubles, and that lady Pekuah had enjoyed much happiness in the world for a long time, and might reasonably expect a change of fortune. They hoped that some good would befal her wheresoever she was, and that their mistress would find another friend who might supply her place.

The princess made them no answer, and they continued the form of condolence, not much grieved in their hearts that the favourite was lost.

Next day the prince presented to the Bassa a memorial of the wrong which he had suffered, and a petition for redress. The Bassa threatened to punish the robbers, but did not attempt to catch them, nor, indeed, could any account or description be given by which he might direct the persuit.

It soon appeared that nothing would be done by authority. Governors, being accustomed to hear of more crimes than they can punish, and more wrongs than they can redress, set themselves at ease by indiscriminate negligence, and presently forget the request when they lose sight of the petitioner.

Imlac then endeavoured to gain some intelligence by private agents. He found many who pretended to an exact knowledge of all the haunts of the Arabs, and to regular correspondence with their chiefs, and who readily undertook the recovery of Pekuah. Of these, some were furnished with money for their journey, and came back no more; some were liberally paid for accounts which a few days discovered to be false. But the princess would not suffer any means, however improbable, to be left untried. While she was doing something she kept her hope alive. As one expedient failed, another was suggested; when one messenger returned unsuccessful, another was despatched to a different quarter.

Two months had now passed, and of Pekuah nothing had been heard; the hopes which they had endeavoured to raise in each other grew more languid, and the princess, when she saw nothing more to be tried, sunk down inconsolable in hopeless dejection. A thousand times she reproached herself with the easy compliance by which she permitted her favourite to stay behind her. "Had not my fondness," said she, "lessened my authority, Pekuah had not dared to talk of her terrours. She ought to have feared me more than spectres. A severe look would have overpowered her; a peremptory command would have compelled obedience. Why did foolish indulgence prevail upon me? Why did I not speak and refuse to hear?"

"Great princess," said Imlac, "do not reproach yourself for your virtue, or consider that as blameable by which evil has accidentally been caused. Your tenderness for the timidity of Pekuah was generous and kind. When we act according to our duty, we commit the event to him by whose laws our actions are governed, and who will suffer none to be finally punished for obedience. When, in prospect of some good, whether natural or moral, we break the rules prescribed us, we withdraw from the direction of superiour wisdom, and take all consequences upon ourselves. Man cannot so far know the connexion of causes and events, as that he may venture to do wrong in order to do right. When we persue our end by lawful means, we may always console our miscarriage by the hope of future recompense. When we consult only our own policy, and attempt to find a nearer way to good, by overleaping the settled boundaries of right and wrong, we cannot be happy even by success, because we cannot escape the consciousness of our fault; but, if we miscarry, the disappointment is irremediably embittered. How comfortless is the sorrow of him, who feels at once the pangs of guilt, and the vexation of calamity which guilt has brought upon him?

"Consider, princess, what would have been your condition, if the lady Pekuah had intreated to accompany you, and, being compelled to stay in the tents, had been carried away; or how would you have born the thought, if you had forced her into the pyramid, and she had died before you in agonies of terrour."

"Had either happened," said Nekayah, "I could not have endured life till now: I should have been tortured to madness by the remembrance of such cruelty, or must have pined away in abhorrence of myself."

"This at least," said Imlac, "is the present reward of virtuous conduct, that no unlucky consequence can oblige us to repent it."

XXXV

THE PRINCESS CONTINUES TO LAMENT[2] PEKUAH

Nekayah, being thus reconciled to herself, found that no evil is insupportable but that which is accompanied with consciousness of wrong. She was, from that time, delivered from the violence of

[2] continues to lament: languishes for want of 2

tempestuous sorrow, and sunk into silent pensiveness and gloomy tranquillity. She sat from morning to evening recollecting all that had been done or said by her Pekuah, treasured up with care every trifle on which Pekuah had set an accidental value, and which might recal to mind any little incident or careless conversation. The sentiments of her, whom she now expected to see no more, were treasured up[3] in her memory as rules of life, and she deliberated to no other end than to conjecture on any occasion what would have been the opinion and counsel of Pekuah.

The women, by whom she was attended, knew nothing of her real condition, and therefore she could not talk to them but with caution and reserve. She began to remit her curiosity, having no great care to collect notions which she had no convenience of uttering. Rasselas endeavoured first to comfort and afterwards to divert her; he hired musicians, to whom she seemed to listen, but did not hear them, and procured masters to instruct her in various arts, whose lectures, when they visited her again, were again to be repeated. She had lost her taste of pleasure and her ambition of excellence. And her mind, though forced into short excursions, always recurred to the image of her friend.

Imlac was every morning earnestly enjoined to renew his enquiries, and was asked every night whether he had yet heard of Pekuah, till not being able to return the princess the answer that she desired, he was less and less willing to come into her presence. She observed his backwardness, and commanded him to attend her. "You are not," said she, "to confound impatience with resentment, or to suppose that I charge you with negligence, because I repine at your unsuccessfulness. I do not much wonder at your absence; I know that the unhappy are never pleasing, and that all naturally avoid the contagion of misery. To hear complaints is wearisome alike to the wretched and the happy; for who would cloud by adventitious grief the short gleams of gaiety which life allows us? or who, that is struggling under his own evils, will add to them the miseries of another?

"The time is at hand, when none shall be disturbed any longer by the sighs of Nekayah: my search after happiness is now at an end. I am resolved to retire from the world with all its flatteries

[3] treasured up: treasured 2

and deceits, and will hide myself in solitude, without any other care than to compose my thoughts, and regulate my hours by a constant succession of innocent occupations, till, with a mind purified from all earthly desires, I shall enter into that state, to which all are hastening, and in which I hope again to enjoy the friendship of Pekuah."

"Do not entangle your mind," said Imlac, "by irrevocable determinations, nor increase the burthen of life by a voluntary accumulation of misery: the weariness of retirement will continue or increase when the loss of Pekuah is forgotten. That you have been deprived of one pleasure is no very good reason for rejection of the rest."

"Since Pekuah was taken from me," said the princess, "I have no pleasure to reject or to retain. She that has no one to love or trust has little to hope. She wants the radical principle of happiness. We may, perhaps, allow that what satisfaction this world can afford, must arise from the conjunction of wealth, knowledge and goodness: wealth is nothing but as it is bestowed, and knowledge nothing but as it is communicated.[4] Goodness affords the only comfort which can be enjoyed without a partner, and goodness may be practised in retirement."

"How far solitude may admit goodness, or advance it, I shall not," replied Imlac, "dispute at present. Remember the confession of the pious hermit. You will wish to return into the world, when the image of your companion has left your thoughts." "That time," said Nekayah, "will never come. The generous frankness, the modest obsequiousness, and the faithful secrecy of my dear Pekuah, will always be more missed, as I shall live longer to see vice and folly."

"The state of a mind oppressed with a sudden calamity," said Imlac, "is like that of the fabulous inhabitants of the new created earth, who, when the first night came upon them, supposed that day never would return. When the clouds of sorrow gather over us, we see nothing beyond them, nor can imagine how they will be dispelled: yet a new day succeeded to the night, and sorrow is never long without a dawn of ease. But they who restrain them-

[4] communicated: 2 *adds* they must therefore be imparted to others, and to whom could I now delight to impart them?

selves from receiving comfort, do as the savages would have done, had they put out their eyes when it was dark. Our minds, like our bodies, are in continual flux; something is hourly lost, and something acquired. To lose much at once is inconvenient to either, but while the vital powers remain uninjured, nature will find the means of reparation. Distance has the same effect on the mind as on the eye, and while we glide along the stream of time, whatever we leave behind us is always lessening, and that which we approach increasing in magnitude. Do not suffer life to stagnate; it will grow muddy for want of motion: commit yourself again to the current of the world; Pekuah will vanish by degrees; you will meet in your way some other favourite, or learn to diffuse yourself in general conversation."

"At least," said the prince, "do not despair before all remedies have been tried: the enquiry after the unfortunate lady is still continued, and shall be carried on with yet greater diligence, on condition that you will promise to wait a year for the event, without any unalterable resolution."

Nekayah thought this a reasonable demand, and made the promise to her brother, who had been advised by Imlac to require it. Imlac had, indeed, no great hope of regaining Pekuah, but he supposed, that if he could secure the interval of a year, the princess would be then in no danger of a cloister.

XXXVI

PEKUAH IS STILL REMEMBERED BY THE PRINCESS[5]

Nekayah, seeing that nothing was omitted for the recovery of her favourite, and having, by her promise, set her intention of retirement at a distance, began imperceptibly to return to common cares and common pleasures. She rejoiced without her own consent at the suspension of her sorrows, and sometimes caught herself with indignation in the act of turning away her mind from the remembrance of her, whom yet she resolved never to forget.

She then appointed a certain hour of the day for meditation on the merits and fondness of Pekuah, and for some weeks retired constantly at the time fixed, and returned with her eyes swollen

[5] remembered by the princess: remembered. The progress of sorrow 2

and her countenance clouded. By degrees she grew less scrupulous, and suffered any important and pressing avocation to delay the tribute of daily tears. She then yielded to less occasions; sometimes forgot what she was indeed afraid to remember, and, at last, wholly released herself from the duty of periodical affliction.

Her real love of Pekuah was yet not diminished. A thousand occurrences brought her back to memory, and a thousand wants, which nothing but the confidence of friendship can supply, made her frequently regretted. She, therefore, solicited Imlac never to desist from enquiry, and to leave no art of intelligence untried, that, at least, she might have the comfort of knowing that she did not suffer by negligence or sluggishness. "Yet what," said she, "is to be expected from our persuit of happiness, when we find the state of life to be such, that happiness itself is the cause of misery? Why should we endeavour to attain that, of which the possession cannot be secured? I shall henceforward fear to yield my heart to excellence, however bright, or to fondness, however tender, lest I should lose again what I have lost in Pekuah."

XXXVII

THE PRINCESS HEARS NEWS OF PEKUAH

In seven months, one of the messengers, who had been sent away upon the day when the promise was drawn from the princess, returned, after many unsuccessful rambles, from the borders of Nubia, with an account that Pekuah was in the hands of an Arab chief, who possessed a castle or fortress on the extremity of Egypt. The Arab, whose revenue was plunder, was willing to restore her, with her two attendants, for two hundred ounces of gold.

The price was no subject of debate. The princess was in extasies when she heard that her favourite was alive, and might so cheaply be ransomed. She could not think of delaying for a moment Pekuah's happiness or her own, but entreated her brother to send back the messenger with the sum required. Imlac, being consulted, was not very confident of the veracity of the relator, and was still more doubtful of the Arab's faith, who might, if he were too liberally trusted, detain at once the money and the captives. He thought it dangerous to put themselves in the power of the Arab, by going into his district, and could not expect that the Arab[6] would so much expose himself as to come into the lower country, where he might be seized by the forces of the Bassa.

It is difficult to negotiate where neither will trust. But Imlac, after some deliberation, directed the messenger to propose that Pekuah should be conducted by ten horsemen to the monastry of St. Antony, which is situated in the deserts of Upper-Egypt, where she should be met by the same number, and her ransome should be paid.

That no time might be lost, as they expected that the proposal would not be refused, they immediately began their journey to the monastry; and, when they arrived, Imlac went forward with the former messenger to the Arab's fortress. Rasselas was desirous to go with them, but neither his sister nor Imlac would consent. The Arab, according to the custom of his nation, observed the laws of hospitality with great exactness to those who put themselves into his power, and, in a few days, brought Pekuah with her maids, by easy journeys, to their place appointed, where he received the stipulated price, and, with great respect, restored her[7] to liberty and her friends, and undertook to conduct them back towards Cairo beyond all danger of robbery or violence.

The princess and her favourite embraced each other with transport too violent to be expressed, and went out together to pour the tears of tenderness in secret, and exchange professions of kindness and gratitude. After a few hours they returned into the refectory of the convent, where, in the presence of the prior and his brethren, the prince required of Pekuah the history of her adventures.

XXXVIII

THE ADVENTURES OF THE LADY PEKUAH

"At what time, and in what manner, I was forced away," said Pekuah, "your servants have told you. The suddenness of the

[6] Arab: Rover 2

[7] he received the stipulated price, and, with great respect, restored her: receiving the stipulated price, he restored her with great respect 2

event struck me with surprise, and I was at first rather stupified than agitated with any passion of either fear or sorrow. My confusion was encreased by the speed and tumult of our flight while we were followed by the Turks, who, as it seemed, soon despaired to overtake us, or were afraid of those whom they made a shew of menacing.

"When the Arabs saw themselves out of danger they slackened their course, and, as I was less harassed by external violence, I began to feel more uneasiness in my mind. After some time we stopped near a spring shaded with trees in a pleasant meadow, where we were set upon the ground, and offered such refreshments as our masters were partaking. I was suffered to sit with my maids apart from the rest, and none attempted to comfort or insult us. Here I first began to feel the full weight of my misery. The girls sat weeping in silence, and from time to time looked up to[8] me for succour. I knew not to what condition we were doomed, nor could conjecture where would be the place of our captivity, or whence to draw any hope of deliverance. I was in the hands of robbers and savages, and had no reason to suppose that their pity was more than their justice, or that they would forbear the gratification of any ardour of desire, or caprice of cruelty. I, however, kissed my maids, and endeavoured to pacify them by remarking, that we were yet treated with decency, and that, since we were now carried beyond pursuit, there was no danger of violence to our lives.

"When we were to be set again on horseback, my maids clung round me, and refused to be parted, but I commanded them not to irritate those who had us in their power. We travelled the remaining part of the day through an unfrequented and pathless country, and came by moonlight to the side of a hill, where the rest of the troop was stationed. Their tents were pitched, and their fires kindled, and our chief was welcomed as a man much beloved by his dependants.

"We were received into a large tent, where we found women who had attended their husbands in the expedition. They set before us the supper which they had provided, and I eat it rather to encourage my maids than to comply with any appetite of my

[8] up to: on 2

own. When the meat was taken away they spread the carpets for repose. I was weary, and hoped to find in sleep that remission of distress which nature seldom denies. Ordering myself therefore to be undrest, I observed that the women looked very earnestly upon me, not expecting, I suppose, to see me so submissively attended. When my upper vest was taken off, they were apparently struck with the splendour of my cloaths, and one of them timorously laid her hand upon the embroidery. She then went out, and, in a short time, came back with another woman, who seemed to be of higher rank, and greater authority. She did, at her entrance, the usual act of reverence, and, taking me by the hand, placed me in a smaller tent, spread with finer carpets, where I spent the night quietly with my maids.

"In the morning, as I was sitting on the grass, the chief of the troop came towards me: I rose up to receive him, and he bowed with great respect. 'Illustrious lady,' said he, 'my fortune is better than I had presumed to hope; I am told by my women, that I have a princess in my camp.' 'Sir,' answered I, 'your women have deceived themselves and you; I am not a princess, but an unhappy stranger who intended soon to have left this country, in which I am now to be imprisoned for ever.' 'Whoever, or whencesoever, you are,' returned the Arab, 'your dress, and that of your servants, show your rank to be high, and your wealth to be great. Why should you, who can so easily procure your ransome, think yourself in danger of perpetual captivity? The purpose of my incursions is to encrease my riches, or more properly to gather tribute. The sons of Ishmael are the natural and hereditary lords of this part of the continent, which is usurped by late invaders, and low-born tyrants, from whom we are compelled to take by the sword what is denied to justice. The violence of war admits no distinction; the lance that is lifted at guilt and power will sometimes fall on innocence and gentleness.'

" 'How little,' said I, 'did I expect that yesterday it should have fallen upon me.'

" 'Misfortunes,' answered the Arab, 'should always be expected. If the eye of hostility could have learned to spare,[9] excellence like yours had been exempt from injury. But the angels of affliction

[9] have learned to spare: learn reverence or pity 2

spread their toils alike for the virtuous and the wicked, for the mighty and the mean. Do not be disconsolate; I am not one of the lawless and cruel rovers of the desart; I know the rules of civil life; I will fix your ransome, give a pasport to your messenger, and perform my stipulation with nice punctuality.'

"You will easily believe that I was pleased with his courtesy; and finding that his predominant passion was desire of money, I began now to think my danger less, for I knew that no sum would be thought too great for the release of Pekuah. I told him that he should have no reason to charge me with ingratitude, if I was used with kindness, and that any ransome, which could be expected for a maid of common rank, would be paid, but that he must not persist to rate me as a princess. He said, he would consider what he should demand, and then, smiling, bowed and retired.

"Soon after the women came about me, each contending to be more officious[1] than the other, and my maids themselves were served with reverence. We travelled onward by short journeys. On the fourth day the chief told me, that my ransome must be two hundred ounces of gold, which I not only promised him, but told him, that I would add fifty more, if I and my maids were honourably treated.

"I never knew the power of gold before. From that time I was the leader of the troop. The march of every day was longer or shorter as I commanded, and the tents were pitched where I chose to rest. We now had camels and other conveniencies for travel, my own women were always at my side, and I amused myself with observing the manners of the vagrant nations, and with viewing remains of ancient edifices with which these deserted countries appear to have been, in some distant age, lavishly embellished.

"The chief of the band was a man far from illiterate: he was able to travel by the stars or the compass, and had marked in his erratick expeditions such places as are most worthy the notice of a passenger. He observed to me, that buildings are always best preserved in places little frequented, and difficult of access: for, when once a country declines from its primitive splendour, the

[1] officious: in the old sense, "kind; doing good offices." Johnson's *Dictionary*.

more inhabitants are left, the quicker ruin will be made. Walls supply stones more easily than quarries, and palaces and temples will be demolished to make stables of granate, and cottages of porphyry.

XXXIX

THE ADVENTURES OF PEKUAH CONTINUED

"We wandered about in this manner for some weeks, whether, as our chief pretended, for my gratification, or, as I rather suspected, for some convenience of his own. I endeavoured to appear contented where sullenness and resentment would have been of no use, and that endeavour conduced much to the calmness of my mind; but my heart was always with Nekayah, and the troubles of the night much overbalanced the amusements of the day. My women, who threw all their cares upon their mistress, set their minds at ease from the time when they saw me treated with respect, and gave themselves up to the incidental alleviations of our fatigue without solicitude or sorrow. I was pleased with their pleasure, and animated with their confidence. My condition had lost much of its terrour, since I found that the Arab ranged the country merely to get riches. Avarice is an uniform and tractable vice: other intellectual distempers are different in different constitutions of mind; that which sooths the pride of one will offend the pride of another; but to the favour of the covetous there is a ready way, bring money and nothing is denied.

"At last we came to the dwelling of our chief, a strong and spacious house built with stone in an island of the Nile, which lies, as I was told, under the tropick. 'Lady,' said the Arab, 'you shall rest a few weeks after your journey[2] in this place, where you are to consider yourself as sovereign. My occupation is war: I have therefore chosen this obscure residence, from which I can issue unexpected, and to which I can retire unpersued. You may now repose in security: here are few pleasures, but here is no danger.' He then led me into the inner apartments, and seating me in the place of honour,[3] bowed to the ground. His women,

---

[2] a few weeks after your journey: after your journey a few weeks 2
[3] in the place of honour: on the richest couch 2

who considered me as a rival, looked on me with malignity; but being soon informed that I was a great lady detained only for my ransome, they began to vie with each other in obsequiousness and reverence.

"Being again comforted with new assurances of speedy liberty, I was for some days diverted from impatience by the novelty of the place. The turrets overlooked the country to a great distance, and afforded a view of many windings of the stream. In the day I wandered from one place to another as the course of the sun varied the splendour of the prospect, and saw many things which I had never seen before. The crocodiles and river-horses were[4] common in this unpeopled region, and I often looked upon them with terrour, though I knew that they could not hurt me. For some time I expected to see mermaids and tritons, which, as Imlac has told me, the European travellers have stationed in the Nile, but no such beings ever appeared, and the Arab, when I enquired after them, laughed at my credulity.

"At night the Arab always attended me to a tower set apart for celestial observations, where he endeavoured to teach me the names and courses of the stars. I had no great inclination to this study, but an appearance of attention was necessary to please my instructor, who valued himself for his skill, and, in a little while, I found some employment requisite to beguile the tediousness of time, which was to be passed always amidst the same objects. I was weary of looking in the morning on things from which I had turned away weary in the evening: I therefore was at last willing to observe the stars rather than do nothing, but could not always compose my thoughts, and was very often thinking on Nekayah when others imagined me contemplating the sky. Soon after the Arab went upon another expedition, and then my only pleasure was to talk with my maids about the accident by which we were carried away, and the happiness that we should all enjoy at the end of our captivity."

"There were women in your Arab's fortress," said the princess, "why did you not make them your companions, enjoy their conversation, and partake their diversions? In a place where they found business or amusement, why should you alone sit corroded

[4] river-horses were: river-horses are 2. Johnson also translated "hippopotami" thus in his Lobo's *Abyssinia*.

with idle melancholy? or why could not you bear for a few months that condition to which they were condemned for life?"

"The diversions of the women," answered Pekuah, "were only childish play, by which the mind accustomed to stronger operations could not be kept busy. I could do all which they delighted in doing by powers merely sensitive,[5] while my intellectual faculties were flown to Cairo. They ran from room to room as a bird hops from wire to wire in his cage. They danced for the sake of motion, as lambs frisk in a meadow. One sometimes pretended to be hurt that the rest might be alarmed, or hid herself that another might seek her. Part of their time passed in watching the progress of light bodies that floated on the river, and part in marking the various forms into which clouds broke in the sky.

"Their business was only needlework, in which I and my maids sometimes helped them; but you know that the mind will easily straggle from the fingers, nor will you suspect that captivity and absence from Nekayah could be much solaced by[6] silken flowers.

"Nor was much satisfaction to be hoped from their conversation: for of what could they be expected to talk? They had seen nothing; for they had lived from early youth in that narrow spot: of what they had not seen they could have no knowledge, for they could not read. They had no ideas but of the few things that were within their view, and had hardly names for any thing but their cloaths and their food. As I bore a superiour character, I was often called to terminate their quarrels, which I decided as equitably as I could. If it could have amused me to hear the complaints of each against the rest, I might have been often detained by long stories, but the motives of their animosity were so small that I could not listen long[7] without intercepting the tale."

"How," said Rasselas, "can the Arab, whom you represented as a man of more than common accomplishments, take any pleasure in his seraglio, when it is filled only with women like these. Are they exquisitely beautiful?"

"They do not," said Pekuah, "want that unaffecting and ignoble

---

[5] sensitive: "having sense or perception, but not reason." Johnson's *Dictionary*.

[6] be much solaced by: receive solace from 2

[7] listen long: listen 2

beauty which may subsist without spriteliness or sublimity, without energy of thought or dignity of virtue. But to a man like the Arab such beauty was only a flower casually plucked and carelessly thrown away. Whatever pleasures he might find among them, they were not those of friendship or society. When they were playing about him he looked on them with inattentive superiority: when they vied for his regard he sometimes turned away disgusted. As they had no knowledge, their talk could take nothing from the tediousness of life: as they had no choice, their fondness, or appearance of fondness, excited in him neither pride nor gratitude; he was not exalted in his own esteem by the smiles of a woman who saw no other man, nor was much obliged by that regard, of which he could never know the sincerity, and which he might often perceive to be exerted not so much to delight him as to pain a rival. That which he gave, and they received, as love, was only a careless distribution of superfluous time, such love as man can bestow upon that which he despises, such as has neither hope nor fear, neither joy nor sorrow."

"You have reason, lady, to think yourself happy," said Imlac, "that you have been thus easily dismissed. How could a mind, hungry for knowledge, be willing, in an intellectual famine, to lose such a banquet as Pekuah's conversation?"

"I am inclined to believe," answered Pekuah, "that he was for some time in suspense; for, notwithstanding his promise, whenever I proposed to dispatch a messenger to Cairo, he found some excuse for delay. While I was detained in his house he made many incursions into the neighbouring countries, and, perhaps, he would have refused to discharge me, had his plunder been equal to his wishes. He returned always courteous, related his adventures, delighted to hear my observations, and endeavoured to advance my acquaintance with the stars. When I importuned him to send away my letters, he soothed me with professions of honour and sincerity; and, when I could be no longer decently denied, put his troop again in motion, and left me to govern in his absence. I was much afflicted by this studied procrastination, and was sometimes afraid that I should be forgotten; that you would leave Cairo, and I must end my days in an island of the Nile.

"I grew at last hopeless and dejected, and cared so little to entertain him, that he for a while more frequently talked with my maids. That he should fall in love with them, or with me, might have been equally fatal, and I was not much pleased with the growing friendship. My anxiety was not long; for, as I recovered some degree of chearfulness, he returned to me, and I could not forbear to despise my former uneasiness.

"He still delayed to send for my ransome, and would, perhaps, never have determined, had not your agent found his way to him. The gold, which he would not fetch, he could not reject when it was offered. He hastened to prepare for our journey hither, like a man delivered from the pain of an intestine conflict. I took leave of my companions in the house, who dismissed me with cold indifference."

Nekayah, having heard her favourite's relation, rose and embraced her, and Rasselas gave her an hundred ounces of gold, which she presented to the Arab for the fifty that were promised.

XL

THE HISTORY OF A MAN OF LEARNING

They returned to Cairo, and were so well pleased at finding themselves together, that none of them went much abroad. The prince began to love learning, and one day declared to Imlac, that he intended to devote himself to science, and pass the rest of his days in literary solitude.

"Before you make your final choice," answered Imlac, "you ought to examine its hazards, and converse with some of those who are grown old in the company of themselves. I have just left the observatory of one of the most learned astronomers in the world, who has spent forty years in unwearied attention to the motions and appearances of the celestial bodies, and has drawn out his soul in endless calculations. He admits a few friends once a month to hear his deductions and enjoy his discoveries. I was introduced as a man of knowledge worthy of his notice. Men of various ideas and fluent conversation are commonly welcome to those whose thoughts have been long fixed upon a single point, and who find the images of other things stealing away. I delighted him with my remarks, he smiled at the narrative of my travels, and was glad to forget the constellations, and descend for a moment into the lower world.

"On the next day of vacation I renewed my visit, and was so fortunate as to please him again. He relaxed from that time the severity of his rule, and permitted me to enter at my own choice. I found him always busy, and always glad to be relieved. As each knew much which the other was desirous of learning, we exchanged our notions with great delight. I perceived that I had every day more of his confidence, and always found new cause of admiration in the profundity of his mind. His comprehension is vast, his memory capacious and retentive, his discourse is methodical, and his expression clear.

"His integrity and benevolence are equal to his learning. His deepest researches and most favourite studies are willingly interrupted for any opportunity of doing good by his counsel or his riches. To his closest retreat, at his most busy moments, all are admitted that want his assistance: 'For though I exclude idleness and pleasure, I will never,' says he, 'bar my doors against charity. To man is permitted the contemplation of the skies, but the practice of virtue is commanded.' "

"Surely," said the princess, "this man is happy."

"I visited him," said Imlac, "with more and more frequency, and was every time more enamoured of his conversation: he was sublime without haughtiness, courteous without formality, and communicative without ostentation. I was at first, Madam,[8] of your opinion, thought him the happiest of mankind, and often congratulated him on the blessing that he enjoyed. He seemed to hear nothing with indifference but the praises of his condition, to which he always returned a general answer, and diverted the conversation to some other topick.

"Amidst this willingness to be pleased, and labour to please, I had always[9] reason to imagine that some painful sentiment pressed upon his mind. He often looked up earnestly towards the sun, and let his voice fall in the midst of his discourse. He would sometimes, when we were alone, gaze upon me in silence with the air of a man who longed to speak what he was yet resolved to suppress.

---

[8] Madam: great princess 2

[9] always: quickly 2

He would sometimes[1] send for me with vehement injunctions of haste, though, when I came to him, he had nothing extraordinary to say. And sometimes, when I was leaving him, would call me back, pause a few moments and then dismiss me.

XLI

THE ASTRONOMER DISCOVERS THE CAUSE OF HIS UNEASINESS

"At last the time came when the secret burst his reserve. We were sitting together last night in the turret of his house, watching the emersion of a satellite of Jupiter. A sudden tempest clouded the sky, and disappointed our observation. We sat a while silent in the dark, and then he addressed himself to me in these words: 'Imlac, I have long considered thy friendship as the greatest blessing of my life. Integrity without knowledge is weak and useless, and knowledge without integrity is dangerous and dreadful. I have found in thee all the qualities requisite for trust, benevolence, experience, and fortitude. I have long discharged an office which I must soon quit at the call of nature, and shall rejoice in the hour of imbecility and pain to devolve it upon thee.'

"I thought myself honoured by this testimony, and protested that whatever could conduce to his happiness would add likewise to mine.

" 'Hear, Imlac, what thou wilt not without difficulty credit. I have possessed for five years the regulation of weather, and the distribution of the seasons: the sun has listened to my dictates, and passed from tropick to tropick by my direction; the clouds, at my call, have poured their waters, and the Nile has overflowed at my command; I have restrained the rage of the dog-star, and mitigated the fervours of the crab. The winds alone, of all the elemental powers, have hitherto refused my authority, and multitudes have perished by equinoctial tempests which I found myself unable to prohibit or restrain. I have administered this great office with exact justice, and made to the different nations of the earth an impartial dividend of rain and sunshine. What must have been the misery of half the globe, if I had limited the clouds to particular regions, or confined the sun to either side of the equator?'

[1] sometimes: often 2

XLII

THE ASTRONOMER JUSTIFIES HIS ACCOUNT OF HIMSELF[2]

"I suppose he discovered in me, through the obscurity of the room, some tokens of amazement and doubt, for, after a short pause, he proceeded thus:

" 'Not to be easily credited will neither surprise nor offend me; for I am, probably, the first of human beings to whom this trust has been imparted. Nor do I know whether to deem this distinction a reward or punishment; since I have possessed it I have been far less happy than before, and nothing but the consciousness of good intention could have enabled me to support the weariness of unremitted vigilance.'

" 'How long, Sir,' said I, 'has this great office been in your hands?'

" 'About ten years ago,' said he, 'my daily observations of the changes of the sky led me to consider, whether, if I had the power of the seasons, I could confer greater plenty upon the inhabitants of the earth. This contemplation fastened on my mind, and I sat days and nights in imaginary dominion, pouring upon this country and that the showers of fertility, and seconding every fall of rain with a due proportion of sunshine. I had yet only the will to do good, and did not imagine that I should ever have the power.

" 'One day as I was looking on the fields withering with heat, I felt in my mind a sudden wish that I could send rain on the southern mountains, and raise the Nile to an inundation. In the hurry of my imagination I commanded rain to fall, and, by comparing the time of my command, with that of the inundation, I found that the clouds had listned to my lips.'

" 'Might not some other cause,' said I, 'produce this concurrence? the Nile does not always rise on the same day.'

" 'Do not believe,' said he with impatience, 'that such objections could escape me: I reasoned long against my own conviction, and laboured against truth with the utmost obstinacy. I sometimes suspected myself of madness, and should not have dared to im-

[2] The astronomer justifies his account of himself: The opinion of the astronomer is explained and justified 2

part this secret but to a man like you, capable of distinguishing the wonderful from the impossible, and the incredible from the false.'

" 'Why, Sir,' said I, 'do you call that incredible, which you know, or think you know, to be true?'

" 'Because,' said he, 'I cannot prove it by any external evidence; and I know too well the laws of demonstration to think that my conviction ought to influence another, who cannot, like me, be conscious of its force. I, therefore, shall not attempt to gain credit by disputation. It is sufficient that I feel this power, that I have long possessed, and every day exerted it. But the life of man is short, the infirmities of age increase upon me, and the time will soon come when the regulator of the year must mingle with the dust. The care of appointing a successor has long disturbed me; the night and the day have been spent in comparisons of all the characters which have come to my knowledge, and I have yet found none so worthy as thyself.

XLIII

THE ASTRONOMER LEAVES IMLAC HIS DIRECTIONS

" 'Hear therefore, what I shall impart, with attention, such as the welfare of a world requires. If the task of a king be considered as difficult, who has the care only of a few millions, to whom he cannot do much good or harm, what must be the anxiety of him, on whom depend the action of the elements, and the great gifts of light and heat!——Hear me therefore with attention.

" 'I have diligently considered the position of the earth and sun, and formed innumerable schemes in which I changed their situation. I have sometimes turned aside the axis of the earth, and sometimes varied the ecliptick of the sun: but I have found it impossible to make a disposition by which the world may be advantaged; what one region gains, another loses by any imaginable alteration, even without considering the distant parts of the solar system with which we are unacquainted. Do not, therefore, in thy administration of the year, indulge thy pride by innovation; do not please thyself with thinking that thou canst make thyself renowned to all future ages, by disordering the seasons. The memory of mischief is no desirable fame. Much less will it become thee to let kindness or interest prevail. Never rob other countries of rain to pour it on thine own. For us the Nile is sufficient.'

"I promised that when I possessed the power, I would use it with inflexible integrity, and he dismissed me, pressing my hand. 'My heart,' said he, 'will be now at rest, and my benevolence will no more destroy my quiet: I have found a man of wisdom and virtue, to whom I can chearfully bequeath the inheritance of the sun.' "

The prince heard this narration with very serious regard, but the princess smiled, and Pekuah convulsed herself with laughter. "Ladies," said Imlac, "to mock the heaviest of human afflictions is neither charitable nor wise. Few can attain this man's knowledge, and few practise his virtues; but all may suffer his calamity. Of the uncertainties of our present state, the most dreadful and alarming is the uncertain continuance of reason."

The princess was recollected, and the favourite was abashed. Rasselas, more deeply affected, enquired of Imlac, whether he thought such maladies of the mind frequent, and how they were contracted.

XLIV

THE DANGEROUS PREVALENCE OF IMAGINATION

"Disorders of intellect," answered Imlac, "happen much more often than superficial observers will easily believe. Perhaps, if we speak with rigorous exactness, no human mind is in its right state. There is no man whose imagination does not sometimes predominate over his reason, who can regulate his attention wholly by his will, and whose ideas will come and go at his command. No man will be found in whose mind airy notions do not sometimes tyrannise, and force him to hope or fear beyond the limits of sober probability. All power of fancy over reason is a degree of insanity; but while this power is such as we can controll and repress, it is not visible to others, nor considered as any depravation of the mental faculties: it is not pronounced madness but when it comes ungovernable, and apparently influences speech or action.

"To indulge the power of fiction, and send imagination out upon the wing, is often the sport of those who delight too much in silent speculation. When we are alone we are not always busy; the labour of excogitation is too violent to last long; the ardour of enquiry will sometimes give way to idleness or satiety. He who has nothing external that can divert him, must find pleasure in his own thoughts, and must conceive himself what he is not; for who is pleased with what he is? He then expatiates in boundless futurity, and culls from all imaginable conditions that which for the present moment he should most desire, amuses his desires with impossible enjoyments, and confers upon his pride unattainable dominion. The mind dances from scene to scene, unites all pleasures in all combinations, and riots in delights which nature and fortune, with all their bounty, cannot bestow.

"In time some particular train of ideas fixes the attention, all other intellectual gratifications are rejected, the mind, in weariness or leisure, recurs constantly to the favourite conception, and feasts on the luscious falsehood whenever she is offended with the bitterness of truth. By degrees the reign of fancy is confirmed; she grows first imperious, and in time despotick. Then fictions begin to operate as realities, false opinions fasten upon the mind, and life passes in dreams of rapture or of anguish.

"This, Sir, is one of the dangers of solitude, which the hermit has confessed not always to promote goodness, and the astronomer's misery has proved to be not always propitious to wisdom."

"I will no more," said the favourite, "imagine myself the queen of Abissinia. I have often spent the hours, which the princess gave to my own disposal, in adjusting ceremonies and regulating the court; I have repressed the pride of the powerful, and granted the petitions of the poor; I have built new palaces in more happy situations, planted groves upon the tops of mountains, and have exulted in the beneficence of royalty, till, when the princess entered, I had almost forgotten to bow down before her."

"And I," said the princess, "will not allow myself any more to play the shepherdess in my waking dreams. I have often soothed my thoughts with the quiet and innocence of pastoral employments, till I have in my chamber heard the winds whistle, and the sheep bleat; sometimes freed the lamb entangled in the thicket, and sometimes with my crook encountered the wolf. I have a dress like that of the village maids, which I put on to help my imagination, and a pipe on which I play softly, and suppose myself followed by my flocks."

"I will confess," said the prince, "an indulgence of fantastick delight more dangerous than yours. I have frequently endeavoured to image the possibility of a perfect government, by which all wrong should be restrained, all vice reformed, and all the subjects preserved in tranquility and innocence. This thought produced innumerable schemes of reformation, and dictated many useful regulations and salutary edicts. This has been the sport and sometimes the labour of my solitude; and I start, when I think with how little anguish I once supposed the death of my father and my brothers."

"Such," says Imlac, "are the effects of visionary schemes: when we first form them we know them to be absurd, but familiarise them by degrees, and in time lose sight of their folly."

XLV

THEY DISCOURSE WITH AN OLD MAN

The evening was now far past, and they rose to return home. As they walked along the bank of the Nile, delighted with the beams of the moon quivering on the water, they saw at a small distance an old man, whom the prince had often heard in the assembly of the sages. "Yonder," said he, "is one whose years have calmed his passions, but not clouded his reason: let us close the disquisitions of the night, by enquiring what are his sentiments of his own state, that we may know whether youth alone is to struggle with vexation, and whether any better hope remains for the latter part of life."

Here the sage approached and saluted them. They invited him to join their walk, and prattled a while as acquaintance that had unexpectedly met one another. The old man was chearful and talkative, and the way seemed short in his company. He was pleased to find himself not disregarded, accompanied them to their house, and, at the prince's request, entered with them. They placed him in the seat of honour, and set wine and conserves before him.

"Sir," said the princess, "an evening walk must give to a man of learning, like you, pleasures which ignorance and youth can hardly conceive. You know the qualities and the causes of all that you behold, the laws by which the river flows, the periods in which the planets perform their revolutions. Every thing must supply you with contemplation, and renew the consciousness of your own dignity."

"Lady," answered he, "let the gay and the vigorous expect pleasure in their excursions, it is enough that age can obtain ease. To me the world has lost its novelty: I look round, and see what I remember to have seen in happier days. I rest against a tree, and consider, that in the same shade I once disputed upon the annual overflow of the Nile with a friend who is now silent in the grave. I cast my eyes upwards, fix them on the changing moon, and think with pain on the vicissitudes of life. I have ceased to take much delight in physical truth; for what have I to do with those things which I am soon to leave?"

"You may at least recreate yourself," said Imlac, "with the recollection of an honourable and useful life, and enjoy the praise which all agree to give you."

"Praise," said the sage, with a sigh, "is to an old man an empty sound. I have neither mother to be delighted with the reputation of her son, nor wife to partake the honours of her husband. I have outlived my friends and my rivals. Nothing is now of much importance; for I cannot extend my interest beyond myself. Youth is delighted with applause, because it is considered as the earnest of some future good, and because the prospect of life is far extended: but to me, who am now declining to decrepitude, there is little to be feared from the malevolence of men, and yet less to be hoped from their affection or esteem. Something they may yet take away, but they can give me nothing. Riches would now be useless, and high employment would be pain. My retrospect of life recalls to my view many opportunities of good neglected, much time squandered upon trifles, and more lost in idleness and vacancy. I leave many great designs unattempted, and many great attempts unfinished. My mind is burthened with no heavy crime, and therefore I compose myself to tranquility; endeavour to abstract my thoughts from hopes and cares, which, though reason knows them to be vain, still try to keep their old possession of the heart; expect, with serene humility, that hour which nature cannot long delay; and hope to possess in a better state that happiness which here I could not find, and that virtue which here I have not attained."

He rose and went away, leaving his audience not much elated with the hope of long life. The prince consoled himself with remarking, that it was not reasonable to be disappointed by this account; for age had never been considered as the season of felicity, and, if it was possible to be easy in decline and weakness, it was likely that the days of vigour and alacrity might be happy: that the noon of life might be bright, if the evening could be calm.

The princess suspected that age was querulous and malignant, and delighted to repress the expectations of those who had newly entered the world. She had seen the possessors of estates look with envy on their heirs, and known many who enjoy pleasure no longer than they can confine it to themselves.

Pekuah conjectured, that the man was older than he appeared, and was willing to impute his complaints to delirious dejection; or else supposed that he had been unfortunate, and was therefore discontented: "For nothing," said she, "is more common than to call our own condition, the condition of life."

Imlac, who had no desire to see them depressed, smiled at the comforts which they could so readily procure to themselves, and remembered, that at the same age, he was equally confident of unmingled prosperity, and equally fertile of consolatory expedients. He forbore to force upon them unwelcome knowledge, which time itself would too soon impress. The princess and her lady retired; the madness of the astronomer hung upon their minds, and they desired Imlac to enter upon his office, and delay next morning the rising of the sun.

XLVI

THE PRINCESS AND PEKUAH VISIT THE ASTRONOMER

The princess and Pekuah having talked in private of Imlac's astronomer, thought his character at once so amiable and so strange, that they could not be satisfied without a nearer knowledge, and Imlac was requested to find the means of bringing them together.

This was somewhat difficult; the philosopher had never received any visits from women, though he lived in a city that had in it many Europeans who followed the manners of their own countries, and many from other parts of the world that lived there with European liberty. The ladies would not be refused, and several schemes were proposed for the accomplishment of their design. It was proposed to introduce them as strangers in distress, to whom the sage was always accessible; but, after some deliberation, it appeared, that by this artifice, no acquaintance could be formed, for their conversation would be short, and they could not decently importune him often. "This," said Rasselas, "is true; but I have yet a stronger objection against the misrepresentation of your state. I have always considered it as treason against the great republick of human nature, to make any man's virtues the means of deceiving him, whether on great or little occasions. All imposture weakens confidence and chills benevolence. When the sage finds that you are not what you seemed, he will feel the resentment natural to a man who, conscious of great abilities, discovers that he has been tricked by understandings meaner than his own, and, perhaps, the distrust, which he can never afterwards wholly lay aside, may stop the voice of counsel, and close the hand of charity; and where will you find the power of restoring his benefactions to mankind, or his peace to himself?"

To this no reply was attempted, and Imlac began to hope that their curiosity would subside; but, next day, Pekuah told him, she had now found an honest pretence for a visit to the astronomer, for she would solicite permission to continue under him the studies in which she had been initiated by the Arab, and the princess might go with her either as a fellow-student, or because a woman could not decently come alone. "I am afraid," said Imlac, "that he will be soon weary of your company: men advanced far in knowledge do not love to repeat the elements of their art, and I am not certain, that even of the elements, as he will deliver them connected with inferences, and mingled with reflections, you are a very capable auditress." "That," said Pekuah, "must be my care: I ask of you only to take me thither. My knowledge is, perhaps, more than you imagine it, and by concurring always with his opinions I shall make him think it greater than it is."

The astronomer, in pursuance of this resolution, was told, that a foreign lady, travelling in search of knowledge, had heard of his reputation, and was desirous to become his scholar. The uncommonness of the proposal raised at once his surprise and curiosity, and when, after a short deliberation, he consented to admit her, he could not stay without impatience till the next day.

The ladies dressed themselves magnificently, and were attended by Imlac to the astronomer, who was pleased to see himself approached with respect by persons of so splendid an appearance. In the exchange of the first civilities he was timorous and bashful; but, when the talk became regular, he recollected his powers, and justified the character which Imlac had given. Enquiring of Pekuah what could have turned her inclination towards astronomy, he received from her a history of her adventure at the pyramid, and of the time passed in the Arab's island. She told her tale with ease and elegance, and her conversation took possession of his heart. The discourse was then turned to astronomy: Pekuah displayed what she knew: he looked upon her as a prodigy of genius, and intreated her not to desist from a study which she had so happily begun.

They came again and again, and were every time more welcome than before. The sage endeavoured to amuse them, that they might prolong their visits, for he found his thoughts grow brighter in their company; the clouds of solicitude vanished by degrees, as he forced himself to entertain them, and he grieved when he was left at their departure to his old employment of regulating the seasons.

The princess and her favourite had now watched his lips for several months, and could not catch a single word from which they could judge whether he continued, or not, in the opinion of his preternatural commission. They often contrived to bring him to an open declaration, but he easily eluded all their attacks, and on which side soever they pressed him escaped from them to some other topick.

As their familiarity increased they invited him often to the house of Imlac, where they distinguished him by extraordinary respect. He began gradually to delight in sublunary pleasures. He came early and departed late; laboured to recommend himself by assiduity and compliance; excited their curiosity after new arts, that they might still want his assistance; and when they made any excursion of pleasure or enquiry, entreated to attend them.

By long experience of his integrity and wisdom, the prince and his sister were convinced that he might be trusted without danger; and, lest he should draw any false hopes from the civilities which he received, discovered to him their condition, with the motives of their journey, and required his opinion on the choice of life.

"Of the various conditions which the world spreads before you, which you shall prefer," said the sage, "I am not able to instruct you. I can only tell that I have chosen wrong. I have passed my time in study without experience; in the attainment of sciences which can, for the most part, be but remotely useful to mankind. I have purchased knowledge at the expence of all the common comforts of life: I have missed the endearing elegance of female friendship, and the happy commerce of domestick tenderness. If I have obtained any prerogatives above other students, they have been accompanied with fear, disquiet, and scrupulosity; but even of these prerogatives, whatever they were, I have, since my thoughts have been diversified by more intercourse with the world, begun to question the reality. When I have been for a few days lost in pleasing dissipation, I am always tempted to think that my enquiries have ended in errour, and that I have suffered much, and suffered it in vain."

Imlac was delighted to find that the sage's understanding was breaking through its mists, and resolved to detain him from the planets till he should forget his task of ruling them, and reason should recover its original influence.

From this time the astronomer was received into familiar friendship, and partook of all their projects and pleasures: his respect kept him attentive, and the activity of Rasselas did not leave much time unengaged. Something was always to be done; the day was spent in making observations which furnished talk for the evening, and the evening was closed with a scheme for the morrow.

The sage confessed to Imlac, that since he had mingled in the gay tumults of life, and divided his hours by a succession of amusements, he found the conviction of his authority over the skies fade gradually from his mind, and began to trust less to an opinion which he never could prove to others, and which he now found subject to variation from causes in which reason had no part. "If I am accidentally left alone for a few hours," said he, "my inveterate persuasion rushes upon my soul, and my thoughts are chained down by some irresistible violence, but they are soon disentangled by the prince's conversation, and instantaneously released at the entrance of Pekuah. I am like a man habitually afraid of spectres, who is set at ease by a lamp, and wonders at the dread which harrassed him in the dark, yet, if his lamp be extinguished, feels again the terrours which he knows that when it is light he shall feel no more. But I am sometimes afraid lest I indulge my quiet by criminal negligence, and voluntarily forget the great charge with which I am intrusted. If I favour myself in a known errour, or am determined by my own ease in a doubtful question of this importance, how dreadful is my crime!"

"No disease of the imagination," answered Imlac, "is so difficult of cure, as that which is complicated with the dread of guilt: fancy and conscience then act interchangeably upon us, and so often shift their places, that the illusions of one are not distinguished from the dictates of the other. If fancy presents images not moral or religious, the mind drives them away when they give it pain, but when melancholick notions take the form of duty, they lay hold on the faculties without opposition, because we are afraid to exclude or banish them. For this reason the superstitious are often melancholy, and the melancholy almost always superstitious.

"But do not let the suggestions of timidity overpower your better reason: the danger of neglect can be but as the probability of the obligation, which, when you consider it with freedom, you find very little, and that little growing every day less. Open your heart to the influence of the light, which, from time to time, breaks in upon you: when scruples importune you, which you in your lucid moments know to be vain, do not stand to parley, but fly to business or to Pekuah, and keep this thought always prevalent, that you are only one atom of the mass of humanity, and have neither such virtue nor vice, as that you should be singled out for supernatural favours or afflictions."

XLVII

THE PRINCE ENTERS AND BRINGS A NEW TOPICK

"All this," said the astronomer, "I have often thought, but my reason has been so long subjugated by an uncontrolable and overwhelming idea, that it durst not confide in its own decisions. I now see how fatally I betrayed my quiet, by suffering chimeras to prey upon me in secret; but melancholy shrinks from communication, and I never found a man before, to whom I could impart my troubles, though I had been certain of relief. I rejoice to find my own sentiments confirmed by yours, who are not easily deceived, and can have no motive or purpose to deceive. I hope that time and variety will dissipate the gloom that has so long surrounded me, and the latter part of my days will be spent in peace."

"Your learning and virtue," said Imlac, "may justly give you hopes."

Rasselas then entered with the princess and Pekuah, and enquired whether they had contrived any new diversion for the next day. "Such," said Nekayah, "is the state of life, that none are happy but by the anticipation of change: the change itself is nothing; when we have made it, the next wish is to change again. The world is not yet exhausted; let me see something to morrow which I never saw before."

"Variety," said Rasselas, "is so necessary to content, that even the happy valley disgusted me by the recurrence of its luxuries; yet I could not forbear to reproach myself with impatience, when I saw the monks of St. Anthony support without complaint, a life, not of uniform delight, but uniform hardship."

"Those men," answered Imlac, "are less wretched in their silent convent than the Abissinian princes in their prison of pleasure. Whatever is done by the monks is incited by an adequate and reasonable motive. Their labour supplies them with necessaries; it therefore cannot be omitted, and is certainly rewarded. Their devotion prepares them for another state, and reminds them of its approach, while it fits them for it. Their time is regularly distributed; one duty succeeds another, so that they are not left open to the distraction of unguided choice, nor lost in the shades of listless inactivity. There is a certain task to be performed at an appropriated hour; and their toils are cheerful, because they consider them as acts of piety, by which they are always advancing towards endless felicity."

"Do you think," said Nekayah, "that the monastick rule is a more holy and less imperfect state than any other? May not he equally hope for future happiness who converses openly with mankind, who succours the distressed by his charity, instructs the ignorant by his learning, and contributes by his industry to the general system of life; even though he should omit some of the mortifications which are practised in the cloister, and allow himself such harmless delights as his condition may place within his reach?"

"This," said Imlac, "is a question which has long divided the wise, and perplexed the good. I am afraid to decide on either part. He that lives well in the world is better than he that lives well in a monastery. But, perhaps, every one is not able to stem the temptations of publick life; and, if he cannot conquer, he may properly retreat. Some have little power to do good, and have likewise little strength to resist evil. Many are weary of their conflicts with adversity, and are willing to eject those passions which have long busied them in vain. And many are dismissed by age and diseases from the more laborious duties of society. In monasteries the weak and timorous may be happily sheltered, the weary may repose, and the penitent may meditate. Those retreats of prayer and contemplation have something so congenial to the mind of man, that, perhaps, there is scarcely one that does not purpose to close his life in pious abstraction with a few associates serious as himself."

"Such," said Pekuah, "has often been my wish, and I have heard the princess declare, that she should not willingly die in a croud."

"The liberty of using harmless pleasures," proceeded Imlac, "will not be disputed; but it is still to be examined what pleasures are harmless. The evil of any pleasure that Nekayah can image is not in the act itself, but in its consequences. Pleasure, in itself harmless, may become mischievous, by endearing to us a state which we know to be transient and probatory, and withdrawing our thoughts from that, of which every hour brings us nearer to the beginning, and of which no length of time will bring us to the end. Mortification is not virtuous in itself, nor has any other use, but that it disengages us from the allurements of sense. In the state of future perfection, to which we all aspire, there will be pleasure without danger, and security without restraint."

The princess was silent, and Rasselas, turning to the astronomer, asked him, whether he could not delay her retreat, by shewing her something which she had not seen before.

"Your curiosity," said the sage, "has been so general, and your pursuit of knowledge so vigorous, that novelties are not now very easily to be found: but what you can no longer procure from the living may be given by the dead. Among the wonders of this country are the catacombs, or the ancient repositories, in which the bodies of the earliest generations were lodged, and where, by the virtue of the gums which embalmed them, they yet remain without corruption."

"I know not," said Rasselas, "what pleasure the sight of the catacombs can afford; but, since nothing else is offered, I am resolved to view them, and shall place this with many other things which I have done, because I would do something."

They hired a guard of horsemen, and the next day visited the catacombs. When they were about to descend into the sepulchral caves, "Pekuah," said the princess, "we are now again invading the habitations of the dead; I know that you will stay behind; let me find you safe when I return." "No, I will not be left," answered Pekuah; "I will go down between you and the prince."

They then all descended, and roved with wonder through the labyrinth of subterraneous passages, where the bodies were laid in rows on either side.

XLVIII

IMLAC DISCOURSES ON THE NATURE OF THE SOUL

"What reason," said the prince, "can be given, why the Egyptians should thus expensively preserve those carcasses which some nations consume with fire, others lay to mingle with the earth, and all agree to remove from their sight, as soon as decent rites can be performed?"

"The original of ancient customs," said Imlac, "is commonly unknown; for the practice often continues when the cause has ceased; and concerning superstitious ceremonies it is vain to conjecture; for what reason did not dictate reason cannot explain. I have long believed that the practice of embalming arose only from tenderness to the remains of relations or friends, and to this opinion I am more inclined, because it seems impossible that this care should have been general: had all the dead been embalmed, their repositories must in time have been more spacious than the dwellings of the living. I suppose only the rich or honourable were secured from corruption, and the rest left to the course of nature.

"But it is commonly supposed that the Egyptians believed the soul to live as long as the body continued undissolved, and therefore tried this method of eluding death."

"Could the wise Egyptians," said Nekayah, "think so grosly of the soul? If the soul could once survive its separation, what could it afterwards receive or suffer from the body?"

"The Egyptians would doubtless think erroneously," said the astronomer, "in the darkness of heathenism, and the first dawn of philosophy. The nature of the soul is still disputed amidst all our opportunities of clearer knowledge: some yet say, that it may be material, who, nevertheless, believe it to be immortal."

"Some," answered Imlac, "have indeed said that the soul is material, but I can scarcely believe that any man has thought it, who knew how to think; for all the conclusions of reason enforce the immateriality of the[3] mind, and all the notices of sense and investigations of science concur to prove the unconsciousness of matter.

"It was never supposed that cogitation is inherent in matter, or that every particle is a thinking being. Yet, if any part of matter be devoid of thought, what part can we suppose to think? Matter can differ from matter only in form, density, bulk, motion, and direction of motion: to which of these, however varied or combined, can consciousness be annexed? To be round or square, to be solid or fluid, to be great or little, to be moved slowly or swiftly one way or another, are modes of material existence, all equally alien from the nature of cogitation. If matter be once without thought, it can only be made to think by some new modification, but all the modifications which it can admit are equally unconnected with cogitative powers."

"But the materialists," said the astronomer, "urge that matter may have qualities with which we are unacquainted."

"He who will determine," returned Imlac, "against that which he knows, because there may be something which he knows not; he that can set hypothetical possibility against acknowledged

---

[3] of the: of 2

certainty, is not to be admitted among reasonable beings. All that we know of matter is, that matter is inert, senseless and lifeless; and if this conviction cannot be opposed but by referring us to something that we know not, we have all the evidence that human intellect can admit. If that which is known may be over-ruled by that which is unknown, no being, not omniscient, can arrive at certainty."

"Yet let us not," said the astronomer, "too arrogantly limit the Creator's power."

"It is no limitation of omnipotence," replied the poet, "to suppose that one thing is not consistent with another, that the same proposition cannot be at once true and false, that the same number cannot be even and odd, that cogitation cannot be conferred on that which is created incapable of cogitation."

"I know not," said Nekayah, "any great use of this question. Does that immateriality, which, in my opinion, you have sufficiently proved, necessarily include eternal duration?"

"Of immateriality," said Imlac, "our ideas are negative, and therefore obscure. Immateriality seems to imply a natural power of perpetual duration as a consequence of exemption from all causes of decay: whatever perishes, is destroyed by the solution of its contexture, and separation of its parts; nor can we conceive how that which has no parts, and therefore admits no solution, can be naturally corrupted or impaired."

"I know not," said Rasselas, "how to conceive any thing without extension: what is extended must have parts, and you allow, that whatever has parts may be destroyed."

"Consider your own conceptions," replied Imlac, "and the difficulty will be less. You will find substance without extension. An ideal form is no less real than material bulk: yet an ideal form has no extension. It is no less certain, when you think on a pyramid, that your mind possesses the idea of a pyramid, than that the pyramid itself is standing. What space does the idea of a pyramid occupy more than the idea of a grain of corn? or how can either idea suffer laceration? As is the effect such is the cause; as thought is, such is the power that thinks; a power impassive and indiscerptible."

"But the Being," said Nekayah, "whom I fear to name, the Being which made the soul, can destroy it."

"He, surely, can destroy it," answered Imlac, "since, however unperishable in itself, it receives from a higher[4] nature its power of duration. That it will not perish by any inherent cause or principle of corruption, may be collected from[5] philosophy; but philosophy can tell no more. That it will not be annihilated by him that made it, we must humbly learn from higher authority."

The whole assembly stood a while silent and collected. "Let us return," said Rasselas, "from this scene of mortality. How gloomy would be these mansions of the dead to him who did not know that he shall never die; that what now acts shall continue its agency, and what now thinks shall think on for ever. Those that lie here stretched before us, the wise and the powerful of antient times, warn us to remember the shortness of our present state: they were, perhaps, snatched away while they were busy, like us, in the choice of life."

"To me," said the princess, "the choice of life is become less important; I hope hereafter to think only on the choice of eternity."

They then hastened out of the caverns, and, under the protection of their guard, returned to Cairo.

XLIX

THE CONCLUSION, IN WHICH NOTHING IS CONCLUDED

It was now the time of the inundation of the Nile: a few days after their visit to the catacombs, the river began to rise.

They were confined to their house. The whole region being under water gave them no invitation to any excursions, and, being well supplied with materials for talk, they diverted themselves with comparisons of the different forms of life which they had observed, and with various schemes of happiness which each of them had formed.

Pekuah was never so much charmed with any place as the convent of St. Anthony, where the Arab restored her to the princess, and wished only to fill it with pious maidens, and to be made

[4] in itself, it receives from a higher: it receives from a superiour 2

[5] cause or principle of corruption, may be collected from: cause of decay, or principle of corruption, may be shown by 2

prioress of the order: she was weary of expectation and disgust, and would gladly be fixed in some unvariable state.

The princess thought, that of all sublunary things, knowledge was the best: She desired first to learn all sciences, and then purposed to found a college of learned women, in which she would preside, that, by conversing with the old, and educating the young, she might divide her time between the acquisition and communication of wisdom, and raise up for the next age models of prudence, and patterns of piety.

The prince desired a little kingdom, in which he might administer justice in his own person, and see all the parts of government with his own eyes; but he could never fix the limits of his dominion, and was always adding to the number of his subjects.

Imlac and the astronomer were contented to be driven along the stream of life without directing their course to any particular port.

Of these wishes that they had formed they well knew that none could be obtained. They deliberated a while what was to be done, and resolved, when the inundation should cease, to return to Abissinia.

Like the Preface to the Dictionary, *Johnson's Preface to his eight-volume edition of Shakespeare is the distillation of many years of work—twenty, in this instance. It was published with the edition in October 1765, separately published shortly thereafter, reprinted with the edition within a few weeks, and at least three more times before Johnson's death. It is now reprinted from the first edition.*

Preface to Shakespeare

That praises are without reason lavished on the dead, and that the honours due only to excellence are paid to antiquity, is a complaint likely to be always continued by those, who, being able to add nothing to truth, hope for eminence from the heresies of paradox; or those, who, being forced by disappointment upon consolatory expedients, are willing to hope from posterity what the present age refuses, and flatter themselves that the regard which is yet denied by envy, will be at last bestowed by time.

Antiquity, like every other quality that attracts the notice of mankind, has undoubtedly votaries that reverence it, not from reason, but from prejudice. Some seem to admire indiscriminately whatever has been long preserved, without considering that time has sometimes co-operated with chance; all perhaps are more willing to honour past than present excellence; and the mind contemplates genius through the shades of age, as the eye surveys the sun through artificial opacity. The great contention of criticism is to find the faults of the moderns, and the beauties of the ancients. While an authour is yet living we estimate his powers by his worst performance, and when he is dead we rate them by his best.

To works, however, of which the excellence is not absolute and definite, but gradual and comparative; to works not raised upon principles demonstrative and scientifick, but appealing wholly to observation and experience, no other test can be applied than length of duration and continuance of esteem. What mankind have long possessed they have often examined and compared, and if they persist to value the possession, it is because frequent comparisons have confirmed opinion in its favour. As among the works of nature no man can properly call a river deep or a mountain high, without the knowledge of many mountains and many rivers; so in the productions of genius, nothing can be stiled excellent till it has been compared with other works of the same kind. Demonstration immediately displays its power, and has nothing to hope or fear from the flux of years; but works tentative and experimental must be estimated by their proportion to the general and collective ability of man, as it is discovered in a long succession of endeavours. Of the first building that was raised, it might be with certainty determined that it was round or square, but whether it was spacious or lofty must have been referred to time. The Pythagorean scale of numbers was at once discovered to be perfect; but the poems of Homer we yet know not to transcend the common limits of human intelligence, but by remarking, that nation after nation, and century after century, has been able to do little more than transpose his incidents, new name his characters, and paraphrase his sentiments.

The reverence due to writings that have long subsisted arises therefore not from any credulous confidence in the superior wisdom of past ages, or gloomy persuasion of the degeneracy of mankind, but is the consequence of acknowledged and indubitable positions, that what has been longest known has been most considered, and what is most considered is best understood.

The poet, of whose works I have undertaken the revision, may now begin to assume the dignity of an ancient, and claim the privilege of established fame and prescriptive veneration. He has long outlived his century, the term commonly fixed as the test of literary merit. Whatever advantages he might once derive from personal allusions, local customs, or temporary opinions, have for many years been lost; and every topick of merriment or motive of sorrow, which the modes of artificial life afforded him, now only obscure the scenes which they once illuminated. The effects of favour and competition are at an end; the tradition of his friendships and his enmities has perished; his works support no opinion with arguments, nor supply any faction with invectives; they can neither indulge vanity nor gratify malignity, but are read without any other reason than the desire of pleasure, and are therefore praised only as pleasure is obtained; yet, thus unassisted by interest or passion, they have past through variations of taste and changes of manners, and, as they devolved from one generation to another, have received new honours at every transmission.

But because human judgment, though it be gradually gaining upon certainty, never becomes infallible; and approbation, though long continued, may yet be only the approbation of prejudice or fashion; it is proper to inquire, by what peculiarities of excellence Shakespeare has gained and kept the favour of his countrymen.

Nothing can please many, and please long, but just representations of general nature. Particular manners can be known to few, and therefore few only can judge how nearly they are copied. The irregular combinations of fanciful invention may delight a-while, by that novelty of which the common satiety of life sends us all in quest; but the pleasures of sudden wonder are soon exhausted, and the mind can only repose on the stability of truth.

Shakespeare is above all writers, at least above all modern writers, the poet of nature; the poet that holds up to his readers a faithful mirrour of manners and of life. His characters are not modified by the customs of particular places, unpractised by the rest of the world; by the peculiarities of studies or professions, which can operate but upon small numbers; or by the accidents of transient fashions or temporary opinions: they are the genuine progeny of common humanity, such as the world will always supply, and observation will always find. His persons act and speak by the influence of those general passions and principles by which all minds are agitated, and the whole system of life is continued in motion. In the writings of other poets a character is too often an individual; in those of Shakespeare it is commonly a species.

It is from this wide extension of design that so much instruction is derived. It is this which fills the plays of Shakespeare with practical axioms and domestick wisdom. It was said of Euripides,[1] that every verse was a precept; and it may be said of Shake-

[1] By Cicero.

speare, that from his works may be collected a system of civil and oeconomical prudence. Yet his real power is not shewn in the splendour of particular passages, but by the progress of his fable, and the tenour of his dialogue; and he that tries to recommend him by select quotations, will succeed like the pedant in Hierocles, who, when he offered his house to sale, carried a brick in his pocket as a specimen.[2]

It will not easily be imagined how much Shakespeare excells in accommodating his sentiments to real life, but by comparing him with other authours. It was observed of the ancient schools of declamation, that the more diligently they were frequented, the more was the student disqualified for the world, because he found nothing there which he should ever meet in any other place. The same remark may be applied to every stage but that of Shakespeare. The theatre, when it is under any other direction, is peopled by such characters as were never seen, conversing in a language which was never heard, upon topicks which will never arise in the commerce of mankind. But the dialogue of this authour is often so evidently determined by the incident which produces it, and is pursued with so much ease and simplicity, that it seems scarcely to claim the merit of fiction, but to have been gleaned by diligent selection out of common conversation, and common occurrences.

Upon every other stage the universal agent is love, by whose power all good and evil is distributed, and every action quickened or retarded. To bring a lover, a lady and a rival into the fable; to entangle them in contradictory obligations, perplex them with oppositions of interest, and harrass them with violence of desires inconsistent with each other; to make them meet in rapture and part in agony; to fill their mouths with hyperbolical joy and outrageous sorrow; to distress them as nothing human ever was distressed; to deliver them as nothing human ever was delivered, is the business of a modern dramatist. For this probability is violated, life is misrepresented, and language is depraved. But

---

[2] The story appears in Dacier's "Life of Hierocles," an Alexandrian philosopher, c. A.D. 430, translated in Rowe's *Life of Pythagoras*, etc., 1707, p. 146: "Another [scholar], who was desirous to sell his house, took a stone of it out of the wall, and carry'd it to the market for a sample." Attributed to a follower of Hierocles.

love is only one of many passions, and as it has no great influence upon the sum of life, it has little operation in the dramas of a poet, who caught his ideas from the living world, and exhibited only what he saw before him. He knew, that any other passion, as it was regular or exorbitant, was a cause of happiness or calamity.

Characters thus ample and general were not easily discriminated and preserved, yet perhaps no poet ever kept his personages more distinct from each other. I will not say with Pope, that every speech may be assigned to the proper speaker,[3] because many speeches there are which have nothing characteristical; but perhaps, though some may be equally adapted to every person, it will be difficult to find, any that can be properly transferred from the present possessor to another claimant. The choice is right, when there is reason for choice.

Other dramatists can only gain attention by hyperbolical or aggravated characters, by fabulous and unexampled excellence or depravity, as the writers of barbarous romances invigorated the reader by a giant and a dwarf; and he that should form his expectations of human affairs from the play, or from the tale, would be equally deceived. Shakespeare has no heroes; his scenes are occupied only by men, who act and speak as the reader thinks that he should himself have spoken or acted on the same occasion: Even where the agency is supernatural the dialogue is level with life. Other writers disguise the most natural passions and most frequent incidents; so that he who contemplates them in the book will not know them in the world: Shakespeare approximates the remote, and familiarizes the wonderful; the event which he represents will not happen, but if it were possible, its effects would probably be such as he has assigned; and it may be said, that he has not only shewn human nature as it acts in real exigences, but as it would be found in trials, to which it cannot be exposed.

This therefore is the praise of Shakespeare, that his drama is the mirrour of life; that he who has mazed his imagination, in following the phantoms which other writers raise up before him, may here be cured of his delirious extasies, by reading human

[3] Pope's Preface to his edition of Shakespeare, 1725.

sentiments in human language; by scenes from which a hermit may estimate the transactions of the world, and a confessor predict the progress of the passions.

His adherence to general nature has exposed him to the censure of criticks, who form their judgments upon narrower principles. Dennis and Rhymer[4] think his Romans not sufficiently Roman; and Voltaire censures his kings as not completely royal. Dennis is offended, that Menenius, a senator of Rome, should play the buffoon; and Voltaire perhaps thinks decency violated when the Danish usurper is represented as a drunkard. But Shakespeare always makes nature predominate over accident; and if he preserves the essential character, is not very careful of distinctions superinduced and adventitious. His story requires Romans or kings, but he thinks only on men. He knew that Rome, like every other city, had men of all dispositions; and wanting a buffoon, he went into the senate-house for that which the senate-house would certainly have afforded him. He was inclined to shew an usurper and a murderer not only odious but despicable, he therefore added drunkenness to his other qualities, knowing that kings love wine like other men, and that wine exerts its natural power upon kings. These are the petty cavils of petty minds; a poet overlooks the casual distinction of country and condition, as a painter, satisfied with the figure, neglects the drapery.

The censure which he has incurred by mixing comick and tragick scenes, as it extends to all his works, deserves more consideration. Let the fact be first stated, and then examined.

Shakespeare's plays are not in the rigorous and critical sense either tragedies or comedies, but compositions of a distinct kind; exhibiting the real state of sublunary nature, which partakes of good and evil, joy and sorrow, mingled with endless variety of proportion and innumerable modes of combination; and expressing the course of the world, in which the loss of one is the gain of another; in which, at the same time, the reveller is hasting to his wine, and the mourner burying his friend; in which the malignity of one is sometimes defeated by the frolick of another; and many mischiefs and many benefits are done and hindered without design.

---

[4] John Dennis (d. 1734), whose *Essay on the Genius and Writings of Shakespear,* 1712, Johnson cites; and Thomas Rymer (d. 1713), whose *Short View of Tragedy,* 1693, is referred to.

Out of this chaos of mingled purposes and casualties the ancient poets, according to the laws which custom had prescribed, selected some the crimes of men, and some their absurdities; some the momentous vicissitudes of life, and some the lighter occurrences; some the terrours of distress, and some the gayeties of prosperity. Thus rose the two modes of imitation, known by the names of *tragedy* and *comedy*, compositions intended to promote different ends by contrary means, and considered as so little allied, that I do not recollect among the Greeks or Romans a single writer who attempted both.

Shakespeare has united the powers of exciting laughter and sorrow not only in one mind but in one composition. Almost all his plays are divided between serious and ludicrous characters, and, in the successive evolutions of the design, sometimes produce seriousness and sorrow, and sometimes levity and laughter.

That this is a practice contrary to the rules of criticism will be readily allowed; but there is always an appeal open from criticism to nature. The end of writing is to instruct; the end of poetry is to instruct by pleasing. That the mingled drama may convey all the instruction of tragedy or comedy cannot be denied, because it includes both in its alternations of exhibition, and approaches nearer than either to the appearance of life, by shewing how great machinations and slender designs may promote or obviate one another, and the high and the low co-operate in the general system by unavoidable concatenation.

It is objected, that by this change of scenes the passions are interrupted in their progression, and that the principal event, being not advanced by a due gradation of preparatory incidents, wants at last the power to move, which constitutes the perfection of dramatick poetry. This reasoning is so specious, that it is received as true even by those who in daily experience feel it to be false. The interchanges of mingled scenes seldom fail to produce the intended vicissitudes of passion. Fiction cannot move so much, but that the attention may be easily transferred; and though it must be allowed that pleasing melancholy be sometimes interrupted by unwelcome levity, yet let it be considered likewise, that melancholy is often not pleasing, and that the disturbance of one man may be the relief of another; that different auditors have different habitudes; and that, upon the whole, all pleasure consists in variety.

The players, who in their edition[5] divided our authour's works into comedies, histories, and tragedies, seem not to have distinguished the three kinds, by any very exact or definite ideas.

An action which ended happily to the principal persons, however serious or distressful through its intermediate incidents, in their opinion constituted a comedy. This idea of a comedy continued long amongst us, and plays were written, which, by changing the catastrophe, were tragedies to-day and comedies to-morrow.

Tragedy was not in those times a poem of more general dignity or elevation than comedy; it required only a calamitous conclusion, with which the common criticism of that age was satisfied, whatever lighter pleasure it afforded in its progress.

History was a series of actions, with no other than chronological succession, independent on each other, and without any tendency to introduce or regulate the conclusion. It is not always very nicely distinguished from tragedy. There is not much nearer approach to unity of action in the tragedy of *Antony and Cleopatra,* than in the history of *Richard the Second.* But a history might be continued through many plays; as it had no plan, it had no limits.

Through all these denominations of the drama, Shakespeare's mode of composition is the same; an interchange of seriousness and merriment, by which the mind is softened at one time, and exhilarated at another. But whatever be his purpose, whether to gladden or depress, or to conduct the story, without vehemence or emotion, through tracts of easy and familiar dialogue, he never fails to attain his purpose; as he commands us, we laugh or mourn, or sit silent with quiet expectation, in tranquillity without indifference.

When Shakespeare's plan is understood, most of the criticisms of Rhymer and Voltaire vanish away. The play of *Hamlet* is opened, without impropriety, by two sentinels; Iago bellows at Brabantio's window, without injury to the scheme of the play, though in terms which a modern audience would not easily endure; the character of Polonius is seasonable and useful; and the Grave-diggers themselves may be heard with applause.

[5] Heming and Condell, fellow-players with Shakespeare. They furnished the materials for the First Folio, 1623.

Shakespeare engaged in dramatick poetry with the world open before him; the rules of the ancients were yet known to few; the publick judgment was unformed; he had no example of such fame as might force him upon imitation, nor criticks of such authority as might restrain his extravagance: He therefore indulged his natural disposition, and his disposition, as Rhymer has remarked, led him to comedy. In tragedy he often writes with great appearance of toil and study, what is written at last with little felicity; but in his comick scenes, he seems to produce without labour, what no labour can improve. In tragedy he is always struggling after some occasion to be comick, but in comedy he seems to repose, or to luxuriate, as in a mode of thinking congenial to his nature. In his tragick scenes there is always something wanting, but his comedy often surpasses expectation or desire. His comedy pleases by the thoughts and the language, and his tragedy for the greater part by incident and action. His tragedy seems to be skill, his comedy to be instinct.

The force of his comick scenes has suffered little diminution from the changes made by a century and a half, in manners or in words. As his personages act upon principles arising from genuine passion, very little modified by particular forms, their pleasures and vexations are communicable to all times and to all places; they are natural, and therefore durable; the adventitious peculiarities of personal habits, are only superficial dies, bright and pleasing for a little while, yet soon fading to a dim tinct, without any remains of former lustre; but the discriminations of true passion are the colours of nature; they pervade the whole mass, and can only perish with the body that exhibits them. The accidental compositions of heterogeneous modes are dissolved by the chance which combined them; but the uniform simplicity of primitive qualities neither admits increase, nor suffers decay. The sand heaped by one flood is scattered by another, but the rock always continues in its place. The stream of time, which is continually washing the dissoluble fabricks of other poets, passes without injury by the adamant of Shakespeare.

If there be, what I believe there is, in every nation, a stile which never becomes obsolete, a certain mode of phraseology so consonant and congenial to the analogy and principles of its respective language as to remain settled and unaltered; this stile is probably to be sought in the common intercourse of life, among those who speak only to be understood, without ambition of elegance. The polite are always catching modish innovations, and the learned depart from established forms of speech, in hope of finding or making better; those who wish for distinction forsake the vulgar, when the vulgar is right; but there is a conversation above grossness and below refinement, where propriety resides, and where this poet seems to have gathered his comick dialogue. He is therefore more agreeable to the ears of the present age than any other authour equally remote, and among his other excellencies deserves to be studied as one of the original masters of our language.

These observations are to be considered not as unexceptionably constant, but as containing general and predominant truth. Shakespeare's familiar dialogue is affirmed to be smooth and clear, yet not wholly without ruggedness or difficulty; as a country may be eminently fruitful, though it has spots unfit for cultivation: His characters are praised as natural, though their sentiments are sometimes forced, and their actions improbable; as the earth upon the whole is spherical, though its surface is varied with protuberances and cavities.

Shakespeare with his excellencies has likewise faults, and faults sufficient to obscure and overwhelm any other merit. I shall shew them in the proportion in which they appear to me, without envious malignity or superstitious veneration. No question can be more innocently discussed than a dead poet's pretensions to renown; and little regard is due to that bigotry which sets candour higher than truth.

His first defect is that to which may be imputed most of the evil in books or in men. He sacrifices virtue to convenience, and is so much more careful to please than to instruct, that he seems to write without any moral purpose. From his writings indeed a system of social duty may be selected, for he that thinks reasonably must think morally; but his precepts and axioms drop casually from him; he makes no just distribution of good or evil, nor is always careful to shew in the virtuous a disapprobation of the wicked; he carries his persons indifferently through right and wrong, and at the close dismisses them without further care, and leaves their examples to operate by chance. This fault the barbarity of his age cannot extenuate; for it is always a writer's duty to make the world better, and justice is a virtue independant on time or place.

The plots are often so loosely formed, that a very slight consideration may improve them, and so carelessly pursued, that he seems not always fully to comprehend his own design. He omits opportunities of instructing or delighting which the train of his story seems to force upon him, and apparently rejects those exhibitions which would be more affecting, for the sake of those which are more easy.

It may be observed, that in many of his plays the latter part is evidently neglected. When he found himself near the end of his work, and, in view of his reward, he shortened the labour, to snatch the profit. He therefore remits his efforts where he should most vigorously exert them, and his catastrophe is improbably produced or imperfectly represented.

He had no regard to distinction of time or place, but gives to one age or nation, without scruple, the customs, institutions, and opinions of another, at the expence not only of likelihood, but of possibility. These faults Pope has endeavoured, with more zeal than judgment, to transfer to his imagined interpolators. We need not wonder to find Hector quoting Aristotle, when we see the loves of Theseus and Hippolyta combined with the Gothick mythology of fairies. Shakespeare, indeed, was not the only violator of chronology, for in the same age Sidney, who wanted not the advantages of learning, has, in his *Arcadia,* confounded the pastoral with the feudal times, the days of innocence, quiet and security, with those of turbulence, violence and adventure.

In his comick scenes he is seldom very successful, when he engages his characters in reciprocations of smartness and contests of sarcasm; their jests are commonly gross, and their pleasantry licentious; neither his gentlemen nor his ladies have much delicacy, nor are sufficiently distinguished from his clowns by any appearance of refined manners. Whether he represented the real conversation of his time is not easy to determine; the reign of Elizabeth is commonly supposed to have been a time of stateliness, formality and reserve, yet perhaps the relaxations of that severity were not very elegant. There must, however, have been always some modes of gayety preferable to others, and a writer ought to chuse the best.

In tragedy his performance seems constantly to be worse, as

his labour is more. The effusions of passion which exigence forces out are for the most part striking and energetick; but whenever he solicits his invention, or strains his faculties, the offspring of his throes is tumour, meanness, tediousness, and obscurity.

In narration he affects a disproportionate pomp of diction and a wearisome train of circumlocution, and tells the incident imperfectly in many words, which might have been more plainly delivered in few. Narration in dramatick poetry is naturally tedious, as it is unanimated and inactive, and obstructs the progress of the action; it should therefore always be rapid, and enlivened by frequent interruption. Shakespeare found it an encumbrance, and instead of lightening it by brevity, endeavoured to recommend it by dignity and splendour.

His declamations or set speeches are commonly cold and weak, for his power was the power of nature; when he endeavoured, like other tragick writers, to catch opportunities of amplification, and instead of inquiring what the occasion demanded, to show how much his stores of knowledge could supply, he seldom escapes without the pity or resentment of his reader.

It is incident to him to be now and then entangled with an unwieldy sentiment, which he cannot well express, and will not reject; he struggles with it a while, and if it continues stubborn, comprises it in words such as occur, and leaves it to be disentangled and evolved by those who have more leisure to bestow upon it.

Not that always where the language is intricate the thought is subtle, or the image always great where the line is bulky; the equality of words to things is very often neglected, and trivial sentiments and vulgar ideas disappoint the attention, to which they are recommended by sonorous epithets and swelling figures.

But the admirers of this great poet have never less reason to indulge their hopes of supreme excellence, than when he seems fully resolved to sink them in dejection, and mollify them with tender emotions by the fall of greatness, the danger of innocence, or the crosses of love. He is not long soft and pathetick without some idle conceit, or contemptible equivocation. He no sooner begins to move, than he counteracts himself; and terrour and pity, as they are rising in the mind, are checked and blasted by sudden frigidity.

A quibble is to Shakespeare, what luminous vapours are to the traveller; he follows it at all adventures, it is sure to lead him out of his way, and sure to engulf him in the mire. It has some malignant power over his mind, and its fascinations are irresistible. Whatever be the dignity or profundity of his disquisition, whether he be enlarging knowledge or exalting affection, whether he be amusing attention with incidents, or enchaining it in suspense, let but a quibble spring up before him, and he leaves his work unfinished. A quibble is the golden apple for which he will always turn aside from his career, or stoop from his elevation. A quibble, poor and barren as it is, gave him such delight, that he was content to purchase it, by the sacrifice of reason, propriety and truth. A quibble was to him the fatal Cleopatra for which he lost the world, and was content to lose it.

It will be thought strange, that, in enumerating the defects of this writer, I have not yet mentioned his neglect of the unities; his violation of those laws which have been instituted and established by the joint authority of poets and of criticks.

For his other deviations from the art of writing, I resign him to critical justice, without making any other demand in his favour, than that which must be indulged to all human excellence; that his virtues be rated with his failings: But, from the censure which this irregularity may bring upon him, I shall, with due reverence to that learning which I must oppose, adventure to try how I can defend him.

His histories, being neither tragedies nor comedies, are not subject to any of their laws; nothing more is necessary to all the praise which they expect, than that the changes of action be so prepared as to be understood, that the incidents be various and affecting, and the characters consistent, natural and distinct. No other unity is intended, and therefore none is to be sought.

In his other works he has well enough preserved the unity of action. He has not, indeed, an intrigue regularly perplexed and regularly unravelled; he does not endeavour to hide his design only to discover it, for this is seldom the order of real events, and Shakespeare is the poet of nature: But his plan has commonly what Aristotle requires, a beginning, a middle, and an end; one event is concatenated with another, and the conclusion follows by easy consequence. There are perhaps some incidents that might be spared, as in other poets there is much talk that only fills up time upon the stage; but the general system makes gradual advances, and the end of the play is the end of expectation.

To the unities of time and place he has shewn no regard, and perhaps a nearer view of the principles on which they stand will diminish their value, and withdraw from them the veneration which, from the time of Corneille, they have very generally received, by discovering that they have given more trouble to the poet, than pleasure to the auditor.

The necessity of observing the unities of time and place arises from the supposed necessity of making the drama credible. The criticks hold it impossible, that an action of months or years can be possibly believed to pass in three hours; or that the spectator can suppose himself to sit in the theatre, while ambassadors go and return between distant kings, while armies are levied and towns besieged, while an exile wanders and returns, or till he whom they saw courting his mistress, shall lament the untimely fall of his son. The mind revolts from evident falsehood, and fiction loses its force when it departs from the resemblance of reality.

From the narrow limitation of time necessarily arises the contraction of place. The spectator, who knows that he saw the first act at Alexandria, cannot suppose that he sees the next at Rome, at a distance to which not the dragons of Medea could, in so short a time, have transported him; he knows with certainty that he has not changed his place; and he knows that place cannot change itself; that what was a house cannot become a plain; that what was Thebes can never be Persepolis.

Such is the triumphant language with which a critick exults over the misery of an irregular poet, and exults commonly without resistance or reply. It is time therefore to tell him, by the authority of Shakespeare, that he assumes, as an unquestionable principle, a position, which, while his breath is forming it into words, his understanding pronounces to be false. It is false, that any representation is mistaken for reality; that any dramatick fable in its materiality was ever credible, or, for a single moment, was ever credited.

The objection arising from the impossibility of passing the first hour at Alexandria, and the next at Rome, supposes, that when the play opens the spectator really imagines himself at Alexandria, and believes that his walk to the theatre has been a voyage to Egypt, and that he lives in the days of Antony and Cleopatra. Surely he that imagines this may imagine more. He that can take the stage at one time for the palace of the Ptolemies, may take it in half an hour for the promontory of Actium. Delusion, if delusion be admitted, has no certain limitation; if the spectator can be once persuaded, that his old acquaintance are Alexander and Caesar, that a room illuminated with candles is the plain of Pharsalia, or the bank of Granicus, he is in a state of elevation above the reach of reason, or of truth, and from the heights of empyrean poetry, may despise the circumscriptions of terrestrial nature. There is no reason why a mind thus wandering in extasy should count the clock, or why an hour should not be a century in that calenture of the brains that can make the stage a field.

The truth is, that the spectators are always in their senses, and know, from the first act to the last, that the stage is only a stage, and that the players are only players. They come to hear a certain number of lines recited with just gesture and elegant modulation. The lines relate to some action, and an action must be in some place; but the different actions that compleat a story may be in places very remote from each other; and where is the absurdity of allowing that space to represent first Athens, and then Sicily, which was always known to be neither Sicily nor Athens, but a modern theatre.

By supposition, as place is introduced, time may be extended; the time required by the fable elapses for the most part between the acts; for, of so much of the action as is represented, the real and poetical duration is the same. If, in the first act, preparations for war against Mithridates are represented to be made in Rome, the event of the war may, without absurdity, be represented, in the catastrophe, as happening in Pontus; we know that there is neither war, nor preparation for war; we know that we are neither in Rome nor Pontus; that neither Mithridates nor Lucullus are before us. The drama exhibits successive imitations of successive actions, and why may not the second imitation represent an action that happened years after the first; if it be so connected with it, that nothing but time can be supposed to intervene. Time is, of all modes of existence, most obsequious to the imagination; a lapse of years is as easily conceived as a passage of hours. In contemplation we easily contract the time of real actions, and therefore willingly permit it to be contracted when we only see their imitation.

It will be asked, how the drama moves, if it is not credited. It is credited with all the credit due to a drama. It is credited, whenever it moves, as a just picture of a real original; as representing to the auditor what he would himself feel, if he were to do or suffer what is there feigned to be suffered or to be done. The reflection that strikes the heart is not, that the evils before us are real evils, but that they are evils to which we ourselves may be exposed. If there be any fallacy, it is not that we fancy the players, but that we fancy ourselves unhappy for a moment; but we rather lament the possibility than suppose the presence of misery, as a mother weeps over her babe, when she remembers that death may take it from her. The delight of tragedy proceeds from our consciousness of fiction; if we thought murders and treasons real, they would please no more.

Imitations produce pain or pleasure, not because they are mistaken for realities, but because they bring realities to mind. When the imagination is recreated by a painted landscape, the trees are not supposed capable to give us shade, or the fountains coolness; but we consider, how we should be pleased with such fountains playing beside us, and such woods waving over us. We are agitated in reading the history of Henry the Fifth, yet no man takes his book for the field of Agencourt. A dramatick exhibition is a book recited with concomitants that encrease or diminish its effect. Familiar comedy is often more powerful on the theatre, than in the page; imperial tragedy is always less. The humour of Petruchio may be heightened by grimace; but what voice or what gesture can hope to add dignity or force to the soliloquy of *Cato*.[6]

A play read, affects the mind like a play acted. It is therefore evident, that the action is not supposed to be real, and it follows that between the acts a longer or shorter time may be allowed to pass, and that no more account of space or duration is to be taken by the auditor of a drama, than by the reader of a narrative,

---

[6] Addison, *Cato*, V.i.

before whom may pass in an hour the life of a hero, or the revolutions of an empire.

Whether Shakespeare knew the unities, and rejected them by design, or deviated from them by happy ignorance, it is, I think, impossible to decide, and useless to enquire. We may reasonably suppose, that, when he rose to notice, he did not want the counsels and admonitions of scholars and criticks, and that he at last deliberately persisted in a practice, which he might have begun by chance. As nothing is essential to the fable, but unity of action, and as the unities of time and place arise evidently from false assumptions, and, by circumscribing the extent of the drama, lessen its variety, I cannot think it much to be lamented, that they were not known by him, or not observed: Nor, if such another poet could arise, should I very vehemently reproach him, that his first act passed at Venice, and his next in Cyprus. Such violations of rules merely positive, become the comprehensive genius of Shakespeare, and such censures are suitable to the minute and slender criticism of Voltaire:

Non usque adeo permiscuit imis
Longus summa dies, ut non, si voce Metelli
Serventur leges, malint a Caesare tolli.[7]

Yet when I speak thus slightly of dramatick rules, I cannot but recollect how much wit and learning may be produced against me; before such authorities I am afraid to stand, not that I think the present question one of those that are to be decided by mere authority, but because it is to be suspected, that these precepts have not been so easily received but for better reasons than I have yet been able to find. The result of my enquiries, in which it would be ludicrous to boast of impartiality, is, that the unities of time and place are not essential to a just drama, that though they may sometimes conduce to pleasure, they are always to be sacrificed to the nobler beauties of variety and instruction; and that a play, written with nice observation of critical rules, is to be contemplated as an elaborate curiosity, as the product of superfluous and

[7] Lucan, *Pharsalia,* III.138–140. "The course of time has not wrought such confusion that the laws would not rather be trampled on by Caesar than saved by Metellus." (tr. J.D. Duff.) Read "servantur."

ostentatious art, by which is shewn, rather what is possible, than what is necessary.

He that, without diminution of any other excellence, shall preserve all the unities unbroken, deserves the like applause with the architect, who shall display all the orders of architecture in a citadel, without any deduction from its strength; but the principal beauty of a citadel is to exclude the enemy; and the greatest graces of a play, are to copy nature and instruct life.

Perhaps, what I have here not dogmatically but deliberatively written, may recal the principles of the drama to a new examination. I am almost frighted at my own temerity; and when I estimate the fame and the strength of those that maintain the contrary opinion, am ready to sink down in reverential silence; as Aeneas withdrew from the defence of Troy, when he saw Neptune shaking the wall, and Juno heading the besiegers.[8]

Those whom my arguments cannot persuade to give their approbation to the judgment of Shakespeare, will easily, if they consider the condition of his life, make some allowance for his ignorance.

Every man's performances, to be rightly estimated, must be compared with the state of the age in which he lived, and with his own particular opportunities; and though to the reader a book be not worse or better for the circumstances of the authour, yet as there is always a silent reference of human works to human abilities, and as the enquiry, how far man may extend his designs, or how high he may rate his native force, is of far greater dignity than in what rank we shall place any particular performance, curiosity is always busy to discover the instruments, as well as to survey the workmanship, to know how much is to be ascribed to original powers, and how much to casual and adventitious help. The palaces of Peru or Mexico were certainly mean and incommodious habitations, if compared to the houses of European monarchs; yet who could forbear to view them with astonishment, who remembered that they were built without the use of iron?

The English nation, in the time of Shakespeare, was yet struggling to emerge from barbarity. The philology of Italy had been transplanted hither in the reign of Henry the Eighth; and the

---

[8] *Aeneid*, II.670.

learned languages had been successfully cultivated by Lilly, Linacer,[9] and More; by Pole, Cheke, and Gardiner;[1] and afterwards by Smith, Clerk, Haddon,[2] and Ascham. Greek was now taught to boys in the principal schools; and those who united elegance with learning, read, with great diligence, the Italian and Spanish poets. But literature was yet confined to professed scholars, or to men and women of high rank. The publick was gross and dark; and to be able to read and write, was an accomplishment still valued for its rarity.

Nations, like individuals, have their infancy. A people newly awakened to literary curiosity, being yet unacquainted with the true state of things, knows not how to judge of that which is proposed as its resemblance. Whatever is remote from common appearances is always welcome to vulgar, as to childish credulity; and of a country unenlightened by learning, the whole people is the vulgar. The study of those who then aspired to plebeian learning was laid out upon adventures, giants, dragons, and enchantments. *The Death of Arthur*[3] was the favourite volume.

The mind, which has feasted on the luxurious wonders of fiction, has no taste of the insipidity of truth. A play which imitated only the common occurrences of the world, would, upon the admirers of *Palmerin*[4] and *Guy of Warwick*,[5] have made little impression; he that wrote for such an audience was under the necessity of looking round for strange events and fabulous trans-

---

[9] William Lily (d. 1522), author of the Latin grammar used even in Johnson's day. Thomas Linacre (d. 1524) taught Greek to Erasmus and Sir Thomas More.

[1] Reginald, Cardinal Pole (d. 1558), called by More as learned as he was noble and as virtuous as he was learned (*Encyclopedia Britannica*). Sir John Cheke (d. 1557) made many Latin translations from the Greek. Stephen Gardiner (d. 1555), bishop and lord chancellor, encouraged the study of Greek at Cambridge.

[2] Sir Thomas Smith (d. 1577), wrote on the pronunciation of Greek as well as on the government of England. Bartholomew Clerke (d. 1590), professor of rhetoric at Cambridge, whom Haddon recommended to be Latin Secretary to Elizabeth after the death of Ascham. Walter Haddon (d. 1571) revised the Latin translation of the Book of Common Prayer. In Johnson's *Milton* he speaks of Haddon and Roger Ascham as "the pride of Elizabeth's reign."

[3] Malory's *Morte d'Arthur* had been printed five times before Shakespeare's death.

[4] *Palmerin of England*, a sixteenth-century chivalric romance.

[5] *Guy of Warwick*, a long fourteenth-century verse romance.

actions, and that incredibility, by which maturer knowledge is offended, was the chief recommendation of writings, to unskilful curiosity.

Our authour's plots are generally borrowed from novels, and it is reasonable to suppose, that he chose the most popular, such as were read by many, and related by more; for his audience could not have followed him through the intricacies of the drama, had they not held the thread of the story in their hands.

The stories, which we now find only in remoter authours, were in his time accessible and familiar. The fable of *As you like it,* which is supposed to be copied from Chaucer's *Gamelyn,*[6] was a little pamphlet of those times; and old Mr. Cibber[7] remembered the tale of *Hamlet* in plain English prose, which the criticks have now to seek in Saxo Grammaticus.[8]

His English histories he took from English chronicles and English ballads; and as the ancient writers were made known to his countrymen by versions, they supplied him with new subjects; he dilated some of Plutarch's lives into plays, when they had been translated by North.

His plots, whether historical or fabulous, are always crouded with incidents, by which the attention of a rude people was more easily caught than by sentiment or argumentation; and such is the power of the marvellous even over those who despise it, that every man finds his mind more strongly seized by the tragedies of Shakespeare than of any other writer; others please us by particular speeches, but he always makes us anxious for the event, and has perhaps excelled all but Homer in securing the first purpose of a writer, by exciting restless and unquenchable curiosity, and compelling him that reads his work to read it through.

The shows and bustle with which his plays abound have the same original. As knowledge advances, pleasure passes from the eye to the ear, but returns, as it declines, from the ear to the eye. Those to whom our authour's labours were exhibited had more skill in pomps or processions than in poetical language, and per-

---

[6] Thomas Lodge's *Rosalynde* (1590), based on the pseudo-Chaucerian *Tale of Gamelyn.*

[7] Colley Cibber (d. 1757), actor and playwright.

[8] Saxo Grammaticus, thirteenth-century Danish historian, in whose *Gesta Danorum* the Hamlet story appears.

haps wanted some visible and discriminated events, as comments on the dialogue. He knew how he should most please; and whether his practice is more agreeable to nature, or whether his example has prejudiced the nation, we still find that on our stage something must be done as well as said, and inactive declamation is very coldly heard, however musical or elegant, passionate or sublime.

Voltaire expresses his wonder, that our authour's extravagances are endured by a nation, which has seen the tragedy of *Cato*. Let him be answered, that Addison speaks the language of poets, and Shakespeare, of men. We find in *Cato* innumerable beauties which enamour us of its authour, but we see nothing that acquaints us with human sentiments or human actions; we place it with the fairest and the noblest progeny which judgment propagates by conjunction with learning, but *Othello* is the vigorous and vivacious offspring of observation impregnated by genius. *Cato* affords a splendid exhibition of artificial and fictitious manners, and delivers just and noble sentiments, in diction easy, elevated and harmonious, but its hopes and fears communicate no vibration to the heart; the composition refers us only to the writer; we pronounce the name of *Cato,* but we think on Addison.

The work of a correct and regular writer is a garden accurately formed and diligently planted, varied with shades, and scented with flowers; the composition of Shakespeare is a forest, in which oaks extend their branches, and pines tower in the air, interspersed sometimes with weeds and brambles, and sometimes giving shelter to myrtles and to roses; filling the eye with awful pomp, and gratifying the mind with endless diversity. Other poets display cabinets of precious rarities, minutely finished, wrought into shape, and polished unto brightness. Shakespeare opens a mine which contains gold and diamonds in unexhaustible plenty, though clouded by incrustations, debased by impurities, and mingled with a mass of meaner minerals.

It has been much disputed, whether Shakespeare owed his excellence to his own native force, or whether he had the common helps of scholastick education, the precepts of critical science, and the examples of ancient authours.

There has always prevailed a tradition, that Shakespeare wanted learning, that he had no regular education, nor much skill in the dead languages. Johnson, his friend, affirms, that *he had small Latin, and no Greek;*[9] who, besides that he had no imaginable temptation to falsehood, wrote at a time when the character and acquisitions of Shakespeare were known to multitudes. His evidence ought therefore to decide the controversy, unless some testimony of equal force could be opposed.

Some have imagined, that they have discovered deep learning in many imitations of old writers; but the examples which I have known urged, were drawn from books translated in his time; or were such easy coincidencies of thought, as will happen to all who consider the same subjects; or such remarks on life or axioms of morality as float in conversation, and are transmitted through the world in proverbial sentences.

I have found it remarked, that, in this important sentence, *Go before, I'll follow,* we read a translation of, *I prae, sequar.*[1] I have been told, that when Caliban, after a pleasing dream, says, *I cry'd to sleep again,* the authour imitates Anacreon, who had, like every other man, the same wish on the same occasion.

There are a few passages which may pass for imitations, but so few, that the exception only confirms the rule; he obtained them from accidental quotations, or by oral communication, and as he used what he had, would have used more if he had obtained it.

The *Comedy of Errors* is confessedly taken from the *Menaechmi* of Plautus; from the only play of Plautus which was then in English. What can be more probable, than that he who copied that, would have copied more; but that those which were not translated were inaccessible?

Whether he knew the modern languages is uncertain. That his plays have some French scenes proves but little; he might easily procure them to be written, and probably, even though he had known the language in the common degree, he could not have written it without assistance. In the story of *Romeo and Juliet* he is observed to have followed the English translation, where it deviates from the Italian; but this on the other part proves nothing against his knowledge of the original. He was to copy, not what he knew himself, but what was known to his audience.

---

[9] Ben Jonson's "To the Memory of my beloved, the Author, Mr. William Shakespeare." Jonson wrote "less Greek."

[1] Zachary Grey's *Notes on Shakespeare,* 1754. The Latin is from Terence's *Andria.*

It is most likely that he had learned Latin sufficiently to make him acquainted with construction, but that he never advanced to an easy perusal of the Roman authours. Concerning his skill in modern languages, I can find no sufficient ground of determination; but as no imitations of French or Italian authours have been discovered, though the Italian poetry was then high in esteem, I am inclined to believe, that he read little more than English, and chose for his fables only such tales as he found translated.

That much knowledge is scattered over his works is very justly observed by Pope, but it is often such knowledge as books did not supply. He that will understand Shakespeare, must not be content to study him in the closet, he must look for his meaning sometimes among the sports of the field, and sometimes among the manufactures of the shop.

There is however proof enough that he was a very diligent reader, nor was our language then so indigent of books, but that he might very liberally indulge his curiosity without excursion into foreign literature. Many of the Roman authours were translated, and some of the Greek; the reformation had filled the kingdom with theological learning; most of the topicks of human disquisition had found English writers; and poetry had been cultivated, not only with diligence, but success. This was a stock of knowledge sufficient for a mind so capable of appropriating and improving it.

But the greater part of his excellence was the product of his own genius. He found the English stage in a state of the utmost rudeness; no essays either in tragedy or comedy had appeared, from which it could be discovered to what degree of delight either one or other might be carried. Neither character nor dialogue were yet understood. Shakespeare may be truly said to have introduced them both amongst us, and in some of his happier scenes to have carried them both to the utmost height.

By what gradations of improvement he proceeded, is not easily known; for the chronology of his works is yet unsettled. Rowe is of opinion, that *perhaps we are not to look for his beginning, like those of other writers, in his least perfect works; art had so little, and nature so large a share in what he did, that for ought I know,* says he, *the performances of his youth, as they were the most vigorous, were the best.*[2] But the power of nature is only the power of using to any certain purpose the materials which diligence procures, or opportunity supplies. Nature gives no man knowledge, and when images are collected by study and experience, can only assist in combining or applying them. Shakespeare, however favoured by nature, could impart only what he had learned; and as he must increase his ideas, like other mortals, by gradual acquisition, he, like them, grew wiser as he grew older, could display life better, as he knew it more, and instruct with more efficacy, as he was himself more amply instructed.

There is a vigilance of observation and accuracy of distinction which books and precepts cannot confer; from this almost all original and native excellence proceeds. Shakespeare must have looked upon mankind with perspicacity, in the highest degree curious and attentive. Other writers borrow their characters from preceding writers, and diversify them only by the accidental appendages of present manners; the dress is a little varied, but the body is the same. Our authour had both matter and form to provide; for except the characters of Chaucer, to whom I think he is not much indebted, there were no writers in English, and perhaps not many in other modern languages, which shewed life in its native colours.

The contest about the original benevolence or malignity of man had not yet commenced. Speculation had not yet attempted to analyse the mind, to trace the passions to their sources, to unfold the seminal principles of vice and virtue, or sound the depths of the heart for the motives of action. All those enquiries, which from that time that human nature became the fashionable study, have been made sometimes with nice discernment, but often with idle subtilty, were yet unattempted. The tales, with which the infancy of learning was satisfied, exhibited only the superficial appearances of action, related the events but omitted the causes, and were formed for such as delighted in wonders rather than in truth. Mankind was not then to be studied in the closet; he that would know the world, was under the necessity of gleaning his own remarks, by mingling as he could in its business and amusements.

Boyle congratulated himself upon his high birth, because it

---

[2] Nicholas Rowe's *Life of Shakespeare,* prefixed to his edition, 1709.

favoured his curiosity, by facilitating his access.[3] Shakespeare had no such advantage; he came to London a needy adventurer, and lived for a time by very mean employments. Many works of genius and learning have been performed in states of life, that appear very little favourable to thought or to enquiry; so many, that he who considers them is inclined to think that he sees enterprise and perseverance predominating over all external agency, and bidding help and hindrance vanish before them. The genius of Shakespeare was not to be depressed by the weight of poverty, nor limited by the narrow conversation to which men in want are inevitably condemned; the incumbrances of his fortune were shaken from his mind, *as dewdrops from a lion's mane.*[4]

Though he had so many difficulties to encounter, and so little assistance to surmount them, he has been able to obtain an exact knowledge of many modes of life, and many casts of native dispositions; to vary them with great multiplicity; to mark them by nice distinctions; and to shew them in full view by proper combinations. In this part of his performances he had none to imitate, but has himself been imitated by all succeeding writers; and it may be doubted, whether from all his successors more maxims of theoretical knowledge, or more rules of practical prudence, can be collected, than he alone has given to his country.

Nor was his attention confined to the actions of men; he was an exact surveyor of the inanimate world; his descriptions have always some peculiarities, gathered by contemplating things as they really exist. It may be observed, that the oldest poets of many nations preserve their reputation, and that the following generations of wit, after a short celebrity, sink into oblivion. The first, whoever they be, must take their sentiments and descriptions immediately from knowledge; the resemblance is therefore just, their descriptions are verified by every eye, and their sentiments acknowledged by every breast. Those whom their fame invites to the same studies, copy partly them, and partly nature, till the books of one age gain such authority, as to stand in the place of nature to another, and imitation, always deviating a little, becomes at last capricious and casual. Shakespeare, whether life or nature be his subject, shews plainly, that he has seen with his own eyes; he gives the image which he receives, not weakened or

[3] Thomas Birch, *Life of Robert Boyle,* 1744.

[4] *Troilus and Cressida,* III.iii.224.

distorted by the intervention of any other mind; the ignorant feel his representations to be just, and the learned see that they are compleat.

Perhaps it would not be easy to find any authour, except Homer, who invented so much as Shakespeare, who so much advanced the studies which he cultivated, or effused so much novelty upon his age or country. The form, the characters, the language, and the shows of the English drama are his. *He seems,* says Dennis, *to have been the very original of our English tragical harmony, that is, the harmony of blank verse, diversified often by dissyllable and trissyllable terminations. For the diversity distinguishes it from heroick harmony, and by bringing it nearer to common use makes it more proper to gain attention, and more fit for action and dialogue. Such verse we make when we are writing prose; we make such verse in common conversation.*

I know not whether this praise is rigorously just. The dissyllable termination, which the critick rightly appropriates to the drama, is to be found, though, I think, not in *Gorboduc* which is confessedly before our authour; yet in *Hieronnymo,*[5] of which the date is not certain, but which there is reason to believe at least as old as his earliest plays. This however is certain, that he is the first who taught either tragedy or comedy to please, there being no theatrical piece of any older writer, of which the name is known, except to antiquaries and collectors of books, which are sought because they are scarce, and would not have been scarce, had they been much esteemed.

To him we must ascribe the praise, unless Spenser may divide it with him, of having first discovered to how much smoothness and harmony the English language could be softened. He has speeches, perhaps sometimes scenes, which have all the delicacy of Rowe, without his effeminacy. He endeavours indeed commonly to strike by the force and vigour of his dialogue, but he never executes his purpose better, than when he tries to sooth by softness.

Yet it must be at last confessed, that as we owe every thing to him, he owes something to us; that, if much of his praise is paid

[5] *Jeronimo,* anonymous play printed in 1605, or perhaps Kyd's *The Spanish Tragedy,* acted in 1592.

by perception and judgement, much is likewise given by custom and veneration. We fix our eyes upon his graces, and turn them from his deformities, and endure in him what we should in another loath or despise. If we endured without praising, respect for the father of our drama might excuse us; but I have seen, in the book of some modern critick,[6] a collection of anomalies, which shew that he has corrupted language by every mode of depravation, but which his admirer has accumulated as a monument of honour.

He has scenes of undoubted and perpetual excellence, but perhaps not one play, which, if it were now exhibited as the work of a contemporary writer, would be heard to the conclusion. I am indeed far from thinking, that his works were wrought to his own ideas of perfection; when they were such as would satisfy the audience, they satisfied the writer. It is seldom that authours, though more studious of fame than Shakespeare, rise much above the standard of their own age; to add a little to what is best will always be sufficient for present praise, and those who find themselves exalted into fame, are willing to credit their encomiasts, and to spare the labour of contending with themselves.

It does not appear, that Shakespeare thought his works worthy of posterity, that he levied any ideal tribute upon future times, or had any further prospect, than of present popularity and present profit. When his plays had been acted, his hope was at an end; he solicited no addition of honour from the reader. He therefore made no scruple to repeat the same jests in many dialogues, or to entangle different plots by the same knot of perplexity, which may be at least forgiven him, by those who recollect, that of Congreve's four comedies, two are concluded by a marriage in a mask, by a deception, which perhaps never happened, and which, whether likely or not, he did not invent.

So careless was this great poet of future fame, that, though he retired to ease and plenty, while he was yet little *declined into the vale of years,*[7] before he could be disgusted with fatigue, or disabled by infirmity, he made no collection of his works, nor desired to rescue those that had been already published from the deprava-

---

[6] John Upton, *Critical Observations on Shakespeare,* 1746.
[7] *Othello,* III.iii.265.

tions that obscured them, or secure to the rest a better destiny, by giving them to the world in their genuine state.

Of the plays which bear the name of Shakespeare in the late editions, the greater part were not published till about seven years after his death, and the few which appeared in his life are apparently thrust into the world without the care of the authour, and therefore probably without his knowledge.

Of all the publishers, clandestine or professed, their negligence and unskilfulness has by the late revisers been sufficiently shown. The faults of all are indeed numerous and gross, and have not only corrupted many passages perhaps beyond recovery, but have brought others into suspicion, which are only obscured by obsolete phraseology, or by the writer's unskilfulness and affectation. To alter is more easy than to explain, and temerity is a more common quality than diligence. Those who saw that they must employ conjecture to a certain degree, were willing to indulge it a little further. Had the authour published his own works, we should have sat quietly down to disentangle his intricacies, and clear his obscurities; but now we tear what we cannot loose, and eject what we happen not to understand.

The faults are more than could have happened without the concurrence of many causes. The stile of Shakespeare was in itself ungrammatical, perplexed and obscure; his works were transcribed for the players by those who may be supposed to have seldom understood them; they were transmitted by copiers equally unskilful, who still multiplied errours; they were perhaps sometimes mutilated by the actors, for the sake of shortening the speeches; and were at last printed without correction of the press.

In this state they remained, not as Dr. Warburton supposes, because they were unregarded,[8] but because the editor's art was not yet applied to modern languages, and our ancestors were accustomed to so much negligence of English printers, that they could very patiently endure it. At last an edition was undertaken by Rowe; not because a poet was to be published by a poet, for Rowe seems to have thought very little on correction or explanation, but that our authour's works might appear like those of his fraternity, with the appendages of a life and recommendatory

[8] Preface to Warburton's edition of Shakespeare, 1747.

preface. Rowe has been clamorously blamed for not performing what he did not undertake, and it is time that justice be done him, by confessing, that though he seems to have had no thought of corruption beyond the printer's errours, yet he has made many emendations, if they were not made before, which his successors have received without acknowledgment, and which, if they had produced them, would have filled pages and pages with censures of the stupidity by which the faults were committed, with displays of the absurdities which they involved, with ostentatious expositions of the new reading, and self congratulations on the happiness of discovering it.

Of Rowe, as of all the editors, I have preserved the preface, and have likewise retained the authour's life, though not written with much elegance or spirit; it relates however what is now to be known, and therefore deserves to pass through all succeeding publications.

The nation had been for many years content enough with Mr. Rowe's performance, when Mr. Pope made them acquainted with the true state of Shakespeare's text, shewed that it was extremely corrupt, and gave reason to hope that there were means of reforming it. He collated the old copies, which none had thought to examine before, and restored many lines to their integrity; but, by a very compendious criticism, he rejected whatever he disliked, and thought more of amputation than of cure.

I know not why he is commended by Dr. Warburton for distinguishing the genuine from the spurious plays. In this choice he exerted no judgement of his own; the plays which he received, were given by Hemings and Condel, the first editors; and those which he rejected, though, according to the licentiousness of the press in those times, they were printed during Shakespeare's life, with his name, had been omitted by his friends, and were never added to his works before the edition of 1664, from which they were copied by the later printers.

This was a work which Pope seems to have thought unworthy of his abilities, being not able to suppress his contempt of *the dull duty of an editor.*[9] He understood but half his undertaking. The duty of a collator is indeed dull, yet, like other tedious tasks, is

[9] Preface to Pope's edition of Shakespeare, 1725.

very necessary; but an emendatory critick would ill discharge his duty, without qualities very different from dulness. In perusing a corrupted piece, he must have before him all possibilities of meaning, with all possibilities of expression. Such must be his comprehension of thought, and such his copiousness of language. Out of many readings possible, he must be able to select that which best suits with the state, opinions, and modes of language prevailing in every age, and with his authour's particular cast of thought, and turn of expression. Such must be his knowledge, and such his taste. Conjectural criticism demands more than humanity possesses, and he that exercises it with most praise has very frequent need of indulgence. Let us now be told no more of the dull duty of an editor.

Confidence is the common consequence of success. They whose excellence of any kind has been loudly celebrated, are ready to conclude, that their powers are universal. Pope's edition fell below his own expectations, and he was so much offended, when he was found to have left any thing for others to do, that he past the latter part of his life in a state of hostility with verbal criticism.

I have retained all his notes, that no fragment of so great a writer may be lost; his preface, valuable alike for elegance of composition and justness of remark, and containing a general criticism on his authour, so extensive that little can be added, and so exact, that little can be disputed, every editor has an interest to suppress, but that every reader would demand its insertion.

Pope was succeeded by Theobald,[1] a man of narrow comprehension and small acquisitions, with no native and intrinsick splendour of genius, with little of the artificial light of learning, but zealous for minute accuracy, and not negligent in pursuing it. He collated the ancient copies, and rectified many errors. A man so anxiously scrupulous might have been expected to do more, but what little he did was commonly right.

In his reports of copies and editions he is not to be trusted,

---

[1] Lewis Theobald attacked Pope's edition in 1726 in *Shakespeare Restored*, and published his own edition in 1733. He made the most famous emendation in Shakespearean criticism, "a babbl'd of green fields" for "a table of green fields," Mistress Quickly describing Falstaff dying in *Henry V*. Pope made him the first hero of *The Dunciad*.

without examination. He speaks sometimes indefinitely of copies, when he has only one. In his enumeration of editions, he mentions the two first folios as of high, and the third folio as of middle authority; but the truth is, that the first is equivalent to all others, and that the rest only deviate from it by the printer's negligence. Whoever has any of the folios has all, excepting those diversities which mere reiteration of editions will produce. I collated them all at the beginning, but afterwards used only the first.

Of his notes I have generally retained those which he retained himself in his second edition, except when they were confuted by subsequent annotators, or were too minute to merit preservation. I have sometimes adopted his restoration of a comma, without inserting the panegyrick in which he celebrated himself for his atchievement. The exuberant excrescence of his diction I have often lopped, his triumphant exultations over Pope and Rowe I have sometimes suppressed, and his contemptible ostentation I have frequently concealed; but I have in some places shewn him, as he would have shewn himself, for the reader's diversion, that the inflated emptiness of some notes may justify or excuse the contraction of the rest.

Theobald, thus weak and ignorant, thus mean and faithless, thus petulant and ostentatious, by the good luck of having Pope for his enemy, has escaped, and escaped alone, with reputation, from this undertaking. So willingly does the world support those who solicite favour, against those who command reverence; and so easily is he praised, whom no man can envy.

Our authour fell then into the hands of Sir Thomas Hanmer,[2] the Oxford editor, a man, in my opinion, eminently qualified by nature for such studies. He had, what is the first requisite to emendatory criticism, that intuition by which the poet's intention is immediately discovered, and that dexterity of intellect which despatches its work by the easiest means. He had undoubtedly read much; his acquaintance with customs, opinions, and traditions, seems to have been large; and he is often learned without shew. He seldom passes what he does not understand, without an attempt to find or to make a meaning, and sometimes hastily makes what a little more attention would have found. He is

[2] Sir Thomas Hanmer's edition was published in 1744–43 [sic]. He was Speaker of the House of Commons.

solicitous to reduce to grammar, what he could not be sure that his authour intended to be grammatical. Shakespeare regarded more the series of ideas, than of words; and his language, not being designed for the reader's desk, was all that he desired it to be, if it conveyed his meaning to the audience.

Hanmer's care of the metre has been too violently censured. He found the measures reformed in so many passages, by the silent labours of some editors, with the silent acquiescence of the rest, that he thought himself allowed to extend a little further the license, which had already been carried so far without reprehension; and of his corrections in general, it must be confessed, that they are often just, and made commonly with the least possible violation of the text.

But, by inserting his emendations, whether invented or borrowed, into the page, without any notice of varying copies, he has appropriated the labour of his predecessors, and made his own edition of little authority. His confidence indeed, both in himself and others, was too great; he supposes all to be right that was done by Pope and Theobald; he seems not to suspect a critick of fallibility, and it was but reasonable that he should claim what he so liberally granted.

As he never writes without careful enquiry and diligent consideration, I have received all his notes, and believe that every reader will wish for more.

Of the last editor it is more difficult to speak.[3] Respect is due to high place, tenderness to living reputation, and veneration to genius and learning; but he cannot be justly offended at that liberty of which he has himself so frequently given an example, nor very solicitous what is thought of notes, which he ought never to have considered as part of his serious employments, and which, I suppose, since the ardour of composition is remitted, he no longer numbers among his happy effusions.

The original and predominant errour of his commentary, is acquiescence in his first thoughts; that precipitation which is produced by consciousness of quick discernment; and that confidence

[3] It was difficult for Johnson to speak of Bishop Warburton's edition partly from the dilemma that Warburton had praised Johnson's first writings on Shakespeare, and that, at the same time, Johnson disapproved of much of Warburton's work.

which presumes to do, by surveying the surface, what labour only can perform, by penetrating the bottom. His notes exhibit sometimes perverse interpretations, and sometimes improbable conjectures; he at one time gives the authour more profundity of meaning, than the sentence admits, and at another discovers absurdities, where the sense is plain to every other reader. But his emendations are likewise often happy and just; and his interpretation of obscure passages learned and sagacious.

Of his notes, I have commonly rejected those, against which the general voice of the publick has exclaimed, or which their own incongruity immediately condemns, and which, I suppose, the authour himself would desire to be forgotten. Of the rest, to part I have given the highest approbation, by inserting the offered reading in the text; part I have left to the judgment of the reader, as doubtful, though specious; and part I have censured without reserve, but I am sure without bitterness of malice, and, I hope, without wantonness of insult.

It is no pleasure to me, in revising my volumes, to observe how much paper is wasted in confutation. Whoever considers the revolutions of learning, and the various questions of greater or less importance, upon which wit and reason have exercised their powers, must lament the unsuccessfulness of enquiry, and the slow advances of truth, when he reflects, that great part of the labour of every writer is only the destruction of those that went before him. The first care of the builder of a new system, is to demolish the fabricks which are standing. The chief desire of him that comments an authour, is to shew how much other commentators have corrupted and obscured him. The opinions prevalent in one age, as truths above the reach of controversy, are confuted and rejected in another, and rise again to reception in remoter times. Thus the human mind is kept in motion without progress. Thus sometimes truth and errour, and sometimes contrarieties of errour, take each others place by reciprocal invasion. The tide of seeming knowledge which is poured over one generation, retires and leaves another naked and barren; the sudden meteors of intelligence which for a while appear to shoot their beams into the regions of obscurity, on a sudden withdraw their lustre, and leave mortals again to grope their way.

These elevations and depressions of renown, and the contradictions to which all improvers of knowledge must for ever be exposed, since they are not escaped by the highest and brightest of mankind, may surely be endured with patience by criticks and annotators, who can rank themselves but as the satellites of their authours. How canst thou beg for life, says Achilles to his captive, when thou knowest that thou art now to suffer only what must another day be suffered by Achilles?[4]

Dr. Warburton had a name sufficient to confer celebrity on those who could exalt themselves into antagonists, and his notes have raised a clamour too loud to be distinct. His chief assailants are the authours of *the Canons of criticism*[5] and of the *Review of Shakespeare's text;*[6] of whom one ridicules his errours with airy petulance, suitable enough to the levity of the controversy; the other attacks them with gloomy malignity, as if he were dragging to justice an assassin or incendiary. The one stings like a fly, sucks a little blood, takes a gay flutter, and returns for more; the other bites like a viper, and would be glad to leave inflammations and gangrene behind him. When I think on one, with his confederates, I remember the danger of Coriolanus, who was afraid that *girls with spits, and boys with stones, should slay him in puny battle;* when the other crosses my imagination, I remember the prodigy in *Macbeth,*

> An eagle tow'ring in his pride of place,
> Was by a mousing owl hawk'd at and kill'd.[7]

Let me however do them justice. One is a wit, and one a scholar. They have both shewn acuteness sufficient in the discovery of faults, and have both advanced some probable interpretations of obscure passages; but when they aspire to conjecture and emendation, it appears how falsely we all estimate our own abilities, and the little which they have been able to perform might have taught them more candour to the endeavours of others.

Before Dr. Warburton's edition, *Critical observations on Shakespeare* had been published by Mr. Upton, a man skilled in languages, and acquainted with books, but who seems to have had

---

[4] *Iliad,* XXI.99.
[5] Thomas Edwards, 1748.
[6] A *Revisal* [sic] *of Shakespeare's Text,* by Benjamin Heath, 1765.
[7] *Macbeth,* II.iv.12: "A falcon tow'ring in her pride of place."

no great vigour of genius or nicety of taste. Many of his explanations are curious and useful, but he likewise, though he professed to oppose the licentious confidence of editors, and adhere to the old copies, is unable to restrain the rage of emendation, though his ardour is ill seconded by his skill. Every cold empirick, when his heart is expanded by a successful experiment, swells into a theorist, and the laborious collator at some unlucky moment frolicks in conjecture.

Critical, historical and explanatory notes have been likewise published upon Shakespeare by Dr. Grey, whose diligent perusal of the old English writers has enabled him to make some useful observations. What he undertook he has well enough performed, but as he neither attempts judicial nor emendatory criticism, he employs rather his memory than his sagacity. It were to be wished that all would endeavour to imitate his modesty who have not been able to surpass his knowledge.

I can say with great sincerity of all my predecessors, what I hope will hereafter be said of me, that not one has left Shakespeare without improvement, nor is there one to whom I have not been indebted for assistance and information. Whatever I have taken from them it was my intention to refer to its original authour, and it is certain, that what I have not given to another, I believed when I wrote it to be my own. In some perhaps I have been anticipated; but if I am ever found to encroach upon the remarks of any other commentator, I am willing that the honour, be it more or less, should be transferred to the first claimant, for his right, and his alone, stands above dispute; the second can prove his pretensions only to himself, nor can himself always distinguish invention, with sufficient certainty, from recollection.

They have all been treated by me with candour, which they have not been careful of observing to one another. It is not easy to discover from what cause the acrimony of a scholiast can naturally proceed. The subjects to be discussed by him are of very small importance; they involve neither property nor liberty; nor favour the interest of sect or party. The various readings of copies, and different interpretations of a passage, seem to be questions that might exercise the wit, without engaging the passions. But, whether it be, that *small things make mean men proud,*[8] and

[8] *2 Henry VI,* IV.i.106: "Small things make base men proud."

vanity catches small occasions; or that all contrariety of opinion, even in those that can defend it no longer, makes proud men angry; there is often found in commentaries a spontaneous strain of invective and contempt, more eager and venomous than is vented by the most furious controvertist in politicks against those whom he is hired to defame.

Perhaps the lightness of the matter may conduce to the vehemence of the agency; when the truth to be investigated is so near to inexistence, as to escape attention, its bulk is to be enlarged by rage and exclamation: That to which all would be indifferent in its original state, may attract notice when the fate of a name is appended to it. A commentator has indeed great temptations to supply by turbulence what he wants of dignity, to beat his little gold to a spacious surface, to work that to foam which no art or diligence can exalt to spirit.

The notes which I have borrowed or written are either illustrative, by which difficulties are explained; or judicial, by which faults and beauties are remarked; or emendatory, by which depravations are corrected.

The explanations transcribed from others, if I do not subjoin any other interpretation, I suppose commonly to be right, at least I intend by acquiescence to confess, that I have nothing better to propose.

After the labours of all the editors, I found many passages which appeared to me likely to obstruct the greater number of readers, and thought it my duty to facilitate their passage. It is impossible for an expositor not to write too little for some, and too much for others. He can only judge what is necessary by his own experience; and how long soever he may deliberate, will at last explain many lines which the learned will think impossible to be mistaken, and omit many for which the ignorant will want his help. These are censures merely relative, and must be quietly endured. I have endeavoured to be neither superfluously copious, nor scrupulously reserved, and hope that I have made my authour's meaning accessible to many who before were frighted from perusing him, and contributed something to the publick, by diffusing innocent and rational pleasure.

The compleat explanation of an authour not systematick and consequential, but desultory and vagrant, abounding in casual allusions and light hints, is not to be expected from any single scholiast. All personal reflections, when names are suppressed, must be in a few years irrecoverably obliterated; and customs, too minute to attract the notice of law, such as modes of dress, formalities of conversation, rules of visits, disposition of furniture, and practices of ceremony, which naturally find places in familiar dialogue, are so fugitive and unsubstantial, that they are not easily retained or recovered. What can be known, will be collected by chance, from the recesses of obscure and obsolete papers, perused commonly with some other view. Of this knowledge every man has some, and none has much; but when an authour has engaged the publick attention, those who can add any thing to his illustration, communicate their discoveries, and time produces what had eluded diligence.

To time I have been obliged to resign many passages, which, though I did not understand them, will perhaps hereafter be explained, having, I hope, illustrated some, which others have neglected or mistaken, sometimes by short remarks, or marginal directions, such as every editor has added at his will, and often by comments more laborious than the matter will seem to deserve; but that which is most difficult is not always most important, and to an editor nothing is a trifle by which his authour is obscured.

The poetical beauties or defects I have not been very diligent to observe. Some plays have more, and some fewer judicial observations, not in proportion to their difference of merit, but because I gave this part of my design to chance and to caprice. The reader, I believe, is seldom pleased to find his opinion anticipated; it is natural to delight more in what we find or make, than in what we receive. Judgement, like other faculties, is improved by practice, and its advancement is hindered by submission to dictatorial decisions, as the memory grows torpid by the use of a table book. Some initiation is however necessary; of all skill, part is infused by precept, and part is obtained by habit; I have therefore shewn so much as may enable the candidate of criticism to discover the rest.

To the end of most plays, I have added short strictures, containing a general censure of faults, or praise of excellence; in which I know not how much I have concurred with the current opinion; but I have not, by any affectation of singularity, deviated from it. Nothing is minutely and particularly examined, and therefore it is to be supposed, that in the plays which are condemned there is much to be praised, and in these which are praised much to be condemned.

The part of criticism in which the whole succession of editors has laboured with the greatest diligence, which has occasioned the most arrogant ostentation, and excited the keenest acrimony, is the emendation of corrupted passages, to which the publick attention having been first drawn by the violence of the contention between Pope and Theobald, has been continued by the persecution, which, with a kind of conspiracy, has been since raised against all the publishers of Shakespeare.

That many passages have passed in a state of depravation through all the editions is indubitably certain; of these the restoration is only to be attempted by collation of copies or sagacity of conjecture. The collator's province is safe and easy, the conjecturer's perilous and difficult. Yet as the greater part of the plays are extant only in one copy, the peril must not be avoided, nor the difficulty refused.

Of the readings which this emulation of amendment has hitherto produced, some from the labours of every publisher I have advanced into the text; those are to be considered as in my opinion sufficiently supported; some I have rejected without mention, as evidently erroneous; some I have left in the notes without censure or approbation, as resting in equipoise between objection and defence; and some, which seemed specious but not right, I have inserted with a subsequent animadversion.

Having classed the observations of others, I was at last to try what I could substitute for their mistakes, and how I could supply their omissions. I collated such copies as I could procure, and wished for more, but have not found the collectors of these rarities very communicative. Of the editions which chance or kindness put into my hands I have given an enumeration, that I may not be blamed for neglecting what I had not the power to do.

By examining the old copies, I soon found that the later publishers, with all their boasts of diligence, suffered many passages to stand unauthorised, and contented themselves with Rowe's regulation of the text, even where they knew it to be arbitrary, and with a little consideration might have found it to be wrong.

Some of these alterations are only the ejection of a word for one that appeared to him more elegant or more intelligible. These corruptions I have often silently rectified; for the history of our language, and the true force of our words, can only be preserved, by keeping the text of authours free from adulteration. Others, and those very frequent, smoothed the cadence, or regulated the measure; on these I have not exercised the same rigour; if only a word was transposed, or a particle inserted or omitted, I have sometimes suffered the line to stand; for the inconstancy of the copies is such, as that some liberties may be easily permitted. But this practice I have not suffered to proceed far, having restored the primitive diction wherever it could for any reason be preferred.

The emendations, which comparison of copies supplied, I have inserted in the text; sometimes where the improvement was slight, without notice, and sometimes with an account of the reasons of the change.

Conjecture, though it be sometimes unavoidable, I have not wantonly nor licentiously indulged. It has been my settled principle, that the reading of the ancient books is probably true, and therefore is not to be disturbed for the sake of elegance, perspicuity, or mere improvement of the sense. For though much credit is not due to the fidelity, nor any to the judgement of the first publishers, yet they who had the copy before their eyes were more likely to read it right, than we who read it only by imagination. But it is evident that they have often made strange mistakes by ignorance or negligence, and that therefore something may be properly attempted by criticism, keeping the middle way between presumption and timidity.

Such criticism I have attempted to practise, and where any passage appeared inextricably perplexed, have endeavoured to discover how it may be recalled to sense, with least violence. But my first labour is, always to turn the old text on every side, and try if there be any interstice, through which light can find its way; nor would Huetius[9] himself condemn me, as refusing the trouble of research, for the ambition of alteration. In this modest industry I have not been unsuccessful. I have rescued many lines from the

---

[9] Pierre Huet (d. 1721), French scholar.

violations of temerity, and secured many scenes from the inroads of correction. I have adopted the Roman sentiment, that it is more honourable to save a citizen, than to kill an enemy, and have been more careful to protect than to attack.

I have preserved the common distribution of the plays into acts, though I believe it to be in almost all the plays void of authority. Some of those which are divided in the later editions have no division in the first folio, and some that are divided in the folio have no division in the preceding copies. The settled mode of the theatre requires four intervals in the play, but few, if any, of our authour's compositions can be properly distributed in that manner. An act is so much of the drama as passes without intervention of time or change of place. A pause makes a new act. In every real, and therefore in every imitative action, the intervals may be more or fewer, the restriction of five acts being accidental and arbitrary. This Shakespeare knew, and this he practised; his plays were written, and at first printed in one unbroken continuity, and ought now to be exhibited with short pauses, interposed as often as the scene is changed, or any considerable time is required to pass. This method would at once quell a thousand absurdities.

In restoring the authour's works to their integrity, I have considered the punctuation as wholly in my power; for what could be their care of colons and commas, who corrupted words and sentences. Whatever could be done by adjusting points is therefore silently performed, in some plays with much diligence, in others with less; it is hard to keep a busy eye steadily fixed upon evanescent atoms, or a discursive mind upon evanescent truth.

The same liberty has been taken with a few particles, or other words of slight effect. I have sometimes inserted or omitted them without notice. I have done that sometimes, which the other editors have done always, and which indeed the state of the text may sufficiently justify.

The greater part of readers, instead of blaming us for passing trifles, will wonder that on mere trifles so much labour is expended, with such importance of debate, and such solemnity of diction. To these I answer with confidence, that they are judging of an art which they do not understand; yet cannot much reproach them with their ignorance, nor promise that they would become in general, by learning criticism, more useful, happier or wiser.

As I practised conjecture more, I learned to trust it less; and after I had printed a few plays, resolved to insert none of my own readings in the text. Upon this caution I now congratulate myself, for every day encreases my doubt of my emendations.

Since I have confined my imagination to the margin, it must not be considered as very reprehensible, if I have suffered it to play some freaks in its own dominion. There is no danger in conjecture, if it be proposed as conjecture; and while the text remains uninjured, those changes may be safely offered, which are not considered even by him that offers them as necessary or safe.

If my readings are of little value, they have not been ostentatiously displayed or importunately obtruded. I could have written longer notes, for the art of writing notes is not of difficult attainment. The work is performed, first by railing at the stupidity, negligence, ignorance, and asinine tastelessness of the former editors, and shewing, from all that goes before and all that follows, the inelegance and absurdity of the old reading; then by proposing something, which to superficial readers would seem specious, but which the editor rejects with indignation; then by producing the true reading, with a long paraphrase, and concluding with loud acclamations on the discovery, and a sober wish for the advancement and prosperity of genuine criticism.

All this may be done, and perhaps done sometimes without impropriety. But I have always suspected that the reading is right, which requires many words to prove it wrong; and the emendation wrong, that cannot without so much labour appear to be right. The justness of a happy restoration strikes at once, and the moral precept may be well applied to criticism, *quod dubitas ne feceris.*[1]

To dread the shore which he sees spread with wrecks, is natural to the sailor. I had before my eye, so many critical adventures ended in miscarriage, that caution was forced upon me. I encountered in every page Wit struggling with its own sophistry, and Learning confused by the multiplicity of its views. I was forced to censure those whom I admired, and could not but reflect, while I was dispossessing their emendations, how soon the same fate might happen to my own, and how many of the readings

[1] "When in doubt, do nothing."

which I have corrected may be by some other editor defended and established.

> Criticks, I saw, that other's names efface,
> And fix their own, with labour, in the place;
> Their own, like others, soon their place resign'd,
> Or disappear'd, and left the first behind.[2] POPE.

That a conjectural critick should often be mistaken, cannot be wonderful, either to others or himself, if it be considered, that in his art there is no system, no principal and axiomatical truth that regulates subordinate positions. His chance of errour is renewed at every attempt; an oblique view of the passage, a slight misapprehension of a phrase, a casual inattention to the parts connected, is sufficient to make him not only fail, but fail ridiculously; and when he succeeds best, he produces perhaps but one reading of many probable, and he that suggests another will always be able to dispute his claims.

It is an unhappy state, in which danger is hid under pleasure. The allurements of emendation are scarcely resistible. Conjecture has all the joy and all the pride of invention, and he that has once started a happy change, is too much delighted to consider what objections may rise against it.

Yet conjectural criticism has been of great use in the learned world; nor is it my intention to depreciate a study, that has exercised so many mighty minds, from the revival of learning to our own age, from the Bishop of Aleria to English Bentley.[3] The criticks on ancient authours have, in the exercise of their sagacity, many assistances, which the editor of Shakespeare is condemned to want. They are employed upon grammatical and settled languages, whose construction contributes so much to perspicuity, that Homer has fewer passages unintelligible than Chaucer. The words have not only a known regimen, but invariable quantities, which direct and confine the choice. There are commonly more manuscripts than one; and they do not often conspire in the same mistakes. Yet Scaliger could confess to Salmasius how little satisfaction his emendations gave him. *Illudunt nobis conjecturae nostrae, quarum nos pudet, posteaquam in meliores codices in-*

---

[2] *Temple of Fame*, ll. 37–40, slightly misquoted.

[3] Joannes Andreas (d. 1480), Bishop of Aleria, a classical scholar, as was Richard Bentley (d. 1742).

cidimus.[4] And Lipsius[5] could complain, that criticks were making faults, by trying to remove them, *Ut olim vitiis, ita nunc remediis laboratur*. And indeed, where mere conjecture is to be used, the emendations of Scaliger and Lipsius, notwithstanding their wonderful sagacity and erudition, are often vague and disputable, like mine or Theobald's.

Perhaps I may not be more censured for doing wrong, than for doing little; for raising in the publick expectations, which at last I have not answered. The expectation of ignorance is indefinite, and that of knowledge is often tyrannical. It is hard to satisfy those who know not what to demand, or those who demand by design what they think impossible to be done. I have indeed disappointed no opinion more than my own; yet I have endeavoured to perform my task with no slight solicitude. Not a single passage in the whole work has appeared to me corrupt, which I have not attempted to restore; or obscure, which I have not endeavoured to illustrate. In many I have failed like others; and from many, after all my efforts, I have retreated, and confessed the repulse. I have not passed over, with affected superiority, what is equally difficult to the reader and to myself, but where I could not instruct him, have owned my ignorance. I might easily have accumulated a mass of seeming learning upon easy scenes; but it ought not to be imputed to negligence, that, where nothing was necessary, nothing has been done, or that, where others have said enough, I have said no more.

Notes are often necessary, but they are necessary evils. Let him, that is yet unacquainted with the powers of Shakespeare, and who desires to feel the highest pleasure that the drama can give, read every play from the first scene to the last, with utter negligence of all his commentators. When his fancy is once on the wing, let it not stoop at correction or explanation. When his attention is strongly engaged, let it disdain alike to turn aside to the name of Theobald and of Pope. Let him read on through brightness and obscurity, through integrity and corruption; let him preserve his comprehension of the dialogue and his interest

[4] J.J. Scaliger (d. 1609), eminent classical editor. Salmasius (d. 1653), French scholar: "Our conjectures make us ridiculous and put us to shame, when later we come upon better manuscripts."

[5] Lipsius (d. 1606), Flemish editor of Tacitus: "Once we toiled over faults, now with corrections."

in the fable. And when the pleasures of novelty have ceased, let him attempt exactness; and read the commentators.

Particular passages are cleared by notes, but the general effect of the work is weakened. The mind is refrigerated by interruption; the thoughts are diverted from the principal subject; the reader is weary, he suspects not why; and at last throws away the book, which he has too diligently studied.

Parts are not to be examined till the whole has been surveyed; there is a kind of intellectual remoteness necessary for the comprehension of any great work in its full design and its true proportions; a close approach shews the smaller niceties, but the beauty of the whole is discerned no longer.

It is not very grateful to consider how little the succession of editors has added to this authour's power of pleasing. He was read, admired, studied, and imitated, while he was yet deformed with all the improprieties which ignorance and neglect could accumulate upon him; while the reading was yet not rectified, nor his allusions understood; yet then did Dryden pronounce "that Shakespeare was the man, who, of all modern and perhaps ancient poets, had the largest and most comprehensive soul. All the images of nature were still present to him, and he drew them not laboriously, but luckily: When he describes any thing, you more than see it, you feel it too. Those who accuse him to have wanted learning, give him the greater commendation: he was naturally learned: he needed not the spectacles of books to read nature; he looked inwards, and found her there. I cannot say he is every where alike; were he so, I should do him injury to compare him with the greatest of mankind. He is many times flat and insipid; his comick wit degenerating into clenches, his serious swelling into bombast. But he is always great, when some great occasion is presented to him: No man can say, he ever had a fit subject for his wit, and did not then raise himself as high above the rest of poets,

Quantum lenta solent inter viburna cupressi."[6]

It is to be lamented, that such a writer should want a commentary; that his language should become obsolete, or his senti-

[6] Dryden, *Essay of Dramatic Poesy,* quoting Virgil, *Eclogue* I.25: "As cypresses rise above the hedgerow thorn."

ments obscure. But it is vain to carry wishes beyond the condition of human things; that which must happen to all, has happened to Shakespeare, by accident and time; and more than has been suffered by any other writer since the use of types, has been suffered by him through his own negligence of fame, or perhaps by that superiority of mind, which despised its own performances, when it compared them with its powers, and judged those works unworthy to be preserved, which the criticks of following ages were to contend for the fame of restoring and explaining.

Among these candidates of inferiour fame, I am now to stand the judgment of the publick; and wish that I could confidently produce my commentary as equal to the encouragement which I have had the honour of receiving. Every work of this kind is by its nature deficient, and I should feel little solicitude about the sentence, were it to be pronounced only by the skilful and the learned.

Johnson began his Life of Milton *in January 1779, finished it in six weeks, and published it in the second volume of his* Prefaces, Biographical and Critical, to the Works of the English Poets *in the spring of 1779. These volumes were not available apart from the whole set of sixty-eight volumes of prefaces and poems, but the lives were at once pirated in Dublin, and in 1781 they were revised and collected as* Lives of the English Poets. *The* Lives *represent Johnson's mature critical judgment, but, infused as usual with strong personal opinion, they were at once attacked. Reprinted from the first edition.*

Life of Milton

The Life of Milton has been already written in so many forms, with such minute enquiry, that I might perhaps more properly have contented myself with the addition of a few notes to Mr. Fenton's elegant Abridgement,[1] but that a new narrative was thought necessary to the uniformity of this edition.

John Milton was by birth a gentleman, descended from the proprietors of Milton near Thame in Oxfordshire, one of whom forfeited his estate in the times of York and Lancaster. Which side he took I know not: his descendant inherited no veneration for the White Rose.

His grandfather John was keeper of the forest of Shotover, a zealous papist, who disinherited his son, because he had forsaken the religion of his ancestors.

His father, John, who was the son disinherited, had recourse for his support to the profession of a scrivener. He was a man eminent for his skill in musick, many of his compositions being still to be found; and his reputation in his profession was such, that he grew rich, and retired to an estate. He had probably more

[1] Elijah Fenton's "Life of Milton" was prefixed to his edition of *Paradise Lost,* 1725. Here and in several of the following notes we are indebted to G.B. Hill's edition of the *Lives of the Poets,* 3 v., Oxford, 1905.

than common literature, as his son addresses him in one of his most elaborate Latin poems. He married a gentlewoman of the name of Caston, a Welsh family, by whom he had two sons, John the poet, and Christopher who studied the law, and adhered, as the law taught him, to the King's party, for which he was awhile persecuted, but having, by his brother's interest, obtained permission to live in quiet, he supported himself by chamber-practice, till, soon after the accession of King James, he was knighted and made a judge; but, his constitution being too weak for business, he retired before any disreputable compliances became necessary.

He had likewise a daughter Anne, whom he married with a considerable fortune to Edward Philips, who came from Shrewsbury, and rose in the Crown-office to be secondary: by him she had two sons, John and Edward, who were educated by the poet, and from whom is derived the only authentick account of his domestick manners.

John, the poet, was born in his father's house, at the Spread-Eagle in Bread-street, Dec. 9, 1608, between six and seven in the morning. His father appears to have been very solicitous about his education; for he was instructed at first by private tuition under the care of Thomas Young, who was afterwards chaplain to the English merchants at Hamburgh; and of whom we have reason to think well, since his scholar considered him as worthy of an epistolary elegy.

He was then sent to St. Paul's School, under the care of Mr. Gill; and removed, in the beginning of his sixteenth year, to Christ's College in Cambridge, where he entered a sizer, Feb. 12, 1624.

He was at this time eminently skilled in the Latin tongue; and he himself, by annexing the dates to his first compositions, a boast of which the learned Politian had given him an example, seems to commend the earliness of his own proficiency to the notice of posterity. But the products of his vernal fertility have been surpassed by many, and particularly by his contemporary Cowley. Of the powers of the mind it is difficult to form an estimate: many have excelled Milton in their first essays, who never rose to works like *Paradise Lost*.

At fifteen, a date which he uses till he is sixteen, he translated or versified two Psalms, 114 and 136, which he thought worthy of the publick eye; but they raise no great expectations: they would in any numerous school have obtained praise, but not excited wonder.

Many of his elegies appear to have been written in his eighteenth year, by which it appears that he had then read the Roman authors with very nice discernment. I once heard Mr. Hampton, the translator of Polybius, remark what I think is true, that Milton was the first Englishman who, after the revival of letters, wrote Latin verses with classick elegance. If any exceptions can be made, they are very few: Haddon and Ascham,[2] the pride of Elizabeth's reign, however they may have succeeded in prose, no sooner attempt verses than they provoke derision. If we produced any thing worthy of notice before the elegies of Milton, it was perhaps Alabaster's *Roxana.*[3]

Of the exercises which the rules of the University required, some were published by him in his maturer years. They had been undoubtedly applauded; for they were such as few can perform: yet there is reason to suspect that he was regarded in his college with no great fondness. That he obtained no fellowship is certain; but the unkindness with which he was treated was not merely negative. I am ashamed to relate what I fear is true, that Milton was the last student in either university that suffered the publick indignity of corporal correction.

It was, in the violence of controversial hostility, objected to him, that he was expelled: this he steadily denies, and it was apparently not true; but it seems plain from his own verses to Diodati,[4] that he had incurred *rustication;* a temporary dismission into the country, with perhaps the loss of a term:

Jam nec arundiferum mihi cura revisere Camum,
Nec dudum vetiti me laris angit amor;
Nec duri libet usque minas perferre magistri,
Caeteraque ingenio non subeunda meo.

I cannot find any meaning but this, which even kindness and reverence can give to the term, *vetiti laris,* "a habitation from which he is excluded;" or how *exile* can be otherwise interpreted.

---

[2] Haddon and Ascham. See Preface to *Shakespeare,* p. 333, n. 2.

[3] William Alabaster (d. 1640) published *Roxana* in 1632.

[4] The lines to Milton's friend Charles Diodati were translated by Cowper: "Nor zeal nor duty now my steps impel/ To ready Cam, and my forbidden cell./ 'Tis time that I a pedant's threats disdain,/ And fly from wrongs my soul will ne'r sustain."

He declares yet more, that he is weary of enduring *the threats of a rigorous master, and something else, which a temper like his cannot undergo.* What was more than threat was evidently punishment. This poem, which mentions his *exile,* proves likewise that it was not perpetual; for it concludes with a resolution of returning some time to Cambridge.

He took both the usual degrees; that of Batchelor in 1628, and that of Master in 1632; but he left the University with no kindness for its institution, alienated either by the injudicious severity of his governors, or his own captious perverseness. The cause cannot now be known, but the effect appears in his writings. His scheme of education, inscribed to Hartlib,[5] supersedes all academical instruction, being intended to comprise the whole time which men usually spend in literature, from their entrance upon grammar, *till they proceed, as it is called, masters of arts.* And in his Discourse *on the likeliest Way to remove Hirelings out of the Church,* he ingeniously[6] proposes, that *the profits of the lands forfeited by the act for superstitious uses, should be applied to such academies all over the land, where languages and arts may be taught together; so that youth may be at once brought up to a competency of learning and an honest trade, by which means such of them as had the gift, being enabled to support themselves (without tithes) by the latter, may, by the help of the former, become worthy preachers.*

One of his objections to academical education, as it was then conducted, is, that men designed for orders in the Church were permitted to act plays, *writhing and unboning their clergy limbs to all the antick and dishonest gestures of Trincalos, buffoons and bawds, prostituting the shame of that ministry which they had, or were near having, to the eyes of courtiers and court-ladies, their grooms and mademoiselles.*

This is sufficiently peevish in a man, who, when he mentions his exile from the college, relates, with great luxuriance, the compensation which the pleasures of the theatre afford him. Plays were therefore only criminal when they were acted by academicks.

He went to the university with a design of entering into the

---

[5] Samuel Hartlib (d. 1670), author of works on education.

[6] *ingeniously: ingenuously* 1783

Church, but in time altered his mind; for he declared, that whoever became a clergyman must "subscribe slave, and take an oath withal, which, unless he took with a conscience that could retch, he must straight perjure himself. He thought it better to prefer a blameless silence before the office of speaking, bought and begun with servitude and forswearing."

These expressions are, I find, applied to the subscription of the Articles; but it seems more probable that they relate to canonical obedience. I know not any of the Articles which seem to thwart his opinions: but the thoughts of obedience, whether canonical or civil, raised his indignation.

His unwillingness to engage in the ministry, perhaps not yet advanced to a settled resolution of declining it, appears in a letter to one of his friends, who had reproved his suspended and dilatory life, which he seems to have imputed to an insatiable curiosity, and fantastick luxury of various knowledge. To this he writes a cool and plausible answer, in which he endeavours to persuade him that the delay proceeds not from the delights of desultory study, but from the desire of obtaining more fitness for his task; and that he goes on, *not taking thought of being late, so it give advantage to be more fit.*

When he left the university, he returned to his father, then residing at Horton in Buckinghamshire, with whom he lived five years; in which time he is said to have read all the Greek and Latin writers. With what limitations this universality is to be understood, who shall inform us?

It might be supposed that he who read so much should have done nothing else; but Milton found time to write the masque of *Comus,* which was presented at Ludlow, then the residence of the Lord President of Wales, in 1634; and had the honour of being acted by the Earl of Bridgewater's sons and daughter. The fiction is derived from Homer's Circe; but we never can refuse to any modern the liberty of borrowing from Homer:

> *——a quo ceu fonte perenni*
> *Vatum Pieriis ora rigantur aquis.*[7]

[7] Ovid, *Amores,* III.ix.25: "from whom as from fount perennial the lips of bards are bedewed with Pierean waters." (Trans. Showerman. Loeb.)

His next production was *Lycidas*, an elegy, written in 1637, on the death of Mr. King, the son of Sir John King, Secretary for Ireland in the time of Elizabeth, James, and Charles. King was much a favourite at Cambridge, and many of the wits joined to do honour to his memory. Milton's acquaintance with the Italian writers may be discovered by a mixture of longer and shorter verses, according to the rules of Tuscan poetry, and his malignity to the Church by some lines which are interpreted as threatening its extermination.

He is supposed about this time to have written his *Arcades;* for while he lived at Horton he used sometimes to steal from his studies a few days, which he spent at Harefield, the house of the Countess Dowager of Derby, where the *Arcades* made part of a dramatick entertainment.

He began now to grow weary of the country; and had some purpose of taking chambers in the Inns of Court, when the death of his mother set him at liberty to travel, for which he obtained his father's consent, and Sir Henry Wotton's[8] directions, with the celebrated precept of prudence, *I pensieri stretti, ed il viso sciolto;* "thoughts close, and looks loose."

In 1638 he left England, and went first to Paris; where, by the favour of Lord Scudamore,[9] he had the opportunity of visiting Grotius,[1] then residing at the French court as ambassador from Christina of Sweden. From Paris he hasted into Italy, of which he had with particular diligence studied the language and literature; and, though he seems to have intended a very quick perambulation of the country, staid two months at Florence; where he found his way into the academies, and produced his compositions with such applause as appears to have exalted him in his own opinion, and confirmed him in the hope, that, "by labour and intense study, which," says he, "I take to be my portion in this life, joined with a strong propensity of nature," he might "leave something so written to after-times, as they should not willingly let it die."

It appears, in all his writings, that he had the usual concomitant of great abilities, a lofty and steady confidence in himself,

[8] Sir Henry Wotton (d. 1639), former Ambassador to Venice.
[9] Scudamore, the Ambassador to France.
[1] Hugo Grotius (d. 1645), author of the first great treatise on international law, *De Jure Belli et Pacis*.

perhaps not without some contempt of others; for scarcely any man ever wrote so much and praised so few. Of his praise he was very frugal; as he set its value high, and considered his mention of a name as a security against the waste of time, and a certain preservative from oblivion.

At Florence he could not indeed complain that his merit wanted distinction. Carlo Dati presented him with an encomiastick inscription, in the tumid lapidary stile; and Francini wrote him an ode,[2] of which the first stanza is only empty noise; the rest are perhaps too diffuse on common topicks; but the last is natural and beautiful.

From Florence he went to Sienna, and from Sienna to Rome, where he was again received with kindness by the learned and the great. Holstenius, the keeper of the Vatican Library, who had resided three years at Oxford, introduced him to Cardinal Barberini, and he, at a musical entertainment, waited for him at the door, and led him by the hand into the assembly. Here Selvaggi praised him in a distich, and Salsilli in a tetrastick; neither of them of much value. The Italians were gainers by this literary commerce; for the encomiums with which Milton repaid Salsilli, though not secure against a stern grammarian, turn the balance indisputably in Milton's favour.

Of these Italian testimonies, poor as they are, he was proud enough to publish them before his poems; though he says, he cannot be suspected but to have known that they were said *non tam de se, quam supra se.*[3]

At Rome, as at Florence, he staid only two months; a time indeed sufficient, if he desired only to ramble with an explainer of its antiquities, or to view palaces and count pictures; but certainly too short for the contemplation of learning, policy, or manners.

From Rome he passed on to Naples, in company of a hermit; a companion from whom little could be expected, yet to him Milton owed his introduction to Manso Marquis of Villa, who

[2] The Latin encomium by Dati and the Italian ode by Francini immediately precede the Latin section of Milton's *Poems,* 1645, as do the Latin verses by Selvaggi and Salsilli mentioned in the next paragraph.

[3] "Not so much about him, as over him." From Milton's preface to his Latin poems.

had been before the patron of Tasso. Manso was enough delighted with his accomplishments to honour him with a sorry distich,[4] in which he commends him for every thing but his religion; and Milton, in return, addressed him in a Latin poem, which must have raised an high opinion of English elegance and literature.

His purpose was now to have visited Sicily and Greece; but, hearing of the differences between the King and Parliament, he thought it proper to hasten home, rather than pass his life in foreign amusements while his countrymen were contending for their rights. He therefore came back to Rome, tho' the merchants informed him of plots laid against him by the Jesuits, for the liberty of his conversations on religion. He had sense enough to judge that there was no danger, and therefore kept on his way, and acted as before, neither obtruding nor shunning controversy. He had perhaps given some offence by visiting Galileo, then a prisoner in the Inquisition for philosophical heresy; and at Naples he was told by Manso, that, by his declarations on religious questions, he had excluded himself from some distinctions which he should otherwise have paid him. But such conduct, though it did not please, was yet sufficiently safe; and Milton staid two months more at Rome, and went on to Florence without molestation.

From Florence he visited Lucca. He afterwards went to Venice; and, having sent away a collection of musick and other books, travelled to Geneva, which he probably considered as the metropolis of orthodoxy. Here he reposed, as in a congenial element, and became acquainted with John Diodati[5] and Frederick Spanheim, two learned professors of divinity. From Geneva he passed through France; and came home, after an absence of a year and three months.

At his return he heard of the death of his friend Charles Diodati; a man whom it is reasonable to suppose of great merit, since he was thought by Milton worthy of a poem, intituled, *Epitaphium Damonis,* written with the common but childish imitation of pastoral life.

He now hired a lodging at the house of one Russel, a taylor in

---

[4] Manso's Latin distich is the first of the complimentary pieces in the Latin poems.

[5] Giovanni Diodati (d. 1649), Swiss Calvinist, translated the Bible into Italian. He was the uncle of Milton's friend Charles.

St. Bride's Churchyard, and undertook the education of John and Edward Phillips, his sister's sons. Finding his rooms too little, he took a house and garden in Aldersgate-street, which was not then so much out of the world as it is now; and chose his dwelling at the upper end of a passage, that he might avoid the noise of the street. Here he received more boys, to be boarded and instructed.

Let not our veneration for Milton forbid us to look with some degree of merriment on great promises and small performance, on the man who hastens home, because his countrymen are contending for their liberty, and, when he reaches the scene of action, vapours away his patriotism in a private boarding-school. This is the period of his life from which all his biographers seem inclined to shrink. They are unwilling that Milton should be degraded to a school-master; but since it cannot be denied that he taught boys, one finds out that he taught for nothing, and another that his motive was only zeal for the propagation of learning and virtue; and all tell what they do not know to be true, only to excuse an act which no wise man will consider as in itself disgraceful. His father was alive; his allowance was not ample, and he supplied its deficiencies by an honest and useful employment.

It is told, that in the art of education he performed wonders; and a formidable list is given of the authors, Greek and Latin, that were read in Aldersgate-street, by youth between ten and fifteen or sixteen years of age. Those who tell or receive these stories, should consider that nobody can be taught faster than he can learn. The speed of the best horseman must be limited by the power of his horse. Every man, that has ever undertaken to instruct others, can tell what slow advances he has been able to make, and how much patience it requires to recall vagrant inattention, to stimulate sluggish indifference, and to rectify absurd misapprehension.

The purpose of Milton, as it seems, was to teach something more solid than the common literature of schools, by reading those authors that treat of physical subjects; such as the Georgick, and astronomical treatises of the ancients. This was a scheme of improvement which seems to have busied many literary projectors of that age. Cowley, who had more means than Milton of knowing what was wanting to the embellishments of life, formed the same plan of education in his imaginary college.

But the truth is, that the knowledge of external nature, and of the sciences which that knowledge requires or includes, is not the great or the frequent business of the human mind. Whether we provide for action or conversation, whether we wish to be useful or pleasing, the first requisite is the religious and moral knowledge of right and wrong; the next is an acquaintance with the history of mankind, and with those examples which may be said to embody truth, and prove by events the reasonableness of opinions. Prudence and justice are virtues, and excellencies, of all times, and of all places; we are perpetually moralists, but we are geometricians only by chance. Our intercourse with intellectual nature is necessary; our speculations upon matter are voluntary, and at leisure. Physical knowledge is of such rare emergence, that one man may know another half his life without being able to estimate his skill in hydrostaticks or astronomy; but his moral and prudential character immediately appears.

Those authors, therefore, are to be read at schools that supply most axioms of prudence, most principles of moral truth, and most materials for conversation; and these purposes are best served by poets, orators, and historians.

Let me not be censured for this digression as pedantick or paradoxical; for if I have Milton against me, I have Socrates on my side. It was his labour to turn philosophy from the study of nature to speculations upon life, but the innovators whom I oppose are turning off attention from life to nature. They seem to think, that we are placed here to watch the growth of plants, or the motions of the stars. Socrates was rather of opinion, that what we had to learn was, how to do good, and avoid evil.

Ὅττι τοι ἐν μεγάροισι κακόν τ' ἀγαθόν τε τέκυται[6]

Of institutions we may judge by their effects. From this wonder-working academy, I do not know that there ever proceeded any man very eminent for knowledge: its only genuine product, I believe, is a small history of poetry, written in Latin by his nephew, of which perhaps none of my readers has ever heard.[7]

---

[6] *Odyssey*, IV.392: "What good, what ill / Hath in thine house befallen." (Trans. Cowper.)

[7] Edward Phillips' "compendious enumeration of the poets . . . from the time of Dante Aligheri to the present age," was appended to his edition of Buchler's *Thesaurus*, 1669. It contains the first praise of *Paradise Lost* in print.

That in his school, as in every thing else which he undertook, he laboured with great diligence, there is no reason for doubting. One part of his method deserves general imitation. He was careful to instruct his scholars in religion. Every Sunday was spent upon theology; in which he dictated a short system, gathered from the writers that were then fashionable in the Dutch universities.

He set his pupils an example of hard study and spare diet; only now and then he allowed himself to pass a day of festivity and indulgence with some gay gentlemen of Gray's Inn.

He now began to engage in the controversies of the times, and lent his breath to blow the flames of contention. In 1641 he published a treatise of *Reformation* in two books, against the Established Church; being willing to help the Puritans, who were, he says, *inferior to the prelates in learning.*

Hall Bishop of Norwich had published an *Humble Remonstrance,* in defence of Episcopacy; to which, in 1641, six[8] ministers, of whose names the first letters made the celebrated word *Smectymnus,* gave their Answer. Of this Answer a Confutation was attempted by the learned Usher;[9] and to the Confutation Milton published a Reply, intituled, *Of Prelatical Episcopacy, and whether it may be deduced from the Apostolical Times, by virtue of those testimonies which are alleged to that purpose in some late treatises, one whereof goes under the name of James lord bishop of Armagh.*

I have transcribed this title to shew, by his contemptuous mention of Usher, that he had now adopted the puritanical savageness of manners. His next work was, *The Reason of Church Government urged against Prelacy, by Mr. John Milton,* 1642. In this book he discovers, not with ostentatious exultation, but with calm confidence, his high opinion of his own powers; and promises to undertake something, he yet knows not what, that may be of use and honour to his country. "This," says he, "is not to be obtained but by devout prayer to that Eternal Spirit that can enrich with all

---

[8] Five: Stephen Marshall, Edmund Calamy, Thomas Young, Matthew Newcomen, and William Spurstow.

[9] James Usher is principally known for his *Annales Veteris et Novi Testamenti,* 1650–54, in which he worked out a chronology of the Bible; his dates are still often found in the margins of the Authorized Version.

utterance and knowledge, and sends out his Seraphim with the hallowed fire of his altar, to touch and purify the lips of whom he pleases. To this must be added, industrious and select reading, steady observation, and insight into all seemly and generous arts and affairs; till which in some measure be compast, I refuse not to sustain this expectation." From a promise like this, at once fervid, pious, and rational, might be expected the *Paradise Lost.*

He published the same year two more pamphlets, upon the same question. To one of his antagonists, who affirms that he was *vomited out of the university,* he answers, in general terms; "The Fellows of the College wherein I spent some years, at my parting, after I had taken two degrees, as the manner is, signified many times how much better it would content them that I should stay.——As for the common approbation or dislike of that place, as now it is, that I should esteem or disesteem myself the more for that, too simple is the answerer, if he think to obtain with me. Of small practice were the physician who could not judge, by what she and her sister have of long time vomited, that the worser stuff she strongly keeps in her stomach, but the better she is ever kecking at, and is queasy: she vomits now out of sickness; but before it be well with her, she must vomit by strong physick.—— The university, in the time of her better health, and my younger judgement, I never greatly admired, but now much less."

This is surely the language of a man who thinks that he has been injured. He proceeds to describe the course of his conduct, and the train of his thoughts; and, because he has been suspected of incontinence, gives an account of his own purity: "That if I be justly charged," says he, "with this crime, it may come upon me with tenfold shame."

The stile of his piece is rough, and such perhaps was that of his antagonist. This roughness he justifies, by great examples, in a long digression. Sometimes he tries to be humorous: "Lest I should take him for some chaplain in hand, some squire of the body to his prelate, one who serves not at the altar, only but at the Court-cupboard, he will bestow on us a pretty model of himself; and sets me out half a dozen ptisical mottos, wherever he had them, hopping short in the measure of convulsion fits; in which labour the agony of his wit having scaped narrowly, instead of well-sized periods, he greets us with a quantity of thumbring posies.——And thus ends this section, or rather dissection, of himself." Such is the controversial merriment of Milton: his gloomy seriousness is yet more offensive. Such is his malignity, *that hell grows darker at his frown.*[1]

His father, after Reading was taken by Essex, came to reside in his house; and his school increased. At Whitsuntide, in his thirty-fifth year, he married Mary, the daughter of Mr. Powel, a justice of the peace in Oxfordshire. He brought her to town with him, and expected all the advantages of a conjugal life. The lady, however, seems not much to have delighted in the pleasures of spare diet and hard study; for, as Philips relates, "having for a month led a philosophical life, after having been used at home to a great house, and much company and joviality, her friends, possibly by her own desire, made earnest suit to have her company the remaining part of the summer; which was granted, upon a promise of her return at Michaelmas."

Milton was too busy to much miss his wife: he pursued his studies; and now and then visited the Lady Margaret Leigh,[2] whom he has mentioned in one of his sonnets. At last Michaelmas arrived; but the lady had no inclination to return to the sullen gloom of her husband's habitation, and therefore very willingly forgot her promise. He sent her a letter, but had no answer; he sent more with the same success. It could be alleged that letters miscarry; he therefore dispatched a messenger, being by this time too angry to go himself. His messenger was sent back with some contempt. The family of the lady were Cavaliers.

In a man whose opinion of his own merit was like Milton's, less provocation than this might have raised violent resentment. Milton soon determined to repudiate her for disobedience; and being one of those who could easily find arguments to justify inclination, published (in 1644) *The Doctrine and Discipline of Divorce;* which was followed by *The Judgement of Martin Bucer concerning Divorce;* and the next year, his *Tetrachordon, Expositions upon the four chief Places of Scripture which treat of Marriage.*

This innovation was opposed, as might be expected, by the clergy; who, then holding their famous assembly at Westminster, procured that the author should be called before the Lords; "but

---

[1] *Paradise Lost*, II.719, paraphrased.

[2] Daughter of the Earl of Marlborough.

that House," says Wood, "whether approving the doctrine, or not favouring his accusers, did soon dismiss him."[3]

There seems not to have been much written against him, nor any thing by any writer of eminence. The antagonist that appeared is stiled by him, *a serving-man turned solicitor.* Howel in his letters mentions the new doctrine with contempt;[4] and it was, I suppose, thought more worthy of derision than of confutation. He complains of this neglect in two sonnets, of which the first is contemptible, and the second not excellent.

From this time it is observed that he became an enemy to the Presbyterians, whom he had favoured before. He that changes his party by his humour, is not more virtuous than he that changes it by his interest; he loves himself rather than truth.

His wife and her relations now found that Milton was not an unresisting sufferer of injuries; and perceiving that he had begun to put his doctrine in practice, by courting a young woman of great accomplishments, the daughter of one Doctor Davis, who was however not ready to comply, they resolved to endeavour a re-union. He went sometimes to the house of one Blackborough, his relation, in the lane of St. Martin's-le-Grand, and at one of his usual visits was surprised to see his wife come from another room, and implore forgiveness on her knees. He resisted her intreaties for a while; "but partly," says Philips, "his own generous nature, more inclinable to reconciliation than to perseverance in anger or revenge, and partly the strong intercession of friends on both sides, soon brought him to an act of oblivion and a firm league of peace." It were injurious to omit, that Milton afterwards received her father and her brothers in his own house, when they were distressed, with other Royalists.

He published about the same time his *Areopagitica, a Speech of Mr. John Milton for the liberty of unlicensed Printing.* The danger of such unbounded liberty, and the danger of bounding it, have produced a problem in the science of government, which human understanding seems hitherto unable to solve. If nothing may be published but what civil authority shall have previously approved, power must always be the standard of truth; if every dreamer of innovations may propagate his projects, there can be

[3] Anthony à Wood, in *Fasti Oxonienses.*
[4] James Howell, a Royalist, in *Epistolae Ho-Elianae: Familiar Letters.*

no settlement; if every murmurer at government may diffuse discontent, there can be no peace; and if every sceptick in theology may teach his follies, there can be no religion. The remedy against these evils is to punish the authors; for it is yet allowed that every society may punish, though not prevent, the publication of opinions, which that society shall think pernicious: but this punishment, though it may crush the author, promotes the book; and it seems not more reasonable to leave the right of printing unrestrained, because writers may be afterwards censured, than it would be to sleep with doors unbolted, because by our laws we can hang a thief.

But whatever were his engagements, civil or domestick, poetry was never long out of his thoughts. About this time (1645) a collection of his Latin and English poems appeared, in which the *Allegro* and *Penseroso*, with some others, were first published.

He had taken a larger house in Barbican for the reception of scholars; but the numerous relations of his wife, to whom he generously granted refuge for a while, occupied his rooms. In time, however, they went away; and the "house again," says Philips, "now looked like a house of the Muses only, though the accession of scholars was not great. Possibly his having proceeded so far in the education of youth, may have been the occasion of his adversaries calling him pedagogue and school-master; whereas it is well known he never set up for a publick school, to teach all the young fry of a parish; but only was willing to impart his learning and knowledge to relations, and the sons of gentlemen who were his intimate friends; and that neither his writings nor his way of teaching ever savoured in the least of pedantry."

Thus laboriously does his nephew extenuate what cannot be denied, and what might be confessed without disgrace. Milton was not a man who could become mean by a mean employment. This, however, his warmest friends seem not to have found; they therefore shift and palliate. He did not sell literature to all comers at an open shop; he was a chamber-milliner, and measured his commodities only to his friends.

Philips, evidently impatient of viewing him in this state of degradation, tells us that it was not long continued; and, to raise his character again, has a mind to invest him with military splendour: "He is much mistaken," he says, "if there was not about this time a design of making him an Adjutant-General in Sir William

Waller's army. But the new-modelling of the army proved an obstruction to the design." An event cannot be set at a much greater distance than by having been only *designed, about some time,* if a man *be not much mistaken.* Milton shall be a pedagogue no longer; for, if Philips be not mistaken, somebody at some time designed him for a soldier.

About the time that the army was new-modelled (1645) he removed to a smaller house in Holbourn, which opened backward into Lincoln's-Inn-Fields. He is not known to have published any thing afterwards till the King's death, when, finding his murderers condemned by the Presbyterians, he wrote a treatise to justify it, and *to compose the minds of the people.*

He made some *Remarks on the Articles of Peace between Ormond and the Irish Rebels.* While he contented himself to write, he perhaps did only what his conscience dictated; and if he did not very vigilantly watch the influence of his own passions, and the gradual prevalence of opinions, first willingly admitted and then habitually indulged, if objections, by being overlooked, were forgotten, and desire superinduced conviction, he yet shared only the common weakness of mankind, and might be no less sincere than his opponents. But as faction seldom leaves a man honest, however it might find him, Milton is suspected of having interpolated the book called *Icon Basilike,* which the Council of State, to whom he was now made Latin secretary, employed him to censure, by inserting a prayer taken from Sidney's *Arcadia,* and imputing it to the King; whom he charges, in his *Iconoclastes,* with the use of this prayer as with a heavy crime, in the indecent language with which prosperity had emboldened the advocates for rebellion to insult all that is venerable or great: "Who would have imagined so little fear in him of the true all-seeing Deity—as, immediately before his death, to pop into the hands of the grave bishop that attended him, as a special relique of his saintly exercises, a prayer stolen word for word from the mouth of a heathen woman praying to a heathen god?"

The papers which the King gave to Dr. Juxon on the scaffold the regicides took away, so that they were at least the publishers of this prayer; and Dr. Birch,[5] who examined the question with

[5] William Juxon, Bishop of London, chosen by Charles to administer the last rites on the scaffold. Thomas Birch originally favored the notion of a forgery in his edition of Milton, 1738, but later reversed himself.

great care, was inclined to think them the forgers. The use of it by adaptation was innocent; and they who could so noisily censure it, with a little extension of their malice could contrive what they wanted to accuse.

King Charles the Second, being now sheltered in Holland, employed Salmasius,[6] professor of polite learning at Leyden, to write a defence of his father and of monarchy; and, to excite his industry, gave him, as was reported, a hundred Jacobuses. Salmasius was a man of skill in languages, knowledge of antiquity, and sagacity of emendatory criticism, almost exceeding all hope of human attainment; and having, by excessive praises, been confirmed in great confidence of himself, though he probably had not much considered the principles of society or the rights of government, undertook the employment without distrust of his own qualifications; and, as his expedition in writing was wonderful, in 1649 published *Defensio Regis.*

To this Milton was required to write a sufficient answer; which he performed (1651) in such a manner, that Hobbes declared[7] himself unable to decide whose language was best, or whose arguments were worst. In my opinion, Milton's periods are smoother, neater, and more pointed; but he delights himself with teizing his adversary as much as with confuting him. He makes a foolish allusion of Salmasius, whose doctrine he considers as servile and unmanly, to the stream of Salmacis, which whoever entered left half his virility behind him. Salmasius was a Frenchman, and was unhappily married to a scold. *Tu es Gallus,* says Milton, *et, ut aiunt, nimium gallinaceus.*[8] But his supreme pleasure is to tax his adversary, so renowned for criticism, with vitious Latin. He opens his book with telling that he has used *persona,* which, according to Milton, signifies only a *mask,* in a sense not known to the Romans, by applying it as we apply *person.* But as Nemesis is always on the watch, it is memorable that he has enforced the charge of a solecism by an expression in itself grossly solecistical, when, for one of those supposed blunders, he says, *propino te grammatistis tuis* vapulandum. From *vapulo,* which has a passive sense, *vapu-*

[6] Claude de Saumaise (d. 1653); a Jacobus was worth a pound.

[7] In *Behemoth,* 1682.

[8] "You are French [or a cock] and, as they say, too much belonging to poultry [i.e., hen-pecked]."

landus can never be derived. No man forgets his original trade: the rights of nations, and of kings, sink into questions of grammar, if grammarians discuss them.

Milton when he undertook this answer was weak of body, and dim of sight; but his will was forward, and what was wanting of health was supplied by zeal. He was rewarded with a thousand pounds, and his book was much read; for paradox, recommended by spirit and elegance, easily gains attention; and he who told every man that he was equal to his King, could hardly want an audience.

That the performance of Salmasius was not dispersed with equal rapidity, or read with equal eagerness, is very credible. He taught only the stale doctrine of authority, and the unpleasing duty of submission; and he had been so long not only the monarch but the tyrant of literature, that almost all mankind were delighted to find him defied and insulted by a new name, not yet considered as any one's rival. If Christina, as is said, commended the *Defence of the People,* her purpose must be to torment Salmasius, who was then at her court; for neither her civil station nor her natural character could dispose her to favour the doctrine, who was by birth a queen, and by temper despotick.

That Salmasius was, from the appearance of Milton's book, treated with neglect, there is not much proof; but to a man so long accustomed to admiration, a little praise of his antagonist would be sufficiently offensive, and might incline him to leave Sweden.

He prepared a reply, which, left as it was imperfect, was published by his son in the year of the Restauration. In the beginning, being probably most in pain for his Latinity, he endeavours to defend his use of the word *persona;* but, if I remember right, he misses a better authority than any that he has found, that of Juvenal in his fourth satire:

> ——*Quid agas cum dira et foedior omni*
> *Crimine* persona *est?*[9]

As Salmasius reproached Milton with losing his eyes in the quarrel, Milton delighted himself with the belief that he had shortened Salmasius's life, and both perhaps with more malignity

[9] "What can you do? this sinister person is more hideous than any crime."

than reason. Salmasius died at the Spa, Sept. 3, 1653; and as controvertists are commonly said to be killed by their last dispute, Milton was flattered with the credit of destroying him.

Cromwel had now dismissed the Parliament by the authority of which he had destroyed monarchy, and commenced monarch himself, under the title of Protector, but with kingly and more than kingly power. That his authority was lawful, never was pretended; he himself founded his right only in necessity: but Milton, having now tasted the honey of publick employment, would not return to hunger and philosophy, but, continuing to exercise his office under a manifest usurpation, betrayed to his power that liberty which he had defended. Nothing can be more just than that rebellion should end in slavery; that he, who had justified the murder of his king, for some acts which to him seemed unlawful, should now sell his services, and his flatteries, to a tyrant, of whom it was evident that he could do nothing lawful.

He had now been blind for some years; but his vigour of intellect was such, that he was not disabled to discharge his office, or continue his controversies. His mind was too eager to be diverted, and too strong to be subdued.

About this time his first wife died in childbed, having left him three daughters. As he probably did not much love her, he did not long continue the appearance of lamenting her; but after a short time married Catherine, the daughter of one Captain Woodcock of Hackney; a woman doubtless educated in opinions like his own. She died within a year, of childbirth, or some distemper that followed it; and her husband has honoured her memory with a poor sonnet.

The first reply to Milton's *Defensio Populi* was published in 1651, called *Apologia pro Rege et Populo Anglicano, contra Johannis Polypragmatici (alias Miltoni) defensionem destructivam Regis et Populi.* Of this the author was not known; but Milton and his nephew Philips, under whose name he published an answer so much corrected by him that it might be called his own, imputed it to Bramhal;[1] and, knowing him no friend to regicides, thought themselves at liberty to treat him as if they had known what they only suspected.

---

[1] John Bramhall (d. 1663), Bishop of Derry.

Next year appeared *Regii Sanguinis clamor ad Coelum*. Of this the author was Peter du Moulin, who was afterwards prebendary of Canterbury; but Morus, or More,[2] a French minister, having the care of its publication, was treated as the writer by Milton, in his *Defensio Secunda,* and overwhelmed by such violence of invective, that he began to shrink under the tempest, and gave his persecutors the means of knowing the true author. Du Moulin was now in great danger; but Milton's pride operated against his malignity, and both he and his friends were more willing that Du Moulin should escape than that he should be convicted of mistake.

In his second Defence he shews that his eloquence is not merely satirical; the rudeness of his invective is equalled by the grossness of his flattery. "Deserimur, Cromuelle,[3] tu solus superes, ad te summa nostrarum rerum rediit, in te solo consistit, insuperabili tuae virtuti cedimus cuncti, nemine vel obloquente, nisi qui aequales inaequalis ipse honores sibi quaerit, aut digniori concessos invidet, aut non intelligit nihil esse in societate hominum magis vel Deo gratum, vel rationi consentaneum, esse in civitate nihil aequius, nihil utilius, quam potiri rerum dignissimum. Eum te agnoscunt omnes, Cromuelle, ea tu civis maximus et gloriosissimus,[4] dux publici consilii, exercituum fortissimorum imperator, pater patriae gessisti. Sic tu spontanea bonorum omnium et animitus missa voce salutaris."

Caesar, when he assumed the perpetual dictatorship, had not more servile or more elegant flattery. A translation may shew its servility; but its elegance is less attainable. Having exposed the unskilfulness or selfishness of the former government, "We were left," says Milton, "to ourselves: the whole national interest fell into your hands, and subsists in your abilities. To your virtue, overpowering and resistless, every man gives way, except some who, without equal qualifications, aspire to equal honours, or who envy the distinctions of merit greater than their own; or who

---

[2] Pierre du Moulin, son of a French Protestant theologian; Alexander More or Moir, son of a Scottish Presbyterian principal of a French College; the son was a professor at Amsterdam.

[3] In Johnson's translation, below, he avoids using Cromwell's name.

[4] "It may be doubted whether *gloriosissimus* be here used with Milton's boasted purity. *Res gloriosa* is an *illustrious thing;* but *vir gloriosus* is commonly a *braggart,* as in *miles gloriosus.*" Johnson.

have yet to learn, that in the coalition of human society nothing is more pleasing to God, or more agreeable to reason, than that the highest mind should have the sovereign power. Such, Sir, are you by general confession; such are the things atchieved by you, the greatest and most glorious of our countrymen, the director of our publick counsels, the leader of unconquered armies, the father of your country; for by that title does every good man hail you, with sincere and voluntary praise."

Next year, having defended all that wanted defence, he found leisure to defend himself. He undertook his own vindication against More, whom he declares in his title to be justly called the author of the *Regii Sanguini clamor.* In this there is no want of vehemence nor eloquence, nor does he forget his wonted wit. "Morus es? an Momus? an uterque idem est?"[5] He then remembers that *Morus* is Latin for a mulberry-tree, and hints at the known transformation:

> ——*Poma alba ferebat*
> *Quae post nigra tulit Morus.*

With this piece ended his controversies; and he from this time gave himself up to his private studies and his civil employment.

As secretary to the Protector he is supposed to have written the declaration of the reasons for a war with Spain. His agency was considered as of great importance; for when a treaty with Sweden was artfully suspended, the delay was publickly imputed to Mr. Milton's indisposition; and the Swedish agent was provoked to express his wonder, that only one man in England could write Latin, and that man blind.

Being now forty-seven years old, and seeing himself disencumbered from external interruptions, he seems to have recollected his former purposes, and planned three great works for his future employment. An epick poem, the history of his country, and a dictionary of the Latin tongue.

To collect a dictionary seems a work of all others least practicable in a state of blindness, because it depends upon perpetual

---

[5] "Are you More or Momus? or is one the same as the other?" The following quotation is Ovid, *Metamorphoses,* IV.51, quoted from memory: "A tree which bore white fruit, and now bears black."

and minute inspection and collation. Nor would Milton probably have begun it, after he had lost his eyes; but, having had it always before him, he continued it, says Philips, *almost to his dying-day; but the papers were so discomposed and deficient, that they could not be fitted for the press.* The compilers of the Latin dictionary, printed afterwards at Cambridge, had the use of them in three folios; but what was their fate afterwards is not known.

To compile a history from various authors, when they can only be consulted by other eyes, is not easy, nor possible, but with more skilful and attentive help than can be commonly obtained; and it was probably the difficulty of consulting and comparing that stopped Milton's narrative at the Conquest; a period at which affairs were not yet very intricate, nor authors very numerous.

For the subject of his epick poem, after much deliberation, *long chusing, and beginning late,* he fixed upon *Paradise Lost;* a design so comprehensive, that it could be justified only by success. He had once designed to celebrate King Arthur, as appears from his verses to Mansus; but *Arthur was reserved,* says Fenton, *to another destiny.*

It appears, by some sketches of poetical projects left in manuscript, and to be seen in a library at Cambridge, that he had digested his thoughts on this subject into one of those wild dramas which were anciently called Mysteries; and Philips had seen what he terms part of a tragedy, beginning with the first ten lines of Satan's address to the Sun. These mysteries consist of allegorical persons; such as Justice, Mercy, Faith. Of the tragedy or mystery of *Paradise Lost* there are two plans:

THE PERSONS	THE PERSONS
Michael.	Moses.
Chorus of Angels.	Divine Justice, Wisdom, Heavenly Love.
Heavenly Love.	The Evening Star, Hesperus.
Lucifer.	Chorus of Angels.
Adam, Eve, } with the Serpent.	Lucifer.
Conscience.	Adam.
Death.	Eve.
	Conscience.

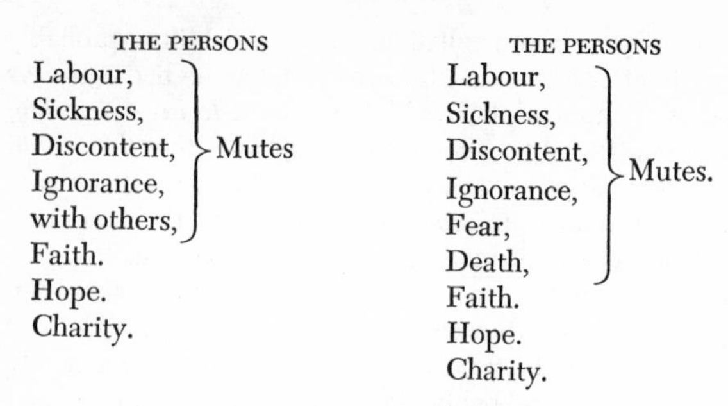

THE PERSONS

Labour,
Sickness,
Discontent,
Ignorance,
with others,
} Mutes
Faith.
Hope.
Charity.

THE PERSONS

Labour,
Sickness,
Discontent,
Ignorance,
Fear,
Death,
} Mutes.
Faith.
Hope.
Charity.

PARADISE LOST

THE PERSONS

Moses, προλογίζει,[6] recounting how he assumed his true body; that it corrupts not, because it is with God in the mount; declares the like of Enoch and Eliah; besides the purity of the place, that certain pure winds, dews and clouds, preserve it from corruption; whence exhorts to the sight of God; tells, they cannot see Adam in the state of innocence, by reason of their sin.

Justice,
Mercy,
Wisdom,
} debating what should become of man, if he fall.

Chorus of Angels singing a hymn of the Creation.

Act II

Heavenly Love.
Evening Star.
Chorus sing the marriage-song, and describe Paradise.

Act III

Lucifer, contriving Adam's ruin.
Chorus fears for Adam, and relates Lucifer's rebellion and fall.

Act IV

Adam,
Eve,
} fallen.

Conscience cites them to God's examination.
Chorus bewails, and tells the good Adam has lost.

---

[6] "In a Prologue."

Act V

Adam and Eve driven out of Paradise.
— — — — — — presented by an angel with
Labour, Grief, Hatred, Envy, War, Famine, Pestilence, Sickness, Discontent, Ignorance, Fear, Death, } Mutes.
To whom he gives their names. Likewise Winter, Heat, Tempest, etc.
Faith, Hope, Charity, } comfort him, and instruct him.
Chorus briefly concludes.

Such was his first design, which could have produced only an allegory, or mystery. The following sketch seems to have attained more maturity.

Adam Unparadised:

The angel Gabriel, either descending or entering; shewing, since this globe was created, his frequency as much on earth as in heaven: describes Paradise. Next, the Chorus, shewing the reason of his coming to keep his watch in Paradise, after Lucifer's rebellion, by command from God; and withal expressing his desire to see and know more concerning this excellent new creature, man. The angel Gabriel, as by his name signifying a prince of power, tracing Paradise with a more free office, passes by the station of the Chorus, and, desired by them, relates what he knew of man; as the creation of Eve, with their love and marriage. After this, Lucifer appears, after his overthrow; bemoans himself, seeks revenge on man. The Chorus prepare resistance at his first approach. At last, after discourse of enmity on either side, he departs: whereat the Chorus sings of the battle and victory in heaven, against him and his accomplices: as before, after the first act, was sung a hymn of the Creation. Here again may appear Lucifer, relating and insulting in what he had done to the destruction of man. Man next, and Eve having by this time been seduced by the Serpent, appears confusedly covered with leaves. Conscience, in a shape, accuses him; Justice cites him to the place whither Jehovah called for him. In the mean while, the Chorus entertains the stage, and is informed by some angel the manner of the Fall. Here the

Chorus bewails Adam's fall; Adam then and Eve return; accuse one another; but especially Adam lays the blame to his wife; is stubborn in his offence. Justice appears, reasons with him, convinces him. The Chorus admonisheth Adam, and bids him beware Lucifer's example of impenitence. The angel is sent to banish them out of Paradise; but before causes to pass before his eyes, in shapes, a mask of all the evils of this life and world. He is humbled, relents, despairs: at last appears Mercy, comforts him, promises the Messiah; then calls in Faith, Hope, and Charity; instructs him; he repents, gives God the glory, submits to his penalty. The Chorus briefly concludes. Compare this with the former draught.

These are very imperfect rudiments of *Paradise Lost;* but it is pleasant to see great works in their seminal state, pregnant with latent possibilities of excellence; nor could there be any more delightful entertainment than to trace their gradual growth and expansion, and to observe how they are sometimes suddenly advanced by accidental hints, and sometimes slowly improved by steady meditation.

Invention is almost the only literary labour which blindness cannot obstruct, and therefore he naturally solaced his solitude by the indulgence of his fancy, and the melody of his numbers. He had done what he knew to be necessarily previous to poetical excellence; he had made himself acquainted with *seemly arts and affairs;* his comprehension was extended by various knowledge, and his memory stored with intellectual treasures. He was skilful in many languages, and had by reading and composition attained the full mastery of his own. He would have wanted little help from books, had he retained the power of perusing them.

But while his greater designs were advancing, having now, like many other authors, caught the love of publication, he amused himself, as he could, with little productions. He sent to the press (1658) a manuscript of Raleigh, called the *Cabinet Council;* and next year gratified his malevolence to the clergy, by a *Treatise of Civil Power in Ecclesiastical Cases, and the Means of removing Hirelings out of the Church.*

Oliver was now dead; Richard was constrained to resign: the system of extemporary government, which had been held together only by force, naturally fell into fragments when that force was taken away; and Milton saw himself and his cause in equal danger. But he had still hope of doing something. He wrote letters, which Toland has published,[7] to such men as he thought friends to the new commonwealth; and even in the year of the Restoration he *bated no jot of heart or hope,* but was fantastical enough to think that the nation, agitated as it was, might be settled by a pamphlet, called *A ready and easy Way to establish a Free Commonwealth;* which was, however, enough considered to be both seriously and ludicrously answered.

The obstinate enthusiasm of the commonwealthmen was very remarkable. When the King was apparently returning, Harrington, with a few associates as fanatical as himself, used to meet, with all the gravity of political importance, to settle an equal government by rotation; and Milton, kicking when he could strike no longer, was foolish enough to publish, a few weeks before the Restoration, *Notes* upon a sermon preached by one Griffiths, intituled, *The Fear of God and the King.* To these notes an answer was written by L'Estrange,[8] in a pamphlet petulantly called *No blind Guides.*

But whatever Milton could write, or men of greater activity could do, the King was now evidently approaching with the irresistible approbation of the people. He was therefore no longer secretary, and was consequently obliged to quit the house which he held by his office; and, proportioning his sense of danger to his opinion of the importance of his writings, thought it convenient to seek some shelter, and hid himself for a time in Bartholomew Close by West Smithfield.

I cannot but remark a kind of respect, perhaps unconsciously, paid to this great man by his biographers: every house in which he resided is historically mentioned, as if it were an injury to neglect naming any place that he honoured by his presence.

The King, with lenity of which the world has had perhaps no other example, declined to be the judge or avenger of his own or his father's wrongs; and promised to admit into the Act of Oblivion all, except those whom the Parliament should except;

---

[7] John Toland's *Life of Milton,* 1698.

[8] James Harrington, author of *Oceana;* Matthew Griffith; Roger L'Estrange, a Royalist and noted journalist.

and the Parliament doomed none to capital punishment but the wretches who had immediately co-operated in the murder of the King. Milton was certainly not one of them; he had only justified what they had done.

This justification was indeed sufficiently offensive; and (June 16) an order was issued to seize Milton's *Defence*, and Godwin's *Obstructors of Justice*,[9] another book of the same tendency, and burn them by the common hangman. The attorney-general was ordered to prosecute the authors; but Milton was not seized, nor perhaps very diligently pursued.

Not long after (August 19) the flutter of innumerable bosoms was stilled by an act, which the King, that his mercy might want no recommendation of elegance, rather called an *act of oblivion* than of *grace*. Godwin was named, with nineteen more, as incapacitated for any publick trust; but of Milton there was no exception.

Of this tenderness shewn to Milton, the curiosity of mankind has not forborn to enquire the reason. Burnet thinks he was forgotten;[1] but this is another instance which may confirm Dalrymple's observation, who says, "that whenever Burnet's narrations are examined, he appears to be mistaken."

Forgotten he was not; for his prosecution was ordered; it must be therefore by design that he was included in the general oblivion. He is said to have had friends in the House, such as Marvel, Morrice, and Sir Thomas Clarges;[2] and undoubtedly a man like him must have had influence. A very particular story of his escape is told by Richardson in his memoirs,[3] which he received from Pope, as delivered by Betterton, who might have heard it from Davenant. In the war between the King and Parliament, Dave-

---

[9] John Goodwin's Ὑβριστοδίκαι, 1649; Goodwin also escaped harm and died 1665.

[1] Gilbert Burnet, in his *History of My Own Times*, says "it was thought a strange omission if he was forgot. . . ." Johnson then paraphrases a remark from Sir David Dalrymple's *Memoirs of Great Britain*, 1771–73.

[2] Andrew Marvell, the poet, who had been Milton's assistant in the Latin secretaryship; Sir William Morice (d. 1676), Secretary of State under Charles II; Clarges was the brother-in-law of General Monk.

[3] *Explanatory Notes and Remarks on Milton's Paradise Lost*, by Jonathan Richardson Father and Son, 1734; as told Pope by the actor Thomas Betterton (d. 1710), who was a member of Sir John Davenant's company in 1661, and might, therefore, Johnson surmises, have heard the story from Davenant.

nant was made prisoner, and condemned to die; but was spared at the request of Milton. When the turn of success brought Milton into the like danger, Davenant repaid the benefit by appearing in his favour. Here is a reciprocation of generosity and gratitude so pleasing, that the tale makes its own way to credit. But if help were wanted, I know not where to find it. The danger of Davenant is certain from his own relation; but of his escape there is no account. Betterton's narration can be traced no higher; it is not known that he had it from Davenant. We are told that the benefit exchanged was life for life; but it seems not certain that Milton's life ever was in danger. Godwin, who had committed the same kind of crime, escaped with incapacitation; and as exclusion from publick trust is a punishment which the power of government can commonly inflict without the help of a particular law, it required no great interest to exempt Milton from a censure little more than verbal. Something may be reasonably ascribed to veneration and compassion; to veneration of his abilities, and compassion for his distresses, which made it fit to forgive his malice for his learning. He was now poor and blind; and who would pursue with violence an illustrious enemy, depressed by fortune, and disarmed by nature?

The publication of the Act of Oblivion put him in the same condition with his fellow-subjects. He was, however, upon some pretence not now known, in the custody of the serjeant in December; and, when he was released, upon his refusal of the fees demanded, he and the serjeant were called before the House. He was now safe within the shade of oblivion, and knew himself to be as much out of the power of a griping officer as any other man. How the question was determined is not known. Milton would hardly have contended, but that he knew himself to have right on his side.

He then removed to Jewin-street, near Aldersgate-street; and being blind, and by no means wealthy, wanted a domestick companion and attendant; and therefore, by the recommendation of Dr. Paget, married Elizabeth Minshul, of a gentleman's family in Cheshire, probably without a fortune. All his wives were virgins; for he has declared that he thought it gross and indelicate to be a second husband: upon what other principles his choice was made, cannot now be known; but marriage afforded not much of his happiness. The first wife left him in disgust, and was brought back only by terror: the second, indeed, seems to have been more a favourite; but her life was short. The third, as Philips relates, oppressed his children in his lifetime, and cheated them at his death.

Soon after his marriage, according to an obscure story, he was offered the continuance of his employment; and being pressed by his wife to accept it, answered, "You, like other women, want to ride in your coach; my wish is to live and die an honest man." If he considered the Latin secretary as exercising any of the powers of government, he that had shared authority either with the Parliament or Cromwel, might have forborn to talk very loudly of his honesty; and if he thought the office purely ministerial, he certainly might have honestly retained it under the King. But this tale has too little evidence to deserve a disquisition; large offers and sturdy rejections are among the most common topicks of falsehood.

He had so much either of prudence or gratitude, that he forbore to disturb the new settlement with any of his political or ecclesiastical opinions, and from this time devoted himself to poetry and literature. Of his zeal for learning, in all its parts, he gave a proof by publishing, the next year (1661) *Accidence commenced Grammar;* a little book which has nothing remarkable, but that its author, who had been lately defending the supreme powers of his country, and was then writing *Paradise Lost,* could descend from his elevation to rescue children from the perplexity of grammatical confusion, and the trouble of lessons unnecessarily repeated.

About this time Elwood the Quaker[4] being recommended to him, as one who would read Latin to him, for the advantage of his conversation; attended him every afternoon, except on Sundays. Milton, who, in his letter to Hartlib, had declared, that *to read Latin with an English mouth is as ill a hearing as law French,* required that Elwood should learn and practise the Italian pronunciation, which, he said, was necessary, if he would talk with foreigners. This seems to have been a task troublesome without use. There is little reason for preferring the Italian pronuncia-

[4] Thomas Ellwood (d. 1713); from Ellwood's autobiography, 1714.

tion to our own, except that it is more general; and to teach it to an Englishman is only to make him a foreigner at home. He who travels, if he speaks Latin, may so soon learn the sounds which every native gives it, that he need make no provision before his journey; and if strangers visit us, it is their business to practise such conformity to our modes as they expect from us in their own countries. Elwood complied with the directions, and improved himself by his attendance; for he relates, that Milton, having a curious ear, knew by his voice when he read what he did not understand, and would stop him, and *open the most difficult passages.*

In a short time he took a house in the Artillery Walk, leading to Bunhill Fields; the mention of which concludes the register of Milton's removals and habitations. He lived longer in this place than in any other.

He was now busied by *Paradise Lost.* Whence he drew the original design has been variously conjectured, by men who cannot bear to think themselves ignorant of that which, at last, neither diligence nor sagacity can discover. Some find the hint in an Italian tragedy; Voltaire tells a wild and unauthorised story of a farce seen by Milton in Italy, which opened thus: *Let the rainbow be the fiddlestick of the fiddle of Heaven.* It has been already shewn, that the first conception was of a tragedy or mystery, not of a narrative, but a dramatick work, which he is supposed to have begun to reduce to its present form about the time (1655) when he finished his dispute with the defenders of the King.

He long before had promised to adorn his native country by some great performance, while he had yet perhaps no settled design, and was stimulated only by such expectations as naturally arose from the survey of his attainments, and the consciousness of his powers. What he should undertake, it was difficult to determine. He was *long chusing, and began late.*

While he was obliged to divide his time between his private studies and affairs of state, his poetical labour must have been often interrupted; and perhaps he did little more in that busy time than construct the narrative, adjust the episodes, proportion the parts, accumulate images and sentiments, and treasure in his memory, or preserve in writing, such hints as books or meditation would supply. Nothing particular is known of his intellectual operations while he was a statesman; for, having every help and accommodation at hand, he had no need of uncommon expedients.

Being driven from all publick stations, he is yet too great not to be traced by curiosity to his retirement; where he has been found by Mr. Richardson, the fondest of his admirers, sitting *before his door in a grey coat of coarse cloth, in warm sultry weather, to enjoy the fresh air; and so, as well as in his own room, receiving the visits of people of distinguished parts as well as quality.* His visiters of high quality must now be imagined to be few; but men of parts might reasonably court the conversation of a man so generally illustrious, that foreigners are reported, by Wood, to have visited the house in Bread-street where he was born.

According to another account, he was seen in a small house, *neatly enough dressed in black cloaths, sitting in a room hung with rusty green; pale but not cadaverous, with chalkstones in his hands. He said, that if it were not for the gout, his blindness would be tolerable.*

In the intervals of his pain, being made unable to use the common exercises, he used to swing in a chair, and sometimes played upon an organ.

He was now confessedly and visibly employed upon his poem, of which the progress might be noted by those with whom he was familiar; for he was obliged, when he had composed as many lines as his memory would conveniently retain, to employ some friend in writing them, having, at least for part of the time, no regular attendant. This gave opportunity to observations and reports.

Mr. Philips observes, that there was a very remarkable circumstance in the composure of *Paradise Lost,* "which I have a particular reason," says he, "to remember; for whereas I had the perusal of it from the very beginning, for some years, as I went from time to time to visit him, in parcels of ten, twenty, or thirty verses at a time (which, being written by whatever hand came next, might possibly want correction as to the orthography and pointing), having, as the summer came on, not been shewed any for a considerable while; and desiring the reason thereof, was answered, that his vein never happily flowed but from the autumnal equinox to the vernal; and that whatever he attempted at other times was never to his satisfaction, though he courted his fancy never so much; so that, in all the years he was about this poem, he may be said to have spent half his time therein."

Upon this relation Toland remarks, that in his opinion Philips has mistaken the time of the year; for Milton, in his *Elegies*, declares that with the advance of the spring he feels the increase of his poetical force, *redeunt in carmina vires.*[5] To this it is answered, that Philips could hardly mistake time so well marked; and it may be added, that Milton might find different times of the year favourable to different parts of life. Mr. Richardson conceives it impossible that *such a work should be suspended for six months, or for one. It may go on faster or slower, but it must go on.* By what necessity it must continually go on, or why it might not be laid aside and resumed, it is not easy to discover.

This dependance of the soul upon the seasons, those temporary and periodical ebbs and flows of intellect, may, I suppose, justly be derided as the fumes of vain imagination. *Sapiens dominabitur astris.*[6] The author that thinks himself weather-bound will find, with a little help from hellebore, that he is only idle or exhausted. But while this notion has possession of the head, it produces the inability which it supposes. Our powers owe much of their energy to our hopes; *possunt quia posse videntur.*[7] When success seems attainable, diligence is enforced; but when it is admitted that the faculties are suppressed by a cross wind, or a cloudy sky, the day is given up without resistance; for who can contend with the course of nature?

From such prepossessions Milton seems not to have been free. There prevailed in his time an opinion that the world was in its decay, and that we have had the misfortune to be produced in the decrepitude of nature. It was suspected that the whole creation languished, that neither trees nor animals had the height or bulk of their predecessors, and that every thing was daily sinking in gradual diminution. Milton appears to suspect that souls partake of the general degeneracy, and is not without some fear that his book is to be written in *an age too late* for heroick poesy.

[5] Literally, "Strength returns to his poetry."

[6] "The wise man will be governed by the stars," quoted from Burton's *Anatomy of Melancholy.*

[7] *Aeneid,* V.231: "they are strong because they think themselves so."

Another opinion wanders about the world, and sometimes finds reception among wise men; an opinion that restrains the operations of the mind to particular regions, and supposes that a luckless mortal may be born in a degree of latitude too high or too low for wisdom or for wit. From this fancy, wild as it is, he had not wholly cleared his head, when he feared lest the *climate* of his country might be *too cold* for flights of imagination.

Into a mind already occupied by such fancies, another not more reasonable might easily find its way. He that could fear lest his genius had fallen upon too old a world, or too chill a climate, might consistently magnify to himself the influences of the seasons, and believe his faculties to be vigorous only half the year.

His submission to the seasons was at least more reasonable than his dread of decaying nature, or a frigid zone; for general causes operate uniformly in a general abatement of mental power: if less could be performed by the writer, less likewise would content the judges of his work. Among this lagging race of frosty grovellers he might still have risen into eminence by producing something which *they should not willingly let die.* However inferior to the heroes who were born in better ages, he might still be great among his contemporaries, with the hope of growing every day greater in the dwindle of posterity. He might still be the giant of the pygmies, the one-eyed monarch of the blind.

Of his artifices of study, or particular hours of composition, we have little account, and there was perhaps little to be told. Richardson, who seems to have been very diligent in his enquiries, but discovers always a wish to find Milton discriminated from other men, relates, that "he would sometimes lie awake whole nights, but not a verse could he make; and on a sudden his poetical faculty would rush upon him with an *impetus*, or *oestrum,* and his daughter was immediately called to secure what came. At other times he would dictate perhaps forty lines in a breath, and then reduce them to half the number."

These bursts of light, and involutions of darkness; these transient and involuntary excursions and retrocessions of invention, having some appearance of deviation from the common train of nature, are eagerly caught by the lovers of a wonder. Yet something of this inequality happens to every man in every mode of exertion, manual or mental. The mechanick cannot handle his hammer and his file at all times with equal dexterity; there are hours, he knows not why, when *his hand is out.* By Mr. Richardson's relation, casually conveyed, much regard cannot be claimed. That, in his intellectual hour, Milton called for his daughter *to secure what came,* may be questioned; for unluckily it happens to be known that his daughters were never taught to write; nor would he have been obliged, as is universally confessed, to have employed any casual visiter in disburthening his memory, if his daughter could have performed the office.

The story of reducing his exuberance has been told of other authors, and though doubtless true of every fertile and copious mind, seems to have been gratuitously transferred to Milton.

What he has told us, and we cannot now know more, is, that he composed much of his poem in the night and morning, I suppose before his mind was disturbed with common business; and that he poured out with great fluency his *unpremeditated verse.* Versification, free, like his, from the distresses of rhyme, must, by a work so long, be made prompt and habitual; and, when his thoughts were once adjusted, the words would come at his command.

At what particular times of his life the parts of his work were written, cannot often be known. The beginning of the third book shews that he had lost his sight; and the Introduction to the seventh, that the return of the King had clouded him with discountenance; and that he was offended by the licentious festivity of the Restoration. There are no other internal notes of time. Milton, being now cleared from all effects of his disloyalty, had nothing required from him but the common duty of living in quiet, to be rewarded with the common right of protection: but this, which, when he sculked from the approach of his King, was perhaps more than he hoped, seems not to have satisfied him; for no sooner is he safe than he finds himself in danger, *fallen on evil days and evil tongues, and with darkness and with danger compass'd round.* This darkness, had his eyes been better employed, had undoubtedly deserved compassion; but to add the mention of danger was ungrateful and unjust. He was fallen indeed on *evil days;* the time was come in which regicides could no longer boast their wickedness. But of *evil tongues* for Milton to complain, required impudence at least equal to his other powers; Milton, whose warmest advocates must allow, that he never spared any asperity of reproach or brutality of insolence.

But the charge itself seems to be false; for it would be hard to recollect any reproach cast upon him, either serious or ludicrous, through the whole remaining part of his life. He persued his studies, or his amusements, without persecution, molestation, or insult. Such is the reverence paid to great abilities, however misused: they who contemplated in Milton the scholar and the wit, were contented to forget the reviler of his King.

When the plague (1665) raged in London, Milton took refuge at Chalfont in Essex;[8] where Elwood, who had taken the house for him, first saw a complete copy of *Paradise Lost,* and, having perused it, said to him, "Thou hast said a great deal upon *Paradise Lost;* what hast thou to say upon *Paradise Found?*"

Next year, when the danger of infection had ceased, he returned to Bunhill-fields, and designed the publication of his poem. A license was necessary, and he could expect no great kindness from a chaplain of the Archbishop of Canterbury. He seems, however, to have been treated with tenderness; for though objections were made to particular passages, and among them to the simile of the sun eclipsed in the first book, yet the license was granted; and he sold his copy, April 27, 1667, to Samuel Simmons for an immediate payment of five pounds, with a stipulation to receive five pounds more when thirteen hundred should be sold of the first edition; and again, five pounds after the sale of the same number of the second edition, and another five pounds after the same sale of the third. None of the three editions were to be extended beyond fifteen hundred copies.

The first edition was of ten books, in a small quarto. The titles were varied from year to year; and an advertisement and the arguments of the books were omitted in some copies, and inserted in others.

The sale gave him in two years a right to his second payment, for which the receipt was signed April 26, 1669. The second edition was not given till 1674; it was printed in small octavo; and the number of books was encreased to twelve, by a division of the seventh and twelfth;[9] and some other small improvements were

[8] *Essex: Bucks* 1783.
[9] *twelfth:* i.e., the tenth.

made. The third edition was published in 1678; and the widow, to whom the copy was then to devolve, sold all her claims to Simmons for eight pounds, according to her receipt given Dec. 21, 1680. Simmons had already agreed to transfer the whole right to Brabazon Aylmer for twenty-five pounds; and Aylmer sold to Jacob Tonson half, August 17, 1683, and half, March 24, 1690, at a price considerably enlarged.

The slow sale and tardy reputation of this poem, have been always mentioned as evidences of neglected merit, and of the uncertainty of literary fame; and enquiries have been made, and conjectures offered, about the causes of its long obscurity and late reception. But has the case been truly stated? Have not lamentation and wonder been lavished on an evil that was never felt?

That in the reigns of Charles and James the *Paradise Lost* received no publick acclamations is readily confessed. Wit and literature were on the side of the Court: and who that solicited favour or the fashion would venture to praise the defender of the regicides? All that he himself could think his due, from *evil tongues in evil days,* was that reverential silence which was generously preserved. But it cannot be inferred that his poem was not read, or not, however unwillingly, admired.

The sale, if it be considered, will justify the publick. Those who have no power to judge of past times but by their own, should always doubt their conclusions. The sale of books was not in Milton's age what it is in the present. To read was not then a general amusement; neither traders, nor often gentlemen, thought themselves disgraced by ignorance. The women had not then aspired to literature, nor was every house supplied with a closet of books. Those indeed, who professed learning, were not less learned than at any other time; but of that middle race of students who read for pleasure or accomplishment, and who buy the numerous products of modern typography, the number was then comparatively small. To prove the paucity of readers, it may be sufficient to remark, that the nation had been satisfied, from 1623 to 1664, that is, forty-one years, with only two editions of the works of Shakespeare, which probably did not together make one thousand copies.

The sale of thirteen hundred copies in two years, in opposition to so much recent enmity, and to a style of versification new to all and disgusting to many, was an uncommon example of the prevalence of genius. The demand did not immediately encrease; for many more readers than were supplied at first the nation did not afford. Only three thousand were sold in eleven years; for it forced its way without assistance: its admirers did not dare to publish their opinion; and the opportunities now given of attracting notice by advertisements were then very few; for the means of proclaiming the publication of new books have been produced by that general literature which now pervades the nation through all its ranks.

But the reputation and price of the copy still advanced, till the Revolution put an end to the secrecy of love, and *Paradise Lost* broke into open view with sufficient security of kind reception.

Fancy can hardly forbear to conjecture with what temper Milton surveyed the silent progress of his work, and marked his reputation stealing its way in a kind of subterraneous current through fear and silence. I cannot but conceive him calm and confident, little disappointed, not at all dejected, relying on his own merit with steady consciousness, and waiting, without impatience, the vicissitudes of opinion, and the impartiality of a future generation.

In the mean time he continued his studies, and supplied the want of sight by a very odd expedient, of which Philips gives the following account:

Mr. Philips tells us, "that though our author had daily about him one or other to read, some persons of man's estate, who, of their own accord, greedily catched at the opportunity of being his readers, that they might as well reap the benefit of what they read to him, as oblige him by the benefit of their reading; and others of younger years were sent by their parents to the same end: yet excusing only the eldest daughter, by reason of her bodily infirmity, and difficult utterance of speech, (which, to say truth, I doubt was the principal cause of excusing her) the other two were condemned to the performance of reading, and exactly pronouncing of all the languages of whatever book he should, at one time or other, think fit to peruse, viz. the Hebrew (and I think the Syriac), the Greek, the Latin, the Italian, Spanish, and French. All which sorts of books to be confined to read, without understanding one word, must needs be a trial of patience almost beyond endurance. Yet it was endured by both for a long time, though the irksomeness of this employment could not be always concealed, but broke out more and more into expressions of uneasiness; so that at length they were all, even the eldest also, sent out to learn some curious and ingenious sorts of manufacture, that are proper for women to learn; particularly embroideries in gold or silver."

In the scene of misery which this mode of intellectual labour sets before our eyes, it is hard to determine whether the daughters or the father are most to be lamented. A language not understood can never be so read as to give pleasure, and very seldom so as to convey meaning. If few men would have had resolution to write books with such embarrassments, few likewise would have wanted ability to find some better expedient.

Three years after his *Paradise Lost* (1670), he published his *History of England*, comprising the whole fable of Geoffry of Monmouth, and continued to the Norman invasion. Why he should have given the first part, which he seems not to believe, and which is universally rejected, it is difficult to conjecture. The stile is harsh; but it has something of rough vigour, which perhaps may often strike, though it cannot please.

On this history the licenser again fixed his claws, and before he would transmit it to the press tore out several parts. Some censures of the Saxon monks were taken away, lest they should be applied to the modern clergy; and a character of the Long Parliament, and Assembly of Divines, was excluded; of which the author gave a copy to the Earl of Anglesea,[1] and which, being afterwards published, has been since inserted in its proper place.

The same year were printed *Paradise Regained*, and *Sampson Agonistes*, a tragedy written in imitation of the ancients, and never designed by the author for the stage. These poems were published by another bookseller. It has been asked, whether Simmons was discouraged from receiving them by the slow sale of the former? Why a writer changed his bookseller a hundred years ago, I am far from hoping to discover. It is certain, that he who in two years sells thirteen hundred copies of a volume in quarto, bought for two payments of five pounds each, has no reason to repent his purchase.

When Milton shewed *Paradise Regained* to Elwood, "This,"

---

[1] Arthur Annesley, first Earl of Anglesey (d. 1686), who apparently had befriended Milton at the Restoration.

said he, "is owing to you; for you put it in my head by the question you put to me at Chalfont, which otherwise I had not thought of."

His last poetical offspring was his favourite. He could not, as Elwood relates, endure to hear *Paradise Lost* preferred to *Paradise Regained.* Many causes may vitiate a writer's judgement of his own works. On that which has cost him much labour he sets a high value, because he is unwilling to think that he has been diligent in vain; what has been produced without toilsome efforts is considered with delight, as a proof of vigorous faculties and fertile invention; and the last work, whatever it be, has necessarily most of the grace of novelty. Milton, however it happened, had this prejudice, and had it to himself.

To that multiplicity of attainments, and extent of comprehension, that entitle this great author to our veneration, may be added a kind of humble dignity, which did not disdain the meanest services to literature. The epick poet, the controvertist, the politician, having already descended to accommodate children with a book of rudiments, now, in the last years of his life, composed a book of logick, for the initiation of students in philosophy; and published (1672) *Artis Logicae plenior Institutio ad Petri Rami methodum concinnata:* that is, "A new Scheme of Logick, according to the Method of Ramus."[2] I know not whether, even in this book, he did not intend an act of hostility against the universities; for Ramus was one of the first oppugners of the old philosophy, who disturbed with innovations the quiet of the schools.

His polemical disposition again revived. He had now been safe so long, that he forgot his fears, and published a *Treatise of true Religion, Heresy, Schism, Toleration, and the best Means to prevent the Growth of Popery.*

But this little tract is modestly written, with respectful mention of the Church of England, and an appeal to the Thirty-nine Articles. His principle of toleration is, agreement in the sufficiency of the Scriptures; and he extends it to all who, whatever their opinions are, profess to derive them from the sacred books. The papists appeal to other testimonies, and are therefore in his opinion not to be permitted the liberty of either publick or private worship; for though they plead conscience, *we have no warrant,*

---

[2] Pierre la Ramée, French logician and opponent of Aristotelianism, killed in the Massacre of St. Bartholomew, 1572.

he says, *to regard conscience which is not grounded in Scripture.*

Those who are not convinced by his reasons, may be perhaps delighted with his wit. The term *Roman Catholick* is, he says, *one of the Pope's bulls; it is particular universal, or Catholick schismatick.*

He has, however, something better. As the best preservative against Popery, he recommends the diligent perusal of the Scriptures; a duty, from which he warns the busy part of mankind not to think themselves excused.

He now reprinted his juvenile poems, with some additions.

In the last year of his life he sent to the press, seeming to take delight in publication, a collection of familiar epistles in Latin; to which, being too few to make a volume, he added some academical exercises, which perhaps he perused with pleasure, as they recalled to his memory the days of youth; but for which nothing but veneration for his name could now procure a reader.

When he had attained his sixty-sixth year, the gout, with which he had been long tormented, prevailed over the enfeebled powers of nature. He died by a quiet and silent expiration, about the tenth of November 1674, at his house in Bunhill-fields; and was buried next his father in the chancel of St. Giles at Cripplegate. His funeral was very splendidly and numerously attended.

Upon his grave there is supposed to have been no memorial; but in our time a monument has been erected in Westminster Abbey *To the Author of Paradise Lost,* by Mr. Benson,[3] who has in the inscription bestowed more words upon himself than upon Milton.

When the inscription for the monument of Philips, in which he was said to be *soli Miltono secundus,* was exhibited to Dr. Sprat, then dean of Westminster, he refused to admit it; the name of Milton was, in his opinion, too detestable to be read on the wall of a building dedicated to devotion. Atterbury, who succeeded him, being author of the inscription, permitted its reception. "And such has been the change of publick opinion," said Dr. Gregory,[4] from whom I heard this account, "that I have seen

[3] The bust by Rysbrach was installed by William Benson in 1737.

[4] The inscription for the poet John Philips (d. 1709), was written by Francis Atterbury (d. 1732) objected to by Thomas Sprat (d. 1713), as reported to Johnson by a Dr. Gregory, probably David Gregory, Dean of Christ Church, Oxford, from 1756 to 1767.

erected in the church a statue of that man, whose name I once knew considered as a pollution of its walls."

Milton has the reputation of having been in his youth eminently beautiful, so as to have been called the Lady of his college. His hair, which was of a light brown, parted at the foretop, and hung down upon his shoulders, according to the picture which he has given of Adam. He was, however, not of the heroick stature, but rather below the middle size, according to Mr. Richardson, who mentions him as having narrowly escaped from being *short and thick.* He was vigorous and active, and delighted in the exercise of the sword, in which he is related to have been eminently skilful. His weapon was, I believe, not the rapier, but the back-sword, of which he recommends the use in his book on Education.

His eyes are said never to have been bright; but, if he was a dexterous fencer, they must have been once quick.

His domestick habits, so far as they are known, were those of a severe student. He drank little strong drink of any kind, and fed without delicacy of choice or excess in quantity. In his youth he studied late at night; but afterwards changed his hours, and rested in bed from nine to four in the summer, and five in winter. The course of his day was best known after he was blind. When he first rose he heard a chapter in the Hebrew Bible, and then studied till twelve; then took some exercise for an hour; then dined; then plaid on the organ, and sung, or heard another sing; then studied to six; then entertained his visiters, till eight; then supped, and, after a pipe of tobacco and a glass of water, went to bed.

So is his life described; but this even tenour appears attainable only in colleges. He that lives in the world will sometimes have the succession of his practice broken and confused. Visiters, of whom Milton is represented to have had great numbers, will come and stay unseasonably; business, of which every man has some, must be done when others will do it.

When he did not care to rise early, he had something read to him by his bedside; perhaps at this time his daughters were employed. He composed much in the morning, and dictated in the day, sitting obliquely in an elbow-chair, with his leg thrown over the arm.

Fortune appears not to have had much of his care. In the civil wars he lent his personal estate to the parliament; but when, after the contest was decided, he solicited repayment, he met not only with neglect but *sharp rebuke;* and, having tired both himself and his friends, was given up to poverty and hopeless indignation, till he shewed how able he was to do greater service. He was then made Latin secretary, with two hundred pounds a year; and had a thousand pounds for his *Defence of the People.* His widow, who, after his death, retired to Namptwich in Cheshire, and died about 1729, is said to have reported that he lost two thousand pounds by entrusting it to a scrivener; and that, in the general depredation upon the Church, he had grasped an estate of about sixty pounds a year belonging to Westminster Abbey, which, like other sharers of the plunder of rebellion, he was afterwards obliged to return. Two thousand pounds, which he had placed in the Excise-office, were also lost. There is yet no reason to believe that he was ever reduced to indigence. His wants being few, were competently supplied. He sold his library before his death, and left his family fifteen hundred pounds, on which his widow laid hold, and only gave one hundred to each of his daughters.

His literature was unquestionably great. He read all the languages which are considered either as learned or polite; Hebrew, with its two dialects, Greek, Latin, Italian, French, and Spanish. In Latin his skill was such as places him in the first rank of writers and criticks; and he appears to have cultivated Italian with uncommon diligence. The books in which his daughter, who used to read to him, represented him as most delighting, after Homer, which he could almost repeat, were Ovid's *Metamorphoses* and Euripides. His Euripides is, by Mr. Cradock's kindness, now in my hands: the margin is sometimes noted; but I have found nothing remarkable.

Of the English poets he set most value upon Spenser, Shakespeare, and Cowley. Spenser was apparently his favourite: Shakespeare he may easily be supposed to like, with every other skilful reader; but I should not have expected that Cowley, whose ideas of excellence were so different from his own, would have had much of his approbation. His character of Dryden, who sometimes visited him, was, that he was a good rhymist, but no poet.

His theological opinions are said to have been first Calvinistical; and afterwards, perhaps when he began to hate the Presbyterians, to have tended towards Arminianism. In the mixed questions of theology and government, he never thinks that he can recede far enough from popery, or prelacy; but what Baudius says of Erasmus seems applicable to him, *magis habuit quod fugeret, quam quod sequeretur.*[5] He had determined rather what to condemn than what to approve. He has not associated himself with any denomination of Protestants: we know rather what he was not, than what he was. He was not of the Church of Rome; he was not of the Church of England.

To be of no church is dangerous. Religion, of which the rewards are distant, and which is animated only by faith and hope, will glide by degrees out of the mind, unless it be invigorated and reimpressed by external ordinances, by stated calls to worship, and the salutary influence of example. Milton, who appears to have had full conviction of the truth of Christianity, and to have regarded the Holy Scriptures with the profoundest veneration, to have been untainted by any heretical peculiarity of opinion, and to have lived in a confirmed belief of the immediate and occasional agency of Providence, yet grew old without any visible worship. In the distribution of his hours, there was no hour of prayer, either solitary, or with his household; omitting publick prayers, he omitted all.

Of this omission the reason has been sought, upon a supposition which ought never to be made, that men live with their own approbation, and justify their conduct to themselves. Prayer certainly was not thought superfluous by him, who represents our first parents as praying acceptably in the state of innocence, and efficaciously after their fall. That he lived without prayer can hardly be affirmed; his studies and meditations were an habitual prayer. The neglect of it in his family was probably a fault for which he condemned himself, and which he intended to correct, but that death, as too often happens, intercepted his reformation.

His political notions were those of an acrimonious and surly republican, for which it is not known that he gave any better

[5] "He was more disposed to flee than to follow." Dominic Baudius, *Epistolae*, cent. II, epist. xxvii.

reason than that *a popular government was the most frugal; for the trappings of a monarchy would set up an ordinary commonwealth.* It is surely very shallow policy, that supposes money to be the chief good; and even this, without considering that the support and expence of a Court is, for the most part, only a particular kind of traffick, by which money is circulated, without any national impoverishment.

Milton's republicanism was, I am afraid, founded in an envious hatred of greatness, and a sullen desire of independence; in petulance, impatient of controul, and pride disdainful of superiority. He hated monarchs in the State, and prelates in the Church; for he hated all whom he was required to obey. It is to be suspected that his predominant desire was to destroy rather than establish, and that he felt not so much the love of liberty as repugnance to authority.

It has been observed, that they who most loudly clamour for liberty do not most liberally grant it. What we know of Milton's character, in domestick relations, is, that he was severe and arbitrary. His family consisted of women; and there appears in his books something like a Turkish contempt of females, as subordinate and inferiour beings. That his own daughters might not break the ranks, he suffered them to be depressed by a mean and penurious education. He thought woman made only for obedience, and man only for rebellion.

Of his family some account may be expected. His sister, first married to Mr. Philips, afterwards married Mr. Agar, a friend of her first husband, who succeeded him in the Crown-office. She had by her first husband Edward and John, the two nephews whom Milton educated; and by her second, two daughters.

His brother, Sir Christopher, had two daughters, Mary and Catherine, and a son Thomas, who succeeded Agar in the Crown-office, and left a daughter, living in 1749 in Grosvenor-street.

Milton had children only by his first wife; Anne, Mary, and Deborah. Anne, though deformed, married a master-builder, and died of her first child. Mary died single. Deborah married Abraham Clark, a weaver in Spital-fields, and lived 76 years, to August 1727. This is the daughter of whom publick mention has been made. She could repeat the first lines of Homer, the *Meta-*

morphoses, and some of Euripides, by having often read them. Yet here incredulity is ready to make a stand. Many repetitions are necessary to fix in the memory lines not understood; and why should Milton wish or want to hear them so often! These lines were at the beginning of the poems. Of a book written in a language not understood, the beginning raises no more attention than the end; and as those that understand it know commonly the beginning best, its rehearsal will seldom be necessary. It is not likely that Milton required any passage to be so much repeated as that his daughter could learn it; nor likely that he desired the initial lines to be read at all; nor that the daughter, weary of the drudgery of pronouncing unideal sounds, would voluntarily commit them to memory.

To this gentlewoman Addison made a present, and promised some establishment; but died soon after. Queen Caroline sent her fifty guineas. She had seven sons and three daughters; but none of them had any children, except her son Caleb and her daughter Elizabeth. Caleb went to Fort St. George in the East Indies, and had two sons, of whom nothing is now known. Elizabeth married Thomas Foster, a weaver in Spital-fields, and had seven children, who all died. She kept a petty grocer's or chandler's shop, first at Halloway, and afterwards in Cock-lane near Shore-ditch Church. She knew little of her grandfather, and that little was not good. She told of his harshness to his daughters, and his refusal to have them taught to write; and, in opposition to other accounts, represented him as delicate, though temperate, in his diet.

In 1750, April 5, *Comus* was played for her benefit. She had so little acquaintance with diversion or gaiety, that she did not know what was intended when a benefit was offered her. The profits of the night were only one hundred and thirty pounds, though Dr. Newton brought a large contribution; and twenty pounds were given by Tonson,[6] a man who is to be praised as often as he is named. Of this sum one hundred pounds was placed in the stocks, after some debate between her and her husband in whose name it should be entered, and the rest augmented their little stock, with which they removed to Islington. This was the greatest

[6] Thomas Newton, editor of *Paradise Lost*, 1749, and Jacob Tonson, the publisher (d. 1767).

benefaction that *Paradise Lost* ever procured the author's descendents; and to this he who has now attempted to relate his Life, had the honour of contributing a prologue.

In the examination of Milton's poetical works, I shall pay so much regard to time as to begin with his juvenile productions. For his early pieces he seems to have had a degree of fondness not very laudable: what he has once written he resolves to preserve, and gives to the publick an unfinished poem, which he broke off because he was *nothing satisfied with what he had done*, supposing his readers less nice than himself. These preludes to his future labours are in Italian, Latin, and English. Of the Italian I cannot pretend to speak as a critic; but I have heard them commended by a man well qualified to decide their merit. The Latin pieces are lusciously elegant; but the delight which they afford is rather by the exquisite imitation of the ancient writers, by the purity of the diction, and the harmony of the numbers, than by any power of invention, or vigour of sentiment. They are not all of equal value; the elegies excell the odes; and some of the exercises on Gunpowder Treason might have been spared.

The English poems, though they make no promises of *Paradise Lost*, have this evidence of genius, that they have a cast original and unborrowed. But their peculiarity is not excellence: if they differ from the verses of others, they differ for the worse; for they are too often distinguished by repulsive harshness; the combinations of words are new, but they are not pleasing; the rhymes and epithets seem to be laboriously sought, and violently applied.

That in the early part of his life he wrote with much care appears from his manuscripts, happily preserved at Cambridge, in which many of his smaller works are found as they were first written, with the subsequent corrections. Such reliques shew how excellence is acquired; what we hope ever to do with ease, we may learn first to do with diligence.

Those who admire the beauties of this great poet, sometimes force their own judgement into false approbation of his little pieces, and prevail upon themselves to think that admirable which is only singular. All that short compositions can commonly attain is neatness and elegance. Milton never learned the art of doing little things with grace; he overlooked the milder excellence of suavity and softness; he was a *lion* that had no skill *in dandling the kid.*

One of the poems on which much praise has been bestowed is *Lycidas;* of which the diction is harsh, the rhymes uncertain, and the numbers unpleasing. What beauty there is, we must therefore seek in the sentiments and images.

It is not to be considered as the effusion of real passion; for passion runs not after remote allusions and obscure opinions. Passion plucks no berries from the myrtle and ivy, nor calls upon Arethuse and Mincius, nor tells of rough *satyrs* and *fauns with cloven heel.* Where there is leisure for fiction there is little grief.

In this poem there is no nature, for there is no truth; there is no art, for there is nothing new. Its form is that of a pastoral, easy, vulgar, and therefore disgusting: whatever images it can supply, are long ago exhausted; and its inherent improbability always forces dissatisfaction on the mind. When Cowley tells of Hervey that they studied together, it is easy to suppose how much he must miss the companion of his labours, and the partner of his discoveries; but what image of tenderness can be excited by these lines?

> We drove a field, and both together heard
> What time the grey fly winds her sultry horn,
> Batt'ning our flocks with the fresh dews of night.

We know that they never drove a field, and that they had no flocks to batten; and though it be allowed that the representation may be allegorical, the true meaning is so uncertain and remote, that it is never sought, because it cannot be known when it is found.

Among the flocks, and copses, and flowers, appear the heathen deities; Jove and Phoebus, Neptune and Aeolus, with a long train of mythological imagery, such as a college easily supplies. Nothing can less display knowledge, or less exercise invention, than to tell how a shepherd has lost his companion, and must now feed his flocks alone, without any judge of his skill in piping; and how one god asks another god what is become of Lycidas, and how neither god can tell. He who thus grieves will excite no sympathy; he who thus praises will confer no honour.

This poem has yet a grosser fault. With these trifling fictions are mingled the most awful and sacred truths, such as ought never to be polluted with such irreverend combinations. The shepherd likewise is now a feeder of sheep, and afterwards an ecclesiastical pastor, a superintendent of a Christian flock. Such equivocations are always unskilful, but here they are indecent, and at least approach to impiety, of which, however, I believe the writer not to have been conscious.

Such is the power of reputation justly acquired, that its blaze drives away the eye from nice examination. Surely no man could have fancied that he read *Lycidas* with pleasure, had he not known its author.

Of the two pieces, *L'Allegro* and *Il Penseroso*, I believe opinion is uniform; every man that reads them, reads them with pleasure. The author's design is not, what Theobald has remarked,[7] merely to shew how objects derive their colours from the mind, by representing the operation of the same things upon the gay and the melancholy temper, or upon the same man as he is differently disposed; but rather how, among the successive variety of appearances, every disposition of mind takes hold on those by which it may be gratified.

The *chearful* man hears the lark in the morning; the *pensive* man hears the nightingale in the evening. The *chearful* man sees the cock strut, and hears the horn and hounds echo in the wood; then walks *not unseen* to observe the glory of the rising sun, or listen to the singing milk-maid, and view the labours of the plowman and the mower; then casts his eyes about him over scenes of smiling plenty, and looks up to the distant tower, the residence of some fair inhabitant; thus he pursues rural gaiety through a day of labour or of play, and delights himself at night with the fanciful narratives of superstitious ignorance.

The *pensive* man, at one time, walks *unseen* to muse at mid-

[7] In his Preface to his edition of Shakespeare.

night; and at another hears the sullen curfew. If the weather drives him home, he sits in a room lighted only by *glowing embers;* or by a lonely lamp outwatches the North Star, to discover the habitation of separate souls, and varies the shades of meditation, by contemplating the magnificent or pathetick scenes of tragick and epic poetry. When the morning comes, a morning gloomy with rain and wind, he walks into the dark trackless woods, falls asleep by some murmuring water, and with melancholy enthusiasm expects some dream of prognostication, or some musick plaid by aerial performers.

Both Mirth and Melancholy are solitary, silent inhabitants of the breast that neither receive nor transmit communication; no mention is therefore made of a philosophical friend, or a pleasant companion. Seriousness does not arise from any participation of calamity, nor gaiety from the pleasures of the bottle.

The man of *chearfulness,* having exhausted the country, tries what *towered cities* will afford, and mingles with scenes of splendor, gay assemblies, and nuptial festivities; but he mingles a mere spectator, as when the learned comedies of Jonson, or the wild dramas of Shakespeare, are exhibited, he attends the theatre.

The *pensive* man never loses himself in crowds, but walks the cloister, or frequents the cathedral. Milton probably had not yet forsaken the Church.

Both his characters delight in musick; but he seems to think that chearful notes would have obtained from Pluto a compleat dismission of Eurydice, of whom solemn sounds only procured a conditional release.

For the old age of Chearfulness he makes no provision; but Melancholy he conducts with great dignity to the close of life.

Through these two poems the images are properly selected, and nicely distinguished; but the colours of the diction seem not sufficiently discriminated. His Chearfulness is without levity, and his Pensiveness without asperity. I know not whether the characters are kept sufficiently apart. No mirth can, indeed, be found in his melancholy; but I am afraid that I always meet some melancholy in his mirth. They are two noble efforts of imagination.

The greatest of his juvenile performances is the *Mask of Comus;* in which may very plainly be discovered the dawn or twilight of *Paradise Lost.* Milton appears to have formed very early that system of diction, and mode of verse, which his maturer judgement approved, and from which he never endeavoured nor desired to deviate.

Nor does *Comus* afford only a specimen of his language; it exhibits likewise his power of description, and his vigour of sentiment, employed in the praise and defence of virtue. A work more truly poetical is rarely found; allusions, images, and descriptive epithets, embellish almost every period with lavish decoration. As a series of lines, therefore, it may be considered as worthy of all the admiration with which the votaries have received it.

As a drama it is deficient. The action is not probable. A masque, in those parts where supernatural intervention is admitted, must indeed be given up to all the freaks of imagination; but, so far as the action is merely human, it ought to be reasonable, which can hardly be said of the conduct of the two brothers; who, when their sister sinks with fatigue in a pathless wilderness, wander both away together in search of berries too far to find their way back, and leave a helpless lady to all the sadness and danger of solitude. This however is a defect over-balanced by its convenience.

What deserves more reprehension is, that the prologue spoken in the wild wood by the attendant Spirit is addressed to the audience; a mode of communication so contrary to the nature of dramatick representation, that no precedents can support it.

The discourse of the Spirit is too long; an objection that may be made to almost all the following speeches: they have not the spriteliness of a dialogue animated by reciprocal contention, but seem rather declamations deliberately composed, and formally repeated, on a moral question. The auditor therefore listens as to a lecture, without passion, without anxiety.

The song of Comus has airiness and jollity; but, what may recommend Milton's morals as well as his poetry, the invitations to pleasure are so general, that they excite no distinct images of corrupt enjoyment, and take no dangerous hold on the fancy.

The following soliloquies of Comus and the Lady are elegant, but tedious. The song must owe much to the voice, if it ever can delight. At last the Brothers enter, with too much tranquillity; and when they have feared lest their sister should be in danger, and hoped that she is not in danger, the Elder makes a speech in praise of chastity, and the Younger finds how fine it is to be a philosopher.

Then descends the Spirit in form of a shepherd; and the Brother, instead of being in haste to ask his help, praises his singing, and enquires his business in that place. It is remarkable, that at this interview the Brother is taken with a short fit of rhyming. The Spirit relates that the Lady is in the power of Comus; the Brother moralises again; and the Spirit makes a long narration, of no use because it is false, and therefore unsuitable to a good being.

In all these parts the language is poetical, and the sentiments are generous; but there is something wanting to allure attention.

The dispute between the Lady and Comus is the most animated and affecting scene of the drama, and wants nothing but a brisker reciprocation of objections and replies to invite attention, and detain it.

The songs are vigorous, and full of imagery; but they are harsh in their diction, and not very musical in their numbers.

Throughout the whole, the figures are too bold, and the language too luxuriant for dialogue. It is a drama in the epic stile, inelegantly splendid, and tediously instructive.

The *Sonnets* were written in different parts of Milton's life, upon different occasions. They deserve not any particular criticism; for of the best it can only be said, that they are not bad; and perhaps only the eighth and the twenty-first are truly entitled to this slender commendation. The fabrick of a sonnet, however adapted to the Italian language, has never succeeded in ours, which, having greater variety of termination, requires the rhymes to be often changed.

Those little pieces may be dispatched without much anxiety; a greater work calls for greater care. I am now to examine *Paradise Lost;* a poem, which, considered with respect to design, may claim the first place, and with respect to performance the second among the productions of the human mind.

By the general consent of criticks, the first praise of genius is due to the writer of an epick poem, as it requires an assemblage of all the powers which are singly sufficient for other compositions. Poetry is the art of uniting pleasure with truth, by calling imagination to the help of reason. Epick poetry undertakes to teach the most important truths by the most pleasing precepts, and therefore relates some great event in the most affecting manner. History must supply the writer with the rudiments of narration, which he must improve and exalt by a nobler art, animate by dramatick energy, and diversify by retrospection and anticipation; morality must teach him the exact bounds, and different shades, of vice and virtue: from policy, and the practice of life, he has to learn the discriminations of character, and the tendency of the passions, either single or combined; and physiology must supply him with illustrations and images. To put these materials to poetical use, is required an imagination capable of painting nature, and realizing fiction. Nor is he yet a poet till he has attained the whole extension of his language, distinguished all the delicacies of phrase, and all the colours of words, and learned to adjust their different sounds to all the varieties of metrical modulation.

Bossu[8] is of opinion that the poet's first work is to find a *moral,* which his fable is afterwards to illustrate and establish. This seems to have been the process only of Milton; the moral of other poems is incidental and consequent; in Milton's only it is essential and intrinsick. His purpose was the most useful and the most arduous; *to vindicate the ways of God to man;* to shew the reasonableness of religion, and the necessity of obedience to the Divine Law.

To convey this moral there must be a *fable,* a narration artfully constructed, so as to excite curiosity, and surprise expectation. In this part of his work, Milton must be confessed to have equalled every other poet. He has involved in his account of the Fall of Man the events which preceded, and those that were to follow it: he has interwoven the whole system of theology with such propriety, that every part appears to be necessary; and scarcely any recital is wished shorter for the sake of quickening the progress of the main action.

The subject of an epick poem is naturally an event of great importance. That of Milton is not the destruction of a city, the conduct of a colony, or the foundation of an empire. His subject

[8] René Le Bossu, *Traité du Poème Epique.*

is the fate of worlds, the revolutions of heaven and of earth; rebellion against the Supreme King, raised by the highest order of created beings; the overthrow of their host, and the punishment of their crime; the creation of a new race of reasonable creatures; their original happiness and innocence, their forfeiture of immortality, and their restoration to hope and peace.

Great events can be hastened or retarded only by persons of elevated dignity. Before the greatness displayed in Milton's poem, all other greatness shrinks away. The weakest of his agents are the highest and noblest of human beings, the original parents of mankind; with whose actions the elements consented; on whose rectitude, or deviation of will, depended the state of terrestrial nature, and the condition of all the future inhabitants of the globe.

Of the other agents in the poem, the chief are such as it is irreverence to name on slight occasions. The rest were lower powers;

> ——of which the least could wield
> Those elements, and arm him with the force
> Of all their regions.

powers, which only the controul of Omnipotence restrains from laying creation waste, and filling the vast expanse of space with ruin and confusion. To display the motives and actions of beings thus superiour, so far as human reason can examine them, or human imagination represent them, is the task which this mighty poet has undertaken and performed.

In the examination of epick poems much speculation is commonly employed upon the *characters.* The characters in the *Paradise Lost,* which admit of examination, are those of angels and of man; of angels good and evil; of man in his innocent and sinful state.

Among the angels, the virtue of Raphael is mild and placid, of easy condescension and free communication; that of Michael is regal and lofty, and, as may seem, attentive to the dignity of his own nature. Abdiel and Gabriel appear occasionally, and act as every incident requires; the solitary fidelity of Abdiel is very amiably painted.

Of the evil angels the characters are more diversified. To Satan, as Addison observes, such sentiments are given as suit *the most exalted and most depraved being.* Milton has been censured, by Clark,[9] for the impiety which sometimes breaks from Satan's mouth. For there are thoughts, as he justly remarks, which no observation of character can justify, because no good man would willingly permit them to pass, however transiently, through his own mind. To make Satan speak as a rebel, without any such expressions as might taint the reader's imagination, was indeed one of the great difficulties in Milton's undertaking, and I cannot but think that he has extricated himself with great happiness. There is in Satan's speeches little that can give pain to a pious ear. The language of rebellion cannot be the same with that of obedience. The malignity of Satan foams in haughtiness and obstinacy; but his expressions are commonly general, and no otherwise offensive than as they are wicked.

The other chiefs of the celestial rebellion are very judiciously discriminated in the first and second books; and the ferocious character of Moloch appears, both in the battle and the council, with exact consistency.

To Adam and to Eve are given, during their innocence, such sentiments as innocence can generate and utter. Their love is pure benevolence and mutual veneration; their repasts are without luxury, and their diligence without toil. Their addresses to their Maker have little more than the voice of admiration and gratitude. Fruition left them nothing to ask, and Innocence left them nothing to fear.

But with guilt enter distrust and discord, mutual accusation, and stubborn self-defence; they regard each other with alienated minds, and dread their Creator as the avenger of their transgression. At last they seek shelter in his mercy, soften to repentance, and melt in supplication. Both before and after the Fall, the superiority of Adam is diligently sustained.

Of the *probable* and the *marvellous,* two parts of a vulgar epick poem, which immerge the critick in deep consideration, the *Paradise Lost* requires little to be said. It contains the history of a miracle, of Creation and Redemption; it displays the power and the mercy of the Supreme Being; the probable therefore is marvellous, and the marvellous is probable. The substance of the

[9] "Author of the *Essay on Study.*" Johnson, 1783. John Clarke's book was published in 1731.

narrative is truth; and as truth allows no choice, it is, like necessity, superior to rule. To the accidental or adventitious parts, as to every thing human, some slight exceptions may be made. But the main fabrick is immovably supported.

It is justly remarked by Addison, that this poem has, by the nature of its subject, the advantage above all others, that it is universally and perpetually interesting. All mankind will, through all ages, bear the same relation to Adam and to Eve, and must partake of that good and evil which extend to themselves.

Of the *machinery,* so called from θεὸς ἀπὸ μηχανῆς, by which is meant the occasional interposition of supernatural power, another fertile topick of critical remarks, here is no room to speak, because every thing is done under the immediate and visible direction of Heaven; but the rule is so far observed, that no part of the action could have been accomplished by any other means.

Of *episodes,* I think there are only two, contained in Raphael's relation of the war in heaven, and Michael's prophetick account of the changes to happen in this world. Both are closely connected with the great action; one was necessary to Adam as a warning, the other as a consolation.

To the compleatness or *integrity* of the design nothing can be objected; it has distinctly and clearly what Aristotle requires, a beginning, a middle, and an end. There is perhaps no poem, of the same length, from which so little can be taken without apparent mutilation. Here are no funeral games, nor is there any long description of a shield. The short digressions at the beginning of the third, seventh, and ninth books, might doubtless be spared; but superfluities so beautiful, who would take away? or who does not wish that the author of the *Iliad* had gratified succeeding ages with a little knowledge of himself? Perhaps no passages are more frequently or more attentively read than those extrinsick paragraphs; and, since the end of poetry is pleasure, that cannot be unpoetical with which all are pleased.

The questions, whether the action of the poem be strictly *one,* whether the poem can be properly termed *heroick,* and who is the hero, are raised by such readers as draw their principles of judgement rather from books than from reason. Milton, though he intituled *Paradise Lost* only a *poem,* yet calls it himself *heroick song.* Dryden, petulantly and indecently, denies the heroism of Adam, because he was overcome; but there is no reason why the hero should not be unfortunate, except established practice, since success and virtue do not go necessarily together. Cato is the hero of Lucan; but Lucan's authority will not be suffered by Quintilian to decide. However, if success be necessary, Adam's deceiver was at last crushed; Adam was restored to his Maker's favour, and therefore may securely resume his human rank.

After the scheme and fabrick of the poem, must be considered its component parts, the sentiments and the diction.

The *sentiments,* as expressive of manners, or appropriated to characters, are, for the greater part, unexceptionably just.

Splendid passages, containing lessons of morality, or precepts of prudence, occur seldom. Such is the original formation of this poem, that, as it admits no human manners till the Fall, it can give little assistance to human conduct. Its end is to raise the thoughts above sublunary cares or pleasures. Yet the praise of that fortitude, with which Abdiel maintained his singularity of virtue against the scorn of multitudes, may be accommodated to all times; and Raphael's reproof of Adam's curiosity after the planetary motions, with the answer returned by Adam, may be confidently opposed to any rule of life which any poet has delivered.

The thoughts which are occasionally called forth in the progress, are such as could only be produced by an imagination in the highest degree fervid and active, to which materials were supplied by incessant study and unlimited curiosity. The heat of Milton's mind might be said to sublimate his learning, to throw off into his work the spirit of science, unmingled with its grosser parts.

He had considered creation in its whole extent, and his descriptions are therefore learned. He had accustomed his imagination to unrestrained indulgence, and his conceptions therefore were extensive. The characteristick quality of his poem is sublimity. He sometimes descends to the elegant, but his element is the great. He can occasionally invest himself with grace; but his natural port is gigantick loftiness.[1] He can please when pleasure is required; but it is his peculiar power to astonish.

He seems to have been well acquainted with his own genius,

---

[1] "Algarotti terms it *gigantesca sublimità Miltoniana.*" Johnson.

and to know what it was that nature had bestowed upon him more bountifully than upon others; the power of displaying the vast, illuminating the splendid, enforcing the awful, darkening the gloomy, and aggravating the dreadful: he therefore chose a subject on which too much could not be said, on which he might tire his fancy without the censure of extravagance.

The appearances of nature, and the occurrences of life, did not satiate his appetite of greatness. To paint things as they are, requires a minute attention, and employs the memory rather than the fancy. Milton's delight was to sport in the wide regions of possibility; reality was a scene too narrow for his mind. He sent his faculties out upon discovery, into worlds where only imagination can travel, and delighted to form new modes of existence, and furnish sentiment and action to superior beings, to trace the counsels of hell, or accompany the choirs of heaven.

But he could not be always in other worlds: he must sometimes revisit earth, and tell of things visible and known. When he cannot raise wonder by the sublimity of his mind, he gives delight by its fertility.

Whatever be his subject, he never fails to fill the imagination. But his images and descriptions of the scenes or operations of nature do not seem to be always copied from original form, nor to have the freshness, raciness, and energy of immediate observation. He saw nature, as Dryden expresses it, *through the spectacles of books;* and on most occasions calls learning to his assistance. The garden of Eden brings to his mind the vale of Enna, where Proserpine was gathering flowers. Satan makes his way through fighting elements, like Argo between the Cyanean rocks, or Ulysses between the two Sicilian whirlpools, when he shunned Charybdis on the *larboard.* The mythological allusions have been justly censured, as not being always used with notice of their vanity; but they contribute variety to the narration, and produce an alternate exercise of the memory and the fancy.

His similies are less numerous, and more various, than those of his predecessors. But he does not confine himself within the limits of rigorous comparison: his great excellence is amplitude, and he expands the adventitious image beyond the dimensions which the occasion required. Thus, comparing the shield of Satan to the orb of the moon, he crowds the imagination with the discovery of the telescope, and all the wonders which the telescope discovers.

Of his moral sentiments it is hardly praise to affirm that they excel those of all other poets; for this superiority he was indebted to his acquaintance with the sacred writings. The ancient epick poets, wanting the light of Revelation, were very unskilful teachers of virtue: their principal characters may be great, but they are not amiable. The reader may rise from their works with a greater degree of active or passive fortitude, and sometimes of prudence; but he will be able to carry away few precepts of justice, and none of mercy.

From the Italian writers it appears, that the advantages of even Christian knowledge may be possessed in vain. Ariosto's pravity is generally known; and though the *Deliverance of Jerusalem* may be considered as a sacred subject, the poet has been very sparing of moral instruction.

In Milton every line breathes sanctity of thought, and purity of manners, except when the train of the narration requires the introduction of the rebellious spirits; and even they are compelled to acknowledge their subjection to God, in such a manner as excites reverence and confirms piety.

Of human beings there are but two; but those two are the parents of mankind, venerable before their fall for dignity and innocence, and amiable after it for repentance and submission. In their first state their affection is tender without weakness, and their piety sublime without presumption. When they have sinned, they shew how discord begins in natural frailty, and how it ought to cease in mutual forbearance; how confidence of the divine favour is forfeited by sin, and how hope of pardon may be obtained by penitence and prayer. A state of innocence we can only conceive, if indeed, in our present misery, it be possible to conceive it; but the sentiments and worship proper to a fallen and offending being, we have all to learn, as we have all to practise.

The poet, whatever be done, is always great. Our progenitors, in their first state, conversed with angels; even when folly and sin had degraded them, they had not in their humiliation *the port of mean suitors;* and they rise again to reverential regard, when we find that their prayers were heard.

As human passions did not enter the world before the Fall, there is in the *Paradise Lost* little opportunity for the pathetick; but what little there is has not been lost. That passion which is peculiar to rational nature, the anguish arising from the consciousness of transgression, and the horrours attending the sense of the Divine displeasure, are very justly described and forcibly impressed. But the passions are moved only on one occasion; sublimity is the general and prevailing quality in this poem; sublimity variously modified, sometimes descriptive, sometimes argumentative.

The defects and faults of *Paradise Lost*, for faults and defects every work of man must have, it is the business of impartial criticism to discover. As, in displaying the excellence of Milton, I have not made long quotations, because of selecting beauties there had been no end, I shall in the same general manner mention that which seems to deserve censure; for what Englishman can take delight in transcribing passages, which, if they lessen the reputation of Milton, diminish in some degree the honour of our country?

The generality of my scheme does not admit the frequent notice of verbal inaccuracies; which Bentley,[2] perhaps better skilled in grammar than in poetry, has often found, though he sometimes made them, and which he imputed to the obtrusions of a reviser whom the author's blindness obliged him to employ. A supposition rash and groundless, if he thought it true; and vile and pernicious if, as is said, he in private allowed it to be false.

The plan of *Paradise Lost* has this inconvenience, that it comprises neither human actions nor human manners. The man and woman who act and suffer, are in a state which no other man or woman can ever know. The reader finds no transaction in which he can be engaged; beholds no condition in which he can by any effort of imagination place himself; he has, therefore, little natural curiosity or sympathy.

We all, indeed, feel the effects of Adam's disobedience; we all sin like Adam, and like him must all bewail our offences; we have restless and insidious enemies in the fallen angels, and in the blessed spirits we have guardians and friends; in the redemption of mankind we hope to be included; and in the description of heaven and hell we are surely interested, as we are all to reside hereafter either in the regions of horror or of bliss.

But these truths are too important to be new; they have been taught to our infancy; they have mingled with our solitary

[2] Richard Bentley's edition of *Paradise Lost* was published in 1732.

thoughts and familiar conversation, and are habitually interwoven with the whole texture of life. Being therefore not new, they raise no unaccustomed emotion in the mind; what we knew before we cannot learn; what is not unexpected cannot surprise.

Of the ideas suggested by these awful scenes, from some we recede with reverence, except when stated hours require their association; and from others we shrink with horror, or admit them only as salutary inflictions, as counterpoises to our interests and passions. Such images rather obstruct the career of fancy than incite it.

Pleasure and terrour are indeed the genuine sources of poetry; but poetical pleasure must be such as human imagination can at least conceive, and poetical terrour such as human strength and fortitude may combat. The good and evil of eternity are too ponderous for the wings of wit; the mind sinks under them in passive helplessness, content with calm belief and humble adoration.

Known truths, however, may take a different appearance, and be conveyed to the mind by a new train of intermediate images. This Milton has undertaken, and performed with pregnancy and vigour of mind peculiar to himself. Whoever considers the few radical positions which the Scriptures afforded him, will wonder by what energetick operation he expanded them to such extent, and ramified them to so much variety, restrained as he was by religious reverence from licentiousness of fiction.

Here is a full display of the united force of study and genius; of a great accumulation of materials, with judgement to digest, and fancy to combine them: Milton was able to select from nature, or from story, from ancient fable, or from modern science, whatever could illustrate or adorn his thoughts. An accumulation of knowledge impregnated his mind, fermented by study, and sublimed by imagination.

It has been therefore said, without an indecent hyperbole, by one of his encomiasts, that in reading *Paradise Lost* we read a book of universal knowledge.

But original deficience cannot be supplied. The want of human interest is always felt. *Paradise Lost* is one of the books which the reader admires and lays down, and forgets to take up again.[3] Its

---

[3] After *again* "None ever wished it longer than it is." Added in 1783.

perusal is a duty rather than a pleasure. We read Milton for instruction, retire harassed and overburdened, and look elsewhere for recreation; we desert our master, and seek for companions.

Another inconvenience of Milton's design is, that it requires the description of what cannot be described, the agency of spirits. He saw that immateriality supplied no images, and that he could not show angels acting but by instruments of action; he therefore invested them with form and matter. This, being necessary, was therefore defensible; and he should have secured the consistency of his system, by keeping immateriality out of sight, and enticing his reader to drop it from his thoughts. But he has unhappily perplexed his poetry with his philosophy. His infernal and celestial powers are sometimes pure spirit, and sometimes animated body. When Satan walks with his lance upon the *burning marle,* he has a body; when in his passage between hell and the new world, he is in danger of sinking in the vacuity, and is supported by a gust of rising vapours, he has a body; when he animates the toad, he seems to be mere spirit, that can penetrate matter at pleasure; when he *starts up in his own shape,* he has at least a determined form; and when he is brought before Gabriel, he has a *spear and shield,* which he had the power of hiding in the toad, though the arms of the contending angels are evidently material.

The vulgar inhabitants of Pandaemonium being *incorporeal spirits,* are *at large, though without number,* in a limited space; yet in the battle, when they were overwhelmed by mountains, their armour hurt them, *crushed in upon their substance, now grown gross by sinning.* This likewise happened to the uncorrupted angels, who were overthrown *the sooner for their arms,* for *unarmed they might easily as spirits have evaded by contraction, or remove.* Even as spirits they are hardly spiritual; for *contraction* and *remove* are images of matter; but if they could have escaped without their armour, they might have escaped from it, and left only the empty cover to be battered. Uriel, when he rides on a sun-beam, is material: Satan is material when he is afraid of the prowess of Adam.

The confusion of spirit and matter which pervades the whole narration of the war of heaven fills it with incongruity; and the book, in which it is related, is, I believe, the favourite of children, and gradually neglected as knowledge is increased.

After the operation of immaterial agents, which cannot be explained, may be considered that of allegorical persons, which have no real existence. To exalt causes into agents, to invest abstract ideas with form, and animate them with activity, has always been the right of poetry. But such airy beings are, for the most part, suffered only to do their natural office, and retire. Thus Fame tells a tale, and Victory hovers over a general, or perches on a standard; but Fame and Victory can do no more. To give them any real employment, or ascribe to them any material agency, is to make them allegorical no longer, but to shock the mind by ascribing effects to non-entity. In the *Prometheus* of Aeschylus, we see Violence and Strength, and in the *Alcestis* of Euripides, we see Death brought upon the stage, all as active persons of the drama; but no precedents can justify absurdity.

Milton's allegory of Sin and Death is undoubtedly faulty. Sin is indeed the mother of Death, and may be allowed to be the portress of hell; but when they stop the journey of Satan, a journey described as real, and when Death offers him battle, the allegory is broken. That Sin and Death should have shewn the way to hell might have been allowed; but they cannot facilitate the passage by building a bridge, because the difficulty of Satan's passage is described as real and sensible, and the bridge ought to be only figurative. The hell assigned to the rebellious spirits is described as not less local than the residence of man. It is placed in some distant part of space, separated from the regions of harmony and order by a chaotick waste and an unoccupied vacuity; but Sin and Death worked up a *mole* of *aggregated soil,* cemented with *asphaltus;* a work too bulky for ideal architects.

This unskilful allegory appears to me one of the greatest faults of the poem; and to this there was no temptation, but the author's opinion of its beauty.

To the conduct of the narrative some objections may be made. Satan is with great expectation brought before Gabriel in Paradise, and is suffered to go away unmolested. The creation of man is represented as the consequence of the vacuity left in heaven by the expulsion of the rebels, yet Satan mentions it as a report *rife in heaven* before his departure.

To find sentiments for the state of innocence, was very difficult; and something of anticipation perhaps is now and then discovered.

Adam's discourse of dreams seems not to be the speculation of a new-created being. I know not whether his answer to the angel's reproof for curiosity does not want something of propriety: it is the speech of a man acquainted with many other men. Some philosophical notions, especially when the philosophy is false, might have been better omitted. The angel, in a comparison, speaks of *timorous deer,* before deer were yet timorous, and before Adam could understand the comparison.

Dryden remarks, that Milton has some flats among his elevations. This is only to say that all the parts are not equal. In every work one part must be for the sake of others; a palace must have passages; a poem must have transitions. It is no more to be required that wit should always be blazing, than that the sun should always stand at noon. In a great work there is a vicissitude of luminous and opaque parts, as there is in the world a succession of day and night. Milton, when he has expatiated in the sky, may be allowed sometimes to revisit earth; for what other author ever soared so high, or sustained his flight so long?

Milton, being well versed in the Italian poets, appears to have borrowed often from them; and, as every man learns something from his companions, his desire of imitating Ariosto's levity has disgraced his work with the *Paradise of Fools;* a fiction not in itself ill-imagined, but too ludicrous for its place.

His play on words, in which he delights too often; his equivocations which Bentley endeavours to defend by the example of the ancients; his unnecessary and ungraceful use of terms of art, it is not necessary to mention, because they are easily remarked, and generally censured, and at last bear so little proportion to the whole, that they scarcely deserve the attention of a critick.

Such are the faults of that wonderful performance *Paradise Lost;* which he who can put in balance with its beauties must be considered not as nice but as dull, as less to be censured for want of candour than pitied for want of sensibility.

Of *Paradise Regained,* the general judgement seems now to be right, that it is in many parts elegant, and every-where instructive. It was not to be supposed that the writer of *Paradise Lost* could ever write without great effusions of fancy, and exalted precepts of wisdom. The basis of *Paradise Regained* is narrow; a dialogue without action can never please like an union of the narrative and dramatick powers. Had this poem been written not by Milton, but by some imitator, it would have claimed and received universal praise.

If *Paradise Regained* has been too much depreciated, *Samson Agonistes* has in requital been too much admired. It could only be by long prejudice, and the bigotry of learning, that Milton could prefer the ancient tragedies, with their encumbrance of a chorus, to the exhibitions of the French and English stages; and it is only by a blind confidence in the reputation of Milton, that a drama can be praised in which the intermediate parts have neither cause nor consequence, neither hasten nor retard the catastrophe.

In this tragedy are however many particular beauties, many just sentiments and striking lines; but it wants that power of attracting the attention which a well-connected plan produces.

Milton would not have excelled in dramatick writing; he knew human nature only in the gross, and had never studied the shades of character, nor the combinations of concurring, or the perplexity of contending passions. He had read much, and knew what books could teach; but had mingled little in the world, and was deficient in the knowledge which experience must confer.

Through all his greater works there prevails an uniform peculiarity of *diction*, a mode and cast of expression which bears little resemblance to that of any former writer, and which is so far removed from common use, that an unlearned reader, when he first opens his book, finds himself surprised by a new language.

This novelty has been, by those who can find nothing wrong in Milton, imputed to his laborious endeavours after words suitable to the grandeur of his ideas. *Our language,* says Addison, *sunk under him.* But the truth is, that, both in prose and verse, he had formed his stile by a perverse and pedantick principle. He was desirous to use English words with a foreign idiom. This in all his prose is discovered and condemned; for there judgement operates freely, neither softened by the beauty nor awed by the dignity of his thoughts; but such is the power of his poetry, that his call is obeyed without resistance, the reader feels himself in captivity to a higher and a nobler mind, and criticism sinks in admiration.

Milton's stile was not modified by his subject: what is shown with greater extent in *Paradise Lost,* may be found in *Comus.* One source of his peculiarity was his familiarity with the Tuscan poets: the disposition of his words is, I think, frequently Italian; perhaps sometimes combined with other tongues. Of him, at last, may be said what Jonson says of Spenser, that *he wrote no language,* but has formed what Butler calls a *Babylonish dialect,*[4] in itself harsh and barbarous; but made by exalted genius, and extensive learning, the vehicle of so much instruction and so much pleasure, that, like other lovers, we find grace in its deformity.

Whatever be the faults of his diction, he cannot want the praise of copiousness and variety: he was master of his language in its full extent; and has selected the melodious words with such diligence, that from his book alone the Art of English Poetry might be learned.

After his diction, something must be said of his *versification. The measure,* he says, *is the English heroick verse without rhyme.* Of this mode he had many examples among the Italians, and some in his own country. The Earl of Surry is said to have translated one of Virgil's books without rhyme;[5] and, besides our tragedies, a few short poems had appeared in blank verse; particularly one tending to reconcile the nation to Raleigh's wild attempt upon Guiana, and probably written by Raleigh himself. These petty performances cannot be supposed to have much influenced Milton, who more probably took his hint from Trisino's *Italia Liberata;*[6] and, finding blank verse easier than rhyme, was desirous of persuading himself that it is better.

Rhyme, he says, and says truly, *is no necessary adjunct of true poetry.* But perhaps, of poetry as a mental operation, metre or musick is no necessary adjunct: it is however by the musick of metre that poetry has been discriminated in all languages; and in languages melodiously constructed, by a due proportion of long and short syllables, metre is sufficient. But one language cannot communicate its rules to another: where metre is scanty and imperfect, some help is necessary. The musick of the English heroick line strikes the ear so faintly that it is easily lost, unless all the syllables of every line co-operate together: this co-operation can

[4] Ben Jonson in *Discoveries,* Butler in *Hudibras,* I.i.93.

[5] *Aeneid* II and IV.

[6] Giorgio Trissino's *Italia Liberata da' Goti,* 1548.

be only obtained by the preservation of every verse unmingled with another, as a distinct system of sounds; and this distinctness is obtained and preserved by the artifice of rhyme. The variety of pauses, so much boasted by the lovers of blank verse, changes the measures of an English poet to the periods of a declaimer; and there are only a few skilful and happy readers of Milton, who enable their audience to perceive where the lines end or begin. *Blank verse,* said an ingenious critick,[7] *seems to be verse only to the eye.*

Poetry may subsist without rhyme, but English poetry will not often please; nor can rhyme ever be safely spared but where the subject is able to support itself. Blank verse makes some approach to that which is called the *lapidary stile;* has neither the easiness of prose, nor the melody of numbers, and therefore tires by long continuance. Of the Italian writers without rhyme, whom Milton alleges as precedents, not one is popular; what reason could urge in its defence, has been confuted by the ear.

But, whatever be the advantage of rhyme, I cannot prevail on myself to wish that Milton had been a rhymer; for I cannot wish his work to be other than it is; yet, like other heroes, he is to be admired rather than imitated. He that thinks himself capable of astonishing, may write blank verse; but those that hope only to please, must condescend to rhyme.

The highest praise of genius is original invention. Milton cannot be said to have contrived the structure of an epick poem, and therefore must yield to that vigour and amplitude of mind to which all generations must be indebted for the art of poetical narration, for the texture of the fable, the variation of incidents, the interposition of dialogue, and all the stratagems that surprise and enchain attention. But, of all the borrowers from Homer, Milton is perhaps the least indebted. He was naturally a thinker for himself, confident of his own abilities, and disdainful of help or hindrance: he did not refuse admission to the thoughts or images of his predecessors, but he did not seek them. From his contemporaries he neither courted nor received support; there is in his writings nothing by which the pride of other authors might be gratified, or favour gained; no exchange of praise, nor solicita-

---

[7] William Locke (d. 1810), "whose taste in the fine arts," says Boswell, was "universally celebrated." (*Life*, IV.43.)

tion of support. His great works were performed under discountenance, and in blindness, but difficulties vanished at his touch; he was born for whatever is arduous, and his work is not the greatest of heroick poems, only because it is not the first.

The Life of Gray *was published in Volume X of Johnson's* Prefaces *(1781), and was reprinted in the same year in his* Lives of the Poets. *It was attacked at once, inasmuch as many of Gray's friends were still alive. Reprinted from the first edition.*

Life of Gray

Thomas Gray, the son of Mr. Philip Gray, a scrivener of London, was born in Cornhill, November 26, 1716. His grammatical education he received at Eton under[1] Mr. Antrobus, his mother's brother;[2] and when he left school, in 1734, entered a pensioner at Peterhouse in Cambridge.

The transition from the school to the college is, to most young scholars, the time from which they date their years of manhood, liberty, and happiness; but Gray seems to have been very little delighted with academical gratifications; he liked at Cambridge neither the mode of life nor the fashion of study, and lived sullenly on to the time when his attendance on lectures was no longer required. As he intended to profess the Common Law, he took no degree.

When he had been at Cambridge about five years, Mr. Horace Walpole, whose friendship he had gained at Eton, invited him to travel with him as his companion. They wandered through France into Italy; and Gray's letters contain a very pleasing account of many parts of their journey. But unequal friendships are easily dissolved: at Florence they quarrelled, and parted, and Mr. Walpole is now content to have it told that it was by his fault. If we look however without prejudice on the world, we shall find that men, whose consciousness of their own merits sets them above the compliances of servility, are apt enough in their association with superiors to watch their own dignity with troublesome and punc-

[1] under: under the care of *in the 1783 edition, hereafter referred to as 1783*. Here and below Johnson has "Eaton," later corrected.
[2] brother: brother, then assistant to Dr. George, *1783*

tilious jealousy, and in the fervour of independance to exact that attention which they refuse to pay. Part they did, whatever was the quarrel, and the rest of their travels was doubtless more unpleasant to them both. Gray continued his journey in a manner suitable to his own little fortune, with only an occasional servant.

He returned to England in September 1741, and in about two months afterwards buried his father, who had, by an injudicious waste of money upon a new house, so much lessened his fortune, that Gray thought himself too poor to study the law. He therefore retired to Cambridge, where he soon after became Bachelor of Civil Law; and where, without liking the place or its inhabitants, or pretending[3] to like them, he passed, except a short residence at London, the rest of his life.

About this time he was deprived of Mr. West, the son of a chancellor of Ireland, a friend on whom he appears to have set a high value, and who deserved his esteem by the powers which he shews in his letters, and in the *Ode to May,* which Mr. Mason has preserved, as well as by the sincerity with which, when Gray sent him part of *Agrippina,* a tragedy that he had just begun, he gave an opinion which probably intercepted the progress of the work, and which the judgement of every reader will confirm. It was certainly no loss to the English stage that *Agrippina* was never finished.

In this year (1742) Gray seems first to have applied himself seriously to poetry; for in this year were produced the *Ode to Spring,* his *Prospect of Eton,* and his *Ode to Adversity.* He began likewise a Latin Poem, *de Principiis Cogitandi.*

It seems to be the opinion[4] of Mr. Mason, that his first ambition was to have excelled in Latin poetry: perhaps it were reasonable to wish that he had prosecuted his design; for though there is at present some embarrassment in his phrase, and some harshness in his lyrick numbers, his copiousness of language is such as very few possess; and his lines, even when imperfect, discover a writer whom practice would quickly have made skilful.

He now lived on at Peterhouse, very little solicitous what others did or thought, and cultivated his mind and enlarged his views without any other purpose than of improving and amusing him-

[3] pretending: professing *1783*

[4] seems to be the opinion: may be collected from the narrative *1783*

self; when Mr. Mason, being elected fellow of Pembroke-hall, brought him a companion who was afterwards to be his editor, and whose fondness and fidelity has kindled in him a zeal of admiration, which cannot be reasonably expected from the neutrality of a stranger and the coldness of a critick.

In this retirement he wrote (1747) an ode on the *Death of Mr. Walpole's Cat;* and the year afterwards attempted a poem of more importance, on *Government and Education,* of which the fragments which remain have many excellent lines.

His next production (1750) was his far-famed *Elegy in the Church-yard,* which, finding its way into a Magazine,[5] first, I believe, made him known to the publick.

An invitation from Lady Cobham about this time gave occasion to an odd composition called *A Long Story,* which though perhaps[6] it adds little to Gray's character, I am not pleased to find wanting in this collection. It will therefore be added to this Preface.

Several of his pieces were published (1753), with designs, by Mr. Bentley; and, that they might in some form or other make a book, only one side of each leaf was printed. I believe the poems and the plates recommended each other so well, that the whole impression was soon bought. This year he lost his mother.

Some time afterwards (1756) some young men of the college, whose chambers were near his, diverted themselves with disturbing him by frequent and troublesome noises.[7] This insolence,

---

[5] *The Magazine of Magazines,* February 1751, in which the poem bore Gray's name, whereas the separate publication, appearing a day earlier, was anonymous.

[6] which though perhaps . . . Preface: which adds little to Gray's character. *1783* (As the poem is not an integral part of the biography, it is omitted from this edition.)

[7] noises: noises, and, as is said, by pranks yet more offensive and contemptuous. *1783*. Gray's house in London had been destroyed by fire, and he had consequently had a rope ladder installed in his rooms in Peterhouse. Some undergraduates early one morning "ordered their man Joe Draper to roar out fire. A delicate white night-cap is said to have appeared at the window; but finding the mistake, retired again to the couch. The young fellows, had he descended, were determined, they said, to have whipped the butterfly up again." (*Correspondence,* ed. Toynbee and Whibley, 1935, III.1220.) The master of the college offended Gray by calling the episode "a boyish frolic," and Gray "migrated" to Pembroke a day or two later. In a letter Gray said that he left "because the rooms were noisy & the People of the house dirty." (Ibid., II.458.)

having endured it a while, he represented to the governors of the society, among whom perhaps he had no friends; and, finding his complaint little regarded, removed himself to Pembroke-hall.

In 1757 he published *The Progress of Poetry* and *The Bard,* two compositions at which the readers of poetry were at first content to gaze in mute amazement. Some that tried them confessed their inability to understand them, though Warburton said that they were understood as well as the works of Milton and Shakespeare, which it is the fashion to praise.[8] Garrick wrote a few lines in their praise. Some hardy champions undertook to rescue them from neglect, and in a short time many were content to be shewn beauties which they could not see.

Gray's reputation was now so high, that, after the death of Cibber, he had the honour of refusing the laurel, which was then bestowed on Mr. Whitehead.

His curiosity, not long after, drew him away from Cambridge to a lodging near the Museum, where he resided near three years, reading and transcribing; and, so far as can be discovered, very little affected by two odes on *Oblivion* and *Obscurity,* in which his lyrick performances were ridiculed with much contempt and much ingenuity.[9]

When the Professor of Modern Languages[1] at Cambridge died, he was, as he says, *cockered and spirited up,* till he asked it of Lord Bute, who sent him a civil refusal; and the place was given to Mr. Brocket, the tutor of Sir James Lowther.

His constitution was weak, and believing that his health was promoted by exercise and change of place, he undertook (1765) a journey into Scotland, of which his account, so far as it extends, is very curious and elegant; for as his comprehension was ample, his curiosity extended to all the works of art, all the appearances of nature, and all the monuments of past events. He naturally contracted a friendship with Dr. Beattie, whom he found a poet, a philosopher, and a good man. The Mareschal College at Aberdeen offered him the degree of Doctor of Laws, which, having omitted to take it at Cambridge, he thought it decent to refuse.

What he had formerly solicited in vain, was at last given him

[8] praise: admire *1783*
[9] Joint productions (1760) of George Colman and Robert Lloyd.
[1] Languages: History *1783*

as a trifle, but it is not a happy trifle. In the first stanza *the azure flowers* that *blow,* shew resolutely a rhyme is sometimes made when it cannot easily be found. Selima, the cat, is called a nymph, with some violence both to language and sense; but there is good use made of it when it is done; for of the two lines,

What female heart can gold despise?
What cat's averse to fish?

the first relates merely to the nymph, and the second only to the cat. The sixth stanza contains a melancholy truth, that *a favourite has no friend;* but the last ends in a pointed sentence of no relation to the purpose; if *what glistered* had been *gold,* the cat would not have gone into the water; and, if she had, would not less have been drowned.

The *Prospect of Eton College* suggests nothing to Gray, which every beholder does not equally think and feel. His supplication to father Thames, to tell him who drives the hoop or tosses the ball, is useless and puerile. Father Thames has no better means of knowing than himself. His epithet *buxom health* is not elegant; he seems not to understand the word. Gray thought his language more poetical as it was more remote from common use: finding in Dryden *honey redolent of spring,* an expression that reaches the utmost limits of our language, Gray drove it a little more beyond common apprehension, by making *gales* to be *redolent of joy and youth.*

Of the *Ode on Adversity,* the hint was at first taken from *O Diva, gratum quae regis Antium;*[8] but Gray has excelled his original by the variety of his sentiments, and by their moral application. Of this piece, at once poetical and rational, I will not by slight objections violate the dignity.

My process has now brought me to the *wonderful wonder of wonders,* the two sister odes; by which, though either vulgar ignorance or common sense at first universally rejected them, many have been since persuaded to think themselves delighted. I am one of those that are willing to be pleased, and therefore would gladly find the meaning of the first stanza of the *Progress of Poetry.*

[8] Horace, *Odes,* I.35

without solicitation. The Professorship of Languages[2] became again vacant, and he received (1768) an offer of it from the Duke of Grafton. He accepted, and retained it to his death; always designing lectures, but never reading them; uneasy at his neglect of duty, and appeasing his uneasiness with designs of reformation, and with a resolution which he believed himself to have made of resigning the office, if he found himself unable to discharge it.

Ill health made another journey necessary, and he visited (1769) Westmoreland and Cumberland. He that reads his epistolary narration wishes, that to travel, and to tell his travels, had been more of his employment; but it is by studying at home that we must obtain the ability of travelling with intelligence and improvement.

His travels and his studies were now near their end. The gout, of which he had sustained many weak attacks, fell upon his stomach, and, yielding to no medicines, produced strong convulsions, which (July 30, 1771) terminated in death.

His character I am willing to adopt, as Mr. Mason has done, from a nameless writer;[3] and am as willing as his warmest friend[4] to believe it true.

> Perhaps he was the most learned man in Europe. He was equally acquainted with the elegant and profound parts of science, and that not superficially but thoroughly. He knew every branch of history, both natural and civil; had read all the original historians of England, France, and Italy; and was a great antiquarian. Criticism, metaphysics, morals, politics, made a principal part of his study; voyages and travels of all sorts were his favourite amusements; and he had a fine taste in painting, prints, architecture, and gardening. With such a fund of knowledge, his conversation must have been equally instructing and entertaining; but he was also a good man, a man of virtue and humanity. There is no character without some speck, some imperfection; and I think the greatest defect in his was an affectation in delicacy, or rather effeminacy, and a visible fastidious-

[2] Languages: History *1783*
[3] nameless writer: letter written to my friend Mr. Boswell, by the Rev. Mr. Temple, rector of St. Gluvias in Cornwall *1783*. (Johnson wrote Boswell in August 1782, saying that he had forgotten the name of the writer, which Boswell had evidently told him after seeing the first edition.)
[4] friend: well-wisher *1783*

ness, or contempt and disdain of his inferiors in science. He also had, in some degree, that weakness which disgusted Voltaire so much in Mr. Congreve: though he seemed to value others chiefly according to the progress they had made in knowledge, yet he could not bear to be considered himself merely as a man of letters; and though without birth, or fortune, or station, his desire was to be looked upon as a private independent gentleman, who read for his amusement. Perhaps it may be said, What signifies so much knowledge, when it produced so little? Is it worth taking so much pains to leave no memorial but a few poems? But let it be considered that Mr. Gray was, to others, at least innocently employed; to himself, certainly beneficially. His time passed agreeably; he was every day making some new acquisition in science; his mind was enlarged, his heart softened, his virtue strengthened; the world and mankind were shewn to him without a mask; and he was taught to consider every thing as trifling, and unworthy of the attention of a wise man, except the pursuit of knowledge and practice of virtue, in that state wherein God hath placed us.

To this character Mr. Mason has added a more particular account of Gray's skill in zoology. He has remarked, that Gray's effeminacy was affected most *before those whom he did not wish to please;*[5] and that he is unjustly charged with making knowledge his sole reason of preference, as he paid his esteem to none whom he did not likewise believe to be good.

What has occurred to me, from the slight inspection of his letters in which my undertaking has engaged me, is, that his mind had a large grasp; that his curiosity was unlimited, and his judgement cultivated; that he was a man likely to love much where he loved at all, but that he was fastidious and hard to please. His contempt however is often employed, where I hope it will be approved, upon scepticism and infidelity. His short account of Shaftesbury I will insert.

> You say you cannot conceive how Lord Shaftesbury came to be a philosopher in vogue; I will tell you: first, he was a lord; secondly, he was as vain as any of his readers; thirdly, men are

[5] Mason, *Gray*, 1775, 403.

> very prone to believe what they do not understand; fourthly, they will believe any thing at all, provided they are under no obligation to believe it; fifthly, they love to take a new road, even when that road leads no where; sixthly, he was reckoned a fine writer, and seems always to mean more than he said. Would you have any more reasons? An interval of above forty years has pretty well destroyed the charm. A dead lord ranks with commoners: vanity is no longer interested in the matter, for a new road is become an old one.[6]

Mr. Mason has added, from his own knowledge, that though Gray was poor, he was not eager of money; and that, out of the little that he had, he was very willing to help the necessitous.

As a writer he had this peculiarity, that he did not write hi pieces first rudely, and then correct them, but laboured every lin as it arose in the train of composition; and he had a notion n very peculiar, that he could not write but at certain times, or happy moments; a fantastick foppery, to which my kindness f a man of learning and of virtue wishes him to have been superi

---

Gray's poetry is now to be considered; and I hope not t looked on as an enemy to his name, if I confess that I contem it with less pleasure than his life.

His ode on *Spring* has something poetical, both in the lang and the thought; but the language is too luxuriant, and thoughts have nothing new. There has of late arisen a practi giving to adjectives, derived from substantives, the termi of participles; such as the *cultured* plain, the *dasied* bank; was sorry to see, in the lines of a scholar like Gray, the *h* spring. The morality is natural, but too stale; the conclus pretty.

The poem on the *Cat* was doubtless by its author cons

[6] From a letter to Stonehewer, August 18, 1758, printed by Mason.
[7] Mason, *Gray*, 335.

Gray seems in his rapture to confound the images of *spreading sound* and *running water*. A *stream of musick* may be allowed; but where does *musick*, however *smooth and strong*, after having visited the *verdant vales, rowl down the steep amain*, so as that *rocks and nodding groves rebellow to the roar?* If this be said of *musick*, it is nonsense; if it be said of *water*, it is nothing to the purpose.

The second stanza, exhibiting Mars's car and Jove's eagle, is unworthy of further notice. Criticism disdains to chase a school-boy to his common places.

To the third it may likewise be objected, that it is drawn from mythology, though such as may be more easily assimilated to real life. Idalia's *velvet-green* has something of cant. An epithet or metaphor drawn from Nature ennobles Art; an epithet or metaphor drawn from Art degrades Nature. Gray is too fond of words arbitrarily compounded. *Many-twinkling* was formerly censured as not analogical; we may say *many-spotted*, but scarcely *many-spotting*. This stanza, however, has something pleasing.

Of the second ternary of stanzas, the first endeavours to tell something, and would have told it, had it not been crossed by Hyperion: the second describes well enough the universal prevalence of poetry; but I am afraid that the conclusion will not rise from the premises. The caverns of the North and the plains of Chili are not the residences of *glory* and *generous shame*. But that Poetry and Virtue go always together is an opinion so pleasing, that I can forgive him who resolves to think it true.

The third stanza sounds big with Delphi, and Egean, and Ilissus, and Meander, and *hallowed fountain* and *solemn sound;* but in all Gray's odes there is a kind of cumbrous splendor which we wish away. His position is at last false: in the time of Dante and Petrarch, from whom he derives our first school of poetry, Italy was over-run by *tyrant power* and *coward vice;* nor was our state much better when we first borrowed the Italian arts.

Of the third ternary, the first gives a mythological birth of Shakespeare. What is said of that mighty genius is true; but it is not said happily: the real effects of his poetical power are put out of sight by the pomp of machinery. Where truth is sufficient to fill the mind, fiction is worse than useless; the counterfeit debases the genuine.

His account of Milton's blindness, if we suppose it caused by study in the formation of his poem, a supposition surely allowable, is poetically true, and happily imagined. But the *car* of Dryden, with his *two coursers*, has nothing in it peculiar; it is a car in which any other rider may be placed.

The Bard appears, at the first view, to be, as Algarotti[9] and others have remarked, an imitation of the prophecy of Nereus.[1] Algarotti thinks it superior to its original; and, if preference depends only on the imagery and animation of the two poems, his judgement is right. There is in *The Bard* more force, more thought, and more variety. But to copy is less than to invent, and the copy has been unhappily produced at a wrong time. The fiction of Horace was to the Romans credible; but its revival disgusts us with apparent and unconquerable falsehood. *Incredulus odi.*[2]

To select a singular event, and swell it to a giant's bulk by fabulous appendages of spectres and predictions, has little difficulty, for he that forsakes the probable may always find the marvellous; and it has little use, we are affected only as we believe; we are improved only as we find something to be imitated or declined. I do not see that *The Bard* promotes any truth, moral or political.

His stanzas are too long, especially his epodes; the ode is finished before the ear has learned its measures, and consequently before it can receive pleasure from their consonance and recurrence.

Of the first stanza the abrupt beginning has been celebrated, but technical beauties can give praise only to the inventor. It is in the power of any man to rush abruptly upon his subject, that has read the ballad of *Johnny Armstrong*.

Is there ever a man in all Scotland—

The initial resemblances, or alliterations, *ruin, ruthless, helm nor hauberk*, are below the grandeur of a poem that endeavours at sublimity.

In the second stanza the Bard is well described; but in the third we have the puerilities of obsolete mythology. When we are told

[9] Count Francesco Algarotti (1712–64), Italian critic.

[1] Horace, *Odes*, I.15

[2] Horace, *Ars Poetica*, l. 188: "Unbelieving, I hate it."

that Cadwallo *hush'd the stormy main,* and that Modred *made huge Plinlimmon bow his cloud-top'd head,* attention recoils from the repetition of a tale that, even when it was first heard, was heard with scorn.

The *weaving* of the *winding sheet* he borrowed, as he owns, from the northern bards; but their texture, however, was very properly the work of female powers, as the art of spinning the thread of life in another mythology. Theft is always dangerous; Gray has made weavers of his slaughtered bards, by a fiction outrageous and incongruous. They are then called upon to *Weave the warp, and weave the woof,* perhaps with no great propriety; for it is by crossing the *woof* with the *warp* that men *weave* the *web* or piece; and the first line was dearly bought by the admission of its wretched correspondent, *Give ample room and verge enough.* He has, however, no other line as bad.

The third stanza of the second ternary is commended, I think, beyond its merit. The personification is indistinct. Thirst and Hunger are not alike; and their features, to make the imagery perfect, should have been discriminated. We are told, in the same stanza, how *towers* are *fed.* But I will no longer look for particular faults; yet let it be observed that the ode might have been concluded with an action of better example; but suicide is always to be had, without expence of thought.

These odes are marked by glittering accumulations of ungraceful ornaments; they strike rather than please; the images are magnified by affectation; the language is laboured into harshness. The mind of the writer seems to work with unnatural violence. *Double, double, toil and trouble.* He has a kind of strutting dignity, and is tall by walking on tiptoe. His art and his struggle are too visible, and there is too little appearance of ease or[3] nature.

To say that he has no beauties would be unjust: a man like him, of great learning and great industry, could not but produce something valuable. When he pleases least, it can only be said that a good design was ill directed.

His translations of Northern and Welsh poetry deserve praise; the imagery is preserved, perhaps often improved; but the language is unlike the language of other poets.

In the character of his *Elegy* I rejoice to concur with the com-

---

[3] ease or: ease and *1783*

mon reader; for by the common sense of readers uncorrupted with literary prejudices, after all the refinements of subtilty and the dogmatism of learning, must be finally decided all claim to poetical honours. The *Church-yard* abounds with images which find a mirrour in every mind, and with sentiments to which every bosom returns an echo. The four stanzas beginning *Yet even these bones* are to me original: I have never seen the notions in any other place; yet he that reads them here, persuades himself that he has always felt them. Had Gray written often thus, it had been vain to blame, and useless to praise him.

Although Johnson encouraged Percy to reprint poetry of the late Middle Ages and early Renaissance, he thought modern imitations ridiculous. The first of the following four poems is a general criticism of Thomas Warton's Poems *of 1777, the second is a parody. The third and fourth attack Percy's version of the simple ballad style in his long original poem,* The Hermit of Warkworth. *Text of the first as recorded by Mrs. Thrale, the rest from Boswell.*

Light Verse

Lines written in ridicule of Thomas Warton's Poems

Wheresoe'er I turn my view,
All is strange, yet nothing new;
Endless labour all along,
Endless labour to be wrong;
Phrase that time has flung away, 5
Uncouth words in disarray:
Trickt in antique ruff and bonnet,
Ode and elegy and sonnet.

Parody of Thomas Warton

Hermit hoar, in solemn cell,
  Wearing out life's evening gray;
Smite thy bosom, sage, and tell,
  Where is bliss? and which the way?

Thus I spoke; and speaking sigh'd; 5

——Scarce repress'd the starting tear;——
When the smiling sage reply'd——
——Come, my lad, and drink some beer.

Parodies of The Hermit of Warkworth

The tender infant meek and mild
Fell down upon a stone;
The nurse took up the squealing child
But yet the child squeal'd on.

I put my hat upon my head
And walk'd into the Strand,
And there I met another man
Who's hat was in his hand.

A Short Song of Congratulation

Johnson wrote only one personal satire—on Thrale's nephew, Sir John Lade, whom he had not advised to marry, as he was "not likely to propagate understanding." Sir John married a prostitute and fulfilled Johnson's forecast in this poem by squandering his fortune.

Long-expected one and twenty
Ling'ring year at last is flown,
Pomp and pleasure, pride and plenty
Great Sir John, are all your own.

Loosen'd from the minor's tether, 5
Free to mortgage or to sell,
Wild as wind, and light as feather
Bid the slaves of thrift farewell.

Call the Bettys, Kates, and Jennys
Ev'ry name that laughs at care, 10

Lavish of your grandsire's guineas,
 Show the spirit of an heir.

All that prey on vice and folly
 Joy to see their quarry fly,
Here the gamester light and jolly 15
 There the lender grave and sly.

Wealth, Sir John, was made to wander,
 Let it wander as it will;
See the jocky, see the pander,
 Bid them come, and take their fill. 20

When the bonny blade carouses,
 Pockets full, and spirits high,
What are acres? What are houses?
 Only dirt, or wet or dry.

If the guardian or the mother 25
 Tell the woes of wilful waste,
Scorn their counsel and their pother,
 You can hang or drown at last.

Letters

To the Right Honourable the Earl of Chesterfield

February, 1755

My Lord,

I have been lately informed, by the proprietor of the World, that two papers, in which my Dictionary is recommended to the publick, were written by your Lordship. To be so distinguished, is an honour, which, being very little accustomed to favours from the great, I know not well how to receive, or in what terms to acknowledge.

When, upon some slight encouragement, I first visited your Lordship, I was overpowered, like the rest of mankind, by the enchantment of your address; and could not forbear to wish that I might boast myself *Le vainqueur du vainqueur de la terre;*[1]—that I might obtain that regard for which I saw the world contending; but I found my attendance so little encouraged, that neither pride nor modesty would suffer me to continue it. When I had once addressed your Lordship in publick, I had exhausted all the art of pleasing which a retired and uncourtly scholar can possess. I had done all that I could; and no man is well pleased to have his all neglected, be it ever so little.

Seven years, my Lord, have now past, since I waited in your outward rooms, or was repulsed from your door; during which time I have been pushing on my work through difficulties, of which it is useless to complain, and have brought it, at last, to the verge of publication, without one act of assistance, one word of encouragement, or one smile of favour. Such treatment I did not expect, for I never had a Patron before.

The shepherd in Virgil grew at last acquainted with Love, and found him a native of the rocks.[2]

---

[1] Modified from Boileau, *L'Art poétique,* III.272.

[2] *Eclogues,* VIII.43.

Is not a Patron, my Lord, one who looks with unconcern on a man struggling for life in the water, and, when he has reached ground, encumbers him with help? The notice which you have been pleased to take of my labours, had it been early, had been kind; but it has been delayed till I am indifferent, and cannot enjoy it; till I am solitary, and cannot impart it; till I am known, and do not want it. I hope it is no very cynical asperity not to confess obligations where no benefit has been received, or to be unwilling that the publick should consider me as owing that to a Patron, which Providence has enabled me to do for myself.

Having carried on my work thus far with so little obligation to any favourer of learning, I shall not be disappointed though I should conclude it, if less be possible, with less; for I have been long wakened from that dream of hope, in which I once boasted myself with so much exultation,

My Lord,
Your Lordship's most humble,
Most obedient servant,
SAM. JOHNSON.

To the Right Honourable the Earl of Bute

MY LORD,

When the bills were yesterday delivered to me by Mr. Wedderburne, I was informed by him of the future favours which his Majesty has, by your Lordship's recommendation, been induced to intend for me.

Bounty always receives part of its value from the manner in which it is bestowed; your Lordship's kindness includes every circumstance that can gratify delicacy, or enforce obligation. You have conferred your favours on a man who has neither alliance nor interest, who has not merited them by services, nor courted them by officiousness; you have spared him the shame of solicitation, and the anxiety of suspense.

What has been thus elegantly given, will, I hope, not be reproachfully enjoyed; I shall endeavour to give your Lordship the only recompense which generosity desires,—the gratification of finding that your benefits are not improperly bestowed. I am, my Lord,

Your Lordship's most obliged,
Most obedient, and most humble servant,
SAM. JOHNSON.

July 20, 1762.

To Miss Susanna Thrale

July, 1783

DEAREST MISS SUSY,[3]

When you favoured me with your letter, you seemed to be in want of materials to fill it, having met with no great adventures either of peril or delight, nor done or suffered any thing out of the common course of life.

When you have lived longer, and considered more, you will find the common course of life very fertile of observation and reflection. Upon the common course of life must our thoughts and our conversation be generally employed. Our general course of life must denominate us wise or foolish; happy or miserable: if it is well regulated we pass on prosperously and smoothly; as it is neglected we live in embarrassment, perplexity, and uneasiness.

Your time, my love, passes, I suppose, in devotion, reading, work, and company. Of your devotions, in which I earnestly advise you to be very punctual, you may not perhaps think it proper to give me an account; and of work, unless I understood it better, it will be of no great use to say much; but books and company will always supply you with materials for your letters to me, as I shall always be pleased to know what you are reading, and with what you are pleased; and shall take great delight in knowing what impression new modes or new characters make upon you, and to observe with what attention you distinguish the tempers, dispositions, and abilities of your companions.

A letter may be always made out of the books of the morning

[3] Susy was thirteen at this date.

or talk of the evening; and any letters from you, my dearest, will be welcome to

SAM. JOHNSON.

To Mrs. Thrale[4]

MADAM

If I interpret your letter right, you are ignominiously married; if it is yet undone, let us once talk together. If you have abandoned your children and your religion, God forgive your wickedness: if you have forfeited your fame and your country, may your folly do no further mischief.

If the last act is yet to do, I who have loved you, esteemed you, reverenced you, and served you, I who long thought you the first of humankind, entreat that, before your fate is irrevocable, I may once more see you. I was, I once was,

Madam, most truly yours,
SAM. JOHNSON.

July 2, 1784.
I will come down, if you permit it.

To Mrs. Thrale

London, July 8, 1784.

DEAR MADAM,

What you have done, however I may lament it, I have no pretence to resent, as it has not been injurious to me: I therefore

[4] Johnson had been intimate with the Thrales for almost twenty years, and on Thrale's death in 1781, had been an executor of his will and a guardian of his children. That Mrs. Thrale was marrying at all would probably have disturbed Johnson, since he loved her, but that she was marrying her children's music teacher, an Italian and a Catholic, was more than he could bear. Hence this rough letter. Mrs. Thrale replied quietly, with dignity and affection, and Johnson's last letter to her shows him in control of his emotions. He died five months later.

breathe out one sigh more of tenderness, perhaps useless, but at least sincere.

I wish that God may grant you every blessing, that you may be happy in this world for its short continuance, and eternally happy in a better state; and whatever I can contribute to your happiness I am very ready to repay, for that kindness which soothed twenty years of a life radically wretched.

Do not think slightly of the advice which I now presume to offer. Prevail upon Mr. Piozzi to settle in England: you may live here with more dignity than in Italy, and with more security: your rank will be higher, and your fortune more under your own eye. I desire not to detail all my reasons, but every argument of prudence and interest is for England, and only some phantoms of imagination seduce you to Italy.

I am afraid however that my counsel is vain, yet I have eased my heart by giving it.

When Queen Mary took the resolution of sheltering herself in England, the Archbishop of St. Andrew's, attempting to dissuade her, attended on her journey; and when they came to the irremeable stream that separated the two kingdoms, walked by her side into the water, in the middle of which he seized her bridle, and with earnestness proportioned to her danger and his own affection pressed her to return. The Queen went forward.——If the parallel reaches thus far, may it go no further.—The tears stand in my eyes.

I am going into Derbyshire, and hope to be followed by your good wishes, for I am, with great affection,

Your most humble servant,

SAM. JOHNSON.

Any letters that come for me hither will be sent me.

In the references, "Misc." *is Hill's* Johnsonian Miscellanies; *all other references are to Hill's Boswell. Page numbers for the latter remain the same for Dr. L.F. Powell's revision, 1934–50.*

Johnson Talking

absurd. When people see a man absurd in what they understand, they may conclude the same of him in what they do not understand. II.466.

absurdity. Let him be absurd, I beg of you: when a monkey is *too* like a man, it shocks one. *Misc.*, I.204.

action. Sir, you must not neglect doing a thing immediately good, from fear of remote evil;—from fear of its being abused. A man who has candles may sit up too late, which he would not do if he had not candles; but nobody will deny that the art of making candles, by which light is continued to us beyond the time that the sun gives us light, is a valuable art, and ought to be preserved. II.188.

What *must* be done, Sir, *will* be done. I.202.

admiration. Very near to admiration is the wish to admire. Every man willingly gives value to the praise which he receives, and considers the sentence passed in his favour as the sentence of discernment. III.411, n.2.

amusements. I am a great friend to publick amusements, for they keep people from vice. II.169.

applause. The applause of a single human being is of great consequence. IV.32.

A man who is used to the applause of the House of Commons, has no wish for that of a private company. A man accustomed to throw for a thousand pounds, if set down to throw for sixpence, would not be at the pains to count his dice. IV.167.

attorney. "He did not care to speak ill of any man behind his back, but he believed the gentleman was an *attorney*." II.126.

authors. Sir, it was like leading one to talk of a book, when the authour is concealed behind the door. I.396.

He is the richest authour that ever grazed the common of literature. I.418, n. 1. [On Dr. Campbell]

Authors are like privateers, always fair game for one another. IV.191, n. 1.

avarice. You despise a man for avarice, but do not hate him. III.71.

barrenness. All barrenness is comparative. III.76.

bawdy-house. Sir, your wife, *under pretence of keeping a bawdy-house,* is a receiver of stolen goods. IV.26.

beauty. Insipid beauty would not go a great way; and . . . such a woman might be cut out of a cabbage, if there was a skilful artificer. V.231.

belief. Every man who attacks my belief, diminishes in some degree my confidence in it, and therefore makes me uneasy; and I am angry with him who makes me uneasy. III.10.

belly. Some people have a foolish way of not minding, or pretending not to mind, what they eat. For my part, I mind my belly very studiously, and very carefully; for I look upon it, that he who does not mind his belly will hardly mind any thing else. I.467.

bishop. A bishop has nothing to do at a tippling-house. IV.75.

books. Mankind could do better without your books, than without my shoes. I.448.

What is written without effort is in general read without pleasure. *Misc.*, II.309.

boredom. Five hours of the four-and-twenty unemployed are enough for a man to go mad in. *Misc.*, I.301.

bores. He talked to me at club one day concerning Catiline's conspiracy—so I withdrew my attention, and thought about Tom Thumb. *Misc.*, I.203.

Boswell. If your company does not drive a man out of his house, nothing will. III.315.

brandy. He who aspires to be a hero must drink brandy. III.381.

bravery. Bravery has no place where it can avail nothing. IV.395.

cant. A man who has been canting all his life, may cant to the last. III.270. [On Dr. Dodd]

Clear your *mind* of cant. IV.221.

character. Derrick may do very well, as long as he can outrun his character; but the moment his character gets up with him, it is all over. I.394.

The greater part of mankind have no character at all. III.280, n.3.

charity. There is as much charity in helping a man down-hill, as in helping him up-hill. V.243.

Chesterfield. This man I thought had been a lord among wits; but, I find, he is only a wit among lords. I.266.

Chesterfield ought to know me better than to think me capable of contracting myself into a dwarf that he may be thought a giant. *Misc.*, I.405, n.2.

I have sailed a long and painful voyage round the world of the English language; and does he now send out two cock-boats to tow me into harbour? *Misc.*, I.405.

Chesterfield's *Letters*. They teach the morals of a whore, and the manners of a dancing master. I.266.

chief. He has no more the soul of a chief, than an attorney who has twenty houses in a street, and considers how much he can make by them. V.378.

cities. A great city is, to be sure, the school for studying life. III.253.

clergy. I have always considered a clergyman as the father of a larger family than he is able to maintain. III.304.

A clergyman's diligence always makes him venerable. III.438.

comedy. I know of no comedy for many years that has so much exhilarated an audience, that has answered so much the great end of comedy—making an audience merry. II.233.

concentration. Depend upon it, Sir, when a man knows he is to be hanged in a fortnight, it concentrates his mind wonderfully. III.167.

conscience. In questions of law, or of fact, conscience is very often confounded with opinion. No man's conscience can tell him the rights of another man; they must be known by rational investigation or historical enquiry. II.243.

contempt. No man loves to be treated with contempt. III.385.

contradiction. What harm does it do to any man to be contradicted? IV.280.

conversation. I never desire to converse with a man who has written more than he has read. II.48, n.2. [On Kelly]

His conversation usually threatened and announced more

than it performed; . . . he fed you with a continual renovation of hope, to end in a constant succession of disappointment. II.122.

A flea has taken you such a time, that a lion must have served you a twelvemonth. II.194.

Never speak of a man in his own presence. It is always indelicate, and may be offensive. II.472.

Questioning is not the mode of conversation among gentlemen. II.472.

Men might be very eminent in a profession, without our perceiving any particular power of mind in them in conversation. It seems strange that a man should see so far to the right, who sees so short a way to the left. IV.19.

We had *talk* enough, but no *conversation;* there was nothing *discussed.* IV.186.

cordiality. Sir, he has no grimace, no gesticulation, no bursts of admiration on trivial occasions; he never embraces you with an overacted cordiality. IV.27.

country. They who are content to live in the country, are *fit* for the country. IV.338.

cow. A cow is a very good animal in the field; but we turn her out of a garden. II.187.

criticism. A fly, Sir, may sting a stately horse and make him wince, but one is but an insect, and the other is a horse still. I.263, n.3.

You *may* abuse a tragedy, though you cannot write one. You may scold a carpenter who has made you a bad table, though you cannot make a table. It is not your trade to make tables. I.409.

I would rather be attacked than unnoticed. For the worst thing you can do to an authour is to be silent as to his works. III.375.

Never let criticisms operate upon your face or your mind; it is very rarely that an authour is hurt by his criticks. The blaze of reputation cannot be blown out, but it often dies in the socket. III.423.

critics. He has a rage for saying something, when there's nothing to be said. I.329. [On Warburton]

Never mind whether they praise or abuse your writings; anything is tolerable, except oblivion. *Misc.*, II.207.

cunning. Cunning has effect from the credulity of others, rather than from the abilities of those who are cunning. It requires no extraordinary talents to lie and deceive. V.217.

death. It matters not how a man dies, but how he lives. The act of dying is not of importance, it lasts so short a time. A man knows it must be so, and submits. It will do him no good to whine. II.106.

I will be conquered; I will not capitulate. IV.374.

If one was to think constantly of death, the business of life would stand still. V.316.

debaters. Why, yes, Sir, they'll do any thing, no matter how odd, or desperate, to gain their point; they'll catch hold of the red-hot end of a poker, sooner than not get possession of it. *Misc.*, II.397.

debt, national. Let the publick creditors be ever so clamorous, the interest of millions must ever prevail over that of thousands. II.127.

description. Description only excites curiosity: seeing satisfies it. IV.199.

despotism. A country governed by a despot is an inverted cone. III.283.

devil. Let him go to some place where he is *not* known. Don't let him go to the devil where he *is* known. V.54.

dictionaries. Dictionaries are like watches, the worst is better than none, and the best cannot be expected to go quite true. I.293, n.3.

dignity. He that encroaches on another's dignity puts himself in his power. IV.62.

dinner. A man seldom thinks with more earnestness of any thing than he does of his dinner; and if he cannot get that well dressed, he should be suspected of inaccuracy in other things. I.467, n.2.

This was a good enough dinner, to be sure; but it was not a dinner to *ask* a man to. I.470.

dirt. By those who look close to the ground, dirt will be seen. II.82, n.3.

dislike. Nothing is more common than mutual dislike, where mutual approbation is particularly expected. III.423.

dispute. Every man will dispute with great good humour upon a subject in which he is not interested. I will dispute very calmly upon the probability of another man's son being hanged. III.11.

I know nothing more offensive than repeating what one knows to be foolish things, by way of continuing a dispute, to see what a man will answer,—to make him your butt! III.350.

distance. Sir, it is surprising how people will go to a distance for what they may have at home. V.286.

distinctions. All distinctions are trifles, because great things can seldom occur, and those distinctions are settled by custom. III.355.

distress. People in distress never think that you feel enough. II.469.

dropped. There are people whom one should like very well to drop, but would not wish to be dropped by. IV.73.

drunkenness. A man who exposes himself when he is intoxicated, has not the art of getting drunk. III.389.

He who makes a *beast* of himself, gets rid of the pain of being a *man.* II.435, n.7.

education. I cannot see that lectures can do so much good as reading the books from which the lectures are taken. I know nothing that can be best taught by lectures, except where experiments are to be shewn. You may teach chymistry by lectures.—You might teach making of shoes by lectures! II.7.

endurance. Where there is nothing to be *done* something must be *endured. Misc.*, I.210.

Englishman. We value an Englishman highly in this country, and yet Englishmen are not rare in it. III.10.

epigram. Why, Sir, he may not be a judge of an epigram: but you see he is a judge of what is *not* an epigram. III.259.

exercise. I take the true definition of exercise to be labour without weariness. IV.151, n.1.

exhibitionism. He wants to make himself conspicuous. He would tumble in a hogstye, as long as you looked at him and called to him to come out. I.432.

fame. Ah! Sir, a boy's being flogged is not so severe as a man's having the hiss of the world against him. Men have a solicitude about fame; and the greater share they have of it, the more afraid they are of losing it. I.451.

Sir, he is one of the many who have made themselves *publick,* without making themselves *known.* I.498. [On Kenrick]

Every man has a lurking wish to appear considerable in his native place. II.141.

flattery. Dearest lady, consider with yourself what your flattery is worth, before you bestow it so freely. IV.341.

You may be bribed by flattery. V.306.

flogging. There is now less flogging in our great schools than formerly, but then less is learned there; so that what the boys get at one end, they lose at the other. II.407.

food. A man does not love to go to a place from whence he comes out exactly as he went in. IV.90.

Frenchman. A Frenchman must be always talking, whether he knows any thing of the matter or not; an Englishman is content to say nothing, when he has nothing to say. IV.15.

friendship. If a man does not make new acquaintance as he advances through life, he will soon find himself left alone. A man, Sir, should keep his friendship *in constant repair.* I.300.

Every heart must lean to somebody. I.515.

Always, Sir, set a high value on spontaneous kindness. He whose inclination prompts him to cultivate your friendship of his own accord, will love you more than one whom you have been at pains to attach to you. IV.115.

Most friendships are formed by caprice or by chance, mere confederacies in vice or leagues in folly. IV.280.

And this is the voice of female friendship I suppose, when the hand of the hangman would be softer. *Misc.*, I.331.

Garrick. No wonder, Sir, that he is vain; a man who is perpetually flattered in every mode that can be conceived. So many bellows have blown the fire, that one wonders he is not by this time become a cinder. II.227.

gaiety. Gayety is a duty when health requires it. III.136, n.2.

Solitude is dangerous to reason, without being favourable to virtue: pleasures of some sort are necessary to the intellectual as to the corporeal health; and those who resist gaiety, will be likely for the most part to fall a sacrifice to appetite; for the solicitations of sense are always at hand, and a dram to a vacant and solitary person is a speedy and seducing relief. *Misc.*, I.219.

genius. A man of genius has been seldom ruined but by himself. I.381.

Sir, a man cannot make fire but in proportion as he has fuel. He cannot coin guineas but in proportion as he has gold. V.229.

gestures. Action can have no effect upon reasonable minds. It may augment noise, but it never can enforce argument. II.211.

Giants' Causeway. Worth seeing, yes; but not worth going to see. III.410.

Goldsmith. He goes on without knowing how he is to get off. His genius is great, but his knowledge is small. II.196.

When people find a man of the most distinguished abilities as a writer, their inferiour while he is with them, it must be highly gratifying to them. II.235.

He was not an agreeable companion, for he talked always for fame. A man who does so never can be pleasing. The man who talks to unburthen his mind is the man to delight you. III.247.

No man was more foolish when he had not a pen in his hand, or more wise when he had. IV.29.

graces. Every man of any education would rather be called a rascal, than accused of deficiency in *the graces*. III.54.

grave. We shall receive no letters in the grave. IV.413.

great. A man would never undertake great things, could he be amused with small. III.242.

grief. All unnecessary grief is unwise. III.136.

Grief is a species of idleness. III.136, n.2.

hanged. Do you think that a man the night before he is to be hanged cares for the succession of a royal family? III.270.

happiness. If a bull could speak, he might as well exclaim,—Here am I with this cow and this grass; what being can enjoy greater felicity? II.228.

hate. Men hate more steadily than they love. III.150.

headache. Nay, Sir, it was not the *wine* that made your head ache, but the *sense* that I put into it. III.381.

heaven. A man who cannot get to heaven in a green coat, will not find his way thither the sooner in a grey one. III.188, n.4.

histories. This is my history; like all other histories, a narrative of misery. IV.362.

hypocrite. No man is a hypocrite in his pleasures. IV.316.

ignorance. A man may choose whether he will have abstemiousness and knowledge, or claret and ignorance. III.335.

ignorant. To help the ignorant commonly requires much patience, for the ignorant are always trying to be cunning. V.217, n.1.

immortality. If it were not for the notion of immortality, he would cut a throat to fill his pockets. II.359.

impressions. Do not, Sir, accustom yourself to trust to *impressions.* There is a middle state of mind between conviction and hypocrisy, of which many are conscious. By trusting to impressions, a man may gradually come to yield to them, and at length be subject to them, so as not to be a free agent, or what is the same thing in effect, to *suppose* that he is not a free agent. IV.122.

inaction. Rather to do nothing than to do good, is the lowest state of a degraded mind. IV.352.

infidel. If he be an infidel, he is an infidel as a dog is an infidel; that is to say, he has never thought upon the subject. II.95. [On Foote]

ingratitude. Why, Sir, a man is very apt to complain of the ingratitude of those who have risen far above him. III.2.

intrepidity. He has an intrepidity of talk, whether he understands the subject or not. V.330.

ivory tower. I hate a fellow whom pride, or cowardice, or laziness drives into a corner, and who does nothing when he is there but sit and *growl*; let him come out as I do, and *bark*. IV.161, n.3.

jealous. Little people are apt to be jealous. III.55.

judge. A judge may be a farmer; but he is not to geld his own pigs. II.344.

kindness. Getting money is not all a man's business: to cultivate kindness is a valuable part of the business of life. III.182.

knowledge. Sir, a desire of knowledge is the natural feeling of mankind; and every human being, whose mind is not debauched, will be willing to give all that he has to get knowledge. I.458.

A man must carry knowledge with him, if he would bring home knowledge. III.302.

If it rained knowledge I'd hold out my hand; but I would not give myself the trouble to go in quest of it. III.344.

labor. No man loves labour for itself. II.99.

language. [Chinese] is only more difficult from its rudeness; as there is more labour in hewing down a tree with a stone than with an axe. III.339.

languages. Languages are the pedigree of nations. V.225.

law. Let us hear, Sir, no general abuse; the law is the last result of human wisdom acting upon human experience for the benefit of the public. *Misc.*, I.223.

lawyers. Sir, a man will no more carry the artifice of the bar into the common intercourse of society, than a man who is paid for tumbling upon his hands will continue to tumble upon his hands when he should walk on his feet. II.48.

Lawyers know life practically. A bookish man should always have them to converse with. III.306.

learning. Their learning is like bread in a besieged town: every man gets a little, but no man gets a full meal. II.363.

In England, any man who wears a sword and a powdered wig is ashamed to be illiterate. III.254.

He has a great deal of learning; but it never lies straight. IV.225.

lectures. Sir, you have sconced me two-pence for non-attendance at a lecture not worth a penny. *Misc.*, I.164, n.5.

letter writing. A short letter to a distant friend is, in my opinion, an insult like that of a slight bow or cursory salutation;—a proof of unwillingness to do much, even where there is a necessity of doing something. I.361.

levellers. Your levellers wish to level *down* as far as themselves; but they cannot bear levelling *up* to themselves. I.448.

liar. As it is said of the greatest liar, that he tells more truth than falsehood; so it may be said of the worst man, that he does more good than evil. III.236.

liberty. The notion of liberty amuses the people of England, and helps to keep off the *taedium vitae*. When a butcher tells you that *his heart bleeds for his country,* he has, in fact, no uneasy feeling. I.394.

Every man has a right to liberty of conscience, and with that the magistrate cannot interfere. People confound liberty of thinking with liberty of talking; nay, with liberty of preaching. II.249.

How is it that we hear the loudest *yelps* for liberty among the drivers of negroes? III.201.

lie. If I accustom a servant to tell a lie for *me,* have I not reason to apprehend that he will tell many lies for *himself?* I.436.

Sir, don't tell me of deception; a lie, Sir, is a lie, whether it be a lie to the eye or a lie to the ear. *Misc.,* II.428.

life. Life is a pill which none of us can bear to swallow without gilding; yet for the poor we delight in stripping it still barer, and are not ashamed to shew even visible displeasure, if ever the bitter taste is taken from their mouths. *Misc.,* I.205.

Life is barren enough surely with all her trappings; let us therefore be cautious how we strip her. *Misc.,* I.345.

literary men. A mere literary man is a *dull* man; a man who is solely a man of business is a *selfish* man; but when literature and commerce are united, they make a *respectable* man. *Misc.,* II.389.

London. No, Sir, when a man is tired of London he is tired of life; for there is in London all that life can afford. III.178.

lords. Great lords and great ladies don't love to have their mouths stopped. IV.116.

love. It is commonly a weak man who marries for love. III.3.

[Love is] the wisdom of a fool and the folly of the wise. *Misc.,* II.393.

luxury. No nation was ever hurt by luxury; for . . . it can reach but to a very few. II. 218.

madness. With some people, gloomy penitence is only madness turned upside down. III.27.

mankind. As I know more of mankind I expect less of them. IV.239.

manners. When you have said a man of gentle manners; you have said enough. IV.28.

Sir, it is very bad manners to carry provisions to any man's house, as if he could not entertain you. To an inferior, it is oppressive; to a superior, it is insolent. V.73.

man of the world. One may be so much a man of the world as to be nothing in the world. III.375.

marriage. I would advise no man to marry, Sir, who is not likely to propagate understanding. II.109, n.2.

[After an unsuccessful first marriage, remarriage is] the triumph of hope over experience. II.128.

A man is in general better pleased when he has a good dinner upon his table, than when his wife talks Greek. *Misc.*, II.11.

All quarrels ought to be avoided studiously, particularly conjugal ones, as no one can possibly tell where they may end; besides that lasting dislike is often the consequence of occasional disgust, and that the cup of life is surely bitter enough, without squeezing in the hateful rind of resentment. *Misc.*, I.246.

melancholy. That distrust which intrudes so often on your mind is a mode of melancholy, which if it be the business of a wise man to be happy, it is foolish to indulge; and if it be a duty to preserve our faculties entire for their proper use, it is criminal. Suspicion is very often a useless pain. III.135.

memory. The true art of memory is the art of attention. IV.126, n.6.

merriment. Nothing is more hopeless than a scheme of merriment. I.331, n.5.

mind. To have the management of the mind is a great art, and it may be attained in a considerable degree by experience and habitual exercise. II.440.

misfortunes. If a man *talks* of his misfortunes, there is something in them that is not disagreeable to him; for where there is nothing but pure misery, there never is any recourse to the mention of it. IV.31.

money. A man who both spends and saves money is the happiest man, because he has both enjoyments. III.322.

morality. The morality of an action depends on the motive from which we act. If I fling half a crown to a beggar with intention to break his head, and he picks it up and buys victuals with it, the physical effect is good; but, with respect to me, the action is very wrong. I.398.

morals. If he does really think that there is no distinction between virtue and vice, why, Sir, when he leaves our houses, let us count our spoons. I.432.

Mrs. Macaulay. To endeavour to make *her* ridiculous, is like blacking the chimney. II.336.

narrowmindedness. A mind as narrow as the neck of a vinegar cruet. V.269. [On Lord North]

nearsightedness. Should I wish to become a botanist, I must first turn myself into a reptile. I.377, n.2.

neglect. All the complaints which are made of the world are unjust. I never knew a man of merit neglected: it was generally by his own fault that he failed of success. A man may hide his head in a hole: he may go into the country, and publish a book now and then, which nobody reads, and then complain he is neglected. IV.172.

old age. Contented with the exchange of fame for ease, [he] e'en resolves to let them set the pillows at his back, and gives no further proof of his existence than just to suck the jelly that prolongs it. *Misc.*, I.282.

There is nothing against which an old man should be so much upon his guard as putting himself to nurse. II. 474.

painting. Painting, Sir, can illustrate, but cannot inform. IV.321.

patriotism. Patriotism is the last refuge of a scoundrel. II.348.

patrons. General truths are seldom applied to particular occasions. . . . Every man believes that mistresses are unfaithful, and patrons capricious; but he excepts his own mistress, and his own patron. I.381.

please. It is very difficult to please a man against his will. III.69.

politeness. It [politeness] is fictitious benevolence. V.82.

politics. We are not to blow up half a dozen palaces, because one cottage is burning. II.90.

Why, Sir, most schemes of political improvement are very laughable things. II.102.

poor. A decent provision for the poor, is the true test of civilization. II.130.

poverty. There is no being so poor and so contemptible, who does not think there is somebody still poorer, and still more contemptible. II.13.

power. Where bad actions are committed at so great a distance, a delinquent can obscure the evidence till the scent becomes cold; there is a cloud between, which cannot be penetrated: therefore all distant power is bad. IV.213.

praise. He who praises every body, praises nobody. III.225, n.3.

Praise is the tribute which every man is expected to pay for the grant of perusing a manuscript. *Misc.*, II.192.

preachers. A man who preaches in the stocks will always have hearers enough. II.251.

proverb. He [a man] should take care not to be made a proverb. III.57.

reading. A man ought to read just as inclination leads him; for what he reads as a task will do him little good. I.428.

When I take up the end of a web, and find it packthread, I do not expect, by looking further, to find embroidery. II.88. [On Mrs. Montagu's *Essay on Shakespear*]

I am always for getting a boy forward in his learning; for that is a sure good. I would let him at first read *any* English book which happens to engage his attention; because you have done a great thing when you have brought him to have entertainment from a book. He'll get better books afterwards. III.385.

A man can tell but what he knows, and I never got any further than the first page. Alas, Madam! how few books are there of which one ever can possibly arrive at the *last* page! *Misc.*, I.332.

No man read[s] long together with a folio on his table: —Books that you may carry to the fire, and hold readily in your hand, are the most useful after all. *Misc.*, II.2.

reason. You may have a reason why two and two should make five; but they will still make but four. III.375.

rebellion. All rebellion is natural to man. V.394.

recommendation. Sir, it is such a recommendation, as if I should throw you out of a two-pair-of-stairs window, and recommend to you to fall soft. IV.323.

religion. Differing from a man in doctrine was no reason why you should pull his house about his ears. V.62.

reputation. You may be wise in your study in the morning, and gay in company at a tavern in the evening. Every man is to take care of his own wisdom, and his own virtue, without minding too much what others think. III.405.

resentment. Resentment gratifies him who intended an injury, and pains him unjustly who did not intend it. IV.367.

retired tradesmen. They have lost the civility of tradesmen, without acquiring the manners of gentlemen. II.120.

rich. Let me smile with the wise, and feed with the rich. II.79.

It is better to *live* rich than to *die* rich. III.304.

We are not here to sell a parcel of boilers and vats, but the potentiality of growing rich, beyond the dreams of avarice. IV.87.

right. Because a man cannot be right in all things, is he to be right in nothing? Because a man sometimes gets drunk, is he therefore to steal? III.410.

rouge. She is better employed at her toilet, than using her pen. It is better she should be reddening her own cheeks, than blackening other people's characters. III.46. [On Mrs. Macaulay]

rudeness. Sir, a man has no more right to *say* an uncivil thing, than to *act* one; no more right to say a rude thing to another than to knock him down. IV.28.

sailors. No man will be a sailor, who has contrivance enough to get himself into a jail; for, being in a ship is being in a jail, with the chance of being drowned. V.137.

schools. Placing him [a timid boy] at a public school is forcing an owl upon day. IV.312.

Scots. The noblest prospect which a Scotchman ever sees, is the high road that leads him to England. I.425.

Much may be made of a Scotchman, if he be *caught* young. II.194.

Sir, it is not so much to be lamented that Old England is lost, as that the Scotch have found it. III.78.

scruples. Whoever loads life with unnecessary scruples, Sir, provokes the attention of others on his conduct, and incurs the censure of singularity without reaping the reward of superior virtue. II.72, n.1.

secrecy. Depend upon it, Sir, he who does what he is afraid should be known, has something rotten about him. II.210.

sense. He grasps more sense than he can hold; he takes more corn than he can make into meal; he opens a wide prospect, but it is so distant, it is indistinct. IV.98. [On Mudge]

serenity. The serenity that is not felt, it can be no virtue to feign. IV.395.

Shakespeare. We must not compare the noise made by your teakettle here with the roaring of the ocean. II.86, n.1.

shooting. You may take a field piece to shoot sparrows; but all the sparrows you can bring home will not be worth the charge. V.261.

singlemindedness. That fellow seems to me to possess but one idea, and that is a wrong one. II.126.

skill. No man I suppose leaps at once into deep water who does not know how to swim. *Misc.*, I.165.

sorrow. There is no wisdom in useless and hopeless sorrow; but there is something in it so like virtue, that he who is wholly without it cannot be loved, nor will by me at least be thought worthy of esteem. III.137, n.1.

The poor and the busy have no leisure for sentimental sorrow. *Misc.*, I.252.

spelling. Never mind it, Sir; perhaps your friend spells *ocean* with an *s*. *Misc.*, II.404.

statistics. Round numbers are always false. III.226, n.4.

stupidity. Such an excess of stupidity, Sir, is not in nature. I.453.

superiority. No, Sir, I won't learn it. You shall retain your superiority by my not knowing it. II.220.

talent. He has not, indeed, many hooks; but with what hooks he has, he grapples very forcibly. II.57. [On Baretti]

talking. People may come to do any thing almost, by talking of it. V.286.

tastes. The lad does not care for the child's rattle, and the old man does not care for the young man's whore. II.14.

tavern. As soon as I enter the door of a tavern, I experience an oblivion of care, and a freedom from solicitude: when I am seated, I find the master courteous, and the servants obsequious to my call; anxious to know and ready to supply my wants: wine there exhilarates my spirits, and prompts me to free conversation and an interchange of discourse with those whom I most love: I dogmatise and am contradicted, and in this conflict of opinions and sentiments I find delight. II.452, n.1.

A tavern chair [is] the throne of human felicity. II.452, n.1.

tenderness. Want of tenderness is want of parts. II.122.

threats. I hope I shall never be deterred from detecting what I think a cheat, by the menaces of a ruffian. II.298. [To Macpherson]

time. He that runs against Time has an antagonist not subject to casualties. I.319, n.3.

travel. Jonas acquired some reputation by travelling abroad, but lost it all by travelling at home. II.122.

If a man comes to look for fishes, you cannot blame him if he does not attend to fowls. V.221.

tricks. Remember that all tricks are either knavish or childish; and that it is as foolish to make experiments upon the constancy of a friend, as upon the chastity of a wife. III.396.

truth. Hume, and other sceptical innovators, are vain men, and will gratify themselves at any expence. Truth will not afford sufficient food to their vanity; so they have betaken themselves to errour. Truth, Sir, is a cow that will yield such people no more milk, and so they are gone to milk the bull. I.444.

I would not keep company with a fellow, who lyes as long as he is sober, and whom you must make drunk before you can get a word of truth out of him. II.188.

Nobody has a right to put another under such a difficulty, that he must either hurt the person by telling the truth, or hurt himself by telling what is not true. III.320.

Every man has a right to utter what he thinks truth, and every other man has a right to knock him down for it. IV.12.

tyranny. There is a remedy in human nature against tyranny, that will keep us safe under every form of government. II.170.

uncharitable talk. Who is the worse for being talked of uncharitably? IV.97.

understanding. Sir, that is the blundering oeconomy of a narrow understanding. It is stopping one hole in a sieve. III.300.

Sir, I have found you an argument; but I am not obliged to find you an understanding. IV.313.

unsettle. They tended to unsettle every thing, and yet settled nothing. II.124. [Dr. Priestley's theological works]

vanity. All censure of a man's self is oblique praise. It is in order to shew how much he can spare. It has all the invidiousness of self-praise, and all the reproach of falsehood. III.323.

No man takes upon himself small blemishes without supposing that great abilities are attributed to him; and, . . . in short, this affectation of candour or modesty [is] but another kind of indirect self-praise, and [has] its foundation in vanity. *Misc.*, II.153.

versatility. Sir, a man may be so much of every thing, that he is nothing of any thing. IV.176.

vex. Publick affairs vex no man. IV.220.

vice. Madam, you are here, not for the love of virtue, but the fear of vice. II.435. [To Mrs. Fermor]

vivacity. Depend upon it, Sir, vivacity is much an art, and depends greatly on habit. II.462.

wag. Every man has, some time in his life, an ambition to be a wag. IV.1, n.2.

watch. He was like a man who resolves to regulate his time by a certain watch; but will not inquire whether the watch is right or not. II.213. [On Burnet]

wealth. The sooner that a man begins to enjoy his wealth the better. II.226.

Sir, the insolence of wealth will creep out. III.316.

woman's preaching. Sir, a woman's preaching is like a dog's walking on his hinder legs. It is not done well; but you are surprized to find it done at all. I.463.

women. Women have a perpetual envy of our vices; they are less vicious than we, not from choice, but because we restrict them; they are the slaves of order and fashion; their virtue is of more consequence to us than our own, so far as concerns this world. IV.291.

No woman is the worse for sense and knowledge. V.226.

words. Don't, Sir, accustom yourself to use big words for little matters. I.471.

world. This I would have you do, not in compliance with solicitation or advice, but as a justification of yourself to the world; the world has always a right to be regarded. II.74, n.3.

writing. No man but a blockhead ever wrote, except for money. III.19.

A man should begin to write soon; for, if he waits till his judgement is matured, his inability, through want of practice to express his conceptions, will make the disproportion so great between what he sees, and what he can attain, that he will probably be discouraged from writing at all. IV.12.

A new manner [of writing]! Buckinger had no hands, and he wrote his name with his toes at Charing-cross for half a crown apiece; that was a new manner of writing! *Misc.*, I.419.